"A Heart Afire," by Netanel Miles-Yepez.

A HEART AFIRE

This book was made possible
with a generous donation by

The Reb Zalman Legacy Project
of the Yesod Foundation

Ron Claman, David Friedman,
Tirzah Firestone,
Thomas D. Hast, Bobbie Zelkind

A HEART AFIRE

Stories and Teachings of the Early Hasidic Masters

Translated and Retold with Commentary by

Zalman Schachter-Shalomi
and Netanel Miles-Yepez

With a Foreword by Arthur Green

2009 • 5769
Philadelphia

JPS is a nonprofit educational association and the oldest and foremost publisher of Judaica in English in North America. The mission of JPS is to enhance Jewish culture by promoting the dissemination of religious and secular works, in the United States and abroad, to all individuals and institutions interested in past and contemporary Jewish life.

The Jewish Publication Society
2100 Arch Street, 2nd floor
Philadelphia, PA 19103
www.jewishpub.org

Design and Composition by Pageworks
Cover design by Claudia Cappelli
Cover illustration by Netanel Miles-Yepez

Manufactured in the United States of America

09 10 11 12 10 9 8 7 6 5 4 3 2 1

ISBN: 978-0-8276-0884-9

Library of Congress Cataloging-in-Publication Data

Schachter-Shalomi, Zalman, 1924-
    A heart afire : stories and teachings of the early Hasidic masters : the circles of the Ba'al Shem Tov & the Maggid of Mezritch / translated and retold with commentary by Zalman Schachter-Shalomi & Netanel Miles-Yepez ; with a foreword by Arthur Green.
        p. cm.
    Includes bibliographical references.
    ISBN 978-0-8276-0884-9
    1. Hasidim—Legends.   2. Rabbis—Legends.   3. Legends, Jewish.
4. Hasidism—History.   I. Miles-Yepez, Netanel   II. Title.
    BM532.S33 2009
    296.8'332—dc22
                                2008028587

JPS books are available at discounts for bulk purchases for reading groups, special sales, and fundraising purchases. Custom editions, including personalized covers, can be created in larger quantities for special needs. For more information, please contact us at marketing@jewishpub.org or at this address: 2100 Arch Street, Philadelphia, PA 19103.

In memory of my *mashpiyyim* in ḤaBaD-Nezhin—Reb Moshe Chekhoval and Reb Barukh Merzel—and the rest of the "Diamond Cutter" *ḥevrah* of Antwerp.

—Zalman Meshullam HaKohen Schachter-Shalomi

For my wonderful aunt and first mentor in *Ḥasidut*, Aurora Wallace y Yepez, who introduced me to the magical books of Chaim Potok and the world of Hasidism.

—Netanel David Miles-Yepez

Acknowledgments

WE WISH TO GIVE A HEARTFELT THANK YOU to those who have helped us with this book: to Rabbi Arthur Green, for writing the foreword and making helpful suggestions; to Maggid Yitzhak Buxbaum, for permission to adapt his stories of Adel Ashkenazi; to Rabbi Leah Novick, who also imparted stories of Adel to us; to Maggid Michael Kagan, for permission to use a portion of his parable "The King's Messenger"; to Rabbi Or Rose, for permission to quote from *God in All Moments;* to Rabbi Bahir Davis, who worked on early versions of some of the stories and teachings; to Rabbi Ruth Gan Kagan, who read portions of the manuscript, made helpful suggestions, and provided sources; to Rabbi Hershy Worch, for providing numerous sources for the Maggid's teachings; to Karen Schnitker, for a number of helpful editing suggestions; to Rena Potok, who was determined in her support for this project and who first encouraged us to move in the direction of a commentary; to the wonderful *menschen* of the Yesod Foundation—Ron Claman, Tirzah Firestone, David Friedman, Thomas Hast, and Bobbie Zelkind—for their generosity and support for this book and The Reb Zalman Legacy Project; to Mary Fulton, for facilitating our work together; and, finally, to our wives, Eve Ilsen and Jennifer Miles, who have been patient and supporting of our work, even on weekends and in the wee hours.

—Z.M.S.-S. and N.M.-Y.

Contents

Part III. The Circle of the Maggid and The Rebbe King

Foreword

IT WAS MANY YEARS AGO, SOMEWHERE ON THE now far side of my own forty years' wandering that I first encountered Jiri Langer's *Nine Gates to the Chassidic Mysteries*. That collection of stories, written by a Jewish seeker from Prague who had "gone East" and become a Belzer Hasid in the years before World War I, made a great impression on me. The warmth and love he felt for the Hasidic masters, their lives, teachings, and tales almost literally rose from every page and sought to draw me into its embrace.

I felt that same loving warmth in reading *A Heart Afire*, the manuscript of my friend and teacher Reb Zalman that you now have before you in finished form. Reb Zalman has done for our generations what Langer did for his. He has retold the story of Hasidism in a way that welcomes us, his readers, and invites us in to become more than visitors in the courts of the Rebbes to whom he introduces us. He and his disciple, Netanel Miles-Yepez, retell the tales not only with grace and style but with an unfailing ear to the question, Who are our readers and what do they need to hear?

Reb Zalman, publishing this book in the ninth decade of his life, has much to give his readers that young Langer did not. In addition to knowing the tales, he and Netanel offer a deep reading of key teachings of Hasidism, translating and offering unique commentary on them. Because both have taught and studied in programs of comparative religion for many years, they offer rich examples of comparison with sources and tales of many faiths, especially drawing on Sufi and Indian parallels to Hasidic insights. Perhaps most important, Reb Zalman draws deeply on his own well of life experience and wisdom. Careful readers of this volume will know that they have before them, in the form of Hasidic narrative, the distilled personal wisdom of a great master of human insight and living.

The story with which Reb Zalman opens the book, that of his own journey to Mezhbizh (Miedzhybozh), is the key to the entire volume. Visiting the Ba'al Shem Tov's grave, he prays that *his* Hasidim, those of the neo-Hasidic Jewish Renewal movement, might somehow be grafted onto the tree of the original master's disciples, so that they, even living very different lives from contemporary Hasidim, might feel themselves authentic continuers of the early movement's path.

Throughout the book, Reb Zalman is engaged in that grafting. He is serving perfectly in the role he has cut out for himself over his long career: being a living bridge between the Hasidism of old, that to which he was exposed in the Belzer *shtibl* in Vienna and in the early Brooklyn years at Lubavitch, and the emerging new Hasidism of North America and Israel at the beginning of the twenty-first century. He thus retells the tales as he heard them from his Rebbe, Rabbi Yosef Yitzhak Schneersohn of Lubavitch, the living branch of Hasidism in his own early memory. His version of Hasidism is that which his Rebbe taught, including the full embrace of the famous Herson *genizah* and all the Lubavitch use of those "sources," even though he tells us more than once that scholars question the authenticity of all these documents. He tells tales as his mentors in Lubavitch told them or as they were printed in the 1930's *Kovetz ha-Tamim*, even though he well knows that this is not what is taught about Hasidism at the Hebrew University. That doesn't matter to him; he is constructing (dare I say "reconstructing"?) a Hasidism that will be useful and accessible to future generations, flowing through him as a branch on the great dynastic tree. To the old materials he adds new or rewritten tales, especially some shaped by contemporary feminist readings, to make the flow work better. Yes, he knows that these were composed in Boulder rather than Berditchev. But that is just the point. Hasidic creativity did not end in 1815, 1880, or 1939. It continues today, even in the most unexpected places.

Hasidic truth and wisdom coming from the most unexpected places. Raising up sparks even in *shtetlakh* called by such odd names as Boulder and Berkeley. Come to think of it, isn't that what Hasidism is all about? Scholars might raise questions, but I have no doubt that the Ba'al Shem Tov would have great *nahas* from this volume. So will you. Enjoy!

—Arthur Green

A Note to the Reader

THIS WORK IS A COLLABORATION BETWEEN TWO AUTHORS, a fact that raised numerous questions with regard to "voice" in our introductions and commentaries. In very objective studies, multiple authors are common and voice is less an issue, as most of an objective work is written in the third person. However, this is a very subjective and personal look at Hasidic teachings and stories; thus it was necessary to use a first person voice throughout. To create a mental continuity for the reader in the introductions and commentaries, we have chosen to use the first person singular ("I") as much as possible. In most cases, we have not distinguished which author the pronoun refers to, finding it largely irrelevant to the subject of discussion and knowing that there was common agreement between us about the opinions and views included in the work. However, it can be said here that most (though not all) of the personal stories and reminiscences in the book belong to Zalman Schachter-Shalomi, while the commentary is fairly evenly distributed between both authors. Nevertheless, the use of the first person plural ("we") was unavoidable in some places, especially in the introduction, in which the book itself is the subject of discussion. It is our hope that this will not create any obstacles for the reader and his or her enjoyment of this work.

As much as possible, we have also attempted to use gender-inclusive language throughout, even bending the rules of grammar and historical accuracy on occasion to do so. These stories and teachings come from a culture and a time of patriarchal dominance, when the masculine "he" was thought to include and encompass the feminine "she." Without making any value judgments about that time, we must nevertheless speak to the more diverse audience of today and for the needs of our own time. Today, women are as much a part of every aspect of spiritual life and discourse as are men. And though our language has not yet evolved a satisfactory gender-neutral pronoun, we must do our best to speak to women and men equally, considering the needs of both as "spiritual consumers" of the teachings in this book. We take some comfort in the fact that the grammatical rule bending we have done in this work is not without linguistic justification. For, as students of historical linguistics are aware, the evolution of language and grammar is primarily effected by common usage and slang invention, not by artificially imposed standards. In common usage, we are already beginning to speak in the gender-inclusive way that we have tried to represent in this work. We are grateful to The Jewish Publication Society for relaxing its high standards in this case to be sensitive to the needs of the readers we are hoping to reach.

As regards God language, we have also avoided terms that would emphasize an era of patriarchal dominance. Instead of "king" and "kingdom," we have most often sought to use "sovereign" and "sovereignty," except where these words may apply specifically to the Divine Masculine (Godhead) in contrast to the Divine Feminine (Presence of God). Likewise, in the Hebrew transliteration, we have broken away from the conventional use of *Adonai* (Lord) for the Tetragrammaton (four-lettered name), *Y-H-V-H*, the unpronounceable name of God. Instead, we have chosen to represent the name in English letters as you see here. When this must be read aloud, we recommend replacing it with the name *Yah*, "Being," which is used at various times in this book. For *Yah* is a part of the divine name and participates in its power and immediacy, but the letters *yud-heh* are not connected to the prohibition on pronunciation. Moreover, *Yah* is not an exclusively masculine name but has both masculine and feminine attributes, making it even more palatable for use by both men and women today.

By special permission of The Jewish Publication Society, the translations from the TANAKH in this work are those of the authors and do not come from *The New JPS Hebrew-English* TANAKH (NJPS). This is because much of Hasidic teaching is based on a particular or alternative translation or interpretation of the Hebrew, and thus the English translations of the TANAKH in our Hasidic translations must be tailored to fit one another in ways that are not possible with a standard English translation. Instead, we give the NJPS translations along with the sources in our notes to illustrate common understanding of these passages.

The sources for the stories and teachings in this book are given as accurately as possible, but because stories (and often teachings) are the currency of Hasidim, passed from hand to hand (and often embellished by each owner), complete accuracy was nearly impossible in all cases. Because this work is intended to be a work that students may study, we have provided the reader with a number of citations for works that have alternative versions of the stories and teachings contained herein. In this way, we hope that students may study both, adding dimension to their understanding as well allowing them to judge for themselves between the merits of our reading and those of others.

For the sake of consistency and clarity for modern readers, we have chosen not to transliterate Hebrew words according to the Ashkenazic pronunciation used by the Hasidic masters and East European Jews, but instead to use the Sephardic pronunciation adopted by Modern Hebrew speakers.

Introduction

IN 2005, I MADE A PILGRIMAGE WITH MY youngest son to the graves of the great Hasidic Rebbes of the 18th century—the Ba'al Shem Tov, the Maggid of Mezritch, Pinhas of Koretz, and many others. My intention was to bring the spirituality of Jewish Renewal and Neo-Hasidism back to the land of my birth and the source of its inspiration in these holy men. My sense was that if what is called Neo-Hasidism today is not firmly rooted in the Hasidism of the Ba'al Shem Tov and these masters then it will lack spiritual depth and the strength to endure for many years to come. This is why I went to the Ukraine.

When I arrived in Mezhbizh—the most important stop on my pilgrimage—I went to the mikveh and then proceeded to the grave of the Ba'al Shem Tov. I began to pray that those of us who are now being called neo-Hasidim should be allowed to connect directly to him. There was no doubt that we were part of the same tree, but it seemed to me that a branch of a branch can begin to feel disconnected in its great distance from the trunk. So my intention was to take this branch of Neo-Hasidism and graft it directly onto the trunk of the tree of Ḥasidut, tapping into the very spirit of the Ba'al Shem Tov himself.

"So what happened?" you might ask.

I don't know how to express it exactly. If I were to convey it in the language of midrash, I would say, "The Ba'al Shem Tov spoke to me"; but we live in different times, and I want to be clear about what I am saying. There were no voices, no appearances, and yet . . . a consciousness arose in me at that moment and I felt I received a "message" from the Ba'al Shem Tov.

There is a divine shefa, a flow that comes from God that descends into our world and creates a holy response in us. That response then returns to the source of the flow . . . like alternating current between us and God. This is what energizes everything we do in the world in relation to the Divine. But, inevitably, someone comes *along and says, "We need to control the flow," someone who appoints him or herself as the guardian of the tradition, limiting access to who may benefit and how. This person wants to say, "Only after you have done all of these preliminaries will we give you a taste of the waters of Eden." These limitations become a kind of dam or sluice gate on the flow, which the guardians lift and close at will. This was the situation in the Ba'al Shem Tov's time, which he attempted to correct by digging underneath that sluice gate to release the flow once more, so that the self-appointed guardians could no longer control it. I now felt as if the Ba'al Shem Tov were saying that the flow had once again become dammed up—over the past 300 years— and was only now being rereleased in our time.*

In that moment, I was deeply certain the holy Ba'al Shem Tov had given us his heksher, *his seal of approval, and the right to connect to him directly.*[1]

In many ways, this book is an outgrowth and a symbol of that pilgrimage to the Ba'al Shem Tov and the early Hasidic Rebbes. Indeed, it is in *itself* a kind of pilgrimage to these same *tzaddikim* whose stories and teachings are translated and retold here. It is an attempt to go back to the source, searching for direct guidance and examples of holiness to inspire us in our own lives today.

NEO-HASIDISM: THE FOURTH TURNING

For many people, Hasidism is identified almost exclusively with the ultraorthodoxy of Jews in Brooklyn and Meah Shearim. But we believe that Hasidism is actually something larger, something perpendicular to a continuum that stretches from the farthest reaches of liberal spirituality to the most strictly defined orthodoxy.[2] That is to say, there is a dimension of holy sincerity and piety associated with living in the authentic presence of God, *nokhaḥ p'nai ha-Shem,* that applies equally to all, whether one is a Reform, Conservative, Reconstructionist, or Orthodox Jew or even, as we have discovered over the years, an evangelical Christian or Universalist Sufi![3] This is the Hasidism that we seek to present here.

Some have called this "Neo-Hasidism." That is to say, it belongs to the spirit and values of a loosely organized movement of people inspired to create their own unique spiritual practice based on the model of the Ba'al Shem Tov. The term "Neo-Hasidism," or new Hasidism, was first used in earnest in the 1950s and 60s to describe the Hasidic-inspired work of people like Martin Buber and Abraham Joshua Heschel. Often it was applied pejoratively, marking that work as inauthentic, as if it were an artificial invention.[4] But this was not the case. Many of the personalities involved in this movement were themselves Hasidim, came from Hasidic families, or were from families that had moved away from Hasidism and who now wished to return in some way. Moreover, those who looked on Neo-Hasidism as an artificial invention had forgotten the historical context in which the prior Hasidic movement had arisen. For Neo-Hasidism was not the first "new" Hasidism to arrive on the scene. In the time of the Ba'al Shem Tov and the Maggid of Mezritch, people spoke of that movement in the same way, likewise calling it "the new Hasidism."[5]

You see, Hasidism had been known before. This is why we like to speak of it as something perennial, arising again and again over the centuries in various group-oriented, contemplative movements in Judaism. Sometimes it even bore the name "Hasidism" in one form or another—the Hasidim ha-Rishonim of the 1st and 2nd centuries B.C.E.; the Hasidei Ashkenaz in 12th- and 13th-century Germany; and the Hasidism of the Ba'al Shem Tov.[6] These are what we tend to think of as the "Three Turnings of Hasidism."[7] And now, it seems, we are on the cusp of a Fourth Turning, the very beginnings of which can be traced to the first years of the 20th century.[8] Therefore, in this volume, we are seeking to bring together the stories and teachings of the Ba'al Shem Tov and the Rebbes of the Third Turning to make them accessible to the neo-Hasidic seekers and future builders of the Fourth Turning.

For this reason, we have tried to find a balance between putting these stories and teachings into an authentic context of the Third Turning and making them accessible to the modern reader. Nevertheless, both of these considerations are secondary to our desire to keep them in a holy context, without reference to the cultural forms of the past or the skeptical eye of modernity. More than anything else, we want them to dwell in the heart, to stir the soul, and to penetrate the mind of the reader, whether male or female, Jewish or non-Jewish. For this, too, is part of the Fourth Turning of Hasidism—balancing the spiritual needs of men and women, welcoming the wisdom that flows behind and through all spiritual traditions, and—most of all—loving and respecting our Mother the Earth. In this way, this book is a kind of dialogue between the Third and Fourth Turnings of Hasidism.

It was for the purpose of connecting these two Turnings that I made my pilgrimage to the grave of the holy Ba'al Shem Tov in Mezhbizh. I prayed there for continuity between the Third Turning and the Fourth; I wanted the holy Ba'al Shem Tov to understand our reasons, as neo-Hasidim, for moving in a new direction. For we too felt that the divine flow was being blocked, often by people who wanted to make sure others would behave according to traditionally defined religious norms before receiving divine blessing and inspiration. Thus the channel of the great flow that had opened in the time of the Ba'al Shem Tov had become so progressively narrowed that barely a trickle of the original flow remained by the middle of the 20th century. Then came the overwhelming release of the 1960s and 70s. In this period, not one person but many began to dig under the sluice gate to release the flow.⁹ This allowed those who could not immediately comprehend and integrate *halakhah*, the laws of Judaism, to taste divine love, compassion, and grace directly. As a result, these previously deprived people began to find new ways of bringing tradition and mitzvot into their lives, ways that were in accord with feminist, ecumenical, and ecological values.

GETTING TO KNOW A REBBE

When the Hasidim of the past went out in search of a Rebbe, they always asked—"Is this the Rebbe for me?" and "How will the Rebbe help me better serve God?" It was a relationship defined by a mutual dedication to *shlemut ha-avodah*, true and complete service to God. Thus it seemed necessary to bring to the sincere seeker—one who has already found some inspiration in Hasidism and who is now beginning to look for something deeper—a book that opens a more sophisticated and intimate door onto the unique personalities of early Hasidism, especially as seen through their stories and a meaningful selection of their teachings. In this way, the modern seeker may be able to answer the same questions asked by seekers of the past.

There was an important academic controversy raging in the 1950s between the famous philosopher and neo-Hasidic enthusiast Martin Buber (1878–1965) and the great academic scholar of Hasidism and Kabbalah Gershom Scholem (1897–1982). At issue was the question of how one should interpret Hasidism in general and how best to understand a Hasidic Rebbe—whether through "legendary anecdotes," the stories of their lives, or through the Rebbe's own theoretical writings.¹⁰

For Martin Buber, Hasidism and Hasidic Rebbes were best understood through what he called the "lived concrete" of the Hasidic stories (*ma'asiot*) and tales (*sippurim*). By this he meant that you could best obtain the essence of a particular Hasidic master through the echo of his "character" preserved in the hagiographic or sacred-biographical stories told about him. The lived concrete was a phrase Buber used to denote an impression left on minds and hearts by a concrete event from life, later preserved in the oral tradition. Even if the oral tradition were corrupt, Buber argued, one could still discern an echo of the living moment in the story, the direct encounter with a unique situation that was significant enough to reach and affect us in our own time.

Buber argued that one learns most from the concrete situations of life. In support of this, he would quote Reb Leib Sarah, who said, "I didn't come to my master to learn the intricacies of Torah; I came to learn how he ties his shoe laces." From this perspective, I have to look at the spectrum of a particular Rebbe's behavior as revealed in his recorded anecdotes if I want to understand him. For this is how the Hasidim themselves attuned to the Rebbe when he wasn't present. Thus the best way to get to know a Rebbe, according to Buber, was through his stories.[11]

Gershom Scholem, as a historian of religion, considered the Hasidic stories of great literary value but thought them of dubious value as historical sources of information about the Hasidic Rebbes and of even less value as sources through which one might determine a kind of essential Hasidic worldview. Instead, Scholem believed that one must rely on the available documents dating from the time of individual Rebbes, especially their own Torah or theoretical writings or the writings of those who knew them and spoke of them or their ideas. After all, these were historically verifiable sources that may have come from the Rebbe himself; surely this would provide the clearest possible picture of *who* the Rebbe was (as much as that might be consistent with what he wrote).[12]

Now, let's conduct a little experiment.

Imagine you are having trouble subscribing to the injunction to love your neighbor as yourself. Either you say it and you don't believe it or you say it and then you don't do it. What is to be done? If you are a Hasid, you might try to immerse yourself in the archetype of Levi Yitzhak of Berditchev (1740–1810). But how do you know who Reb Levi Yitzhak was? If you accept Buber's point of view, you might look into a story, a *ma'aseh*, for inspiration.

One day, Reb Levi Yitzhak of Berditchev is walking down the street when he notices an old Yiddeleh greasing the wheels of his wagon while still wearing his tallit and tefillin and hurriedly mumbling his prayers! At that moment, a passerby sees the same sight and cries out, "Shaygetz! What are you doing greasing your wheels in tallit and tefillin!" But Reb Levi Yitzhak looked heavenward in the sight of both men and cried aloud, "Oy! Ribbono shel Olam—what remarkable servants You have! Even when they're greasing the wheels of their wagons they can't take their minds off of You!"[13]

With this story, the Hasid attempts to feel the kind of love that Reb Levi Yitzhak feels for this old man, someone whom most others disdain. The Hasid begins to re-form his or her own feelings in Reb Levi Yitzhak's gestalt, which looks at others through rose-colored glasses. For in the stories of Reb Levi Yitzhak, he is always insinuating good into a situation. But is this the only Reb Levi Yitzhak that is available to us? Not at all.

A more intellectually oriented Hasid might say (in line with Scholem), "You think that you can know all about Reb Levi Yitzhak of Berditchev just by reading stories about him? Reb Levi Yitzhak left us a book called *Kedushat Levi*. If you want to understand Reb Levi Yitzhak, read what he taught in his writings. This is what he wanted to transmit; if you don't read what he was teaching, how could you possibly understand who he was?"

So let us look at a teaching, or Torah, of Reb Levi Yitzhak from his book *Kedushat Levi*.

Why do the rabbis promise that all questions will be answered by Eliyahu ha-Navi when he comes to announce the Mashiah and not by Moshe himself, who will be resurrected at that time? Moshe died, and we cannot hope to be helped in our current problems by Moshe, peace be upon him, who completed his life.

Since that time, the Torah has been placed in our hands, and if one's soul is from the side of grace (hesed), everything is pure, permitted, and kosher; and if it is from the side of rigor (gevurah), the opposite holds true. Yet each person according to their own rung is a vehicle for the word of the living God. This is why the sages, realizing the need for grace in this world, set the halakhah down according to the teachings of Hillel, for this is according to the world's need.

Now, one who is alive in this world is aware of the needs of the time and the attributes we need to live by. But one who is not alive on this plane does not know the attributes we need to live by in this world. Since Eliyahu is yet existing and alive, never having tasted the taste of death, remaining connected to this plane, he is suited like no other to resolve our doubts."[4]

Now, in this, we can clearly see the sophisticated genius of Reb Levi Yitzhak. Thus Scholem might say that the *Kedushat Levi* shows Reb Levi Yitzhak to be a brilliant and clearly reasoning teacher who writes in a noble rabbinic style, much in contrast with the warmly charismatic mystic of Buber's *ma'asiot* or stories of the lived concrete.

But do these sources really reveal two different Rebbes? *Not for the Hasid.*

Who is right in such an academic discussion is irrelevant to the Hasid. Perhaps not for a Hasid who is *also* a scholar, but certainly from the perspective of *Hasidut* itself. For as a wise Hasid once observed, "An objective Hasid is not a Hasid."[15] The Hasid is only concerned with what is of transformational value in the story or teaching and is equally grateful to the Rebbe of both the *ma'aseh* and the Torah. For Hasidim, there is only one Rebbe; the differences between stories and teachings simply reveal different dimensions of a multifaceted character, enhancing the aura of mystery and sanctity around the Rebbe.

With this in mind, we have chosen to honor *both* Buber and Scholem, presenting *ma'asiot* and Torah together as texts to be studied and contemplated equally and side by side.[16] Indeed, these differences hardly seem to matter, for whether writing about a *ma'aseh* or a Torah, there always seemed to be a teaching that illustrated a story or a story that illustrated a teaching. This, in fact, is a clear example of how Hasidim create their own portrait of the Rebbe. Thus the Rebbe Nahman of Bratzlav of Arthur Green's *Tormented Master* is quite different from that of Aryeh Kaplan's in *Until the Mashiach,* and the Ba'al Shem Tov of Martin Buber's *Legend of the Baal-Shem* is different from that of Yitzhak Buxbaum's in *The Light and Fire of the Baal Shem Tov.* Every *ma'aseh,* every Torah learned from a particular Rebbe serves only to add another layer of depth to the portrait formed in the mind and the heart of the Hasid.[17] In this way, the long dead Rebbes of the Hasidic tradition live again in our own reconstructions of them, concatenated portraits composed of little fragments of personal significance to each and every Hasid.[18]

This book is no different.

The teachings and stories we have translated and chosen to retell represent a selection that is personally significant to us or that we thought might be significant to others. Sometimes we have consciously tried to bring together popularly known Rebbes with the lesser-known aspects of their stories and teachings. To this end, we have occasionally used minor traditions and radical teachings more in line with our own values and have retold stories from our own perspectives (a fairly common practice in Hasidic storytelling). In a few places, we have even sought to use materials that traditional Hasidim and other writers on Hasidism have rejected in the past, often because they come from "non-kosher" sources or from the enemy camp or simply because of personal preference.[19]

Likewise, without any pretense of presenting history, we have incorporated historical sources and arranged the material in such a way as to create an intelligible portrait of each individual Rebbe's life—from the cradle to the grave—in a fusion of biography and hagiography. This is simply a part of the hyphenated reality of Hasidim today. For while the Hasid may not be objective about being a Hasid, we still live in and are part of a society that values objective standards. We need not be ashamed of either our subjectivity *or* our objectivity; for one who is only subjective is not responsible, and one who is only objective is not human. Thus we wanted to find some balance between the archetypal Rebbe of myth and tradition and the accessible Rebbe of history and human psychology.

We want the reader to get the *feel* of real people in these pages, people who struggled and were transformed. Very often when we encounter hagiography, the description of the lives of saints, the Rebbes of the past often seem like plaster-cast statues or two-dimensional iconic representations. That is not how we need to approach the Ba'al Shem Tov or any other Rebbe today. Sociologists call these hagiographic depictions of tradition "archetypal models"—models that so perfectly embody our ideals that they are very difficult for us to emulate, so perfect as to be above the human situation. In contrast to these are what sociologists call "accessible models"—models that seem relatively realistic and inspire us to say, "I can become like that" or "I too can live like that."[20]

In the Jewish tradition, Abraham, Isaac, and Jacob are generally treated as archetypal models, but the Rabbis of the Talmud also say to us, "You should say to yourself, 'When will my actions approach the actions of my parents?' "[21] Do you understand? What we need from Abraham is not perfection, but that he should be accessible enough for us to emulate his actions, that *his* hospitality, for instance, should be a model for *us* in becoming that kind of being. Today, we think the Ba'al Shem Tov also needs be an accessible model for people; we need to make ourselves aware of the narrow ridge that he had to walk and learn to walk it ourselves.

THE *FARBRENGEN* BOOK

My papa, Reb Shlomo Schachter, of blessed memory, was a Belzer Hasid, and once I remember he told me a secret he had learned in Belz. In Poland, before the Holocaust, they used to make a green-tinted schnapps called *pyellum bronfen*. It was made with bitter herbs (hence its greenish tint) and was supposed to be good for the stomach. But Papa told me he had learned in his time among the Belzer Hasidim that "you should never buy *pyellum bronfen* from a Hasid." "Why?" I asked. "Because a Hasid doesn't let it steep long enough . . . he drinks a lot faster than the ordinary person!"

A lot of books about Hasidism written by non-Hasidim are like *pyellum bronfen* from a Hasid; they don't let you "steep" long enough. And while it is true that Hasidim used to drink their schnapps a lot faster that the ordinary person, that is *not* how they approached the teachings of their Rebbes. In these they would soak themselves completely, drinking them in very slowly—over days, weeks, even years—with a refined appreciation. Thus we have tried to make this a book for steeping and drinking slowly. It is a collection of stories and teachings (translated from Yiddish and Hebrew) that have set our insides ablaze, like that green-tinted vodka, and in which we have steeped ourselves for years, growing in our appreciation of their complexity and richness.

Because they are diverse stories and teachings from across the spectrum of Hasidic spirituality, they needed some corralling into a logical arrangement and a bit of commentary to bind them together. Nevertheless, our desire is always to lead the reader up to them, like an attendant at a *mikveh*—waiting while one dips—then providing them with a towel as they are led out. But there are also occasions when the attendant must do more than simply show you where the water is. When a person is new to the mitzvah of *tevilah* (immersion), the *mikveh* attendant must also make some attempt to teach them the ways of the *mikveh* and perhaps even something of its *kavanah* (intention). In our case, the attendant commentary seeks to give the reader a sense of the authentic flavor of the Hasidic milieu, or rather to contextualize and ready the senses for the experience of authentic Ḥasidut.

This is why our commentary in this volume, such as it is, is *not* (for the most part) filled with the usual scholarly minutiae and explanations, pointing out what is "really going on" in these translations and stories. Nevertheless, there were many occasions when we felt that omitting this material just wasn't possible, fearing that we might be abandoning our readers in the middle of heavily predicated or abstruse and paradoxical teachings that may have no meaning to them otherwise. But whenever possible, we truly sought to let the readers draw their own conclusions, putting the weight of storytelling and teaching clearly on the shoulders of the texts themselves. Thus we hope that our commentary will be seen more as a series of contextual "preludes" and "postludes" than as answers to questions.

To do this, we modeled our chapters on the situational dynamic of a Hasidic *farbrengen*, literally, "time spent together," during which Hasidim would gather for the purpose of telling stories, singing, drinking, and learning the teachings of the Rebbes.[22] Thus our preludes and postludes are filled with stories of the Rebbes, the stories behind the teachings, insights, and meditations on the atmosphere of Hasidic living and learning, and reminiscences of our own love affair with Hasidism—that is, with memories from the intimacy of our own experience of being *in love* with Hasidism. Nor were these included in any artificial process. Throughout the writing of this volume, which we called "The *Farbrengen* Book," we sat down together (nearly every week over a three-year period) to enter into dialogue on these same Hasidic masters in the spirit of a *farbrengen*—all the while remembering teachings, translating, discussing our own questions, and telling favorite stories to one another. And though we have polished these dialogues considerably, this is basically what is represented in the chapters that follow. We can only hope that our own joy in the process is evident to you as you read these pages.

In our previous work, *Wrapped in a Holy Flame,* we also brought together biographical portraits and gave commentary on selected fragments of Hasidic teaching, but this was done more as an introduction to Hasidism for the general reader—namely, to present the great intellectual sophistication and contemplative depth available in the Hasidic tradition. The biographical portraits there are more straightforward and tighter in structure, whereas here they depend on stories from the tradition and translations from various sources. The commentary in that work is likewise more detailed and free flowing, though based on smaller fragments of teachings, which are given in full in the present volume. For this reason, *Wrapped in a Holy Flame* should be considered as a companion to *A Heart Afire,* and readers of this book will benefit by consulting its introductions, biographies, and teachings throughout.

As *A Heart Afire* assumes a certain familiarity with Judaism, Hasidism, and Kabbalah, we would like to recommend several books to readers who may find this material challenging or unfamiliar. The first are *Jewish with Feeling: A Guide to Meaningful Jewish Practice* (with Joel Segel) and *Credo of a Modern Kabbalist* (with Daniel Siegel), both of which will provide readers with an understanding of Judaism and Jewish spiritual practice in the light of Jewish mysticism. For those who would like to deepen their understanding of Hasidic prayer and spiritual practice, we highly recommend the classic *Your Word Is Fire: The Hasidic Masters on Contemplative Prayer,* by Arthur Green and Barry W. Holtz; and *God in All Moments: Mystical & Practical Wisdom from Hasidic Masters,* by Or Rose and Ebn Leader. For those in need of good maps to the difficult terrain of Jewish mysticism, we recommend *God Is a Verb: Kabbalah and the Practice of Mystical Judaism,* by David Cooper; *Ehyeh: A Kabbalah for Tomorrow,* by Arthur Green; and *Innerspace: Introduction to Kabbalah, Meditation and Prophecy,* by Aryeh Kaplan. These works will give you good introductions to the language and concepts of the Kabbalah.

PART I

The Hidden Tradition and
The Ba'al Shem Tov

1

A Hidden Light: The Ba'alei Shem
and the Hidden *Tzaddikim*

WHEN WE THINK OF THE BA'AL SHEM TOV, we usually think of him as something new and without precedent in Judaism. But this is not entirely accurate. As we mentioned in the introduction, Judaism had already known various Hasidic movements before the time of the Ba'al Shem Tov. According to the Hasidic tradition, especially as it was taught by my Rebbe, Yosef Yitzhak Schneersohn of Lubavitch (1880–1950), there were others who preceded the holy Ba'al Shem Tov in the "office" of ba'al shem.[1] Of course, this is in no way intended to lessen his uniqueness and significance for us but merely to put him into his proper context.[2] For the Ba'al Shem Tov, while certainly bringing a new light to the world, was also coming out of an older tradition of Ashkenazi Hasidism, and he led this "new" Hasidic movement using a title we know his predecessors had used before him.

Before the time of Yisra'el ben Eliezer, the Ba'al Shem Tov (1698–1760), many others had borne the title *ba'al shem*, or master of the divine name. Even in the writings of Hai Ga'on (939–1038) and Yehudah HaLevi (1075–1141) there are references to certain ba'alei shem.[3] In his own time, these ba'alei shem were typically itinerant folk healers of one sort or another. Nevertheless, there were at least three ba'alei shem known to the Hasidic tradition in the generations that immediately preceded Yisra'el ben Eliezer who were clearly *more* than simple folk healers but also prominent leaders and teachers like himself.[4]

3

ELIYAHU, THE BA'AL SHEM OF WORMS

The first of these ba'alei shem was Rabbi Eliyahu ben Moshe Loanz (1565–1636), the Ba'al Shem of Worms (Wormiza), who was active in the Rhineland of Germany. This is the area where, several hundred years before, the Hasidei Ashkenaz had also been prominent under the leadership of Rabbi Yehudah the Hasid of Regensburg (12th to 13th centuries) and his disciple, Rabbi Eleazar Rokeah of Worms (ca. 1176–1238). Though there is little evidence for it, it is not impossible that Reb Eliyahu Ba'al Shem might somehow have been distantly connected with a remnant of the Hasidic lineage of the Hasidei Ashkenaz.

Reb Eliyahu Ba'al Shem is known to have taught Kabbalah and esoteric spiritual disciplines to his disciples, a practice that, if not yet wholly disreputable in the eyes of the normative authorities, was certainly considered suspicious. In his *Likkutei Dibburim,* Reb Yosef Yitzhak of Lubavitch describes how the reputation of Reb Eliyahu Ba'al Shem had spread far and wide in his own day and how with this increase in fame came opposition from many traditionalists. One scholar in particular, Rabbi Pinhas Zelig of Speyer, had gone so far as to excommunicate him. Because Reb Eliyahu Ba'al Shem was living near Prague at the time, this was something that the famous Rabbi Yehudah Loew, the Maharal of Prague (1525–1609), felt he needed to investigate personally. He took his son and visited the famous ba'al shem. What passed between them at that time is a mystery, but we do know that when the Maharal returned from his visit, he published a complete vindication of Reb Eliyahu Ba'al Shem and his teachings.[5]

According to the Rebbe, the disciples of Reb Eliyahu Ba'al Shem not only studied Kabbalah but were also well versed in Torah. In his *yeshivot* or seminaries, the young men all studied both *nigleh* and *nistar,* the revealed as well as the hidden Torah. Their spiritual practice was based in the Kabbalah of the day but also had a distinctly social element to it, an element that is characteristic of Hasidism. Thus, in addition to noting their Kabbalah-based practices—*yihudim* (unifications), *kavanot* (mystical intentions), solitude, fasting, and self-mortification—the Rebbe described how groups of three to five men would go into a forest or a field to study *musar* or *aggadah* and would "rebuke each other. Each man would lay bare the ailments that plagued his soul: one of them would bemoan his inclination to pride; another—to falsehood, or envy, or slander, and other such undesirable attributes."[6]

Among his students familiar to us today was the renowned Rabbi Yom-Tov Lippman Heller (1577–1654), who went on to become a distinguished rabbinic authority.[7] And we also know the name of Rabbi Eliyahu's successor in the role of ba'al shem.

YOEL, THE BA'AL SHEM OF ZAMOSHTCH

At his passing, it seems that Reb Eliyahu Ba'al Shem transferred his authority to Rabbi Yoel ben Yitzhak Heilprin, the Ba'al Shem of Zamoshtch (Zamocz). Like that of his master, Reb Yoel Ba'al Shem's holy charisma, coupled with genuine talmudic and kabbalistic learning, made him a highly regarded sage in 17th-century Poland. However, today he is mostly remembered as a wonder worker.

Unlike Reb Eliyahu Ba'al Shem, about whom we know mainly external details, there are actually *ma'asiot*, stories of Reb Yoel Ba'al Shem, which impressed themselves on the folk imagination and are preserved to this day. In these *ma'asiot*, Reb Yoel Ba'al Shem is less a leader and teacher than a heroic shaman or a *ba'al mofet* (master of miracles) of considerable power.

ONE DAY, REB Yoel Ba'al Shem was called to the house of a pregnant woman and her husband. Both were wonderful people, giving tzedakah generously and living a good Jewish life, but Oy! nebukh, all six of their children had died in infancy. Now that the woman was pregnant again, they were justifiably worried that they would lose their seventh child. Having heard about the miracles of Reb Yoel Ba'al Shem, both the woman and her husband sent word to him in desperation, asking him to come and supervise the birthing and to see the child safely through its first month.

This is how Reb Yoel Ba'al Shem came to be in the house of the poor couple. Barukh ha-Shem, the child was born safely. However, they were not out of danger yet. Some of the other children had been born safely too, but none had lived longer than a month! So Reb Yoel had taken precautions. Using a piece of charcoal, he and his talmidim (disciples) had made a circle of protection around the house and written kamayot (amulets) for the child's health. More important, they continued their prayers for the child's protection both night and day.

This went on for seven days until Wachnacht, the night before the brit.

The tradition of *Wachnacht*, or "watch night," actually goes back to antiquity. It is the practice of watching over a child until morning, protecting it from any harm that might come to it before entering the *brit* or "covenant."[8]

This comes from the idea that it is just before we are about to do something spiritually powerful that the forces of negativity attempt to subvert our good intentions.

DURING THIS WACHNACHT, *Reb Yoel Ba'al Shem decided to keep the watch himself, stationing his* talmidim *just outside the door where they recited holy verses. But there must have been a hole in their defenses, for an unfamiliar cat silently entered the room after midnight. Almost before the Ba'al Shem could react, it leaped toward the crib, and even as it was pouncing, the cat grew to enormous proportions! Just in time, Reb Yoel Ba'al Shem lifted his iron-tipped cane to parry the cat in midair and poked out one of its eyes! The cat let out a terrifying shriek and quickly began to shrink in size. Before he could catch it, the cat managed to escape from the house.*

The next day, the brit *was delayed while everyone waited for the midwife to arrive. After a while, a messenger was sent to look for her. The messenger returned soon after saying, "She is at home in bed with a bandaged eye!"*

The explanation is that this midwife had sold her soul to the Evil One. It was she who had taken all the children born in that household and had killed them for Lilith, the mother of all demons.[9]

Another tale tells of how Reb Yoel Ba'al Shem dealt with *sheidim* (demons) who were making trouble in a family's cellar. But neither this nor the previous story is quite the edifying kind of tale we like today. We hear them and think "superstition" and "ignorance"; nevertheless, they are what has survived in the popular imagination about Reb Yoel Ba'al Shem, and they also tell us a great deal about folk beliefs and the many domestic tragedies of shtetl life.[10]

I feel it is important to deal with them here, even if only in a minor way, because I don't think we need to be ashamed of these stories the way we once were. For a long time, educated Jews tended to censor these kinds of stories out of embarrassment; they were afraid that the stories would reflect on them and they would be labeled backward and irrational. In a time when the philosopher Hermann Cohen (1842–1918) was marketing Judaism as *Die Religion der Vernunft* or "the religion of reason," many people didn't want to translate stories like these. But when we read Carlos Castaneda today and wonder, "Don't we have something like that?" we have to come back to these supposedly disreputable tales.

ADAM, THE BA'AL SHEM OF ROPSHITZ
AND THE *TZADDIKIM NISTARIM*

The successor of Reb Yoel Ba'al Shem was Adam of Ropshitz, called Adam Ba'al Shem. Very few people in all of Jewish history have been named Adam, so he tends to stand out as a bit of a mystery. We know so little about him, and what we do know is found mainly in the early stories of his successor, Yisra'el Ba'al Shem Tov. But even then, the information is mostly tangential. We are told that he was supposed to be in possession of a book filled with profoundly sacred, esoteric writings intended only for the eyes of the current ba'al shem. Toward the end of his life, Reb Adam was to turn the book over to the next ba'al shem, the new leader of the *tzaddikim nistarim* or "hidden righteous ones."[11]

Reb Eliyahu Ba'al Shem and Reb Yoel Ba'al Shem were known to have sent their disciples out as emissaries, traveling incognito from place to place on secret errands in an effort to spread the teachings of the Kabbalah. However, it seems that in the later years of Reb Yoel's leadership and throughout that of Reb Adam the mission of the *tzaddikim nistarim* broadened considerably. Of course, they continued to spread the holy influence of their own mystically oriented Judaism, enriching the often dry observance of the rabbinic intelligentsia, but now they also began to aid and console the downtrodden of the Jewish community while reviving the spirit of Torah within them. You see, many simple Jews of that period had become physically, emotionally, and spiritually destitute in the wake of the terrible violence visited upon them by the Cossacks, and perhaps not less by their own grinding poverty. Abandoned by the Torah elite of the time, their only material and spiritual respite came through the hidden messengers of Reb Adam Ba'al Shem.[12]

It was once a common custom for Christians and Jews all over Europe to travel the countryside as penitents and pilgrims. People who had something to atone for would travel from town to town and see themselves as being "in exile." Imagine, God forbid, you committed involuntary manslaughter and you feel very guilty and feel as if you had to atone for it. How would you gain what they call in Christianity "indulgence"? How could you make sure that you would not be punished in purgatory for this act? Can you pay *now* so you don't have to pay *later*? Well, this is a notion that Jews also embraced.

The kabbalists had spelled out "tariffs" long before this time: Such and such a sin required so many fast days, rolling in the snow naked, or sitting on an anthill! It seems silly to us today, but if you really felt a burden of guilt in those days and you wanted to wash it away, you could do so almost literally by, for example, entering a freezing cold *mikveh*. If you wanted to feel contrite physically, you might do so by wearing a hair shirt or sackcloth and ashes, saying, "Dear God, I am so sorry; I hope that the pain and discomfort that I am experiencing will make up for what I have done."

So it was expected in those days that people would travel the countryside doing penance. And because it was not considered polite to ask many questions of these people, the *tzaddikim nistarim*, these hidden saints, were able to travel from town to town on righteous errands for the ba'al shem in almost complete anonymity.

Who were these hidden *tzaddikim* and how did one come to live that lifestyle?

Imagine a young man growing up in the shtetl; he has a good heart and a decent head on his shoulders and is used to a life of labor. He doesn't mind the work, but it is not enough for him either. He wants to serve God in other ways. He knows it is probably not his destiny to sit in a traditional *beit midrash* day after day, and he may not even have any desire for that life.

One day, a traveler comes into the shtetl. He sets himself up as a sharpener of knives and fixer of tools on the edge of the village. Our young man strikes up a conversation with him in passing one day and finds that the stranger holds a peculiar fascination for him. Something about his presence is a just a little bit different, and there are small hints now and again that speak of unsuspected depths. The young man comes to talk to the fixer more and more and begins to realize that something is being teased out of him in these conversations. Finally, he comes upon the fixer at his prayers, and he now knows what has been hidden from his sight. He hadn't come upon this scene by chance. He had been expected and is now being invited into a life of special holiness.

Soon it is time for the itinerant fixer to move on, and the young man is naturally invited to come with him for a time. He goes along and learns much from the fixer until the day they arrive at the door of Reb Adam Ba'al Shem, where the young man receives further instruction and is fully initiated into the secret fellowship.

In my own mind's eye, this was probably the way in which Eliezer, the father of the Ba'al Shem Tov, came to join the *tzaddikim nistarim*.

ELIEZER, THE FATHER OF
THE BA'AL SHEM TOV

There is not much in the tradition about Reb Eliezer's life as a *tzaddik nistar*, but there are a few tales about the special holiness of him and his wife, Sarah, and how they merited having such a son as the holy Ba'al Shem Tov. One tale goes like this . . .

ONCE, WHILE TRAVELING *on an errand for the* tzaddikim nistarim, *Reb Eliezer was taken captive by bandits and sold as a slave in the markets of Istanbul. While he is being displayed on an auction block in the market, the vizier of the sultan happens by and looks Reb Eliezer over. He doesn't look like much of a worker, mind you, but the vizier thinks that he looks like an intelligent person. He buys him for a companion and a manservant.*

Eliezer, it seems, has picked up a little Turkish in his travels, and the vizier finds to his delight that he is able to have good conversations with his new manservant. Most of the day, Reb Eliezer takes care of the vizier's clothes and manages the household while the vizier is at the court of the sultan. When the vizier returns home in the evening, he begins to share his woes with Reb Eliezer . . . "Oy! what a day I had at the court! The sultan wants this . . . the sultan wants that . . . and I don't know what to tell him!" Every once in a while, Reb Eliezer answers, "Well, if I were you, sir, I would suggest to the sultan that he . . ." and this is precisely what the vizier recommends to the sultan the next morning. The sultan was always pleased.

Then one day the vizier found himself in a real quandary. A terrible thing had happened. The sultan had been at war with a certain territory for years and years with no result—he simply couldn't conquer it. The capital city was too well defended. On one side it was surrounded by mountains, and on the other was a harbor that had been mined. Finally, the sultan threw up his hands in frustration and said to his vizier, "If you don't give me an answer to this problem tomorrow, here's a yellow silk rope for you."

This was a clear message to the vizier: It meant that he could hang himself if he didn't come up with an answer. This is what the failed messiah, Shabbetai Tzvi (1626–1676), got from the sultan of Istanbul when the sultan began to feel that the would-be messiah's movement was becoming a threat. In this case, it was an ultimatum: Convert to Islam or commit suicide with this rope. Shabbetai Tzvi converted. So you can imagine how the vizier feels when he returns home that night.

THAT NIGHT, THE vizier says to Reb Eliezer, "Look what I got today at the court,"
and he tells him the story. Very concerned for his friend, as well as for himself, *Reb*
Eliezer says to him, "You know, I've been thinking about this, and what you need
to do is have some rafts made. Take prisoners who are already condemned to death
and offer them freedom in exchange for a dangerous service. They will man those
rafts and navigate a path through the mines, marking a safe route for your ships to
follow into the harbor. Then the sultan should be able to take the city easily since it
is not otherwise well defended."

The vizier takes the idea to the sultan the next morning. The sultan eyes him
curiously for a moment and says, "You have been coming up with some very good
solutions lately; I can't believe that you figured these things out yourself. Who is
helping you?" The vizier has to admit the truth—his manservant, Eliezer, is the real
source of the ideas. The sultan cuts off the vizier's head in disgust and makes Reb
Eliezer vizier in his place, giving him his own daughter as a wife.

Now Reb Eliezer had been the vizier's confidant for long enough to know that he
didn't want this job. He was safer as a slave. To be at the whim of this capricious
sultan was definitely worse. And he had another problem . . . the sultan's daughter.

Reb Eliezer was already married when he was taken captive, so he is forced to
play a difficult and dangerous game, trying to remain faithful to his wife while not
offending the sultan's daughter. After a few weeks of this game, the sultan's daugh-
ter has had enough, and she says to him, "What is the matter; am I not beautiful?
Why do you stay away from me?"

He is forced to confess. "It is not that you are not beautiful, but that I am not
free to love you. I am a Jew taken captive from my homeland in Wallachia where I
have a wife to whom I am trying to remain faithful. What else can I do?"

Seeing that the situation is hopeless with a man faithful to another woman, the
sultan's daughter says to him, "Take some of my jewelry, and I will help you to
escape so that I can have a life for myself." In this way, he manages to get back to
his wife, Sarah. When he embraces her again, he hears a voice saying, "You have
managed this temptation well; you can expect great favor from Heaven."[3]

But there are other stories told of why Reb Eliezer and his wife, Sarah, merited the honor of becoming the parents of the holy Ba'al Shem Tov. In many
ways, this next *ma'aseh* tells us more about what the Ba'al Shem Tov could
have learned from his parents in the short time they spent together.

AFTER REB ELIEZER returned from Istanbul, he purchased an inn with the riches the
sultan's daughter had given him. He made it into a kind of Shabbat hotel; before

long, it was well known throughout the region that the inn of Reb Eliezer and his wife, Sarah, was a place of refuge for anyone who needed a place to eat and sleep for Shabbat, even if they were short of funds.

Now Reb Eliezer's inn had a special arrangement. In the common room, there were three large tables. At the first table, he would seat the great lamdanim (those who were learned in rabbinics), so that in the middle of the eating and drinking and singing zemirot (table songs), they could also discuss the most abstruse parts of Torah.

At the second table, Reb Eliezer would seat those who knew a shtikel Humash and a shtikel midrash. They were not as learned as the lamdanim, but they weren't ignorant either. They would discuss the sedra (Torah portion) of the week, saying, "What do you think Pinhas really did? Why did he do it?" and "Why did God reward him for that?" They would go back and forth with this kind of Torah discussion.

At the third and last table, he would seat the pashute Yidden, the simple Jews and shnorrers who would mostly sing zemirot. Then one of the people from the second table would come and join them and tell them about the sedra of the week, just as someone from the first table would come to the second and discuss deeper Torah. In this way, everyone in Reb Eliezer's inn learned at their level but also grew in their understanding of Torah while enjoying Shabbat.

Late one Friday evening, there is a knock at the door of the inn. It is already well into Shabbat, but Reb Eliezer rushes to the door and opens it. There he finds a mud-caked traveler with a rough-hewn staff just off the road. He greets him kindly with a "Shalom aleikhem!" But the traveler responds with only a gruff snort and asks, "Is there food here?" Reb Eliezer nods and tries to make the man comfortable, acting as if he were unaware of the stranger's gruffness.

Thinking it best to give him special attention, Reb Eliezer brought the stranger over to sit with him at the first table among the lamdanim. Well, you can imagine the impression that this coarse and dirty traveler made on this group. Perhaps it would have been different had he sat in silence, but he didn't. He tended to scoff with rough disdain whenever one of the lamdanim made a point, sometimes even swearing under his breath! Soon, a lamdan pulled Reb Eliezer aside and said, "Reb Eliezer, if he sits at this table any longer, we're going to have to leave." So Reb Eliezer took him to the second table and sat down with him there. But someone again pulled Reb Eliezer aside and said, "Listen, he's certainly not fit to sit with the lamdanim, but he isn't fit for us either; we didn't come here to be insulted by this paskudniak who shows up in the middle of Shabbat!" Reb Eliezer then takes him to the last table, but even the shnorrers don't want to sit with him! Without uttering a complaint, Reb Eliezer goes and finds a little table and sets it up in the corner of the room. He feeds the stranger and keeps him company while he eats. Before he has even finished eating, he falls asleep on the table, snoring loudly.

In the morning, when all the other guests in the inn have come in to daven
*together—the stranger isn't there. The other guests murmur about his absence; he
is clearly testing everyone's patience. Finally,* Shabbat *is over,* Havdalah *has been
made, and the stranger says, "I gotta go." "Alright," says Reb Eliezer, "I'll walk with
you down the road to show you which way to go." He grabs his coat and a little
traveling food (and a few rubles) to give to the stranger and heads out the door to
catch up with him.*

*They walk together for a few minutes before the man turns unexpectedly on Reb
Eliezer and says, "Look at me!"*

*A little startled, Reb Eliezer looks at him as if for the first time, looking deeply
into his eyes. Suddenly he is confronted by someone else entirely—no longer is he
looking at the foul-mouthed traveling* shnorrer, *but at Eliyahu ha-Navi!*

*Eliyahu ha-Navi then says, "Eliezer, I have come with a message for you. There
is a very special soul waiting to come down, and I have come to find a couple who
can be appropriate hosts for this soul. We have judged you and your wife to be
that couple. You may expect a son in the next year who is to be a light unto his
generation."*[14]

These are the "hosts" that Heaven sought for the child Yisra'el ben Eliezer,
parents who could teach him to care for all *Yiddelakh,* all Jews everywhere and
of every kind. Who else but the Reb Eliezer of this *ma'aseh* could have taught
him to love so well?

It is also clear from these stories that it is a special gift to be a parent to
such a child, even if the parents are not fated to be with him for long. Sarah
dies young, and Reb Eliezer dies just a few years later. But before he does,
he calls his son over and says to him, "Yisrolickel [little Yisra'el], I have to
go now, but I want to tell you two things first: Do not fear anything in the
whole wide world except God, and every bit of love that you have, offer it to a
fellow Jew." With that, he dies, and Yisra'el ben Eliezer is orphaned at just five
years old.[15]

THE HIDDEN HISTORY OF THE BA'AL SHEM TOV

The following piece is a wonderful autobiographical letter that tradition says
was written by the holy Ba'al Shem Tov himself. In it he writes to a *tzaddik
nistar* named Mordechai of Tartary, who has asked to hear the story of how the
Ba'al Shem Tov came to meet his master and, more important, how the Ba'al
Shem Tov came into his own divine inheritance.

Scholars have long questioned the authenticity of this letter, and most today consider it a forgery. Nevertheless, its content has so deeply informed the Hasidic imagination that historical authenticity is hardly relevant to the Hasid whose soul has been enriched by its truth. I ask you to suspend your critical judgment temporarily and enter into the holy *olam ha-mashal* (the world of the imagination) as the Ba'al Shem Tov tells the story of his own life up to his 36th year. As much as possible, we would like the Rebbes and the Hasidim to tell the story of their own lives and of the lives of their masters.

To my beloved friend, the silent pillar of fire, Reb Mordechai of Tartary[16]—
 I received your letter through our friend and colleague, and I have decided to fulfill your request, my holy friend, to reveal to your ears the known cause from the beginning of how the blessed name has brought me to my present situation.
 I apologize for the condition of the paper, but as you know—finding my meditation in these quiet fields—I cannot carry large sheets of paper with me and am forced to write on these thin pages that tend to blot.

I was born in the holy city of Okkup in the year 1698 (5458).
 When I was only five years old, I was orphaned from my mother and father, of blessed memory, and passed into the hands of the local congregation in matters of food, drink, clothing, and tuition. When the leaders of the city saw no sign of blessing in my studies, they abandoned me, and I drifted from city to city and settlement to settlement, until I came with the help of the blessed name to the holy city of Brod. It was then that I turned eighteen and was made a tutor of children.

In most Hasidic books, these events in the early life of the Ba'al Shem Tov are often treated *casually* and without comment, as if they were merely props to support the significance of a significant life. This is the way of most hagiography (sacred biography): biographical details and circumstances are reported simply, while moments of realization and actions modeling special holiness are presented in great detail. Today's hagiography cannot afford to be so casual. We have paid the price for putting our spiritual teachers on pedestals, expecting them to model our own ideals of perfection. They inevitably fail, and we lose the opportunity to take responsibility for our own spiritual lives.

As we look at the life of the Ba'al Shem Tov today, we have no desire to lose the experience of the child called Yisroyel (or Yisrolickel) in the saintly supe-riority of the adult Ba'al Shem Tov, to lose the humanity of a little boy in trag-ic circumstances in favor of a legend. If the Ba'al Shem Tov elicits love and admiration from us today, it should be with his humanity intact and through his response to the challenge of his own frailties and the frailties of others. So take notice of what he says here and contemplate it with an open heart—do not pass over the words "orphaned," "abandoned," and "drifted" without recalling the lonely child who must have come before the great saint.

Nevertheless, the Ba'al Shem Tov does not say much more than the hagio-graphers in this letter. Perhaps it is simply for brevity's sake (in a letter meant to answer different questions) or perhaps these are memories in his inner garden too painful and too sensitive to be brought out without need.

In the literature of Hasidism, there are many tales about this period in the Ba'al Shem Tov's life. But for now we will let the Ba'al Shem Tov tell his own story, and we will respect his silence on these matters.[17]

IN BROD DWELT the holy master Reb Gershon, in whose house there was an orphan whom he asked me to tutor in Torah. In this way, I met my wife, who was Reb Gershon's sister, and thus I became his brother-in-law. But at that time, thank God, I was completely unaware of the elevated soul that was within me.

In this passage, the Ba'al Shem Tov says only, "I met my wife, who was Reb Gershon's sister." But I just cannot leave it at that; I am much too enamored of the tale of how the Ba'al Shem Tov met his wife to leave it out. I will, how-ever, try to be brief in telling it, even though it is slightly at variance with what the Ba'al Shem Tov wrote to Reb Mordechai of Tartary.

> Once, the distinguished rabbi Efraim of Brod became involved in a legal dispute while traveling through the little town where the young Yisra'el ben Eliezer was then living. As many people in that town took their disputes to "Reb Yisroyel," he too agreed to hear what the judicious young man would say. Reb Yisroyel heard the complaints of each of the parties and made a suggestion that was agreeable to both. Pleased with the judgment, Reb Efraim sat down to talk with the young man and, before long, offered him his daughter, Hannah, in marriage. Young Yisra'el agreed, and they drew up the documents. However, Reb Efraim died in his carriage before reaching home. When the contract was discovered among

his belongings, only the name of the intended—Yisra'el ben Eliezer—was mentioned. The paper gave no clue as to where such a person could be found or what merits the intended had to recommend him. Reb Efraim's son, Rabbi Gershon of Kittov, therefore put the document aside until the man came to claim his sister.

Just as Reb Gershon was beginning to think no one would come, Yisra'el arrived in Brod to claim his wife. Now Reb Gershon—who was one of the most respected talmudists and kabbalists of the region—was appalled at the sight of this Yisra'el ben Eliezer. He looked like a peasant, and talked like one too! The prospect of his sister marrying this seemingly uncouth and uncultured young man was not to be borne. He asked the young man to wait and went to urge his sister, Hannah, to have the engagement annulled. Realizing that this was probably what Reb Gershon was saying to her, Yisra'el spoke up and asked if he might have a word with Hannah in private. Reb Gershon looked at his sister, and she nodded her consent. After a few minutes, she came out of the room and approached her brother, saying that she agreed to the marriage. Reb Gershon was astonished and urged her to reconsider, but Hannah would not hear of it, saying only, "Our beloved father made this contract, so we need not worry about it—it is certainly God's will."[18]

Oh how I would have loved to have eavesdropped on that conversation! What could the holy Reb Yisra'el have possibly said to convince her that he was more than the rough, uneducated peasant that he seemed? Tradition tells us nothing of this, so we can only speculate.

Another important statement in this passage of the letter is, "But, at that time, thank God, I was completely unaware of the elevated soul that was within me." Many stories of the Ba'al Shem Tov would have you believe that he was always conscious of his elevated soul, that even in his early years, he was conscious of it and was consciously hiding it. This letter doesn't suggest that at all; it doesn't suggest anything more than he grew in spiritual depth gradually, like all of us, unaware of exactly what kind of soul we have, knowing only that we keep having to turn back to God in repentance. The Ba'al Shem Tov has the humility to say this. For all the amazing experiences he is about to tell us, there isn't a note of pride in it.

I suppose because I am a "name" in certain religious circles, people sometimes ask me, "When did you 'wake up'?" Or they say, "Tell me about one of your great theophanies!" And while there have been powerful experiences, each time I am asked, I feel I have to parry this question with a Zen answer— "I'm not Rinzai, I'm Soto!" In Zen Buddhism, the Rinzai school talks about "sudden enlightenment," whereas the Soto school recognizes gradual enlightenment and used to be called "farmer's Zen." Well, whatever has happened with me has been gradual. There is always a lot happening below the horizon, simmering for quite a while before it finally breaks through. While I have had a sense of things churning, I have never been able to say, "suddenly there was light where before there had been only darkness!" Throughout the Ba'al Shem Tov's letter, there is the suggestion that, although he may be relating great experiences, the shift was gradual. This is important. While many people *do* have strong and sudden experiences of realization, these experiences can only become (and must be) integrated with the whole being over time.

THEN ON THE *Friday of the Torah portion Va-yeshev, in the winter of 1716, at one past noon, I fell into a deep tranquility and saw an old man coming toward me, asking, "Yisrolickel, do you know who I am?"*

I answered, "No."

Then he said, "I am sent from Heaven to teach you. No one is to know of this; not even your wife. Therefore, every day you shall travel to the place between the great mountains, and I will come and teach you there. God willing, I will uncover your true identity and reveal your inner character. Tell no one of this dream until I ask you to do so."

Then I asked him his name, and he answered, "In time, God willing, you will become aware of everything." With that, the holy elder disappeared and I awoke. I dismissed the experience as only a dream and put it out of my mind. I then went to bathe in honor of Shabbat.

It is important to pay attention to his doubts here. For a spiritual seeker, this is a romantic story, and there is a danger in thinking that what you get in elevated visions and dreams is better than what you get *down here* on this plane of reality. It is good to keep a measure of doubt handy after you have had such an experience, saying, "Yes, that was something, but it was still a dream, and here is where the work is."

I ENTERED THE *mikveh, and just as my head went under and I was completely immersed, I opened my eyes—as is my custom—and I trembled with awe and fear.*

There he was again, right in front of me! Immediately, I felt transformed into another person, and ever since, a spirit of holiness engulfs me at the receiving of the holy Shabbat.

After this, the people of the community stared at me strangely, and I didn't understand why. That evening, that venerable one, my master and teacher, who is known to you, came to me once again in a dream, saying, "Yisrolickel, it was no mere dream you had today. Know for certain that it is completely true. The sign of this truth you will see, God willing, this Sunday when you will go to the outskirts of the city and find me between the second and the third hill. However, for Heaven's sake, before you come, immerse in the mikveh four times." He then disappeared and I awoke from my sleep. I now understood that this was no ordinary dream, but a heavenly visitation.

I told myself, "This must be from the merit of my holy parents! They must have exerted themselves in such prayer and intercession before the throne of glory that Heaven caused this mercy to come upon me and elevated me to this higher awareness."

At the morning service of the holy Shabbat, I was called to the Torah to read the maftir, and this was still more amazing to me, for never had I been so honored among the congregation, as my holy brother-in-law used to conduct the calling to the Torah himself. Later that day, at the third meal of the holy Shabbat, in the house of my brother-in-law, Reb Gershon called me to him and said, "Yisrolick, what is it that I notice in you? I see a great change in your face! Are you by any chance, God forbid, not in perfect health?" I could not answer him at that time as I was sworn to silence by my teacher and holy master. At the conclusion of the Shabbat, after the Havdalah in my own house, just as I was singing Eliyahu's hymn, my wife also asked, "Why is it that you are so pale?" And I was sorry that I could not answer her either, being bound by my promise.

Three times our attention is drawn to the fact that the Ba'al Shem Tov somehow seems changed in appearance to the people around him. First, it is the community who seems to stare at him strangely. Then it is his brother-in-law who takes notice of him, as if for the first time, and gives him the honor of reading from the Torah. This is interesting, because there is just the barest, most humble suggestion here of what is repeated in all the tales of the Ba'al Shem Tov, that his brother-in-law, who later became one his greatest disciples, at first found him ignorant and contemptible and thought him unworthy of marriage to his sister, as we have already said.[19] Last, we have his wife asking him why he is so pale. This is wonderful, because there *are* experiences after which you don't look the same to people. There is something about your face, your presence: When Moses came down from Sinai, they said his face shone with light.

On the Sunday of the Torah portion Mikkets, a heavy blizzard descended on us. Still, I did what I had to do, and the hour before noon, I went to immerse four times in the mikveh and afterward went quickly to the outskirts of the city. Fortunately, I was wearing a heavy fur and was warm enough for the five-mile trek to the second mountain. As I walked, a gentile traveling from the city in a sleigh took pity on me and invited me to share the ride.

As we reached the second hill, which was to be the place of meeting, I descended from the sleigh and walked into the vale between the second and the third hill. Suddenly, the venerable one, my teacher and holy master, appeared right in front of me, saying, "Follow me." I followed him until, unexpectedly, a door opened to a cave in the cleft of the rock! I looked and saw that it was full of light, and inside was a table and two chairs. My holy teacher and master sat on the first chair and said to me, "Sit, my child." I sat in the second chair. He then took a book from his pocket and laid it on the table. The name of this book I mustn't yet reveal.[20]

He began from its beginning and said to me, "My son—look!" His face was shining and dazzling like starlight—it was as if a celestial soul had entered me. I began to read aloud from the book, and he lifted his hands above my head in blessing. Though I had never seen this holy book before, I found my understanding was immense. My eyes were illumined, and the paths of Heaven were laid out before me. The gates of understanding were opened to me as they had been at the Revelation at Mount Sinai.

After nearly two hours, he said to me, "My child, enough. God willing, you will come again tomorrow and find me in the cave just as you did today. God forbid that you should tell anyone of this."

I then asked my teacher and holy master, "What is your name?"

He answered, "It isn't yet time for you to know this. When the time comes, you will become aware of it by yourself." He took me by his right hand, and we both went out of the holy cave together.

He accompanied me all the way to the gates of the city and then put his two holy hands on my head, blessing me, but I was not able to hear the blessing clearly. It was the same on the morrow—and on and on—and still I did not know the name of my holy teacher.

Can you imagine what it would have been like to have followed the directions of such a vision and then to actually find someone there? The fear, the wonder, the delight—*and the fear again!* He had good reason for being cautious about revealing his inner landscape, even to a *tzaddik nistar* such as Reb Mordechai. For immediately, the discursive mind asks—"How is it possible? Was he hallucinating?"

The truth is, it doesn't matter. Whether this was a shamanic or imaginal journey or a trip into the natural landscape where the veil between worlds is almost transparent, the Ba'al Shem Tov's experience remains the same, the transformative effect on his consciousness remains the same. We need only know that *something* happened to him.

We have no real record of the Ba'al Shem Tov sitting and learning anything except for this mysterious book and the book sent to him by Reb Adam, the Ba'al Shem of Ropshitz.[21] Whether it was the same book or not, we have no idea. Nor do we have much of an idea about his formal education other than what he tells us in this letter. One thing is certain, his education was quite different from that of Dov Baer, the Maggid of Mezritch, his successor, who attended a formal *yeshiva* and was considered one of the most learned rabbis in Europe. This makes it all the more amazing that he was able to garner the respect of the Maggid and many other learned teachers. By his own account, he seems to have attended a *ḥeder* like other Jewish children, but the rest seems to have come from his wanderings in the woods or from the hidden *tzaddikim* who may have raised him after he was abandoned by the community or—if we can stretch our minds to believe it—from his holy teacher and this mysterious book.

Another interesting part of this story for me is the way in which his teacher addresses him—"my child," "my son." What an effect these simple words must have had on this young man, an orphan, ever looking for a reflection of his own father in others. Here is someone who is the archetype and essence not only of the strong and gentle father but also of the greatest of spiritual teachers.

THE SUMMER BEFORE we finally took leave of one another, near the gates of the city, he told me his name, and a great fear and wonder fell on me as I realized the immensity of the blessing I had received in Torah and learning from so holy and awesome a master. I fainted and fell to the ground. With the help of the blessed name, I was brought back to health, and he then told me that I must move from the city of my dwelling to a village.

Even though he does not mention his teacher's name in this letter, we can assume from his reaction that he recognized the name on hearing it and understood something of its significance. It is only in the writings of the Ba'al Shem Tov's senior disciple, Ya'akov Yosef of Polonoye (d. 1782), that we learn the holy teacher of the Ba'al Shem Tov was none other than the biblical prophet Ahiyah ha-Shiloni, the teacher of Prophet Elijah. Clearly the Ba'al Shem Tov and Reb Mordechai of Tartary, to whom the letter is addressed, belong to the same fellowship of hidden saints, and it is also clear that Reb Mordechai already knows of the master on some level. Whatever the case may be, it would have been imprudent to reveal the name in a letter that might be read by the uninitiated.[22] Remember, this was not long after the time of the failed messiah, Shabbetai Tzvi, when people were very conscious of heresy.

It is also interesting that his teacher waited so long to reveal his name. He doesn't say anything except, "I will teach you." And young Yisra'el, unburdened by a "name," is able to absorb that teaching purely, and with depth, because there are no distractions. He doesn't have to base his trust in the teacher's name, only in the behavior of the teacher and the teaching itself. Somehow, when you name something, then it has a label and you stop learning about it in depth. If Ahiyah ha-Shiloni had given him his name too soon, Yisra'el might have stopped looking closely at him for everything he could know about him, paying attention to his every breath, his every move.

But the name of Ahiyah ha-Shiloni and this whole experience also takes us back to the Ba'al Shem Tov's implicit reluctance to tell of these things, as seen in the opening paragraph of the letter. For whom can you tell about an initiation so deep? An initiation from Ahiyah ha-Shiloni himself, the teacher of Prophet Elijah! Even the Ari ha-Kodesh, Rabbi Yitzhak Luria (1534–1572), learned from the student of Ahiyah ha-Shiloni. Here is a boy of 18, who *appears* to be no more than a peasant, learning from the ascended master of Prophet Eliyahu—how can you talk about that? And why should anyone believe you? If you go around telling tales like this about yourself, you are sure to be thought crazy, an egotist, or a megalomaniac.

I can imagine a *mitnaged* (an opponent of Hasidism) of the time yelling, "Outrageous! You take your 'kitchen wisdom' and treat it as if it came from the highest Heavens!" And it is not just the *mitnagdim* on the outside that we need to worry about but the powerful lures of the ego within. This is the real reason for the many prohibitions in our traditions around talking about our spiritual experiences. Imagine, if you will, what process the Ba'al Shem Tov has to go through before he finally decides he is going share this with somebody. Despite the fact that we don't know much about who Mordechai of Tartary was, we can imagine what kind of intimacy there must have been between them before the Ba'al Shem Tov consented to tell him this story.

---

*W*ITH THE HELP *of God, and through the efforts of my saintly brother-in-law, I moved to a village near Kittov. I established an inn there, and from Shabbat to Shabbat, I was in meditation and solitude until this day, spending my time between the mountains.*

Every Shabbat eve, I returned to my house, but on the weekdays I was blessed to face my holy teacher and master who has disclosed the secrets of the mysteries to me, until now, thank God, no secret escapes me. However . . . and this causes me pain . . . it is already a month less one day since my holy teacher and master came to me in the morning watch (between two and six A.M.), saying, "Yisrolickel, you know, my child, that the time will soon come when you must be revealed. It was decreed, written, and signed from Heaven that when you become 36 years old, you must be revealed."[23]

The letter ends with the news that it is time for Yisra'el, the hidden *tzaddik*, to come out of the closet and become the Ba'al Shem Tov.

Why is this a cause for pain?

Just imagine the life he has been leading up to this point, a life among the hidden *tzaddikim*, whose highest commitment is to a kind of "karma yoga," a service to God without the thought of reward, without the slightest recognition from the people around them, whom they are directly benefiting. To dedicate your life to this kind of selfless service is not a light commitment, and to suddenly have your life's mission turned upside down must have seemed like a disaster. More than that, there was a certain comfort in the anonymous life he had been living. Days with his master, time for deep prayer and meditation, freedom from the endless responsibilities of communal life; these would have been heavy losses, and it is no wonder that the retiring Yisra'el should have felt torn between the silent life and the pull of the future.[24]

A LETTER FROM ADAM BA'AL SHEM

Right on the heels of this earth-shattering news, the Ba'al Shem Tov received a letter from Reb Adam of Ropshitz, his predecessor in the role of ba'al shem. Tradition holds that a copy of this letter was sent by the Ba'al Shem Tov to his brother-in-law, Gershon of Kittov.

I HAVE HEARD from our teacher and master, the holy one—

IN THE YEAR 1572 (5333), *there lived in the holy city of S'fat a simple and unlearned man who prayed in simplicity and was perfect in his actions, living humbly and attracting no one's attention.*

One night, while he was performing the Tikkun Ḥatzot (midnight prayer), he heard a knock at the door. When he asked who it was, he received the answer, "Eliyahu ha-Navi," and immediately he opened the door.

As Eliyahu ha-Navi entered, a luminous glow filled even the corners of the room. There was such joy and elation that even the man's children began to dance in their cribs. Then the man said to him, "Please, sit, Rabbi, and be at peace."

He then sat down and said to the man, "I am here to reveal the time of the Mashiaḥ's coming to you. But I do so only on the condition that you reveal one thing to me: What special thing did you do on the day of your bar mitzvah? For on account of this deed, it was decreed from above that you merited to have me reveal myself to you and to reveal the hidden mysteries."

Then, the man answered him, "Whatever I have done, I have done it only for the sake of the Holy One's blessed name. How can I reveal this to anyone except the Holy One? If you, my holy teacher and honored master, will not reveal these exalted things to me because of my refusal, then I do not need them. I have it by tradition that whatever a Jew does should be hidden from others, so that it may be for the sake of the blessed name alone."

Suddenly, Eliyahu ha-Navi vanished.

Above there was a great tumult on account of this man's simplicity, refusing even Eliyahu ha-Navi so that his deed should be only for the sake of Heaven! Nevertheless, it was decreed with the agreement of the entire heavenly tribunal that Eliyahu ha-Navi must reveal himself to the man again and teach him Torah, revealing all of the hidden mysteries.

And so it was.

If the heavenly assembly was so upset with him, why was he still rewarded? Because, in the middle of their righteous indignation, Prophet Elijah said to them, "Look, you don't get it—he may not have answered our question, but he told us something much more valuable, that whatever the deed was, it was done 'only for the sake of the Holy One's blessed name.' " When this was understood, the assembly agreed that the hidden mysteries should be revealed to him by Prophet Elijah. A story . . .

Toward the end of his life, the Ba'al Shem Tov searched for someone who might help him in his task. He was then led unexpectedly to a young shepherd tending his flock. He ducked behind a bush to watch the shepherd and what he saw next amazed him. The shepherd, thinking himself alone, began to talk to God, saying, "Oh God, what can I do to serve you out here?" He looked around for a moment and then said, "If it will please you, I'll jump this ditch for you!" So he jumped across the ditch. Then he jumped back, and continued to jump back and forth across the ditch until he fell down in exhaustion! When he saw this, the Ba'al Shem Tov knew that this was the person who could help him in his task.[25]

This is a good question for all of us to ask of ourselves. "What is it that I have done for God alone—*that no one else in the world knows*—that is simply my own special love gift to God?"

ELIYAHU SHOWED HIMSELF to the man again and taught him the many mysteries of the holy Torah. In time, he became distinguished in his generation, a perfect tzaddik in hiding. No one knew of his holiness and greatness.

And when this tzaddik passed from this world in his old age, they set him a place above in the very mansion where the holy mothers and fathers dwell. But the advocates of good stirred, saying, "He deserves a greater reward, seeing that he was such a great tzaddik, hiding himself that no one should know his deeds, which were done, in deepest truth, for the sake of Heaven alone. Thus he deserves an immensely great and good reward."

So the tribunal of Heaven decreed—

"Being that the world was not worthy to sense the fragrance of the spirit of his Torah, this holy soul shall once again descend into the material world, and Heaven shall move this soul to reveal herself. A renewing way shall be revealed through this soul until the world will be filled with knowledge, bringing the nearness of completion."

NOW, IN THE name of our holy teacher and master, I must reveal that you, my holy brother, are this same blessed soul who has come to this world again to scent it with the fragrance of purity and to purify it with the spirit of holiness. Thus, very soon, you must reveal yourself and illuminate the hearts of everyone with a renewing

light. May the name of Heaven be sanctified through your hand, and the redemption brought near in our day.
　　Amen—thus be the will.[26]

———————

Hearing this, the Ba'al Shem Tov knew it was truly his time to be revealed and he consented. But he was not to be without support in this task. There is a ḤaBaD teaching that says:

> When the souls of the Ba'al Shem Tov, the Maggid of Mezritch, and Reb Shneur Zalman of Liadi were told that they had to come down to Earth again for this purpose, each of them said, "I will not go unless I have a cadre of 60 warriors to come with me." For it is said that around the bed of King Solomon there were 60 swordsmen to protect him from the terrors of the night. Each of them asked for these *shishim gebborim* (60 mighty ones) to accompany them. And if we look at the extraordinary companions and disciples of these three, we have to believe that this wish was granted to each.[27]

I have a sense that this demand was based in a very real feeling that said, "If you are going to send me down with this kind of consciousness in me—a consciousness that most people won't be able to tune into—then I'm going to seem like a crazy man. I will have such a burden on me; to fulfill my mission is going to be difficult because of the doubts that will constantly be assailing me, saying, 'Maybe I'm crazy.' At the very least, I will need 60 companions to accompany me, people I can rely on and who will have a notion of what my consciousness is about."

It is important to have spiritual teachers and friends, people who speak the same language, or at least accept you in your uniqueness. We need to know we're not alone, and certainly not crazy. But we also have to remember that spiritual work done in loneliness, without reality checks from people we trust, can often breed delusions of grandeur and harmful behavior. It is important to ask yourself, as Kurt Vonnegut liked to put it his highly idiosyncratic language, "Who do I have in my 'karass'?"[28]

2

A Heart Afire: The Revelation of the Ba'al Shem Tov

AFTER THE BA'AL SHEM TOV'S LONG APPRENTICESHIP, THE time had finally come for him to reveal himself to the world. But how was this man who had spent most of his life learning to hide going to go about making himself known? How was he going to reveal the message he was born to give and do it without it leading directly into the ego inflation he most feared?

It was a difficult problem; one that he shared with most of the great messengers of the world's spiritual traditions. I am reminded most of the situation of the Buddha Gautama (ca. 463–383 B.C.E.) . . .

> After his awakening under the Bodhi Tree in India, the Buddha Gautama was not inclined to teach the message of "dependent co-arising" that had been imparted to him. For seven weeks he sat and meditated on the problem in the vicinity of that tree, asking himself, "How will I find the words to convey such a message? And who will have the ears to hear it?" After much deliberation, he decided that it simply wasn't possible.
>
> Seeing that the Buddha had finally reached a decision, God, in the form of Brahma, suddenly appeared before the Buddha and implored him to teach, saying, "Blessed Buddha, it will indeed be difficult to teach the truth of dependent co-arising; humanity as a whole goes about with dust caked in its eyes and yet knows it not.

But it is not equally so for all people; some are quite blind, while others may begin to see clearly with a little help." The Buddha realized that it had been so for him as well. Then, suddenly overwhelmed with compassion, he knew that he must seek to be the servant of this message to others. He decided to seek out others like himself first, people who might be able to grasp the message, and who in time could help him in the work of refining it for those whose eyes were still quite blind.[1]

Like the Buddha, the holy Ba'al Shem Tov had also grasped a message of integral wholeness, which for him was conveyed in the teaching of *hashgahah pratit* or specific personal providence. But as we have already mentioned, he was very reluctant to become a "known" teacher, concerned that he would only be misunderstood or, worse, become filled with an unholy pride. Nevertheless, through the intervention of his teacher, Ahiyah ha-Shiloni, and his predecessor, Adam Ba'al Shem, he was finally convinced of the necessity of this fateful step.

But how would he go about it? And to whom would he take this message first? As with the Buddha, he chose those in whom—with but a little help—the "dust caked in their eyes" might easily be removed. It was not that the Ba'al Shem Tov was in any sense an elitist—indeed, we will see later that he was in fact quite the opposite—but that he needed to enlist the help of those who were already themselves gifted in order to spread the message. Thus he began to draw to himself Torah scholars and kabbalists who were already on the cusp of a breakthrough.

DIVINE PROVIDENCE

The following story is a unique treasure among Hasidic teaching tales, and though less well known than other conversion tales of the Ba'al Shem Tov, it is one of the few that allows us a glimpse at the integral sophistication with which he "ensnared" the great rabbis of his generation. The teachings that follow it will show how he kept them as well as how he taught his Hasidim to succeed in the path that he himself had taken.

IN THE HEART *of one of the great rabbis of the time—great not only in Torah, but also in wisdom and God consciousness—there stirred an overwhelming desire to meet the Ba'al Shem Tov so that he might form a judgment based on more than mere hearsay.[2] He hoped to engage the Ba'al Shem Tov in a dispute so as to convince him to repent from his deviant ways!*

And so, as he set out on his journey to the Ba'al Shem Tov's home, he entreated God to protect him from the schemes of this reformer and his followers, so that he would not be ensnared in the net of their heresies.

A common motif in stories of the Ba'al Shem Tov is "the enemy turned into a friend." Rabbi Gershon of Kittov is at first dismissive of and embarrassed by his seemingly coarse brother-in-law; Rabbi Ya'akov Yosef rails against the Ba'al Shem Tov from the pulpit; and Rabbi Dov Baer, the Maggid of Mezrich, is disgusted by the Ba'al Shem Tov's "simple peasant tales" before finally realizing their true message. In this case, this basic motif becomes "the would-be-converter who is himself converted."

THE BA'AL SHEM Tov, *who was already acquainted with this rabbi's bitter opposition to his movement and its ideology, welcomed him with warm hospitality and an attitude of friendliness and goodwill. He asked about his welfare, seated him, and then encouraged him to speak his mind, to argue with him in his quest for truth.*

"I am well aware," said the Ba'al Shem Tov, "that your heart is turned against me and that my way vexes your spirit. Tell me, what wrong have you found in me? What report has reached you to discredit me? I beg you, challenge me with your questions and objections. Only then will I be able to know what to answer and how to clear myself before you. After all, our common goal is truth and faith. No honor and glory will be granted to the victor, whether it be you or I. In the face of the glory of the ever present to whom all glory is due, of what use is the empty honor of an argument won?"

The rabbi thought for a while before responding, weighing his words carefully so that he might express them with utmost precision. His thoughts now organized, he began:

"If, in the heat of this discussion, I address you improperly, do not judge me as one who presumes against one's master, since I have not become your disciple. Is it not the way of the Torah, that in matters concerning the faith, one neither flatters nor respects a person's status? Thus I put to you these weighty issues."

The very civilized opening of this debate reveals two distinct perspectives on the debate itself. The Ba'al Shem Tov's opening remarks make it clear that this is, from his perspective, a holy argument for "the sake of Heaven"—it is irrelevant who wins or loses such an argument as long as truth prevails. Nevertheless, the *mitnaged*'s (opponent's) preface to his own remarks tell us that something very different is on the line for him, even if he has not yet fully accepted the idea. Whether because he feels threatened by the Ba'al Shem Tov's reputation for converting enemies to his cause (and is trying to puff himself up) or because he already feels mysteriously drawn to him, the *mitnaged* betrays himself by putting the matter of master and disciple, Rebbe and Hasid, on the table without its ever being raised by the Ba'al Shem Tov.

"IT WAS TOLD to me by trustworthy people that you credit yourself with the possession of an occult and mysterious form of worship, one unknown to the sages of previous generations. Your disciples describe it as a secret discovery in the faith, some of them going so far as attributing to it the validity of a dogma, as if it were a new addition to the faith! I was further told that in order to realize it, one must be graced with an exalted soul and a special predisposition.

"In my opinion, those who maintain such ideas must be held accountable for heresy. One who claims 'innovation,' adding to the fundamentals of the faith, is subject to suspicion of heresy, for they transgress the commandment saying, 'You shall not add' to the commandments (Deut. 13:1).[3]

"Your disciples also claim in your name that your Torah secrets are imparted to you from Heaven. Then they say that those who formulate Torah insights from the reason of their own mind and do not channel the Torah from above are presenting Torah that is inauthentic, a mere manipulation of words and empty discourse. This, in our eyes, is spiritual arrogance, a lying conceit arising from your own heart. You claim ruaḥ ha-kodesh, the prophecy of the Holy Spirit, for yourself and derogate all ordinary Torah to rungs lower than your own.

"When I scrutinize all of your homilies and explications, I come to the conclusion that they are all contrived distortions and concepts that run contrary to prescribed Torah exegetics. Typically, your teachings disregard the apparent meanings of the Torah and belittle the rabbis and students who pore over it day and night.

"Who and what compels you to strike out on a new path? From whom did you receive your tradition? Who has handed to you the authority over Torah and prayer that you claim as yours? Please, tell me something of your early upbringing, of your childhood, so that I might understand your conduct accordingly."

From the rabbinic perspective of the time, the *mitnaged* is wholly justified in raising these objections with the Ba'al Shem Tov. Undoubtedly, the new

Hasidim, convinced of their master's spiritual elevation by what they had themselves seen, had begun to sing his praises rather *too* loudly in their own towns and villages. By attempting to convince others with words of what they had seen with their own eyes, these new Hasidim were naturally driven into making impulsive and inflated claims on behalf of their new master and thus caused him a lot of unnecessary headaches (just as they would his successor, the Maggid of Mezritch).

The zeal of disciples is often a master's most difficult test. In this case, their pious exaggerations, stories taken out of context, and words imparted without the proper understanding, did not bolster the reputation of their master, as they had hoped, but only brought it into question by those who, like the *mitnaged*, were more mature and sober in their judgments.

THE BA'AL SHEM *Tov expressed his satisfaction over the clarity with which the rabbi presented his case, and replied:*

"My father worked hard to achieve simple integrity and virtue. As a small child, I was completely joined to him. My own simple openness stems from him. I recall how before his death, he called me to his side and said to me, 'Always remember, my child, that God is with you. Never let go of this awareness. Nurture it in all your ways. Conceal it from everyone so that no one can sense it in you, and so that you appear as one who is ignorant.' These words have remained anchored in my heart and engraved in my memory."[4]

In this very simple way, without reprimanding his own disciples before a stranger or calling the *mitnaged*'s "trustworthy" sources into question, the Ba'al Shem Tov is making it known that it would be foreign to him to make such claims for himself as he has been accused of making. At the same time, he has also begun to answer the question about his origins.

We also see in his father's advice the telltale signs of a *tzaddik nistar*, a hidden righteous one.

"AFTER MY DEAR father surrendered his body, I used to seek solitude in the forests and the fields, and there I would meditate on the holy teaching that the blessed and Holy One fills all being and is with me mamash *(palpably)!*

"In order to serve God our maker in my own secret way, I became a behelfer *(a teacher's helper), training the children in the blessings over food and the responses of 'Blessed is God' and 'Blessed is the name' and 'Amen' for each benediction. Also,*

I would joyfully and loudly proclaim the Shema *with them. In this way, was I able to invest my work with the* kavanah, *with the divine intentionality that my father first taught me. Later on, I became a caretaker in the synagogue. There, I was also able to practice in secret the* kavanot *(mystical intentions) during the night.*

"When the proper time arrived, I found in the sister of Rabbi Gershon of Kittov a wonderful wife, and we settled down in a small house situated between two mountains. For a while, I earned my livelihood by digging clay and transporting it to town. Then we rented a home in the village, not too far from a small meditation hut in the nearby forest. I spent most of my time in that hut, and upon returning to the village, I would busy myself at the inn, receiving guests and plying them with food, drink, and accommodations.

"In the course of time, I acquired knowledge of both the nigleh *(manifest) and* nistar *(hidden) parts of Torah. However, this was not as important to me as my work to sanctify my thoughts and to deepen in myself the kind of awareness my father had taught me. My studies, prayers, and actions served as the means to realize this intent."*

So we have been taken once again through some of the events of the Ba'al Shem Tov's early life, some of which are very similar to what we have learned in the autobiographical letter sent to the hidden *tzaddik* Mordechai of Tartary. It also speaks discreetly of the values of the *tzaddikim nistarim* without naming them or mentioning his exalted teacher—neither of which would have been prudent—but conveying the message of the teaching just the same. Thus having brought his *mitnaged* interlocutor up to the present, he continues answering his objections.

" 'ONE IS LED *along the path one wishes to follow.'⁵ Through every occurrence I sought to see, to hear, to sense, and to find meaning and purpose. I found myself continually proceeding toward my goal. At each step, I saw through my inner eyes the manifestation of divinity. In each word I heard God. In each experience, I felt sacredness. I felt divine purpose at work in everything, a dynamic form of* hashgahah pratit *(specific personal providence). At the rung upon which I then stood, every secular workday act would—upon reflection—take on the sacred quality of Torah and prayer. Every focused deed felt like a holy mitzvah."*

Some might call this fooling oneself, but what the Ba'al Shem Tov is actually talking about is a sacred, intentional, and contemplative *investment*. He is looking out on the world in all of its perfection, investing in the understanding of the inherent perfection of its design.

I once composed a chant for attuning to the four worlds (*arba olamot*) of Jewish mysticism that says, "It is perfect, you are loved, all is clear, and I am holy." "It is perfect," refers to the world in which we live, the world of *assiyah*, the world of action. Now, "perfection" may not seem to make sense in a world where so many things obviously appear to be wrong. But neither the chant nor the Ba'al Shem Tov is suggesting that there not pain, loss, or destruction in the world but, rather, that there is an attunement to perfection, love, clarity, and holiness in attitude that is healing for the heart and for the planet as well.

In this way, the Ba'al Shem Tov was able to see, with sacred eyes, the miraculous order of creation. He was able to look at the natural world and the seemingly ordinary and see the magic and miracle inherent in them.

"OPEN YOUR HEART! Anyone who describes my path as new—and as a newly invented deviation from faith and service—is completely in error, as is anyone who thinks of my way as a gratuitous addition in the service of God. For in truth, the stirring that I evoke in the hearts of those who desire closeness to God is nothing new, nor is there in this any 'addition' to that which was already known to such individuals as were peculiarly well versed in the faith; nor is there anything 'added' to what we have received from our ancestors and teachers whom God, our sustainer, calls forth in every generation. On the contrary, all of my teaching constitutes but a reminder and a reinforcement of the content and intent of faith, which, due to the many vicissitudes and trials that have beset us, has been forgotten from the hearts of many masters of Torah. And if this happened to the great, how much more so to the rest of the people. Therefore, give me your ear and listen as I try to help you to understand."

These last three sentences refer to the spiritual drought and suffering experienced by the Jews in eastern Europe in the decades before the coming of the Ba'al Shem Tov. In the wake of their recent messianic disappointments and the terrible pogroms led by Chmielnicki and his mounted Cossacks, the Jews of eastern Europe were in a serious depression, almost devoid of hope. Compounding the problem was the terribly rigid division between the learned Torah scholars and the unlearned and underprivileged Jews of the shtetl, which created a barrier that had largely blocked the flow of genuine spirituality to both groups.

"*There is no doubt that the belief in the existence of God is the main foundation and root of the entire Torah. Obviously, we need not discuss here those who in their life are already dead—the wicked who arbitrarily dismiss the existence of God—for such have momentarily lost their celestial minds and have throttled their own faith. Leaving them aside, there are also those who assert God's divinity and yet deny God's providence. Thus we find that there are those who believe and deny in the same breath. What gain is there in their assertion that the blessed creator created all creatures and invested great wisdom and proper intention in them, if they also assert that this creator then removed providence from the world, leaving creation to carry on by itself?*"

I used to challenge people who suggested that the abbreviation for Jesus' name, (*Yeshu*) *yud-shin-vav*, actually stood for *y'imah sh'mo v'zikhro*, "may his name be blotted out." I would ask them, "Do you believe in divine providence (*hashgaḥah pratit*)? Because if there is such a thing as divine providence and you believe in it, you have to ask, 'What was happening when Jesus was born?' Was God saying, 'Oops, I forgot to look!' Did Jesus or the Buddha somehow happen outside of God's providence?" How could God not have taken into account the birth of such figures; how could it not be part of God's plan? The Ba'al Shem Tov says, "Even a leaf falling from a tree and blown by the wind falls on a particular side because of *hashgaḥah pratit!*"[6] If you believe in *hashgaḥah pratit*, then you have to believe that all that we find in the religious world is also *ki lo yidokh, mimenu nidokh*, God making certain that every nation has access to the Divine in the forms that fit the ethnic and environmental ways of that people.

"*In asserting this, they remove from God the attributes of intender, caller-into-being, invigorator, sustainer, creator, and renewer—leaving only the history of a God who once created the world long ago but who no longer creates or cares to be involved. What good is a God who created the world thousands of years ago if at this moment we behold that God as deaf, blind, and unaware? There is no practical difference between this notion of God and that of those who altogether deny the existence of God.*

"*A true believer is one who affirms the relationship of all creation to the creator, who affirms that the creator's existence is self-sufficient, independent of any other being or existence, knowing itself and creation through self-knowledge, effecting all acts with specific intent toward known ends, who is inclusive of all perfections that are absolutely good. In other words, God is simple, free willed, and absolute omnipotence. God's wisdom is not conditioned and acquired from the outside; God's will does not depend on the will of another, on effects that other causes bring to that will. Dependent on other causes, God would not be free, not simple, for the will, too, would be conditioned by a cause. Thus God's omnipotence means that there is no possible function that God could not fulfill. Now, such is the true concept of God's awesome and honored name, which every true believer has to understand and to realize. In other words, God as invigorator, as the caller-into-existence, as the sustainer, who, with great graciousness, renews daily all of the acts of creation."*

For the Ba'al Shem Tov, it is not enough to *talk* about God or even to *believe* in the existence of God; one must be in *relationship* with God, the living God of the prophets. The divine "clock maker" of the 18th-century Deists is for all intents and purposes little better than the godlessness of atheists. Nor is the God of theology or rabbinics—who can be spoken of in the third person—of much more use to him. It is not that he is rejecting the thought of the sages but that he is pointing out how meaningless it is to talk *about* God if that talk is not accompanied by a knowing wink, acknowledging God's hidden presence in every place and every moment. For if God is not also radically and palpably present, theological speculations are like coordinates on a fictional map to nowhere. God is truly a verb, continually creating and communicating with us—indeed, keeping us in existence every moment!

There is another reason that the simple acknowledgment or belief in God's existence is not enough for the Ba'al Shem Tov: the very notion to him is regressive and demonstrates a lack of understanding. It is not that I believe in God, but that *God believes me into existence,* creating a space in which I can become conscious of my own self and can ultimately discover the divine source of that self. God does not occupy a portion of existence over and against us, a divine territory in what we call existence or the universe; God, quite simply, *is* existence! When God is existence, then all is God and everything that we encounter is but a symbol "transparent to transcendence."7

This pantheistic notion terrified many rabbis in the Ba'al Shem Tov's day and for long after. However, today, it is becoming the only tenable position. For as we free ourselves from the limiting notion of God as some kind of territorial overlord, we find that the only God that will suffice cannot be limited in any way whatsoever—whether in space or time. God simply *is.* God is all in everything.[8] Thus the holy Ba'al Shem Tov spells out in a plethora of theological and philosophical erudition the ways in which God cannot and should not be limited in our thinking or in our hearts.[9]

"IN GENERAL, FAITH is sufficient to the observance of the Torah and the mitzvot, even at the shallow level on which many students of Torah accept it. Nevertheless, they too, err in their imagination and think that this God sits on the highest plane, beyond all the Heavens, climbing up and down, leaving everyone to act as their heart desires in the ways of their own free choice, without divine intervention of God's power and might. Such people also believe that the existence of creation separates the creator from the creation, that God is blessedly abstract, sundered and separated from all the world in complete and utter separation. They believe that God looks down from an extremely high place and sees all things that are done under the sun as well as such other things that have no apparent reason behind them. But due to the fact that, in the end, their belief in the providence and supervision of God is strong and since they do believe that God beholds and knows all that occurs and that it is in God's power to ordain reward and consequence—this faith of theirs can shelter them from pollution and bring them close to merit.

"Higher than this level of faith is that of those who believe and have realized that the Holy One infuses God-presence into all of creation, and that the letters of the Torah are celestial lights. People of this category believe that the sanctuaries, synagogues, and houses of study are filled with the glories of God's radiance and that most of the dreams of the tzaddikim are true and that the authentic tzaddik is, at times, affected by an echo of heavenly intelligence and merits the ascension to, and revelation of ruaḥ ha-kodesh (the Holy Spirit). Believers such as these rise one rung above the category I mentioned before, and most people who serve God and are sensitive to the word of God belong to this group.

"However, those who read the Torah, taking the pains of allowing her to speak to them—who behold her with open and focused eyes—will rise far above any of the levels mentioned before. They will find that all her intentions are concentrated on instilling pure faith in the Holy One. This is the central theme on which the 613 mitzvot and all the segments of the Torah converge. We must implant this deeply in our hearts. No existence has existence other than the self-existence of God. Hence even that which at first glance seems as separated and sundered from divinity is itself absolute divinity. Likewise, all that is brought into the existence and renewal of the active world, even though their manifest causes are results of natural accidents and a person's choice or intervention, nevertheless, the inner cause is rooted in hashgaḥah pratit, the particular providence and wisdom of God, which radiate visibly to the eyes of such has merit to see it, as a subtle brilliance of divine wisdom.

"Having affirmed that it is of the infinite One's omnipotence to do anything and everything, it is therefore possible to believe that God is capable of concentrating on concealing God's self in such an amazing manner that God may be simultaneously manifest and hidden, visible and invisible, and that the average eye cannot see anything but the externals of manifest phenomena. But the believer whose mind is alert to behold and see everything in its innermost spiritual dimensions and state of holiness can thus discover the divine power that is intertwined and combined with all the separate atoms of all beings—seeing in this power the design that furthers a particular intention."

This is the key to the Ba'al Shem Tov's emphasis on divine providence, indeed his whole conception of *hashgaḥah pratit* in regard to the minutiae of daily life: "No existence has existence other than the self-existence of God. Hence even that which at first glance seems as separated and sundered from divinity is itself absolute divinity." You see, when God is the place of the world, then there is nothing that is not divine, that is not a manifestation of divinity. Thus every encounter becomes a divine opportunity to be taken hold of, like a golden chain of consciousness leading one back to the source. Divinity itself is the secret meaning, the holy significance buried in every thing, every breath, and every thought. Once we have acknowledged that divinity, then we naturally begin to reflect on its particular meaning for us in this moment, in the four worlds of our own consciousness.

"YOU SURELY RECALL the story in the Talmud:

" 'And thus it occurred to Rabbi Akiva. He set out on a journey, taking with him an ass, a cock, and a light. Arriving at a village, he sought food and lodging at the inn but was denied both. He then exclaimed, "Gam zu l'tovah" (Everything ordained from Heaven is for the good). Leaving the village, he set up camp for the night in a nearby field. During the night, a lion attacked and killed his ass, a panther ate his cock, and a powerful gust of wind extinguished his light. Again, he exclaimed, "Everything ordained from Heaven is for the good." The following morning, he passed through the village a second time to continue his journey, when he found it deserted and in ruins. A lone villager explained that a gang of bandits had attacked the village during the night, killing, plundering, and kidnapping. Akiva then realized how true his exclamations had been. His ass and his cock could have made noises and drawn the attention of the marauders, as could his light had it not been extinguished.'[10]

"Now each of these incidents are really distinct from one another, rooted in dif-

ferent causes. Viewed separately, each episode was the result of free choice and nat-
ural instinct, for the innkeeper was a man of free choice, the animals were only fol-
lowing their instincts as hungry predators, and it is natural for a gust of wind to
extinguish a light. Anyone whose thinking is undisciplined will thus attribute these
events to accident and nature, but a holy person, like Rabbi Akiva, found in these
episodes nothing but the hand of God. He did not dismiss the innkeeper's refusal of
hospitality as simply 'free choice,' nor did he attribute the loss of his animals and
his light only to beastly instincts and natural causes. Instead, Rabbi Akiva saw God
face to face in each event."

It is important to notice here that the Ba'al Shem Tov does not simply dismiss reason and natural causes in a headlong quest for spiritual significance. He begins by openly acknowledging that these events, when viewed separately, are quite "distinct from one another," and "rooted in different causes." Then why does he call an attribution of events to "accident and nature" an "undisciplined" way of thinking? Because this attribution is taking into consideration only one source of human knowledge.

You see, the Ba'al Shem Tov believed in an integral process of understanding—distilling information from the world of the senses, the world of emotion, the world of the intellect, and the world of intuition—in what might be called "four worlds thinking." This more "disciplined" approach, similar to G. I. Gurdjieff's Objective Reason, takes into account the fact that the only things we truly experience directly are the contents of consciousness—what we *perceive* as coming from the senses, from our feelings, from our minds, and from our intuitive faculty.[11] We do not dismiss any of them, but neither is it necessary to give the most authority to sensation simply because it has the *appearance* of objectivity. Rather, one must hold the paradox of seemingly conflicting information, engaging and embracing the entirety of the situation, taking all of these factors into account. It is not that one is true and another is false simply because they would seem to be in conflict; it is that they are giving one different types of information on which to make an integrated appraisal of the situation.

Thus when the Ba'al Shem Tov speaks of Rabbi Akiva as having "found in these episodes nothing but the hand of God," he is saying that Rabbi Akiva took a holistic approach to the situation. Surely the information from the senses and reason was of God also, as we have already discussed (there being nothing but God), but it was not all the information there was to be had. To this he added the percepts of feeling and intuition from which he grasped the whole as a divine event of personal significance to him, seeing "God face to face in each event."

"THE FOLLOWING HAPPENED to one of our acquaintances. He was roused from his sleep one night by the bite of an insect. Leaping from his bed, he ran into the outer room, upsetting a barrel of water, which then spilled on the floor and extinguished some coals that were about to burst into flame and burn down the house. Returning to his bed, he found that the post holding up the ceiling had cracked and the ceiling had collapsed over his bed. Had he still been in bed, he would have been killed.

Now, had this man been one of the undisciplined who cast off the divine yoke, he would have viewed each of these occurrences as separate incidents, totally unrelated to one another. And if he who experienced this would have seen it in such a manner, how much more so would those to whom he would have related it. But one who believes with perfect faith sees the visage of God face to face in the coinciding of all these accidents. Those who have meditated several times to see things in such a manner, their only strength being in their faith, attribute all such experiences to hashgahah pratit (special providence). Even in situations that are not as conspicuously recognizable as this, they can see the hand of God. As they accustom themselves to this perception in service, they will realize that there is nothing outside of God. Thus we interpret the sentence, 'There is none else besides God' (Deut. 4:39)¹² in its very simple meaning.

"Myriad thoughts arise in a person every second. Those that pass momentarily, sparking and lighting up in one moment and being extinguished in the next, may be nothing more than hollow thoughts with which we need not concern ourselves. However, the thought that lingers for a moment and remains more persistently, I say is a thought of Torah and of the faith. The tarrying and lingering of that thought is a stirring and a reminder coming from above, rooted in the Divine. One must seize such thoughts and realize them more fully.

"But since the minds of people are not all the same, and since each mind contains many details, each believer must realize that he or she is being stirred with subtle hints from above. Such hints are branches of the cosmic knowing, prepared especially for that individual because they are attached to the very root of that person's soul. Such individuals are thus capable of visualizing the subtle realities, of seeing angels, divine energies, as they influence the growth of every single blade of grass."¹³

Just as sensation and intellect are naturally paired, so are feeling and intu-

ition—though all are inextricably linked. According to the Sufi mystic Hazrat
Inayat Khan (1882–1927), intuition first expresses itself in the language of
feeling. That feeling, he said, then spreads "within the horizon of the mind,
shapes itself and becomes more narrative of its idea." But this is also problematic, for a person who is not mature in discerning a simple thought from
intuition or a thought reacting to that intuition from the intuition itself may
become confused about which is which. And if one then takes the thought for
intuition and pursues it to a disappointing end, one tends to lose confidence
in one's own intuition, "and that faculty diminishes." Therefore, one needs to
become very discerning with regard to the workings of the mind through the
practice of meditation.[14]

"INDEED, THEY ARE actually able to hear the sound of that angelic messenger com-
manding that blade of grass to grow. People who have such wisdom are also able
to hear all heavenly echoes and proclamations resonating in the world.

"Unlike those whose superficial perception allows them to believe such experiences possible only in situations specifically sanctified for such encounters, people of
the subtle level of mind realize that all situations are sanctified. Thus they believe
that not only prophecy and vision come from Heaven but that every word that is
intentionally heard and related to is an emissary of God. Upon proper reflection,
they can find in it specific aim and intention. Such people are able to draw heaps
of insight from things that seem meaningless to others.

"To these rare souls, who have realized the amazing mystery that all is holy,
there is no distinction between synagogue and woods, as both are suitable places for
prayer. For through kavanah (conscious intent) the praying soul sanctifies even the
forest. And as they intensify their deep perception, thus adhering to the creator in
deveikut; there remains no distinction to them between the word of Torah,
Mishnah; Talmud, midrash, aggadah, or discourses that seem meaningless for having originated in the marketplace!

"Even when people are speaking, unconscious of the hidden meaning in their
words, they cannot obscure the hand of the creator who gave humanity the power
of speech and furnished us with a mouth through which we can speak. For God
places many secondary intentions in our mouths, hiding in them amazing things
that we ourselves may not have intended in our communication. Not only this, but
those who are in the habit of hearing the subtle meaning and the inner voice are
easily aroused, even when they fall from their absorbing deveikut in God. For they
hear in every thing a voice calling to them to return to service, even if the one who
spoke the rousing word did not intend it."

There is a species of miracle that might be called ordinary, which may be the most important of all miracles. Consider the situation the famed psychologist Carl Jung once found himself in after a wedding . . .

> **When the wedding meal was ready, Jung was seated opposite a distinguished looking man who turned out to be a lawyer. Quite naturally, the two men began an animated conversation about criminal psychology. But when Jung, in order to answer a question that the man had asked, began to make up a detailed hypothetical story to illustrate his point, the lawyer's expression began to change drastically. Jung, seeing this dramatic change, clearly felt that something had gone wrong and quickly excused himself, going out for a cigar. Within minutes, another guest came out and reproached him for his frightful indiscretion. Jung would write of this many years later: "To my amazement and horror it turned out that I had told the story of the man opposite me, exactly and in all its details. I also discovered, at this moment, that I could no longer remember a single word of the story—even to this day I have been unable to recall it."[15]**

This is a very important teaching.

We must not fall into the error of deifying our spiritual teachers simply because wisdom seems to flow through them. Often we are amazed by this phenomenon and tend to assume all of our lives are laid bare before the teacher, that they are speaking with complete consciousness of how their words are affecting us. This is how it was in the Ba'al Shem Tov's time as well. Often the Hasidim would leave a talk by him, all assuming he had spoken exclusively to them and their particular issues. There is no denying that his insight was acute, but the Ba'al Shem Tov is telling us himself that it is *God* who has affixed the most significant messages onto the carrier wave of our speech and actions and thus it is *God* who must be praised.

"IN THE SAME manner, when the Moabite parents of Ruth gave her the name Ruth, they had no inkling that from her would come David ha-Melekh with song and praise for God, as the meaning of the word 'Ruth' implies. Nor did the parents of the Spies (during the Exodus journey) know that the names they chose for their sons spoke of their sons' future. All this is due to the fact that the Holy One moved events that caused the parents to make the appropriate associations for naming their children as they did, or that in the Moabite language caused the parents of Ruth to call

her by that particular name. The sages had this notion in mind when they studied the scriptural passage, 'God Who has placed desolations *(shamot, which also translates as* shemot, *names) in the world' (Ps. 46:9).*[16]

"For true believers, there is no distinction between readings from sacred literature and the utterances of a child or even of an idolater; for as soon as they carefully examine any associated thoughts that are sparked in their hearts and that tarry with them for a while, these too become as words of Torah. This even applies to such thoughts that arise in the heart when we are preoccupied with thoughts of inclination for darkness and lust. For if we feel that such thoughts arise repeatedly and return continuously, they too may be purposeful thoughts, though not yet developed. They may contain in them ever so subtle sparks of the germ of a second thought that has not yet fully been assimilated properly and, therefore, cannot be fully dressed in a garment of speech, nor can it yet become a complete concept. Thus the preoccupation itself is a sign that there is something in the root of the soul that relates to this particular thought. Moreover, such a thought may also be a stirring originating from above, concerned with our spiritual well-being, with some aspect of ourselves that needs mending. It is also possible that a person was born to realize only that particular point or thought, and that this point or thought is the entire purpose for his or her descent into this world.

"This insight is taught also through the passage in the Torah that says, 'If one seduces a virgin,' in other words, if you will unfold a virgin thought, 'who has not been betrothed,' meaning that it hasn't developed sufficiently to be expressed by your lips, 'and has lain with that virgin,' meaning that you have been preoccupied with this virgin thought, 'they shall surely be married,' for this is an excellent sign that this thought was designated for you during the six days of Creation and that it came to you only now so that you might find the hidden treasures contained in it, which, for whatever reasons, you needed to discover at this moment (Exod. 22:15).[17]

"Now, I know very well that there are many Torah students who believe that this manner of exegesis represents an outright distortion; they see my Torah insights, or those of my disciples, as sacrilegious mockery."

———————

At the very least, there was much in what the Ba'al Shem Tov was saying and doing that was threatening to the guardians of religion and official piety. It is the age-old tension between shaman and priest, between the living experience of spirituality and the time-honored traditions of the past. Ultimately, both are necessary, but there is nevertheless a tension between the two at all times. Shamanism is always threatening chaos and the priesthood is always falling into irrelevance. In the healthiest of all situations, as we have with the Ba'al Shem Tov and early Hasidism, a marriage between the two is achieved.[18] But for those who are clearly on one side or the other, the Ba'al Shem Tov was either a sell-out or a dangerous deviant!

"*But, to us, it doesn't matter if they mock our method, for we believe that any incentive that the mind can find to reinforce virtuous behavior, in any verse of Torah or statements by the Rabbis, is good and wholesome, as long as the association and texts stimulate the thought and thus serve as pegs on which to hang the memory of ideas that are useful in the service of God* (avodat ha-Shem).

"*Although it may seem that the original textual meaning is being distorted, the process is justified on the full validation of the resulting insight, when it becomes engraved on the tablets of your heart. At the very moment you utter the words of the text, your entire mind and being have been immersed in that idea, your knowledge and feeling surrounds it and is surrounded by it as well. In such a manner these thoughts are able to penetrate the hearts of those who receive them. This is how we interpret the meaning of 'words that come from the heart, enter the heart'—that when you utter such words, you are standing in the very place of your heart.*

"*I repeat these ideas intentionally. They were forgotten from the hearts of most rabbis, and the majority of Torah students have lost the skill of such exegetic exercises. These cardinal principles have been all but abandoned in favor of forced answers to farfetched questions and hair-splitting casuistry that do not raise up those who hear them and are of no benefit to their condition.*"

In these few paragraphs, the Ba'al Shem Tov *ever so subtly* describes the foundations of contemplative practice in the Hasidic tradition, the practice known as *hitbonenut* in the ḤaBaD tradition of Hasidism. He then contrasts the "skill" required for such holy "exegetic exercises" with the *pilpul* or hair-splitting casuistry associated with Torah exegetics in his own day and for generations to come. In this, he is advocating contemplative depth over the clever manipulation of knowledge.

"*Torah scholars ought to be valued, and we apportion to them the honor due to their Torah knowledge. Nevertheless, it is our task to point out to them the fact that in their scholastic preoccupations they do little good. There are insights to be pruned from the Torah that can spark real transformations in a person toward respect of God, toward improved morality and virtuousness—far greater objectives than the inconsequential finer points of abstruse lore. Blessed is a generation in which the greater are great enough to listen to the lesser, for in no way will the very greatest lack by absorbing another opinion or virtue, even if it necessitates their mending of previous methods and habits."*

During their conversation, a gentile tinker knocked on the window and asked whether any pots, pans, or barrels were in need of mending. "Go in peace," the Ba'al Shem Tov answered him with a smile, "with me and with my house, everything is in a perfect state." The tinker replied, "Check well, for you will find that there are places that do need mending." At this point, the Ba'al Shem Tov turned to his guest and said:

"Behold and meditate on this. Was that man not an emissary of divine providence? Were his words not holy utterances? Is it not true indeed that everyone, upon inspecting their inner furnishings and utensils, will find that they stand in need of being mended, that their heart and soul are split, that their mind and emotions need correction? This is my way of believing with perfect faith that no accidents happen in the world, and through this realization I feel that I am constantly being guided from above. As my soul lives, at this moment I feel immense gratitude in the depths of my heart to the creator of the beginning for the call of this tinker, for his words were perfect testimony to the very point of our conversation.

"My mind was just struck by how one of the commentators on the Torah explained the verse: 'Get yourselves up from the midst of this congregation' (Num. 17:10).[19] He wrote as follows: 'From time to time, each of us must raise him- or herself from the congregation and feel separate from the masses, for to truly be tzaddikim we need to annihilate all of our selfhood and, at times, to do things that seem correct only in our personal opinion, though lacking the support and agreement of the masses.'

"Obviously, therefore, each person must be concerned with his or her own soul without caring whether their opinions are agreed on by their friends. I know that for this reason: Because I preach personal and unpopular opinions, I have gained many enemies. But our sages taught that in a place where there is a possibility of profaning God's name, one responds even if it means to forgo honor toward the prominent masters.[20]

"In these ideas, then, you will find all the essence of my thinking, and it is from these premises that I would thus be able to answer all your questions. If it is your wish to accept my words by your goodwill and allow them some place in your heart, then remain in my home for a while, and we will converse of these things until they will have become fastened like bridge heads in the depths of your thoughts. Then, sentences like M'lo khol ha-aretz k'vodo (The world is full of God's glory) (Isa. 6:3)[21] and Shiviti Y-H-V-H l'negdi tamid (I have placed Yah before me always) (Ps. 16:8)[22] will radiate with tremendous brilliance and affect even your slightest action."

The rabbi nodded. He had been sunk in deep thought during the time the Ba'al

Shem Tov was speaking. He rose from his seat and paced nervously back and forth across the room as one driven by unsettling thoughts. Then he turned to the Ba'al Shem Tov and said:

"In many of your words I find much agreement and reason, but that which you repeated and reiterated—that empty talk spoken in the street is Torah and that even the circumstantial utterances of a passing heathen could be a message of the most high and that their chatter can be prophecy—these ideas are not only incomprehensible to me but seem like heresy. According to your way of thinking, the celestial holiness would then dwell even in their heresy and pornography, and sparks of the Shekhinah's (the Divine Presence's) splendor would be found in lustful thoughts and deranged madness! I cannot, under any circumstances, accept such an idea, nor would the Torah agree to it. Thus people as you, who hold such an opinion and remain loyal to it, deserve to be punished. I'm sure that under no circumstances could I ever accept such a notion as my own."

This is an old argument, and one that is often seen when the logic and internal consistency of the pantheistic notion of God pushes someone into a corner, provoking an emotional response—"How could *God* be within dog crap! *Never!* I refuse to believe that holiness could be found in such lowly things; it is not possible!"

This is entirely understandable. The paradox is very difficult to hold because it raises so many new questions, shaking the very foundations of a person's previously solid existence. One must be careful in pushing someone too far, too fast, which *seems* to be the case here—but just wait. It will soon become clear that the Ba'al Shem Tov has only taken him to the edge, to the jumping-off place.

THE BA'AL SHEM Tov waited for the rabbi to complete his response and said:

"It is not that you are unable to accept this idea. It is that you are unwilling. You can, but you won't. You are quite capable of accepting this opinion but you do not wish to. For it all depends on the desire and will and the abilities you already have. There is nothing that truly arrests one's will. Change the 'I cannot' to 'I will not' and then I will declare that you are right. It is not that you cannot accept the words of the tinker as words of prophecy and holiness, but that you will not."

At that, the rabbi became quite frustrated and departed abruptly. He left the Ba'al Shem Tov's village immediately and set off on the road leading back to his own town. Along the way, a peasant driving a wagon loaded with stones suddenly lost control of his ox and the wagon turned over. Looking around desperately for someone to help, the peasant spotted the approaching rabbi and called out to him, "Jew! Please come and help me with this load! I cannot raise it myself! Please come and help me!"

The rabbi replied, "I'm too weak. I have no strength. I can't help you."

"You can't," the peasant retorted, "or you don't want to? I think you can, but you won't. It's in your power, but not your will. Will it, I beg you, so you will be able to help!"

The rabbi was stunned by his words. He did not know whether he should rush to the Ba'al Shem Tov and tell him what had just happened or whether he should first help the peasant. In this incident, however, the rabbi transcended his thoughts by action and called to some of his fellow Jews that they, too, might come and help the peasant. As soon as the wagon had been uprighted, the rabbi hurried back to the house of the Ba'al Shem Tov, his heart pounding wildly within him, not knowing whether to go to the right or to the left.

The Ba'al Shem Tov greeted him warmly at the door and asked, "Have you perchance found out that you were able, that you could do it, but did not will it? Have you been subject to an experience that pointed this out, even to you?"

At that moment, the rabbi decided to remain with the Ba'al Shem Tov and to speak with those who had already become allied with him, to hear from their mouths concerning this great concept. And so he did. Open-eyed, he beheld all that the Ba'al Shem Tov had taught him, and a short while later, he became an ardent Hasid, sanctifying the ways of the Ba'al Shem Tov in all his own ways. And, in time, he became a perfect tzaddik.[23]

We may be tempted to scorn the rabbi's arrogance for walking away at first, but it would not be just. The truth is, words are not enough; the testimony of personal experience must enter into relationship with the words before an honest turning is possible. Even the holy Ba'al Shem Tov's words could not substitute for the rabbi's personal choice and *teshuvah,* a repentance based on his own experience.

THE HEART AFIRE

This teaching of the Ba'al Shem Tov deals with *teshuvah* or repentance in particular as well as with many of the same issues addressed in the story we have just learned, only from another perspective.

In 1783, 23 years after the passing of the Ba'al Shem Tov and 11 years after that of his successor, the Maggid of Mezritch, a debate took place in the city of Minsk between Rabbi Shneur Zalman of Liadi (1745–1813), representing Hasidism, and several leading rabbinic authorities representing the *mitnagdim* (opponents of Hasidism). As a preliminary to the debate, Reb Shneur Zalman allowed himself to be tested in talmudic knowledge and scholarship because the *mitnaged* contingent would not lower themselves to a debate with anyone who was not sufficiently knowledgeable in Talmud. However, Reb Shneur Zalman agreed to this preliminary only on the condition that the *mitnagdim* would also agree to be tested by him afterward.

As one of the most brilliant talmudists and halakhic (legal) authorities of his time, Reb Shneur Zalman answered all of their most difficult questions with ease. He then set about his own interrogation, asking a series of questions that none of the *mitnagdim* could solve, even though there were famous scholars among them.

His credentials having been accepted, the *mitnagdim* then asked Reb Shneur Zalman to defend two particular Hasidic doctrines of the Ba'al Shem Tov that they found objectionable. The first had to do with the seemingly inordinate praise the Ba'al Shem Tov accorded to the prayer and psalm recitation of the unlearned, simple Jews, who had only the slightest notion of what they were saying. This, the *mitnagdim* argued, made these simple Jews undeservedly proud, puffing them up with self-importance, while diminishing the wholly deserved prestige of the Torah scholars.

Their second objection centered around the Ba'al Shem Tov's teaching that even the *tzaddikim* (the righteous) must serve God by *teshuvah* (turning or repentance), as common sinners do. This was untenable to them, that the saint and scholar should be classed with the lowly sinner in need of repentance! In their eyes, this undermined the whole of the Torah and damaged the dignity of the righteous scholars of Torah.[24]

Reb Shneur Zalman listened carefully to their objections, then, when it was time for him to speak, he told them that the foundation of these Hasidic doctrines—to which they took so much exception—was to be found in the first revelation of Moses, our teacher. He then gave over the quintessential teaching of the Ba'al Shem Tov, which he had heard from the mouth of his own teacher, the Maggid of Mezritch.

This oral teaching was passed down through the ḤaBaD lineage to my own master, Rabbi Yosef Yitzhak Schneersohn of Lubavitch, and to my other teachers, from whom I received it.

IT IS WRITTEN, "And the messenger of God showed (vayyera) itself to him in the heart of the fire, in the midst of the thorn-bush. And he saw to his amazement that, although the thorn-bush was burning, it was not consumed! Then Moshe said, 'Let me turn from here to see this great sight' " (Exod. 3:2–3).[25]

Now, it is important to understand the setup here, the transition that Moses makes as he comes into this particular moment and encounters the Divine Presence, going from an inspired curiosity about an unusual fire to a true "fear and trembling" before the Holy Presence in that fire. It becomes necessary to ask ourselves, "What was Moses' connection with the living God before this seminal moment in Jewish myth and history?"

This is difficult to answer with any certainty, but we might do well to speculate about Moses the Egyptian prince and Moses the son-in-law of the Priest of Midian as opposed to Moshe Rabbeinu, the prophet of the God of Yisra'el.

Once, when my wife, Eve, and I were staying with Jean Houston in Oregon, I had a wonderful experience of the Egyptian Moses.[26] You see, growing up as a traditional Orthodox Jew, the only Moses I ever knew was a Jewish Moses. But Jean wanted to help me get in touch with a younger, Egyptian Moses. She put me in a room with an original Egyptian statue of the goddess Sekhmet and said, "Why don't you sit with Sekhmet for a while? It's very likely that Moses had something to do with her in his youth." Well, I'll tell you, the Moses of my heart and mind is still a Jewish Moses, but ever since that day, I have had a very strong sense of Moses' earlier Egyptian identity and the kind of mythological context in which he must have been raised. I think it is worthwhile to consider how Moses, during his time in Egypt, probably received a thorough education in Egyptian spiritual beliefs and perhaps even initiation into their mysteries.

I also tend to see Moses as a shepherd-apprentice to his father-in-law,

Jethro, who for me is a Beduin chief and shaman, something like Carlos Castaneda's Don Juan. Then let's say that between Egypt, his silent years, and his shamanic apprenticeship with Jethro, Moses' insight and spiritual awareness was growing in important and powerful ways, but that he still hadn't quite broken through to the deepest experience of the Divine Presence. At least not until he sees the burning bush from a distance and says, "Let me go away from here to get closer to there to see this great sight."

Think about how many times you have had to overcome the distance from the *here* to *there* in order to see what was happening in your own life. If you really take a look at this on the inside, you begin to understand that this is part of the structure of the spiritual path, the necessity and the ability to make transitions from *here* to *there*—to go from the parking lot to the shul, from everyday awareness into meditation, from one level of spiritual initiation to another—you have to leave the here *to go* there, to sacrifice the here *for* there. These few words hint at the transition that is about to occur for Moses as well as the work that has to be done in our own lives.

And what happened next? He comes closer, and all of a sudden he is shaken by a voice that says, "Take the shoes from off your feet, for you stand on holy ground!" (Exod. 3:4–5).[27] We say a "voice" and immediately think of it as coming from the outside, but outside or inside, what matters is that it was experienced as an imperative. In that moment, he knew both the *mysterium fascinans* and the *mysterium tremendum*. These are the terms that Rudolf Otto (1869–1937) used to describe the paradoxical experience of the holy, which, on the one hand, attracts you and draws you closer (*mysterium fascinans*) and, on the other hand, overwhelms you with its intensity, causing an awe that almost sends you reeling (*mysterium tremendum*).[28]

The Hebrew says, *"shal n'alekha m'al ragleḥa"* (Remove the shoe from off your foot). The Hasidic reading of this is, "Unlock yourself from your habits, for you are standing on holy ground," because *n'al*, which means "shoe," also means "lock," something that locks you in, and *regel*, which means "foot," also means "habit." So in this holy place, you must release yourself from your habitual mind, for here everything is new, unprecedented.

So this is the setup and this is the moment we and Moses have come to at the very beginning of the holy Ba'al Shem Tov's teaching.

ONKELOS THE PROSELYTE *renders the verse, "the messenger of God showed Itself" as "the messenger of God revealed Itself," replacing the Hebrew* vayyera *with the Aramaic word "v'itgali."*

Onkelos the Proselyte (ca. 35–120) was a Roman nobleman who converted to Judaism and later translated the Torah into Aramaic, the vernacular of the Jews in Palestine. Instead of making a literal translation, Onkelos created a new work, translating not just the words but also the *sense* of the words. Thus the *Targum Onkelos*, though a translation of the Torah, also became a much-studied commentary on the Torah, an interpretation from the perspective and paradigmatic understanding of the 2nd-century sages.

The *Targum Onkelos* usually avoids anthropomorphic references to God. For instance, when the Torah says, "the mouth of the Lord," Onkelos renders this "the word (*memra*) of the Lord." And so, as we see from this example, when the Torah uses a word that implies a physical presence, like *vayyera* (showed), Onkelos tries to get at the sense of this by using the Aramaic word "*v'itgali*" (revealed), instead.

NOW, THE INTENT *of "revealing" is that everyone should be able to perceive the revelation according to his or her own capacity, for the real meaning of revelation is fulfilled only when the most humble are conscious of that revelation. It is for this reason that Onkelos also translates "And Y-H-V-H descended (vayyered) upon Mount Sinai" (Exod. 19:18)[29] as "Y-H-V-H revealed (v'itgali) Itself on Mount Sinai." "Revealing" refers to the "descent" of revelation down to the most humble level. Now, just as the revealing of the Torah on Mount Sinai was intended not only for Moshe on his exalted level but for all of the people, even down to the most humble of Yisra'el, and all were able to perceive it according to their level, so was the first revelation to Moshe before the burning bush.*

You see, this interpretation is based on the relationship between the Hebrew and its Aramaic translation. The Hebrew of the Torah is not forgotten; rather, it is in a creative dance with both Onkelos and the Ba'al Shem Tov. For the Ba'al Shem Tov sees the Hebrew *vayyered* (descended) and the Aramaic *v'itgali* (revealed) as being in an intrinsic, two-way relationship. Not only is *v'itgali* a commentary on *vayyered* but *vayyered* is also a commentary on *v'itgali*; their identification with one another adds dimension to our understanding of the passage. Thus because *vayyered* means "descended," it follows that there are tiers or levels of understanding what is *v'itgali* (revealed). That is to say, the revelation descends on "stairs" that represent each one of us, from the simplest to the most sophisticated; it is the same revelation seen through many different eyes. And because there is an intrinsic relationship between revealing and descent, one could also say it is the purpose of revelation to reach all people, on all levels, even the most humble. The Ba'al Shem Tov makes it clear that revelation is not fulfilled until *all* people are "conscious of that revelation."

Now, for some people, this may seem like mere word juggling, and that is all it would be were it not for one sacred ingredient. And because of that ingredient, the connections come and speak of what *must* be true. For what good is a revelation that does not have a message for everyone? This is what I often tell people about *gematria*, the kabbalistic interpretive technique of using the numerical value of Hebrew words to create connections with other words; without the element of sacred intuition, it is only a game. Intuition is what makes it effective, what creates its effect on the heart and mind and what makes it more than just clever but also . . . *true*. This is the message that was described so clearly in the story of divine providence we learned earlier.

Moreover, Rashi renders the phrase "b'labat esh" (in the midst of the fire) as "b'shalhevet shel esh, libo shel esh" (in the flame of fire, the heart of fire). So where does the messenger of the God become known? In the heart afire, which is the sincere and simple inner intention of the heart.

You see here again that Rashi (Rabbi Shlomo Yitzhaki, 1040–1105) is using language in much the same way as Onkelos, in an attempt to get at the sense of the original words, to derive contemporary meaning from them. But more important is the fact that the Ba'al Shem Tov is slowly building a case for equality among Jews, for a kind of spiritual democracy. First he demonstrates how revelation is received by all, each in his or her own uniqueness and according to each one's own capacity. But since this still leaves room for elitists and those who attach themselves to rigid hierarchies, he levels the playing field by nullifying inherent capacity in the face of an act of will, "the sincere and simple inner intention of the heart." This is the heart afire, and the place from which God speaks.

And where is this "heart of fire" to be found? "In the midst of the thorn bush." Rashi asks, "Why in the thorn bush and not in some grander tree? Because it says, 'with that one I am in the narrow place (tzarah)' " (Ps. 91:15).[30] Now, the narrow place is this world, because it is here where we are squeezed and in which the infinite light of God (Or Ain Sof) is constricted, condensed, and concealed in Nature. Where it shines freely, it is called "Open Space."

The intentional purpose of creation and the manifest world is that through the service and the study of holiness, the narrow place (tzarah) becomes transformed into a window (tzohar), illuminating the worlds.[31]

Now that the Ba'al Shem Tov has leveled the playing field, he begins to create a new, spiritually just hierarchy, one that would make the lowest the highest and the highest the lowest. It is not to be based on knowledge or capacity but, as he has already shown, on sincerity and simple intention (*kavanah*) and now . . . humility.

Why do we talk about humility?

"The heart of fire" was found in the humble thorn bush and not in a glorious tree. Why is that? Because it is symbolic of God's compassion and of God's holy desire for us. God is available to us in this world, a narrow place in which we often feel confined and constricted, just as the light of divinity is confined and constricted by the fragmentation of consciousness inherent in the world. This is to be contrasted with the place where the light of divinity shines freely, called "Open Space," which would be analogous to the grander tree.

"Well," you might say, "if the light of divinity shines freely in the Open Space, why then shouldn't we identify with the grander tree?" This is a good question, and one whose answer is implied throughout the teachings of the Ba'al Shem Tov. It is a teaching that marks the first glimmering of the dawn of a new paradigm in consciousness. Wholeness lives in paradox. Whether inside or outside, high or low, you still have to go through, from here to there. But the salient point of this passage is simply this: follow God's example. If God did not try to identify solely with the Open Space but sought to inhabit the narrow place as well, we must not seek to identify solely with the grand tree of our nature but to seek the humility of the lowly thorn bush. One must go *into* and *through* this world, this narrow place (*tzarah*), making a window (*tzohar*) within it, through which one can see Open Space.

More words will not say more about this matter; it requires some chewing.

IT IS ALSO written, "The human being is like a tree of the field" (Deut. 20:19).[32] There are fruit trees, which Rabbi Yohanan compares to the wise scholars (talmidei hakhamim), and there is the humble bush (sneh) that bears no fruit, representing the people of the earth (am ha-aretz).[33] And yet, the heart afire is in the thorn bush. To be sure, the scholars engaged in Torah study are filled with fire, for Torah is called "fire";[34] but they cannot claim "yet it is not consumed," for they can quench *their thirst with the insights they gain in study. Not so the humble thorn bushes, the humble and unlearned Jews who are the very heart of fire. With their simple and sincere prayer, in their holy ignorance, they are the flame that is not quenched; their thirst can never be satisfied.*

So here it is, the definitive answer to the first objection of the *mitnagdim* with whom Reb Shneur Zalman of Liadi is debating and thus the reason for his repeating this oral teaching of the Ba'al Shem Tov: The low, ignorant, and humble people of the earth (*am ha-aretz*) are in actuality the most high because their fire is never consumed. Whereas the scholars of holiness (*talmidei hakhamim*), who conceive of themselves as the most high or accomplished, are actually the lowest because they become bloated with their own knowledge and extinguish the flame in the heart. The fire needs oxygen to burn, but in neglecting humility and the narrow place (*tzarah*), they have no opportunity to create a window (*tzohar*) through which fresh oxygen might enter from the Open Space.

This is always the big pitfall for the intellectual, thinking that one knows it already, or has it. What do they know? They know only what they knew before. So the intellectuals, if they want to continue to be honored, will either accept the consensus reality of their peers or seek to impose a reality on others that will reinforce their own sense of knowing. Now this issue of "consensus reality" is very important, because every religion needs to have a consensus reality for its adherents, a consensus of the pious that tells us the norm of how we are to worship in this group. But when the intellectuals begin to see themselves as the elite, in charge of forming the consensus reality, then the fire is going to go out and the flow is going to be blocked.

An interesting fact about this teaching is that it was not given by the Ba'al Shem Tov to the *mitnagdim*, as Reb Shneur Zalman is doing; he was actually teaching it to his own disciples. For while the Ba'al Shem Tov was no elitist, his inner circle of disciples were basically drawn from the congregation of the learned elite and held many of the same prejudices. Thus the Ba'al Shem Tov was trying to tell them just what was so special about those simple Jews, a specialness that they were themselves lacking. It was as if he were saying, "They are the burning bush that has not been consumed. But *you* see a burning bush, and you say, 'Ah-ha! I know what *that* is; it's a burning bush! You have to deal with it this way, and it has these five meanings,' and you already have Rudolf Otto at the ready and start talking about *mysterium fascinans* and *mysterium tremendum* without ever being fascinated or 'tremend-ized'!"

The Ba'al Shem Tov is trying to show them that, when they empathize with the simple people, appreciating their uncomplicated yearning, then they may come to recognize that their present attainment is nothing compared to that which is drawing them still further. Even Goethe had it in his own way when Mephisto finally wants to take Faustus's soul, saying, "Now you've got everything you wanted." But Doctor Faustus says, "No, the eternally feminine draws me further." I'm still not satisfied, I still have this hunger.

This teaching is particularly concerned with reframing ideas—of righteousness and repentance, pride and humility, knowledge and ignorance—in an attempt to overcome oversimplified notions like "the righteous are above repentance," "ignorance is stupidity," and "knowledge is superiority." An example of just how Hasidism turns such notions upside down is given by Nahman of Bratzlav, the great-grandson of the Ba'al Shem Tov. He taught that there are two kinds of ignorance in one's disciples and thus two different approaches the teacher must take with them. First, there are students who are ignorant because they simply don't know, so they must be taught and instructed properly in what they should know. But then there are students who know, and know that they know, and are, therefore, obstructed from going deeper. With them, the teacher must break through that knowledge so that they come to the place of unknowing, which is a *desirable* ignorance.[35] Thus the *Kena Upanishad* says, "The one who knows, does not know; but the one who knows he does not know . . . knows."[36] And it is to the former that this teaching is addressed.

This brings us to Reb Shneur Zalman's answer to the second objection of the *mitnagdim,* and the prescription the Ba'al Shem Tov makes for the health of his inner circle of disciples.

THUS IT IS *written, "And Moshe said, 'Let me turn aside from here to see this great sight.' " Rashi suggests that he meant, "Let me turn aside from* here *to approach* there." *Which is to say, Moshe understood the holy message revealing the superiority of the "ignorance" of the humble ones over the "knowledge" of the scholars— that the heart afire is only in the thorn bush—and thus he made* teshuvah *(a turning in repentance). Even though Moshe was himself a* tzaddik *(a righteous person), he experienced a repentant heart, saying, "Let me turn aside from where I am to come close to that place." So the teaching is, one must never be satisfied with one's humility before God; from the higher to the lower and the lower to the higher, there is always room for repentance.*[37]

Originally, the Ba'al Shem Tov wished to call his new movement *ba'alei teshu-*

vah, emphasizing the enormous importance of repentance in his thought. As we have seen, this emphasis on *teshuvah* (especially as it applied to the *tzaddikim*) inspired the particular enmity of the *mitnagdim*, many of whom looked on themselves as models of righteousness, leading lives dedicated exclusively to Torah study. So they asked, "Why do you demand that *tzaddikim* should have to do *teshuvah*? This is the same as denying their status as *tzaddikim*!" Well, the basic answer given to them was simple, because our sages say, "In the place where the *ba'alei teshuvah* stand, the righteous cannot stand." When this answer was reported to some of the leaders of the *mitnagdim*—some say to the Vilna Ga'on himself—the response was this: "The reason why it is said that 'In the place where the *ba'alei teshuvah* stand, the *tzaddikim* cannot stand' is because it stinks there! Yes, they have been forgiven and have overcome all kinds of evil, but they still bring the smell of impiety with them."

When someone takes this attitude, what can you possibly say to convince them? But if that person is ever to be convinced, it will be because a precedent can be found in Torah, and this teaching is such a precedent. For it says in Torah, "The man, Moses, was exceedingly humble, more than any person on the face of the Earth." (Num. 12:3).[38] And by demonstrating the relationship between humility, repentance, and ignorance, all with regard to Moses' first revelation, the Ba'al Shem Tov was not only creating an appreciation for simple, unlearned Jews but was also opening up a truly limitless path for his disciples based on humility and ignorance.

For even if one has been able to separate oneself from sinful actions or does great good in the world, there is always more work to be done on the inside. You see, one of the obstacles both for the people of that time and for us in ours is the attribution of a static identity to oneself and to other people. Thus, in the time of the Ba'al Shem Tov, one man is righteous because he does nothing but study Torah all day and performs all of the mitzvot perfectly, and another is not because he works as a laborer, can't read, and sometimes mangles the blessings. In our own secular society, one person is thought good because she votes Democratic and drives a fuel-efficient hybrid, while another is not because he was once in prison and doesn't talk much. But when the so-called righteous scholar and ecologically sensitive Democrat both treat their spouses and the people of their general acquaintance poorly because they tend to judge them as being less righteous than themselves, and when the ignorant laborer and the mean ex-convict turn out to be humble, sincere individuals who have grown because of their disadvantages and have learned from their mistakes, then these rigid identifications are shattered. Thus the Ba'al Shem Tov and Hasidism invest great effort in tying to point out the fallacy in this kind of thinking, constantly revealing the unlimited nature of the spiritual path.

One of the most problematic static identities is that of the so-called "enlightened." In Hasidism, this is the *tzaddik gamur* or the completely right-eous person. And though Hasidism is guilty of promoting an "I've got it" or "he's got it" identity at different times, this teaching of the Ba'al Shem Tov basically undermines it in all of its varieties.[39] He says, "One must never be satisfied with one's humility before God, from the higher to the lower and the lower to the higher, there is always room for repentance." Thus the Sufi mas-ter Pir Vilayat Inayat Khan once said, "Enlightenment is like a receding wave; no matter how far you might wade out into the water, the wave is always mov-ing on."[40] So there is enlighten-*ing*, but no enlighten-*ment*. You can't put a ceiling on infinity, and that is an important point here. The heart afire has a flame that cannot be quenched, and the secret of its eternal flame is a contin-ual peeling away of the layers of the ego, revealing a simpler, humbler, and more direct prayer in the presence of God.

THE WORD ARK

Now we would be negligent if we did not say something about the Ba'al Shem Tov's prayer. For prayer was at the heart of the holy Ba'al Shem's life and teaching. His prayer was said to be so awesome that while he prayed the grain in nearby barrels vibrated with his intensity and the water in various vessels would tremble and sway.[41]

My favorite teaching on prayer from the Ba'al Shem Tov is found in a work called *Sefer ha-Ba'al Shem Tov*. This work is a collection of fragments and reports of teachings from the Ba'al Shem Tov organized in the manner of most Hasidic books, which is to say, according to the *sedra* (Torah portion) of the week. In the *sedra* of Noaḥ, we find the following teaching . . .

"MAKE A SKYLIGHT for the ark, and leave it open for a cubit above" (Gen. 6:16).[42]

Rabbi Yisra'el Ba'al Shem Tov said:
The word that a person speaks in Torah and tefillah *(prayer) should be filled with light. In every word are entire worlds (olamot), souls (neshamot), and divin-ity (elehut). And when spoken with this light illuminating them, the words begin to*

shine and rise up, letters binding themselves to one another, becoming unified into words, all in communion and oneness with God.

Immediately, the Ba'al Shem Tov shifts the meaning of these biblical sentences by playing on the possible meanings of Hebrew words—in this case, *tevah* (ark) and *tzohar* (window). For *tevah* in Hebrew is simply a "box" but may also refer to a "word," which is how the Ba'al Shem Tov uses it here. Then he exchanges the Hebrew *tzohar* (window), for the word *zohar* (shining or radiant). So now "Make a skylight for the ark" becomes "The word that you use in prayer should shine." Moreover, the sense of the "skylight" is still there, so that when you are *davenen* (praying), you know that it has to be open to the higher levels; it has to have a vertical connection!

What does he mean by "letters binding themselves to one another"?

If every letter is illumined, then every word has a still greater illumination. Every sentence has a greater illumination than the word. In the spirit of the Ba'al Shem Tov, we might say, "The *bet* which loves the *resh* which loves the *vav* which loves the *khaf,* all of which unite in love to form the *barukh* of "Blessed are You, *Yah,* our God!" Do you see the magic that the Ba'al Shem Tov sees in everything?

A PERSON MUST *include worlds, souls, and divinity, each of the three categories in his or her own soul. Then the words will rise up, and great joy will emerge from them—there is no end to the ecstasy that these may cause.*

"This is the way in which God instructed Noah to make the ark . . . make it with lower, middle, and upper decks" (Gen. 6:15–16).[43] *These refer to the worlds (olamot), souls (neshamot), and divinity (elehut). The lower level is the spoken word, the middle level is the word felt, and the upper level is the word known. Above is the skylight through which the infinite may enter, infusing the letters and words with life. Then you shall hear the words you are saying, for it shall be the* Shekhinah *(Divine Presence) who speaks and not you; you shall be her groomsman. This is how one gives pleasure to the creator.*

One needs great faith for this.

The *Shekhinah* is called the "belief of the artist." Without *emunah*, without faith, you create separation. Therefore, you really have to believe in the significance of your acts. Elsewhere, the Ba'al Shem Tov says, "Sometimes you will find *tzaddikim* who say to themselves, 'I am such a spiritual person,' 'I am great in my *davenen;*' don't take it as pride—it is what they need to do at that time to get out from their depression and to invest in the service of God." When you are depressed, you say, "So what? What does it matter? What can I do?" It is then that you need to have faith, saying, "What do you mean? *What does it matter—what can I do?* The world depends on your actions! For you the world was created! God is waiting for you to say, *Barukh ata* (blessed are you) . . . because this will bring healing into the world!"

". . . [A]ND LEAVE IT open for a cubit above." This means that you should not hold onto the word once you have spoken it. Let it arise and pass through the skylight.

Remember, "Come into the ark with all of your household" (Gen. 7:1),[44] enter into the word with all of your strength.[45]

Once the word has left your mouth, give it to God—don't hold on to it. Allow it to pass through that skylight and be as if consumed from above.

Now, we come to the big summation: God says to Noah, *Bo el ha-tevah* (Come into the ark), which the Ba'al Shem Tov reads as, "Enter into the word."[46] And what is Noah to bring with him? All of his "household." In other words, the whole kit and caboodle: his sons, their wives, the children, the animals, the food, everything. That is to say, load the *word-ark* of your *davenen* with everything that you have: everything that makes up your physical life, everything that makes up your emotional life, everything that makes up your mental or imaginal life; bring it all into the word of your *davenen* so that it creates feeling in your prayer.

This is so different from the advice of those who say, "Leave all of those things behind; go into *davenen* without any of these interferences." The Ba'al Shem Tov, in contrast, says, "Bring it all in!" There are deep connections between this advice, the teachings of Reb Shneur Zalman of Liadi on *hitbonenut* (discursive meditation), and the Ba'al Shem Tov's teaching on divine providence; one would do well to explore these connections thoroughly.

A JOURNEY OF HEAVENLY ASCENT

The following letter, written by the Ba'al Shem Tov to his brother-in-law, Gershon of Kittov, is one of the great documents of Hasidic literature and is believed by scholars to be authentic. It describes nothing less than the Ba'al Shem Tov's *aliyat ha-neshamah* or ascent of the soul to the higher regions and the palaces of the Messiah.

ON ROSH HASHANAH, 1747 (5507), I made a journey of heavenly ascent, the nature of which you are well aware. At that time, I saw visions such as I have never seen before, and what I saw and learned upon that ascent is impossible to express in words.

"A journey of heavenly ascent" is a conscious ascent of the soul to Heaven. Occasionally, this is referred to as an "adjuration," which means that the spiritual journey was accomplished by use of a divine or angelic name that "forced" or "bound" a particular spiritual entity to accomplish it. But this is certainly not the case here. The Ba'al Shem Tov was opposed to such coercive means of spiritual accomplishment and was known to have achieved his "rungs" by great *kavanah* and simple faith.[47]

It is interesting to note that the Ba'al Shem Tov says "the nature of which you are well aware" to his student and brother-in-law. Clearly such journeys were not the province of the Ba'al Shem Tov alone, but were also accomplished by his students, or at least one of his students, even if not in equal measure to his own "travels." Nevertheless, he finds it difficult to express what he has seen.

It used to be that computers communicated with peripherals through one of two options: a serial cable or a parallel cable. A serial cable allowed for only one signal at a time, but a parallel cable allowed several signals to be sent simultaneously. Now, for the human being, the mouth is a serial instrument, but the mind is clearly a parallel instrument. While it is possible for us to receive parallel information with our minds, our mouths cannot communicate it as we receive it. The mouth is serial, being able to say only one thing at a time. Thus it is difficult to convey the complexity of any of our experiences, and *especially* those that are spiritual in nature.

An interesting story found in the *Shivḥei ha-Ari* . . .

One day, as Yitzhak Luria, the Ari ha-Kodesh, rested during his midday nap, his disciple Avraham Brukhim watched him from an adjoining room. After a few moments, Reb Avraham noticed something odd: The Ari's lips seemed to be moving as he slept. Thinking perhaps the master was awake, or God forbid, sick, he entered the room very quietly and leaned in very close to him. The Ari did not appear to be unwell, but he clearly wasn't awake either. Curiosity overcame Reb Avraham, and he thought, "What heavenly Torah would come from the master's dreams!" He knelt down with the greatest care, and inclined his ear close to the Ari's mouth, but he could hear only the faintest whisper. Suddenly, the Ari's eyes opened and Reb Avraham jumped up in fright and shame. "Forgive me, master!" he said. "At first, I thought perhaps something was amiss, but when I found that it was not, and seeing your lips moving, I leaned in close to listen." The Ari laughed and said with a smile and a sigh, "Avraham, I wish I could tell you the secret lore my soul received in my short nap. But Heaven and Earth will witness that were I to have 80 years with you, I could not tell you all of what I have just learned concerning the mystery surrounding Ba'alam's donkey!"

WHEN I RETURNED *to the paradise of the lower* Gan Eden *(Garden of Eden), I saw many souls of the deceased and the living. Some I knew, while others were in numberless masses, moving about and ascending from world to world by way of the columns well known to the knowers of hidden wisdom.*

It is interesting that he mentions the "souls of the deceased and the living." Most people might expect for the Ba'al Shem Tov to see the souls of the deceased here, but I think many are surprised by the presence of the souls of the living. Nevertheless, in the mystical tradition of Judaism, the entirety of the soul is seen as extending beyond the confines of the human body, being in continual contact with other worlds of spiritual experience. It is also said that in sleep, souls "come to themselves" in the higher life, only to return to a more limited, wakening consciousness in the morning.

But what are we to think of these "columns"?

Perhaps you can imagine these as being similar to the poles on which firefighters slide from floor to floor in the fire station—except that these poles run between the worlds described in Kabbalah, and souls rise up as well as down on them. The Ba'al Shem Tov tells us that these are "well known to the knowers of hidden wisdom," which is to say, initiates in the wisdom of Kabbalah. These columns have been interpreted in Hasidic literature in many ways, but we might best understand them as being related to the spinal column in both the human being and the supreme spiritual archetype of the human being, *Adam Kadmon*, as a ladder on which the angels of God rise and descend. If you think about this internally, you really get a sense of what the kundalini of Hindu tantra is talking about; a current of energy, of consciousness rising on the three columns of the subtle body and interacting with nexus points (chakras) of increasingly subtle spiritual realities. This is the subtle spiritual counterpart of the spinal column, our own information superhighway, carrying electrical signals to and from the brain. Except here, it is not simple command functions being conveyed but the carrier signals of intentional energy and revelatory information.

What does that mean? It means that we are continually sending information about our intentions, both positive and negative, up these columns into the supercomputer of spiritual life, or the morphogenic field, if you will. Based on that information, we get a karmic response. It is worthwhile to consider what kind of intentions we are sending up the spiritual information superhighway—whether they are of greed, perversion, anger, or jealousy, or of love, concern for the planet, or greater harmony and unification. Can you imagine what this could mean for the planet if we really got serious about clarifying intentions in our daily lives?

THEY ALL DID *this with a joy so immense that it would tire the mouth to tell of it and the ear to hear of it. Many of those who had fallen into sin turned round, and their pollution was cleansed by forgiveness. It was a time of great benevolence, which even in my view seemed extraordinary.*

We learn from the Ba'al Shem Tov here—and this is relevant to the earlier teaching on the heart afire—that *teshuvah* (repentance), literally, "turning," is possible in the spiritual realms. For the living, this might refer to a spiritual echo of their *teshuvah* on the earthly plane, or perhaps to "repairs" made on their behalf on the subtle plane that then trickled down into manifestation.

Even more interesting, given that the Ba'al Shem Tov does not say whether this refers to the souls of the living or the dead, is the fact that he may be referring to *teshuvah* for the souls of the dead! This would contradict the usual view that the human being cannot change anything after this life is over. But the teachings of the Ba'al Shem Tov and his great-grandson Reb Nahman of Bratzlav suggest that this is indeed possible.[48] The Ba'al Shem Tov once remarked that the reason his *Minḥah* prayer lasted so long on Friday afternoon before *Shabbat* was because he was assisting the souls of the dead who flocked about him in search of ways to make amends and to achieve a *tikkun* or repair for their souls.

Reb Gershon of Kittov, to whom this letter is addressed, once declared to the Ba'al Shem Tov that he wanted to do the same thing, but after the Ba'al Shem Tov gave him the pneumatic keys to open himself to this experience, Reb Gershon was overwhelmed by the rush of souls that came to him for mending and fainted!

MANY WERE ACCEPTED *in their* teshuvah—*even some whom you know. Such great joy reigned among them that they, too, made their ascent.*

All of them pleaded with me, even to the point of embarrassment, saying, "Due to the profound level of your Torah, God has graced you with exceeding understanding to attain and to know of such things; come with us to be our helper and support!" Because of the great joy that I saw among them, I agreed to ascend with them. I then asked my teacher and master to come along with me, for to go into the higher worlds is something fraught with danger. Since the day in which I began to act in such matters, I still have not risen to the great heights that he has attained.

In this moment, the Ba'al Shem Tov overcomes the Promethean urge to do it himself.

I remember one day as I was about to cross the street, I told my little son to hold my hand. He pulled away and said, "Abba, I can hold my own hand!" and tried to do just that. He didn't see the danger and thought that holding his hand was simply a part of crossing the street that he could do himself. This is the place we often get into, saying, "I don't need a Rebbe" or "a guide; I can do it myself." But even the Ba'al Shem Tov, who is tremendously accomplished at this point in his life, humbles himself, and seeks the help of his spiritual master.

What was the danger for the Ba'al Shem Tov? One was certainly the danger of ego inflation. You have to be careful, especially during elevated mystical experiences like this one, for the ego is bound to come along and say, "Ahhhhh!" and fill itself with pride in the accomplishment. The best way to handle this situation is to have a *mashpiyya* (a mentor) or a Rebbe with you, being in constant connection with that person, asking them, "Is this the right direction? What about this?" and then waiting for an answer.

So I ROSE from level to level, until I entered into the palace of the Mashiaḥ, *where the* Mashiaḥ *teaches Torah together with all the masters of the Mishnah, the saints, and the seven shepherds. There I saw a profound joy and did not know the cause of it. For a moment, I thought this joy was caused by my being freed of this world.*

The "seven shepherds" are Abraham, Isaac, Jacob, Moses, Aaron, Joseph, and David, and are similar to the seven *rishis* (seers) of the Hindu tradition.

But what is really interesting in this passage is when the Ba'al Shem Tov says, "For a moment, I thought this joy was caused by my being freed of this world." In other words, he thought they were happy because he had died in the course of the ascent and was now free to remain with them.

Even in mundane, chemically assisted "ascents of the soul," you sometimes get into a situation where you think, "This is it—I've passed the threshold between life and death. I can't go back." This is often accompanied by a great tightening of fear in your gut. It sometimes happens in deep meditation as well—you get the feeling that if you were to take just one more step, you would be pulled into the fatal abyss yawning in front of you. One more step, and your whole ego structure would simply dissolve. At that point, there is such a great fear that these things often turn into what were once called "bummers." The best thing to do when that fear takes you is to say, "Oh, what a wonderful way to cross over" and, depending on the situation, perhaps to add, "but it's not my time," and then to move back without fear.

I am sure that most of us know of someone who has passed on in a difficult or less than dignified situation. Wouldn't you rather go in the middle of such a wonderful meditation? It's not likely to happen at that time, but the fear is very real, and so we have to find a way of dealing with it that is not merely a whimpering surrender to the ego. A Jew in the time of the Ba'al Shem Tov didn't speak so much of dying as of *nifter veren* (literally, "gotten rid of"), which is transcending the role one plays in the world. One can return to the true being, the true ontological self, to that which is not obscured or hidden by a role or personality that one had to use in this world.

In *Romeo and Juliet*, Shakespeare described how just as Juliet is about to fall asleep, she is suddenly possessed by a fear, wondering whether she has actually taken poison and is dying. There is always that moment of paranoia, and it is so beautiful how the Ba'al Shem Tov is not ashamed to write about it.

<hr>

THEY INFORMED ME *afterward that I had not yet been freed of the world below, but that they greatly enjoyed my effecting unifications here below through their holy Torah. However, the essence of the joy and its cause I still do not know.*

<hr>

What is a "unification"? Well, there are unifications and there are *unifications.* But if we are to begin to understand what these are about, we must first think of a unification as an "ah-ha!" moment. An *ah-ha!* usually comes upon us in the moment when we finally reconcile two seeming opposites that have been troubling us. Today, we have very little patience for paradox; we don't like the tension of it. Thus when we come upon a seeming contradiction, question, or paradox, we usually affirm one side and deny the other.

But if we stay in the tension—even though it can be crucifying at times— in the end, there is an *ah-ha!,* a reconciliation, the connection of opposites, a unification. And we say, "Yes! *Both* tradition and renewal belong to the same universe! This insight, born of the terrible tension that we have gone through, is going to help us plot the rest of the path that we have to travel. The experience of tension has toughened us up enough to allow us to walk that path." So rather than yield to one side or the other, stay in the creative tension until it yields an *ah-ha!* unification for you. Tension is good. Don't try to get rid of it. It is part of what makes one a *Yisra'eli,* a God-wrestler.

<hr>

I ASKED MASHIAḤ, "When will the Mashiaḥ come?"

The reply was, "By this sign will you know—when your teachings have been published and become manifest in the world, and your sources spread outward. When that which I have taught you, and which you have attained, will be known by the masses; then they too will be able to effect such unifications, and such ascendances as you do. Then all the rinds and shells will be effaced, and it will then be a time of goodwill and salvation."

I pondered greatly over this, and felt immense pain for the long time that this would take. When would this come about? I wondered.

<hr>

Do you remember how the Ba'al Shem Tov made it clear in the teaching of the heart afire that revelation is not fulfilled until all people are "conscious of that revelation"?

Once, I was sitting in a car on Eastern Parkway near the Lubavitch headquarters with one of my wonderful old ḤaBaD friends. I was still a card-carrying Lubavitcher Hasid, but the word was already out, "Zalman is into retreats and meditation," and I had already written a booklet called *A First Step: A Primer of a Jew's Spiritual Life,* which was basically a guide to ḤaBaD *hitbonenut* meditation.[49] And this colleague says to me, "Oy! Zalman, Zalman. What's the matter with you. You want everybody to attain *ahavah ba'-tanugim* (the love of ecstasy) in one easy lesson." That is to say, to get to this great place of the love of God in one easy lesson. And I responded, "You're darn right."

Often in Judaism there is so much emphasis on observance that the joy in relating to God gets lost. Many teachers want to get a lot of observance mileage out of people before they will even give them a crumb of God-experience. But my sense is that we need to give people a taste of that experience, an experience of that light, and let God lead them further in the direction of observance and to the particular level of observance that God wants from them.

In the Bible, Pharaoh says to Moses, "Why do you need to take all of the people and their belongings into the desert?" Moses answered, "*Va'anḥnu lo neda' mah na'avod et Yah ad bo'enu shamah*" (We know not how we will serve Yah, our God, until we get there). I would like to have this sentence inscribed over everything having to do with Jewish Renewal. For you don't know yet what is going to be required. First, make the connection, and if the connection is strong, the rest is going to come. Observance of the mitzvot must first come according to your capacity, and the more you get involved in it, the deeper the observance grows in you. But if you demand that the checklist of observance be completed before you get a taste of divine honey, the likelihood is that people are going to invest so heavily in the surface of the tradition that they will become hollow on the inside, sending a lot of energy into shadow. Or they are simply going to shop for the spirit elsewhere.

So you can understand how the Ba'al Shem Tov must have felt about this messianic prerequisite and how it effected his mission. He knew he needed to juice people up with the best there was to offer on whatever level they could receive it. But how? Imagine what he was facing; how was he going to do this in a depressed society, under the thumb of oppressive neighbors and grinding poverty? What deficit had to be filled before he could bring them to these high places?

HOWEVER, I LEARNED *of three* segullot *(charms) while I was there, and three holy* shemot *(names) that are easy to learn and to explain, and by them my anxiety was temporarily cooled. I thought that because this is possible, my fellow seekers will be able to reach as high a level as I have. That is to say, that they too will be able to ascend, to learn, and to attain as I have. However, it turned out that I was not permitted to reveal these within my lifetime. I asked them to permit me to teach them to you, but they did not permit this either.*

———————

This was like saying, "If you give the code away, it won't work. You get the password, but if the password gets used before the time is right or by the wrong person, it shuts down the whole system." These were only for the Ba'al Shem Tov, which points to the fact that he was operating on a unique level in his time and could not use this "technology" to bring a new paradigm to the consciousness of the people before they were ready for it. He was allowed to challenge the current paradigm, but he was not allowed to burst it apart by moving faster than the learning process could accommodate.

A *segullah* or a charm acts like a catalyst in some transcendental manner, but does not cause any direct effect. *Segullot* traditionally partake of sympathetic, magical devices, but here it seems that the Ba'al Shem Tov is talking about pneumatic keys sure to open the paths of expanded consciousness![50]

———————

So I say, steer your course toward the God of our sustenance. Let them not make light of your prayer and your learning, because every word and every utterance of your lips is capable of effecting a unification. In every letter there are worlds, souls, and divinity, beings that rise and are bound and unified with these letters. Out of the letters a word is made, and it is through this word that a unification is made with the Divine. Your soul is included in them, and every category of the above.

———————

It may seem like the Ba'al Shem Tov is veering away from his disappointment about the *segullot* he was not permitted to share in all this discussion of "worlds, souls, and divinity," but he is actually revealing something important about the technology behind these potencies and names. He says, enter into the words, do it with such an intensity of concentration, with such a unification of will, intellect, and emotion, at such a level of presence to the ever present that the barriers cannot help but part before you, revealing the absolute in all its splendor (even if some of the secondary effects of rising up may be missing from your experience).

The concentration on the "word" here is what leads one from *moḥin d'katnut* (lesser mind), or compressed or limited conscious, to *moḥin d'gadlut* (mind of expansion), or the vast consciousness. The Ba'al Shem Tov is saying, you don't know what power you have within you to transform your life and inner landscape. *Daven* (pray), and in your *davenen*, pay attention to your utterance. For "in every letter there are worlds, souls, and divinity, beings that rise and are bound and unified with these letters."

You will no doubt have noticed the clear connections and parallels between this teaching and his teaching on the *sedra* (Torah portion) of Noah.

THEN ALL THE *worlds are unified together, and they ascend; an infinite joy and a pleasure are caused, and if you truly understand what the joy of the bride and groom is when seen in a microcosmic and physical way, how much more will you be able to understand these things on the higher level. Then, God the sustainer will be your helper, no matter which way you turn, and you will succeed!*

They "ascend." Have you ever watched a soap bubble fly? Think of your *davenen* as this kind of a bubble, and remember what Reb Pinhas of Koretz said: "I am my prayer."

> Once, the Ba'al Shem Tov came to a town and wanted to enter the shul there, but immediately turned round upon entering the door. His students asked him, "What's the matter?"
> He answered, "It is full of prayer."
> "Nu?" they said, "This is good, isn't it?"
> He looked at them gravely and said, "No, prayers should rise . . . but these are all still here."

The shul was constipated with prayers that couldn't rise!

It is also interesting to note that the Ba'al Shem Tov is not afraid of using sexual language in a sacred context, challenging us to expand our limited notions of intercourse and union. He is saying, think of "the joy of the bride and groom" and that will give you just the smallest notion of how it is with God. Sexual pleasure is small in comparison, but that pleasure—the expansion of consciousness and the loss of the sense of separateness—will help you to understand what this higher experience of union is about.[51]

"GIVE A SLIGHT *hint to a wise person and they will become even wiser*" (Prov. 9:9).[52]

Did you hear that? He is saying, "I have just given you a hint about what I cannot disclose in full . . . go and figure it out and do what you need to do!"

On his ascent, he was given the tools and told that he could not teach them. So he was put in the position of having to say, "I know what you need to do, but I can't tell you." But you know, all spiritual teachers are put in this position. For often it is better for students to discover it themselves. We simply can't digest it all at once, and we have to learn how to use one tool before we can have another. This is one of the biggest secrets teachers need to learn, how not to take the initiative away from their students, whether because of ego or out of compassion.

Here we have the Ba'al Shem Tov saying, "I know what you need to do; I'm not going to tell you what it is . . . *but a hint.* No, I cannot tell you . . . *but a hint.* Do you understand?" With this and all the teachings, you see, it is like a scavenger hunt; there is a little here and a little there, and you have to find the ways to put these things together. My sense is that if we study carefully what the Ba'al Shem Tov has said to us, we are going find more and more of those hints, eventually allowing us to sneak through the cracks in reality.

For the Hasidim, this letter didn't survive by chance and certainly not as a historical document, nor is it any longer just a communication from the Ba'al Shem Tov to his brother-in-law. It is a holy message from the Ba'al Shem Tov to all Hasidim, everywhere. It is an invitation to deepen your own awareness and to enter the path trodden by the Ba'al Shem Tov himself.

How? By taking his clues about the word into your *davenen* or by following him in an imaginal ascent of the soul. You may not be able to do what the Ba'al Shem Tov did at that time, not having access to his keys or to his toolbox, but you may still follow in his footsteps in your imagination.

3

The Wheel of Fate and Fortune: Whispers of the Ba'al Shem Tov

IN MANY TALES, THE BA'AL SHEM TOV PLAYS a supporting role, often showing up only to bring things into focus for someone else. This seems to have been a major part of his teaching, especially for those who were not among his inner circle, or who were just on the periphery of it. It is in these *ma'asiot* that we find the Ba'al Shem Tov who was so appealing to the popular imagination, the magician of meaning, like Merlin in the Arthurian tales, coming in and out of the larger story to punctuate *ah-ha!* moments for others. Sometimes it is a one-liner he delivers to bring the whole story together or to show how intimately acquainted he is with the karmic strings of the universe. These he would pull ever so slightly to create the right effect: to teach something to a disciple that would be passed on through the generations, to obtain a useful pneumatic key bringing worlds together, to answer a simple question or give someone just the right push, to teach a lesson in compassion, or to bring about *teshuvah*. The stories in this chapter are all of this kind and were transmitted like holy gossip from one generation to the next until they reached our own ears and hearts.

WINE DROPS ON THE EYELASHES

I first heard this *ma'aseh* from Reb Berel Baumgarten,[1] who heard it from Reb Dovid Nosson the *shammes* of the Hayyim Berlin Yeshiva, who heard it from the Komarner Rebbe, who heard it from the Zydachover, and he from Reb Ya'akov Yitzhak, the Ḥozeh of Lublin, who heard it from Reb Dov Baer, the Maggid of Mezritch, who himself heard it from Reb Hayyim, to whom these events happened.

REB HAYYIM WAS a yoshev (sitter) at the court of the Ba'al Shem Tov, sitting and learning Torah day and night for the good of the community. In return for this ser-vice, every Tuesday (the day on which God twice said, "It is good"), the Ba'al Shem Tov would give Reb Hayyim a stipend for his family's maintenance.

In Europe, there was a practice that was inspired by the Mishnah, which says, "Any city that does not have ten *batlanim* does not deserve to be called a city."[2] Now, *batlanim* translates as "idlers" or "loafers," but that is not the true sense of it. In this context, it means ten contemplatives who are supported by the city and who are always available for communal functions. The work of the *batlan* is identical to the work of a *yoshev*, a "sitter" like Reb Hayyim. Sitters are Hasidim designated by their devotion to stay in the Rebbe's town and in the Rebbe's *beit ha-midrash* (house of study), learning and doing contempla-tive work. These people were the continuity, as it were, for the community.

My papa used to tell me that when he would visit Belz and the court of the Belzer Rebbe as a young man, one of the older Hasidim, a *yoshev*, would share his own bowl of soup with him with two spoons, which was a way of bringing him close and teaching him the appropriate consciousness of eating and other aspects of Hasidic life. So *yoshevim* (sitters) were also very much *mash-piyyim* (mentors) who would teach the younger Hasidim the principles of Ḥasidut.

In the HaBaD Hasidic lineage, the word "*yoshev*" was used mostly in the second through the fourth generations. In the time of Reb Shneur Zalman of Liadi (1745–1813), he already had three levels of *hadarim* (schools) and groups that he had set aside according to their capacity to study and to contemplate, so the *yoshev*-designate was not so necessary. But when the *hadarim* came apart after the Napoleonic War, there were again designated *yoshevim* in the time of the Reb Dov Baer of Lubavitch (1773–1828), the Tzemah Tzedek Menachem Mendel of Lubavitch I (1789–1866), and Reb Shmuel of Lubavitch (1834–1882). However, the fifth Lubavitcher Rebbe, Reb Shalom Dov Baer of Lubavitch (1860–1920) wasn't satisfied with this situation and wanted to have a formal HaBaD Hasidic *yeshiva*, and that is how Yeshiva Tomḥei T'mimim was begun.

In the time of his son, Reb Yosef Yitzhak of Lubavitch (1880–1950), my own Rebbe, I too studied in Yeshiva Tomḥei T'mimim in Crown Heights, Brooklyn. And like those *yoshvim* of the past, I did not have to pay while I studied; I was provided with food and a bed in the dormitory, all paid for by the *yeshiva*. From time to time, I also received a little receipt redeemable for a new suit. The manufacturer would give a certain number of these receipts to the *yeshiva* that were redeemable for suits by the *yeshiva bokherim* (students).

Later on, in 1950, when I went out to collect money for the *yeshiva*, I was doing this so that other people would have the same benefit I had, and so this mitzvah would continue to be fulfilled by our community. Even today, when my son was studying in Bat Ayin in Israel, he was provided with living quarters and also received a stipend. This is what they call a *kollel* now.

BUT ONE TUESDAY, *Reb Hayyim waited in vain at the Ba'al Shem Tov's door. He waited and waited, but he was not called to receive his stipend that day. He returned home to his wife empty-handed, and when she asked him for the money, he told her that the Ba'al Shem Tov had not called him. "It must have been an oversight; surely the holy Ba'al Shem Tov will call me in next week and correct the mistake."*

"What should we do in the meantime?" she pressed him.

"Pawn the pillows."

Grudgingly, she pawned the pillows, and Reb Hayyim studied on for another week.

The next Tuesday, Reb Hayyim stood at the Ba'al Shem Tov's door again, waiting, praying in his heart and trying to send his thoughts through the door to the Rebbe . . . "Rebbe, it's me, Hayyim, behind the door! Rebbe, please remember my stipend! There was none last week and I . . . Rebbe, please hear me!"

But Reb Hayyim was not called that day.

"Hayyim! Hayyim! What now?" his wife demanded.

"Borrow again! Pawn the candlesticks!" he said. "The Rebbe will remember; I'll stand near him at the evening service—he won't forget us!"

That week, the studies soured on Reb Hayyim; the flavor was all gone for him. All he could think was, "What will become of us? Will we be ruined? No, no, the Rebbe will remember!"

Tuesday came and Reb Hayyim stood at the door again, waiting. This time, his wife had also come and was pacing up and down outside in front of the Ba'al Shem Tov's house. Hours passed but, like a sentry at her post, she refused to leave. Reb Hayyim gathered his courage and knocked on the door. Timidly, he entered and faced the Ba'al Shem Tov, who looked at him quizzically, with an expression that said, "Have I sent for you?"

Reb Hayyim interpreted this simple expression as disapproval and thought, "What could I have done?" He began to launch into an explanation:. "Rebbe . . . I had no idea that I had displeased you. What should I do? Perhaps you no longer want me here, but now I have three weeks of debt!"

Then the Ba'al Shem Tov said, "Did you and I have an agreement that I would go on supporting you forever?"

Reb Hayyim was stunned into silence. When he recovered, he said, "But Rebbe, what will I do instead? How will I take care of this debt?"

The Ba'al Shem Tov reached into his drawer and took out some coins for Reb Hayyim. "This," he said, "is enough to cover the debt, and the extra you will use to go into business."

"Business?" Reb Hayyim asked, "I have been a yoshev all these years . . . I don't even know what business is!" And this was true.

Then the Ba'al Shem Tov said to him, "Before long you will be offered a deal, and the first thing that you are offered, you will buy with the surplus of this money. You will see, things will work out from there." And he blessed him to succeed in his new venture.

Hearing this, Reb Hayyim took heart and said, "Thank you, Rebbe; I know there is a purpose in this and I will do my best to serve ha-Shem in this business!"

Thus Reb Hayyim became a merchant, and a good one. The Ba'al Shem Tov's blessing—"With God's help, Reb Hayyim, you will find favor in the eyes of those who look upon you"—immediately proved potent. The seed money quickly became a goose; the goose, a turkey; the turkey, a goat; the goat . . . ba'kitzur—to make a long story a little shorter—Reb Hayyim was soon the proud owner of a general store. He even had a jewelry counter, which he soon turned into a profitable jewelry business!

Before long, he learned that his gem supplier bought the gems in Leipzig. "Leipzig," he thought, "I can also shop there and cut out the middle man!" Some purpose was driving Reb Hayyim; he was off to Leipzig where he could buy the gems directly and increase his profit. He began to see in the world other Jews, minyanim, and rabbonim, but since Reb Hayyim compared them all with Mezhbizh and the Ba'al Shem Tov, none of them really measured up.

Leipzig was a dizzying education—the crowds, the fair, the noise of it all, the variety of gems. "What? The gems didn't come from Leipzig either? Where did they come from then? Amsterdam?" Reb Hayyim thought as long as he had come all the way to Leipzig, he might as well travel on to Amsterdam and get a better price!

Finally, Reb Hayyim reached Amsterdam. "What? The diamonds came from Africa?" Something urged Reb Hayyim on; he had to go to the source! To Africa!

The journey to Africa was long and the sea was wide. The former yoshev was ill; he wasn't used to sea travel. There was a storm, and the ship was being tossed on the waves, up and down . . . can I say it better than the psalmist?

> They go down to the sea in ships,
> Their work is in the mighty water,
> Such wonders they have witnessed,
> God's miracles in the bottomless ocean.
> God roared and there whipped up a gale,
> And the waves rose up high.
> Tossed skyward and hurled down,
> Into the chasm, retching their souls,
> Reeling like drunks, their wits were consumed.
> (Ps. 107:23–27)[3]

A rock amidst the waves? A hole in the ship? Whatever it was, the ship sank, and a terrified Reb Hayyim ended up holding onto a broken board for dear life. Tossed back and forth on the waves, the immediacies of preserving his life left him no time to think about the strange fate that brought him to his predicament. Tossed up and down, forward and back, wave after wave crashed over his head; suddenly, with a jarring impact he was deposited on an unknown shore. Exhausted, he dragged himself up the beach and sank into a forgetful sleep on a small sand dune.

He awoke after untold hours and looked about, wondering, "Where are my tallit and tefillin? What island is this?" He looked around and was surprised to see smoke. "A fire? People? Barukh ha-Shem! Blessed is the Creator who provides for us!" Reb Hayyim ran awkwardly (though with excitement) toward the source of the smoke and found a village. There was no one about so he entered a house. "Barukh ha-Shem! A mezuzah! Jews! . . . Blessed are You who bestows such kindness on the undeserving!"

He surveyed the simple furnishings on the table: a bottle of schnapps, a few pieces of lekakh honeycake, a tallit, and two pairs of tefillin—Rashi's and Rabbeinu Tam's![4] He donned them, and lo and behold the knots were tied just like his own, they turned outward, just like in Mezhbizh! And the way in which he davened in them! Oy! those tallit and tefillin really prayed by themselves, and his soul wafted upward.

> Yah, You alone;
> Have made the Heavens,
> The Heavens of the Heavens,
> All those that serve you there,

Earth and all that is on her,
The oceans and all that they contain.
And You are mehayeh—invigorating![5]

"Ah, mehayeh!" Reb Hayyim enjoyed this prayer so much. He waited for the impression of tefillin straps on his hand to pass away and then helped himself to a drink, saying "L'hayyim!" which he really meant at that point.

Drinking is not supposed to be done in solitude, so we always say, "*l'hayyim,*" both in greeting and as a blessing, even when we are alone. Long ago, when people were convicted of capital crimes and waiting to be executed, they were always given something to drink, so that they would not go to their deaths suffering. One of the daughters of Jerusalem would be selected to hand the condemned man a drink before his execution. He would ask her, "Is this *l'hayyim* (to life) or *l'mavet* (to death)," meaning, "is this the poison by which I will meet my death?" So she would answer, "*L'hayyim.*" Since that time, we have continued to say *l'hayyim* before we drink.

One Friday morning, a Hasid arrived in Lublin for the coming *Shabbat* and went to greet the Lubliner, Ya'akov Yitzhak, the Hozeh of Lublin. The Rebbe, who doesn't ordinarily look up at his Hasidim, looked up from under his big eyebrows and said, "Do me a favor; don't come here for *Shabbat*—please go away."

The Hasid is shocked and says, "Why Rebbe? I've come a long way."

The Lubliner sighs and says, "You are going to die this *Shabbat* during the *tish,* at my *table,* and people are going to get upset, and the *Shabbat* will be disturbed. So do me a favor, go away, die someplace else, and I will see about helping you out on the other side. You'll get a good incarnation, but go away."

Oy! The poor guy gets a ride on a wagon and starts to head back home to die. Along the way, he stops at a roadhouse where he meets other Lubliner Hasidim heading to Lublin. They say, "Hey Hershel, what's with the long face? You're going in the wrong direction!"

With tears in his eyes, he tells them that the Rebbe sent him home, saying that he doesn't want him to die there on *Shabbat* during the *tish.* "Oh," his friends say, "never mind what the Rebbe says—if you are going to die, you are going to die—but we are going to stand right next to you the whole time. If you die, we'll hold you up and walk you out quietly so that nobody should make a fuss!"

Now they say to him, "How much money do you have on you?" "Twenty rubles," he answers.

"All right," they say, "you'll need about 10 rubles to ship your carcass back to town for burial, but then you'll have 10 rubles left-over . . . let's buy a keg of schnapps with it! So they buy the schnapps, and they catch a ride on a wagon going back to Lublin for *Shabbat*. As they travel they start drinking and say over and over again, "*L'ḥayyim! L'ḥayyim! L'ḥayyim! L'ḥayyim!*"

Arriving in Lublin, they go through the line to greet the Rebbe, and when Hershel the Hasid comes before the Rebbe, the Lubliner once again lifts his eyebrows, looks up, and says, "What Hasidim can do with their '*L'ḥayyim!*' even a Rebbe can't do!"

They had saved his life.

HE NOTICED A volume of Talmud at hand and so he took the opportunity for a little study. Soon, the owner of the house will come, he was sure. After all, there was a pot of soup boiling on the stove, and the owner will surely invite him to eat. Oh! the questions he will ask then! "Has the Ba'al Shem Tov ever been to this island before? Perhaps when he tried to go to the Holy Land?"

After studying and waiting a considerable time (for a castaway), Reb Hayyim heard his stomach rumble and could not wait any longer; he helped himself to the soup. "Ah, meḥayeh!"

"But this is very strange; where are all the people? Who leaves a pot of soup on the fire and doesn't come to check on it?" Reb Hayyim began to visit the other houses and found them the same as the previous one, with not a soul to be seen. He despaired and wondered, "What is going on?" Soon, he felt tired and made himself comfortable, and before long he was fast asleep.

The next day there was still not a soul to be seen, but the bottle had been refilled, the lekakh replaced, and the pot of soup was a-boil again . . . yet not a soul was around. A third day dawned the same, and still no one. Reb Hayyim despaired (albeit comfortably); he saw no one, ergo he wouldn't see anyone. With this naïveté, and pained only for the lack of company, he accepted his fate and went to bed that Thursday night.

In the morning he woke to the sound of furious activity. "To the shoḥet (butcher) with the chickens! To the sea for fish! Vegetables from the garden and fruits!"

Men, women, and children, all in an eager rush to make Shabbat, woke Reb Hayyim from his sleep of resignation.

Reb Hayyim turned to one of them, surprised! "Please tell me who you are? What you are? Where are you from? What are you doing here?"

But talking to them was just like talking to people during their prayers. Engaged in a mitzvah, doing God's will, how could they be interrupted?

Reb Hayyim wanted to help prepare for the Shabbat, but no one answered his desire to help. Reb Hayyim, like an orphaned shadow, wandered around the town, watching everyone prepare for the Shabbat while his own soul ached over his isolation. "Oh, how I would like to be part of it all!"

In the afternoon he went to the bath house, and there, enveloped in steam, with the other people preparing for the Shabbat, he saw their joy and still was not a part of it.

Toward sunset, everyone proceeded to the synagogue, including Reb Hayyim. The cantor began to daven, and Reb Hayyim—who had been to many places on that long journey, who had been to many cities in Poland, to Leipzig and even to Amsterdam, and who was on his way to Africa—hadn't heard such davenen since he left Mezhbizh and the Ba'al Shem Tov. Suddenly, Reb Hayyim felt at home. "Ah-h-h! the taste of olam ha-ba (the world to come)!

The cantor began again: "Come let us sing unto our sustainer! Let us chant to the rock of our salvation!" Oh, that singing, that chanting! The ecstasy of that prayer! Oh, yes, Reb Hayyim felt at home and really began to merge with those people.

The cantor sang, "Come, O friend, to meet the Bride! Let us meet the Shabbat!" The melodies, though they were not the same, had the same lilt, the same taste as those of Mezhbizh, the home of the Ba'al Shem Tov. But, before long—all too soon—the service was over.

The shammes approached Reb Hayyim and asked him to be the guest of the rabbi. It was the first time someone had really taken notice of him, so Reb Hayyim was both overjoyed that someone actually spoke to him and only too glad to accept the kind offer. Now, he supposed, "I will get some answers!"

So Reb Hayyim followed the rabbi to his home. Seated at the table he listened as the rabbi bid the angels welcome. "Shalom aleikhem Mal'akhei Hasharet" (Peace be unto you, angels of peace)! Reb Hayyim could almost feel the clasp of the angel's hands in his as he too said, "Shalom aleikhem" (Peace be unto you).

The rabbi intoned the eshet hayil: "A woman of valor, who can find? Her worth is far above rubies. The heart of her husband is secure in her." Reb Hayyim was immediately transported into the realm in which God sings this song to his Shekhinah.

Then came the Kiddush. The cup of wine glistened in the rabbi's hand. "It is

evening, it is morning, the sixth day. And the Heavens and the Earth were whole"
(Gen. 1:31).⁶ Before his mind's eye, Reb Hayyim saw the integration of the universe,
how God hallows this day and prepares to rest, and Reb Hayyim stood as a witness
to this sublime fact of all creation, the Shabbat. *Oh, such spiritual* ta'am Gan Eden
(the taste of the Garden of Eden). It was as if the tendrils of his sensory nerves were
connected to his very neshamah *(soul), feeling with his soul the delights of this*
world through the Shabbat!

Very soon, the rest of the guests gathered around the rabbi's table for the tish,
and he began to teach Torah based on the parsha *(the portion of the week).*

Reb Hayyim had heard preachers in many parts of Poland, preachers in Leipzig,
preachers in Amsterdam, but such preaching, such fervor, such ecstasy, such a feel-
ing of hearing the Shekhinah *(Divine Presence) talking through the throat of*
Moshe, this feeling he had only at Mezbhizh and now, here again! Reb Hayyim was
amazed and wondering.

It was very late when the hevra (fellowship) broke up; each headed home, each
one to their own place, and Reb Hayyim went to the place where he had stayed all
week, and he rested. All the anxieties of the week were gone. But in the back of his
mind he still wondered: "Who? What? Where? When? How?" He thought, "There
will be time to ask."

Behold it was the Shabbat *morning.*

Reb Hayyim rose and went down to the sea for a ritual dip. Refreshed and
renewed, he was able to pronounce with the rest of the congregation, "Everything
that breathes adores Your Name, Yah, our God; all flesh is raised to ecstasy as it
becomes aware of You."⁷ Reb Hayyim's very flesh was enthralled at the song of his
own soul to God.

Then the Torah was being read; the words floated through the air like intricate
designs of fire. All the people stood erect for the reading of the Torah. No one dared
to talk at the time when God speaks to each person's mind and soul through the
words of the Torah being read from the reader's desk.

Then the haftarah, *the reading from the prophetic books. Oh, Reb Hayyim could*
see the prophet on the hilltop addressing the throng surrounding him. He felt, even
in the denunciation of the prophets, the tender mercies of God. He knew at
that moment the voice of God still spoke in Mezbhizh as well as in this place. "Oh,"
Reb Hayyim sighed, "if only in the other cities of Poland, if Leipzig and Amsterdam
. . ."

The Musaf *(the additional service) began, and at the* Kedushah *(the sanctifi-*
cation of God's name), Reb Hayyim joined the rest of the congregation and felt as
if he were an angel standing in the presence of the throne of glory, approaching that
throne and placing the crown, wrought by Yisra'el's prayers the world over, on the
head of God!

"Keter yitnu leḥa" (The crown they give unto You), Reb Hayyim chanted. "Holy, holy, holy . . . The sustainer of hosts." Reb Hayyim too felt like one of the celestial serafim in Heaven, chanting God's praise.

When they came to the passage, "And the sacrifice of this Shabbat we shall render unto You in love," Reb Hayyim had an insight, something he had never felt before or fully understood. Reb Hayyim had always wondered, "How is it possible to make up the required sacrifice of this Shabbat even at the time of the coming of the Mashiaḥ?" And now Reb Hayyim understood! "The sacrifice of this Shabbat, this very Shabbat, which we cannot sacrifice unto You, O God, in the life of an animal or on the altar in Yerushalayim, the sacrifice of this Shabbat, our sustainer, we sacrifice to You in love . . . by loving You!"

This passage, "And the sacrifice of the *Shabbat* we shall render unto You in love," is based on the fact that we do not offer sacrifices anymore. But because the prophet Hosea has said, "We shall pay for the bullocks with our lips" (Hosea 14:3),[8] the true lip service was begun, and people would recite the passage on sacrifices in prayer, and that would stand in place of the traditional sacrifices. So when Reb Hayyim came to this passage and said, "the sacrifice of this *Shabbat* we shall render unto You in love," which originally meant, "we will offer the sacrifice *lovingly*," he now read as, "by *loving* You." Because it is no longer possible to offer the sacrifice, love becomes a noun and not an adjective describing how the sacrifice was to be offered.

REB HAYYIM JOINED in the jubilation of the Ain Keloheinu, "There is no God like our God." After the service was over, Reb Hayyim went back to his host, the rabbi, and for the first time in his life, he fully understood the meaning of the saying that the first meal on the Shabbat was established by Avraham, the second meal of the Shabbat by Yitzhak, and the third by Ya'akov. The first and the last meals Reb Hayyim could always enjoy. But somehow Yitzhak frightened him. It was at that moment, sitting at the rabbi's table, being in that sublime atmosphere, for the first time in his life, he was able to say to Yitzhak, "You are my father, my grandfather." Strange . . . Yitzhak became familiar to him as he mirrored his own loneliness and isolation and the sense of fellowship with the one who was lonely in this universe for God.

There are moments when our souls feel like Isaac bound on the altar . . . you cannot even count on your father to rescue you; you know that you have been chosen to give up your life to God; all the survival instincts of your body rise up against that; what power does it take to hold on and to say, "Thy will be done" under those circumstances? This moment is so impressive; anyone who ever had or has to offer their life in a sacramental-sacrificial way must tune in to this moment with Isaac. That is the *gevurah*, the strength or the discipline of *mesirat nefesh*, of offering one's soul.

THE TORAH OF *the second meal was also worth hearing, repeating, remembering, and meditating upon.* Shabbat *lasted, and this meal lasted until* Minḥah *(afternoon) prayers, when the people again assembled in the synagogue. With tremendous joy in his heart, and with the premonition of the parting of the* Shabbat *adding tartness to the flavor he felt in his soul, Reb Hayyim said the words, "You are One, and Your name is One, and who is likened unto Your people Yisra'el, one nation upon the Earth."*

At the third meal of the Shabbat *not much was said, but the melodies that were wafting from person to person as they sat around the table in the synagogue; the melodies were of the kind Reb Hayyim hadn't heard anywhere else. Reb Hayyim had been to many cities in Poland, to Leipzig, and to Amsterdam, but he hadn't heard melodies of this quality since he left Mezhbizh. Yet, he knew these melodies, he recognized them; they must have been the melodies that the Levites chanted in the holy Temple!*

The Shabbat *was then over. The* Ma'ariv *(evening) prayer was being said and the* Havdalah *separation was being made between* Shabbat *and the week, and Reb Hayyim wanted to ask his questions. His curiosity had reappeared as the new week was dawning. Just as Reb Hayyim opened his mouth to ask the rabbi, the* Havdalah *candle was raised, and the rabbi intoned, "Hiney El yeshuati" (Behold the God of my salvation)!*

Back in his weekday state of mind, beholding God was a terrifying thing; Reb Hayyim stood as one paralyzed. At the end of the Havdalah *ceremony, the rabbi doused the* Havdalah *candle with the leftover wine in his* Havdalah *cup and everyone stepped forward to dip their little fingers into the wine, touching them to their eyelids. Lo and behold, as they touched them to their eyelids, they disappeared, one by one, the rabbi being the last. Just as suddenly as they had come, they had disappeared! Now Reb Hayyim knew, somehow he was sure, that all during the week he would have to endure the same loneliness he did the week before.*

The *minhag* or custom of dipping one's little finger into the wine seems to be of ancient origin, and putting the wine drops on the eyelids is for the purpose of bringing the light of *Havdalah* (discrimination) to our eyes that we should be able to see what is necessary to see during the week and be able to discriminate between the real and the false, the positive and the negative, the holy and the profane, which is so easy to discern on *Shabbat*.

ALTHOUGH HIS WANTS *were well taken care of, and his schnapps replenished, and the cake was there every day, as was the soup, Reb Hayyim's wonderment and the many theories that he spun grew larger and larger. He knew Friday morning he would wake up and they would be there again. He made up his mind, come Saturday night, he would ask the rabbi his questions; he would prevent him, if need be, from dipping his fingers into the wine before he touched his eyelids—in order to know the truth. Again the Shabbat went, and again Reb Hayyim felt as if transported into a higher world, a supernatural, more sublime world.*

Again the rabbi intoned: "Behold, God is my salvation, I shall trust and never fear." And the way in which he said it started Reb Hayyim thinking, as if that were the answer to his own problems, as if that sentence of the Bible would tell him that he must trust and never fear. So he was caught in meditation until that time too all the people and the rabbi were gone.

For next week, Reb Hayyim devised a plan. He would not listen to Havdalah; he would make Havdalah afterward and keep his fingers in his ears and not even listen, because he knew that were he to listen he would again be transformed by a new way of looking at that sentence.

This time Reb Hayyim was prepared.

Just as the rabbi was about to dip his fingers in the wine, Reb Hayyim grabbed his hands and said, "Rabbi, you must tell me! Who are you? Where are you from? What does it all mean?"

A cloud descended on the rabbi's eyes, he heaved a sigh and said, "Hayyim, why did you have to ask? Hayyim, you cannot remain with us any longer in the same way that you have during the past. Hayyim, you must now make a choice and decide one way or the other. I will tell you our story, after which your decision must be made, a decision that will be irrevocable."

"It was in the time of the First Temple, in the time of Eliyahu ha-Navi, when a group of our parents approached the prophet and said to him, 'Master, your servants desire to leave this land, which is so full of holiness but also of idolatry. We do not wish our children or ourselves to become polluted by the idolatry that you are so hard pressed to fight. If you grant us permission, we shall leave this country and settle somewhere far away, on an island, where we can serve God according to the dictates of our conscience, according to the way in which we recognize God's truth.' "

The context of the period in which Prophet Elijah lived is important for this story. Prophet Elijah was known as a defender of the faith, at odds with King Ahab; he was engaged in spiritual warfare with the idolatrous priests of Ba'al, who were supported by the king (1 Kings 16–22). Thus the parents of the people of our story do not seek the king's or the priests' permission to settle in a new land, for these are the very idolators they are escaping. For this reason, they turn to Prophet Elijah, their Rebbe. For them, as an acknowledged servant of the true God, he is their only legitimate leader. To my mind, it is only a short stretch to envision these people as belonging to the *b'nai ha-neviim* (the disciples of the prophets), those individuals and families who were loosely allied with the prophets who, like Elijah, lived on the outskirts of society. In time, it is likely that the community of the disciples of the prophets influenced or evolved into the first Hasidic communities, like those we find at Qumran. Thus, in some sense, the meeting of Reb Hayyim with the inhabitants of this holy island is a reunion between two different streams of Hasidism.

"AND THE PROPHET agreed. Moreover, he gave them the sacred name Kefitzat ha-Derekh." Kefitzat ha-Derekh means the "jumping of the way." It is as if a long road were made shorter. It is as if all of space became warped and distances no longer remained distances and could be traversed with ease.

The term *"kefitzat ha-derekh"* is first used in the Midrash to explain how various individuals got from one place to another when the biblical text offers no explanation.[9] From there it entered into popular consciousness as a kind of pneumatic key used by saints and miracle workers to traverse great distances in a short time. But nowhere is it more important than in the tales of the Ba'al Shem Tov, and we shall soon see how this *ma'aseh* relates to the Ba'al Shem Tov's usage of this particular name.

"WE SENT A group of spies. They found this island on which we are now. They came back, reported to us, and we held hands, standing in a great circle, and a holy and terrible name was pronounced. When we opened our eyes, we found ourselves on this island where we built what we built and made ourselves at home and continued to worship God.

The island sanctuary for those loyal to the God of Yisra'el in a time of idolatry is reminiscent of the Jews of the island of Djerba off the coast of Tunisia, North Africa. On that island, Jews have lived for centuries and kept to very specific customs. For example, there are two congregations in Djerba: one is a congregation of *Kohanim* (that is, made up of families of the priestly heritage) and the other is a congregation of Yisra'el (that is, made up of the families of Yisra'el generally). The rule among these two congregations was that the rabbi of the *Kohanim* had to come from the Yisra'el congregation, and the rabbi of the Yisra'el congregation had to come from the *Kohanim*. And for many years they had a very beautiful way of keeping their community *minhagim* and their respective liturgies. Then the Alliance Israelite began to make overtures to the Jewish community of Djerba, trying to make sure that they would bring in modern schools and modernize their society. But when they began to pressure them more seriously, the people of Djerba raised money to pay the Alliance Israelite off so that they wouldn't trouble them anymore. Then they could continue in their own traditions, as these kept them together and kept them pure over the centuries.

"BEFORE EVERY ONE *of the three pilgrimage holidays—before Pesah, before Shavuot, and before Sukkot—one third of our community would be delegated to go on the pilgrimage to the holy Temple and to offer the sacrifices on our behalf, as well as on their own behalf. Our entire community would walk with them to the edge of the sea, and there, after song and dance and tender leave taking, the chosen ones would hold hands, close their eyes, utter the name, and be transported. The day after the holiday, we would again gather by the shore to await them. So we did, year after year.*

"Then one year, a group we had sent for Sukkot came back, and gone were their festive garments—instead they were clothed in sackcloth and ashes; and as we wondered why, with no answer forthcoming, we knew and realized their terrible tidings. The Temple, the House of God, the place where God had chosen to dwell had been destroyed! We wept, all of us, our youngest and our oldest. We wept until our souls could stand it no longer and finally separated from our bodies, and we found ourselves before the great tribunal on high.

"Even there they didn't know what to do with us. Some argued that even Heaven, with Avraham, with Yitzhak, and with Moshe, was not good enough for us. We did not think it so, yet they were adamant and none knew where we were to be placed.

"Suddenly, there came a voice from the throne of glory, saying, 'What is the greatest reward I have in my treasury? The greatest reward that awaits a human being is that he or she return again to the body, that the soul and the body become

one. But with one important difference. That whereas now it is the body that receives its realization from the soul, then the soul will receive its realization from the flesh.' For the flesh is in some ways closer to the inscrutable, ineffable heights."

The rabbi explained, "Is it not so? Only the flesh can hide the light of God from the soul. Therefore, the origin of the flesh is in its root much higher and much more sublime. It stems directly and immediately from the Divine Ayin (the No-Thing), without having to become subject to innumerable transmutations and developmental steps like the soul. All the angels on high agreed, and so it was decided.

"All week we were to be in Heaven and our souls were to receive their reward: the reward, where the righteous sit with crowns on their heads and bask in the radiance of the Shekhinah. *Before* Shabbat, *we were to be returned to Earth, because those who do not work for the* Shabbat, *who do not prepare for the* Shabbat, *what will they eat on the* Shabbat? *And the Friday is as much of the* Shabbat *as the* Shabbat *itself. The more preparation, the higher the rejoicing of the* Shabbat *itself. The more preparation, the higher the rejoicing of the* Shabbat, *the deeper the draught of life that the soul will derive from the body. On the* Shabbat *we are granted the resurrection, the bodily resurrection here on Earth."*

Reb Shalom Dov Baer of Lubavitch (1860–1920) taught that when the resurrection of the dead will come, the soul will no longer teach the body, as it does now, but rather the soul will then receive its teaching directly from the body. Thus, when the time came for the people of the holy island to be rewarded for their exemplary lives, what else could be given to them? They had their heavenly reward during the week in *Gan Eden,* but the real reward was to receive everything that the body could give and enjoy on *Shabbat* on Earth, including the preparation for *Shabbat.*

Similarly, Reb Nahman of Bratzlav (1772–1810) said that you have to teach your body everything that the soul knows, because the soul is ephemeral, and its teachings evaporate quickly. The body, in contrast, has memory, the body can arouse the soul again and again through memory. Now, today, the healing of our planet depends a great deal on what we can learn from our bodies and the body of the planet. As long as we continue to take *only* a top-down approach, mind over matter, soul over body, the mess that we have gotten ourselves into will lead us toward inevitable destruction. We can no longer afford to allow our voracious minds to consume the planet in endless material schemes, nor can we afford a spirituality that subjugates the body and advocates a harsh separation between spirit and matter. Right now, Earth is crying out to us, "Honor the flesh, honor the substance, listen to the needs of My body." So this is one of the most important messages of this story, to realize that the soul teaches the body, but the body can also teach the soul, and this is embodied in the holy islanders' relationship to the week and *Shabbat*.

DESPITE HIS AMAZEMENT, *Reb Hayyim somehow understood.*

The rabbi turned to Reb Hayyim and said, "Hayyim, now you must make up your mind; either you become one of us and dip your fingers in the wine and disappear like the rest of us, or else, Hayyim, you must leave this island. I will see to it that you find transportation. The name of Kefitzat ha-Derekh *shall help you arrive where you have to arrive."*

Reb Hayyim thought and thought very deeply. Such an opportunity! Souls wait for eons and eons for this chance, and he too would have to wait if he returned home. To have all of eternity, even higher than Heaven, at his fingertips! Surely he should avail himself of this opportunity. But then Reb Hayyim thought of his wife, deserted, chained, never able to remarry, never finding solace, not knowing whether her husband was dead or alive . . . and he missed her. Then Reb Hayyim thought of the opportunity of the soul again; but what is an opportunity of the soul if one must renege on God's mitzvot of kindness and love of others, if it is purchased at the price of forgetting a fellow human being?

With a sigh, Reb Hayyim declared his decision to the rabbi, saying, "This is an opportunity that I desire greatly, yet my choice must be to return home."

The rabbi lifted his hands and said, "Blessed are you, Hayyim, for making this choice; may the Heavenly Husband be so considerate of his Earthly Bride; may God so think of His people Yisra'el as you think of your wife and becoming reunited with her, finding your redemption through her."

"Amen," said Reb Hayyim.

When I first heard the story, I was told that Reb Hayyim had said that he could not accept such an offer, no matter how tempting, without the advice of his Rebbe, the Ba'al Shem Tov. Later I heard it from another source with the above-mentioned motive for returning—namely that Reb Hayyim did not want to leave his wife an *agunah*, an "anchored" and chained woman who could not marry, there being no evidence that she was a widow. How could he enjoy such a blessed state at such a great expense to his wife and children? I liked this ending better and usually tell it this way. However, even this pity that he shows for his wife and children is not quite satisfactory from our perspective. What of love? Sadly, that was not such a strong value in many such stories, partly because familial love was more often the norm than romantic love and because many in that paradigm might have seen such a motive as an unseemly attachment to the material world. Not so today.

THE RABBI TOLD *Reb Hayyim to open his hand. He did so, and in the palm of his hand the rabbi placed the name of Kefitzat ha-Derekh, telling Reb Hayyim to close his eyes and to see himself where he wanted to arrive, and there he would be.*

"But Hayyim," he warned him, "on your arrival, you must throw this terrible name of Kefitzat ha-Derekh heavenward, or else you will be a child of death."

Reb Hayyim nodded his understanding and closed his eyes. Naturally the place where he imagined himself was in Mezhbizh. As he opened his eyes he then found himself in the marketplace of Mezhbizh! He began to throw the terrible name of Kefitzat ha-Derekh heavenward when a hand suddenly took hold of his and Reb Hayyim screamed, "Murderer, let go of my hand!"[10]

Then he heard the gentle voice of the Ba'al Shem Tov saying to him, "Hayyim, it was for this name that you were sent where you were sent."

It was for the sake of obtaining the *Kefitzat ha-Derekh* that Reb Hayyim was sent on this journey. As I mentioned before, it comes up time and again in the tales of the Ba'al Shem Tov, how he seems to bend time in his journeys and holy errands to serve God's purposes.

Many people may be familiar with the corruption of the term *"kefitzat ha-derekh"* used in Frank Herbert's *Dune,* where the messianic figure sought by the Bene Gesserit is called the Kwisatz Haderach, "the one who can be many places at once."[11] In that novel, the "shortening of the way" is a concept explored from several different perspectives. It is first seen in the idea of "fold-space," a theory of space travel by which ships are brought across oceans of time and space in a fraction of the time it would take a ship to travel an "unfolded" linear trajectory. This folding of space is accomplished by "navi-gators." These are beings who are able to look down a line of development into the future and then to manipulate the very fabric of space to connect their point of origin with their intended destination. But the Kwisatz Haderach in *Dune* is different; he is an axis of events, having access to both the past memories of all his genetic forbears and to multiple lines of development in the future. Thus he is "the one who can be many places at once." There is something in both of these ideas that is relevant for us and our understanding of this particular *ma'aseh* today.

In Reb Hayyim's story, linear continuity and cyclical continuity, time travel and dimensional travel are important recurring themes. At first, our refugees from King Ahab's idolatrous kingdom leave Yisra'el in search of a place in which they may practice the religion of Yisra'el in freedom, according to the ways of their forebears. They settle on an island protected and isolated from the vicissitudes of worldly civilization and the changing fortunes of Yisra'el. While this could not stop small inexorable evolutionary shifts from occurring in their lives, it certainly slowed them down. Because they had been gifted with the *Kefitzat ha-Derekh,* they could also continue in their Temple observances, overcoming time and distance to be present at the yearly pilgrimage holy days. But after several generations, in the year 586 B.C.E., they were again confronted with devastating historical reality: Although they may have slowed the changes in their own world, change continued to come swiftly in the world outside. That year, the holy Temple in Jerusalem was destroyed by the Babylonians. So greatly were they shaken by this that they despaired of their existence and their souls abandoned their bodies.

However, as we have seen, they were once again returned to their island, but this time with a new solution. Whereas before they lived a linear existence and traveled through time, now they were reintroduced into a world of cyclical existence, and instead of using the *Kefitzat ha-Derekh* to overcome time and distance, they used it to shift dimensions. Living a heavenly existence for five and half days, they returned to Earth for the *Shabbat,* which is lived the same from week to week and is not subject to evolutionary shifts, not if there is no weekday existence in the world!

This is reminiscent of Friedrich Gerstäcker's fictional German village of Germelshausen, which appears out of the mists only one day every 100 years, allowing its inhabitants to maintain their blessed existence without disturbance through the centuries. There is just one catch, no one may ever leave the village or the enchantment will be broken and the village and all its inhabitants will disappear into the mist forever.[12] Thus every day the village of Germelshausen lives in an idyllic world, changing in 100 years only as much as that idyllic paradigm can change in a single day. And now Reb Hayyim finds himself in a similar situation to the young man who wanders into Germelshausen on its miraculous day and falls in love with a girl from the village; either he must leave his world entirely to be with her or watch her slip away from him forever in the interval of 100 years.

If we look for parallels to this in our own world, we find that what today's Hasidim in Brooklyn and Meah Shearim are trying to do in their communities is entirely understandable—they are trying to create just such a holy island as we find in our story. There is something beautiful about this desire to create an enclave in which they can be *shomrei Shabbat,* living fully and totally according to their own understanding of God's demands on them. Anyone who has ever tasted this life in the best of all circumstances knows that it is a little bit of Heaven on Earth. The question is, do they impose their ethic on other people? Can someone come and go from that world?

Because they have not been given the second gift of cyclical and dimensional jumping, their island enclave has to be more like the first gift given to the islanders. And like the islanders, to make themselves safe, the Hasidim today have mostly chosen to set up barriers against incursions of modernity, sometimes declaring harsh social sanctions on those who would not voluntarily comply with their rules, making it very difficult for anyone to come and go.

The difficulty in this situation always lies on the borders of the enclave, where their circle meets the outside world. This is where it always becomes less beautiful, turning into a contrast and clash of ideals, bringing out the worst qualities of both sides. Those of us who identify as neo-Hasidim have largely defined ourselves against more traditional Hasidim because we wish to live without being defined by those walls. In doing so, we have sometimes been critical of those on the other side of the divide. Nevertheless, there is beauty there that is lacking here. And while we have chosen to live on this side of that wall, identifying with the neo-Hasidic principles of freedom and adaptive vitality, believing that we too have something of beauty and value, we must still remember to honor the community that would like to preserve that rare golden flower of Hasidic spirituality as it has been known for centuries.

From this side, we might also ask, "What was the purpose of Reb Hayyim's mission? What can it teach us? Why did the holy Ba'al Shem Tov send him into the holy island, knowing that he would make the choice to return and, on returning, bring back a great secret? Perhaps we might take from this story a lesson based on these questions: What do we need to learn from our holy brothers and sisters in the more exclusive Hasidic enclaves? What can they teach us about *Shabbat*? For Neo-Hasidism is seeking more than what is *new*, it also seeks to *renew* the wisdom and forms of the past, reinvesting them with meaning for our own lives today, saying, "What was that *minhag* meant to do originally? How can it do that for us today?" I just want to say that it may yet be important for us to be able to "jump" into that world where the guardians of our tradition do their best to preserve the Jewish tradition as it was known in the past, and to "shorten the way" between our two worlds. We should have a place where, from time to time, we may experience *Shabbat* in that very sweet and very beautiful way and then be able to jump back out. Our own *Kefitzat ha-Derekh* may simply be a good passport between worlds, helping us stay rooted in tradition while remaining adaptable and open to changing circumstances, being in "many places at once."

IF YOU WANT to know what happened to Reb Hayyim, I can tell you. Reb Hayyim sold all his possessions and became a yoshev again with the Ba'al Shem Tov, and the Ba'al Shem Tov had the Kefitzat ha-Derekh. But what does the end of the story matter?[13]

Years after I first heard this story in the oral tradition, I found the same story in a book, but there it had become flat and lifeless, mere hagiography to get you to say, "Oy! what a *tzaddik* the Ba'al Shem Tov was!" But when I first heard this from Reb Berel Baumgarten, much as I have translated it here, it really lit a fire in me. I would often tell this story when I conducted a retreat. It set the mood for the participants to be in a state altered from their everyday routine consensus reality. It provided us with our own *kefitzat ha-derekh* state in which miraculous quantum jumps could be made to transformative insights. It is a pleasure to share this story in the hope that you too may experience a *kefitzat ha-derekh*. So jump ahead!

A TRIP TO POSEN

This *ma'aseh* takes us along on one of the Ba'al Shem Tov's mysterious journeys and is told from the perspective of the Hasid who witnessed these events. We can assume that it must have come after the story that we have just told, for the Ba'al Shem Tov uses the *Kefitzat ha-Derekh* in it.

AMONG THE DISCIPLES of the Ba'al Shem Tov was a young man who came from the city of Posen. He had been living in Mezhbizh for two or three years and had not been home for a visit in all that time. Then, one day, the Ba'al Shem Tov asked the young man, "Would you like to accompany me on a trip to Posen?"

The young man responded enthusiastically, "Of course!" Already he had begun to think of his mother's cooking and how impressed the Ba'al Shem Tov would be by the hospitality his family would show them.

Soon after Shabbat they loaded themselves into the wagon and Alexi the balagula, the Ba'al Shem Tov's personal coachman, turned the horses around and they began to make their way.[14] *But after they had traveled for what seemed a long time, it appeared to the young man—who knew the way to Posen—as if they had-n't really gotten anywhere in all that time. They went here, they went there, wend-ing their way, but never really getting anywhere! By Wednesday they were still on the road and nothing seemed to be happening; now the young man was really get-ting anxious to get someplace, anyplace. That night they slept over in the forest, and on Thursday, early in the afternoon, they finally arrived at a little pond where Alexi stopped the horses, as if at a destination.*

The Ba'al Shem Tov seemed to think it was a destination as well and immedi-ately descended from the carriage. He walked over to the little pond, took his clothes off and dipped in the pond as if it were the holiest of mikvaot! The holy Ba'al Shem Tov gestured to the young man to dip in the pond as well, and "Wow!" he was very happy to do it and even sensed something out of the ordinary about this place, but still he didn't have any idea why they had stopped to do this at this particular pond. There were so many other ponds along the way—why this one? Nevertheless, he said nothing.

It is not the usual way of disciples to ask questions before they have observed well and spent time contemplating what they have seen and heard. Only after they have chewed on a thing for a while and considered it careful-ly is it acceptable for a disciple to ask a question of the Rebbe.

Perhaps the most famous and instructive example of this principle is to be found in the story told of Rabbi Joshua ben Levi (3rd century C.E.) and Prophet Elijah . . .

Once upon a time, the great sage Joshua ben Levi was visited by Prophet Elijah and offered a wish. He asked that he be allowed to accompany the prophet on his travels. Prophet Elijah agreed to fulfill this request, but on one condition: Joshua was not to ques-tion any of his actions, no matter how extraordinary they may seem. If he did, they would immediately have to part ways. Joshua readily agreed, not knowing the difficult test he was about to face.

On the first stop of their journey, they came to the door of a man who offered them food and lodging without hesitation. He was a poor man and had little to give, but all that he had he gave willingly and with joy. Joshua ben Levi noticed that the poor man had an ailing wife and though he was a farmer, he had only one cow. In the morning, as Elijah and Joshua departed, Joshua heard

Prophet Elijah whisper a prayer that the poor man's only cow might die! Before they were out of earshot, Joshua heard the wail of the poor man crying over his dead cow.

Rabbi Joshua ben Levi was horrified; it was not in his wildest imaginings that Prophet Elijah would do such a thing! He opened his mouth to protest, but Prophet Elijah cut him short and reminded him of his promise. Joshua closed his mouth quickly but was nevertheless stunned by what he had seen and heard.

Late in the afternoon, they reached the house of a rich man to ask for accommodation. Before they had even completed a sentence, he slammed the door in their faces and sent a servant to drive them off. Later, they sneaked into his barn to sleep for the night. With no food in their bellies, or water, it was a long, uncomfortable night. In the morning, they woke with stones and hay pressed in their skin, and Joshua ben Levi heard Prophet Elijah whisper a prayer that a particular wall that had cracked (and would soon fall) in the rich man's house would be repaired without anyone ever having noticed. Joshua was once again astonished— prayers of harm for the good poor man and prayers of good for the selfish rich man! But he held his tongue, remembering his promise.

The next evening they came to a richly decorated synagogue whose members were clearly people of means. But none of the members even deigned to look at them, even as they sent them off with bread and water. As they were departing, once again Joshua ben Levi heard Prophet Elijah whisper a prayer: "Please God, make them all heads and leaders!" While in the next town, after they had met with people of a generous synagogue and a wonderful community, he heard the prophet whisper: "Please God, give them only one head!"

"Enough already!" said Joshua ben Levi, knowing that his journey with the prophet must end. "What is this all about?"

Then Prophet Elijah answered. "Joshua ben Levi, this is what you have seen and not understood. You observed that the poor man who was kind to us had a sickly wife, did you not? Well, she was about die. Thus I prayed to God that the cow might die so that his wife might live. As for the rich man who turned us away, I prayed that the wall might be repaired without his knowledge, for within it was hidden a great treasure that would have served only to make him more miserly. Likewise, it was no blessing I gave to the haughty synagogue that they should have many heads and leaders among them, for a congregation with too many heads and leaders will not last long, whereas for the righteous community, I asked that they should have only one head, so that they have clear vision and unity among them, and may prosper for many years!"[15]

SO THE BA'AL Shem Tov, *the young Hasid, and Alexi stayed overnight in the forest, and the next morning, Friday, they began to make their way again. At about noon, the carriage came to a stop in front of a broken-down shack. The Ba'al Shem Tov descended from the carriage slowly and with great reverence, as if he had just arrived at the palace of a king. He proceeded to knock at the door with the same air of great occasion. The door opened and out came a man—a wreck of a man, really—beaten, broken down, and so wounded that just to look upon him broke one's heart, as it did the heart of the young man from Posen. Suspecting that the Ba'al Shem Tov must have come to heal this man, he was then astonished to see the holy Ba'al Shem Tov reach out to him, hugging and kissing him as he would a long lost brother, after which the two of them went into the shack and closed the door. The young man waited with Alexi and the horses for half an hour before the Ba'al Shem Tov finally came out and they resumed their journey. Though he was full of questions, the young man said nothing.*

By this time, it was already afternoon and the Shabbat would soon be arriving, and though they were surely far from Posen, the Ba'al Shem Tov showed no sign of concern. Inexplicably, in the late afternoon, just before evening was to descend, the horses found their way into the city of Posen! The young man was ecstatic now, looking proudly on his city and the sites he would show his Rebbe. But instead of turning in the direction that would lead to his father's house, where they could expect the best hospitality, the horses turned onto a street called der Schulergasse *(the student's street). Alarmed, the young man almost yelled, "Rebbe, we can't go down this street! This is where the German students of the university live . . . Jews are always beaten up on this street!"*

It is important to note that Posen was quite cosmopolitan compared to Mezhbizh. Located in Silesia, on the edge of Poland, Posen had a German university, many educated citizens, and a more bourgeois populace generally. The Jews of Posen were mostly *mitnagdim,* and it was not the kind of environment where the Ba'al Shem Tov would be very welcome, whether by Jews or non-Jews. In fact, it is somewhat extraordinary that this young Hasid of the

Ba'al Shem Tov had made his way from Posen to Mezhbizh and had chosen a life very different from that off his contemporaries.

THE BA'AL SHEM Tov responded, "Listen, during this entire journey, we haven't told the horses where to go, and we're not about to start now, okay?"
   The young man nodded but remained concerned, for no Jew was even permitted on der Schulergasse, except the Jewish tailor and his apprentices who lived in a building near the middle of the street. There, the tailor and his family lived, the lone exception to the rule. This was because the German students were so often dueling with one another that they were constantly in need of someone to patch their clothes! Thus the tailor's family was permitted to live in that place.
   The horses stopped in front of the tailor's house and the Ba'al Shem Tov got out and knocked on the door. The tailor answered, and the Ba'al Shem Tov asked if they might stay for Shabbat, asking also to let them put the horses in the stable.
   The terrified tailor said, "Rabbi, you can't stay here; we're going to get into trouble! No Jew is permitted—"
   The Ba'al Shem Tov interrupted him, "Look, you don't have to worry; you and your family and the apprentices are eight, and if you allow the two of us in, we'll make a minyan so we can all daven here on Shabbat."
   The tailor reluctantly agreed.
   It was nearly Shabbat already, so the Ba'al Shem Tov went and washed up, put on his Shabbat clothes, proceeded over to the window looking out on the street, and began to daven Psalm 107 with a loud voice, shaking in his intensity:

> Thank You, Yah—You are so good,
> So constant in Your generosity!
> Have you been rescued by Yah,
> Rescued from the claws of the oppressor?
> Then say it . . .
> [Thank You, Yah—You are so good,
> So constant in Your generosity!] (Ps. 107:1–2).[16]

BEFORE LONG, ONE of the university students walked by and was struck by the sight of a Jew standing there, praying loudly and making funny motions. He naturally went and called the other students over; and soon there was a rowdy crowd of students laughing at the Ba'al Shem Tov and mimicking him.[17] Then one of the students stooped to pick up a stone and was about to throw it through the window at the holy Ba'al Shem Tov when suddenly he froze and fell to the ground cat-aleptic!

The students who saw what happened panicked; they didn't know what to do with their friend. Something so serious required that they get help for him, so they ran across the street to the house of one of the professors and rang the bell. The professor came out to see what was the matter with the frozen student. He took one look at him and immediately issued orders for them to carry the boy into his house and to call for the doctor. After several of the boys ran off to do this, he asked the others who remained, "What happened?"

They pointed to the tailor's window where the Ba'al Shem Tov continued to pray and said that they were making fun of the Jew yelling and gesticulating wildly when their friend had decided he was going to throw a rock through the window at the strange Jew.

The professor looked up with wonder at the Ba'al Shem Tov praying in the window and then lowered his head and sighed. He said, "Pass the word; if anybody even thinks of molesting the tailor and his family—or anybody in his household—for the next 48 hours, I will make certain that they end up in cartzer *(incarcerated)* as a penalty. You are to leave them alone; do you understand?"

They all nodded their understanding and quickly disappeared.

The professor walked back to his house, went inside for a moment, grabbed a frock coat, and left again, walking across the street to the tailor's house. He knocked on the tailor's door, which the tailor answered timidly, shaking because of this whole gesheft. Before the obviously frightened tailor could speak, the professor said, "I understand that there was a disturbance here before and I want to assure you that there won't be another one tonight. Please allow me to sit here just inside the door so that I might guarantee this; I promise that I will not interfere in any way with your prayers or meal; I just want to make sure that you will not be disturbed."

Even if he had wanted to object to this unusual request, the tailor was too frightened by what had happened and agreed immediately.

While all of this was going on, the Ba'al Shem Tov went about preparing for the Shabbat as if nothing was wrong, paying no attention whatsoever to the professor near the door. He made Kiddush and conducted a wonderful tish, the likes of which this tailor had never seen, and the tailor quickly realized that his guest was a holy man. In the middle of the meal, the seudah, the Ba'al Shem Tov began to say a devar Torah, a deep, deep, Torah teaching.

Now, the young man from Posen was again puzzled. He, of course, understood what the holy Ba'al Shem Tov was teaching, at least on his own level, but he looked around at the tailor and his apprentices, and said to himself, "Why is he teaching this to these people who can't have any idea what he is really saying?"

They recited the Birkat ha-Mazon *(grace after the meal), and just as they were about to lock up, the professor said, "What time will you be starting up in the morning? I'll be back then."*

And so he came back again in the morning and took up the same position as he had the night before, like a sentry near the door. He stayed the entire day—observing in the way only a professor can observe—while the Ba'al Shem Tov again said Torah at the Shabbat *table, and then once again at* shalosh seudot *(the third meal).*

As soon as Shabbat *was over, the Baal Shem Tov declared to his host and to his disciple, "After we make* Havdalah, *we will be leaving immediately and heading back home to Mezhbizh."*

The young man was taken aback and asked, "Without seeing my parents?"

The Ba'al Shem Tov answered, "I never said we were going to see your parents; I asked you if wanted to come to Posen. You've come, and now we're going back."

After Havdalah, *they were back in the carriage and the Hasid could not contain himself any longer, "Rebbe, all of this has been very strange, and I cannot make head or tail of it; may I know what all of this was about? I mean, this whole business, driving around aimlessly until Thursday to dip in that pond, the sadly battered old man? And why did we have to be in this tailor's house for* Shabbat *and no longer?"*

The Ba'al Shem Tov looked at him indulgently and said, "About the first two things, I will tell you; the other you will understand in time.

"That pond, as I am sure you sensed, was no ordinary pond. You have heard, of course, that the Well of Miriam travels all over the world, and so it was necessary for us to pursue it until the time and the place was right for us to dip in it. You should consider yourself blessed to have dipped in the sacred Well of Miriam."

According to tradition, a well followed the people of Yisra'el through the desert on their wanderings because of the righteousness of Miriam the Prophetess. It remained with them until the day of her death, when it began to travel all over the Earth. This is how the Ba'al Shem Tov came to dip in it. But there were other Rebbes who had this honor as well . . .

Just before *Kol Nidrei,* the service on the eve of Yom Kippur, the Kalaver Rebbe, Reb Yitzhak Eisik of Kalev, called the wealthy and pious Ya'akov Fisch and asked him to have his carriage brought out. Though the people were already gathered in the synagogue, the two hopped inside and were soon off to Ya'akov

Fisch's fields, where they stopped in front of a small body of water. Without a word, Reb Yitzhak Eisik stripped off his clothes, dipped in the water the required number of times, got out, and dressed again. Reb Ya'akov watched in amazement, but before he could say anything, the two were back in the carriage and heading back to the synagogue.

After Yom Kippur was over, Ya'akov Fisch went back to the spot where they had stopped in his fields, but he found no water there, nor had he ever seen water in that spot before, though he had walked those fields a thousand times. He finally went to see the Kalever Rebbe for an answer. "Reb Ya'akov," the Kalever Rebbe explained, "if Miriam's Well passes through our country again, you would do well to dip in it too, instead of standing there amazed."[18]

"AND WHO WAS the old man?" asked his disciple.

The Ba'al Shem Tov answered, "That 'old man' was Mashiaḥ. You see, Mashiaḥ can come at any moment, but in order for that to be true, there has to be one person who is designated to fill the role of Mashiaḥ in potential at all times."[19]

"Why was he so wounded?"

"Because it says, 'he is wounded for all our iniquities and is bearing them' (Isa. 53). Thus, as his time on Earth was coming to an end, I came to thank him for his service—for having waited in the wings all this time in the event that the moment of grace should arrive—bearing all our sufferings. I wanted to thank him for this, and also to ask him about the next in potential. Who that is, is none of your business."

Then the young man asked, "What about this trip to Posen?"

"Ah," said the Ba'al Shem Tov. "You'll find out in time."

Just as the holy Ba'al Shem Tov finished this sentence, they arrived back in Mezhbizh— their entire trip having taken only the length of their conversation! For an explanation of this miracle, the young Hasid didn't even bother to ask. It was well known that the holy Ba'al Shem Tov had long possessed the secret of "shortening the way."

Years passed and the Ba'al Shem Tov had gone with them, and this young man was now in his middle years, living in Posen again, a good citizen doing business in different towns and cities. Occasionally, he had to be away for Shabbat. Because he had once been with the Ba'al Shem Tov, he knew that the best thing that he could do was to inquire about the rabbi of the town and then to ask the rebbetzin (rabbi's *wife), "Would you please put me up for Shabbat, for meals, so I can enjoy the rabbi's company, hear Torah, and also be certain about kashrut?"*

And so on one of these occasions when he had to be away for Shabbat, he came to a town and arranged to stay with the rabbi. The rabbi took an immediate liking to him, escorted him to shul, and they came back Friday night and were sitting at the table singing zemirot when the rabbi began to say Torah.

Suddenly, the Hasid realized that this was the very Torah the holy Ba'al Shem Tov taught that strange Friday night in Posen!

Unable to contain himself, he interrupted, "How did you come by that Torah?" The rabbi merely smiled.

Shabbat afternoon, it was the same thing, and then once again at shalosh seudot. All three of the Ba'al Shem Tov's Torahs spoken in Posen!

The Hasid waited with an eager expectancy. When Shabbat was over, the rabbi said to him, "So you didn't recognize me? . . . I was the professor."

The Hasid's mouth dropped open, but now he kept silent to hear the full explanation of this situation.

The rabbi-professor continued, "At the time of your visit to Posen, I was a scholar and professor of Old Testament and Hebrew at the university. I had long felt a desire to convert to Judaism, but I also had my doubts; actually, there were three questions that I needed answered before I converted. When you came, and I saw the strange effect on the young student who was about to throw the stone at your master, I knew that he might be the person to answer my questions. Without me so much as voicing a single one of them, all of them were answered in succession through the three Torahs he gave that Shabbat!

"So, with my doubts finally resolved, I left the university and traveled away to where I could undergo conversion, but since learning was already in my blood, it wasn't very difficult for me to achieve the status of rabbi after only a short time. And so I got this position of rabbi here in this town. When you came to the door yesterday, I recognized you immediately and I was glad to see you. So now you know all there is to know of my story."

Now, of course, I know what you are thinking, because I have been wondering the same thing for years: "What were the three Torahs? And what questions did they answer?" I wish I knew, but we are not privileged to know them. Nevertheless, we all have three such questions, and we can imagine them into this story.

THE MAN WHO WASN'T IN NEED OF BLESSINGS

ONE DAY, A rich man comes to visit the Ba'al Shem Tov, and the Ba'al Shem Tov asks him, "Is there anything that you need? A blessing for children? For money?"

"No, no," the rich man answers, "I am fine with everything: I am well off, I have a good wife, good children and good sons-in-law, good health, and a good house— everything that a man needs; I am not in need any kind of blessings, thank you."

So the Ba'al Shem Tov says, "Well, if that's the case, perhaps you won't mind hearing a story?"

The rich man says, "Glad to hear a story."

"Years ago," the Ba'al Shem Tov begins, "there were two boys in a little town who were 'milk brothers,' sharing the same wet nurse. Their names were Reuven and Shimon. These two boys grew up together, loved each other, and were insepa-rable; the two of them were the best of friends. They studied in ḥeder together, they studied in yeshiva together, and they were both brilliant. Soon enough, the rich men of the area who were looking for good sons-in-law came and bought them for their daughters.

"Now these two milk brothers lived in different towns in the houses of their fathers-in-law where they sat and studied Torah each day. Because they couldn't talk each day as they were used to doing, they began to write each other letters every day so they could discuss what each of them was studying.

"After a while, the time came when they finally had to start taking care of busi-ness, and before long they were writing only once a week . . . then once a month . . . and then once a year. They were both busy men and successful in their respec-tive businesses; both had become pretty rich fairly quickly because they started with rich money from their fathers-in-law.

"Then it happened . . .

"Reuven's business took a turn for the worse, and he suddenly found himself with no cash. If he couldn't pay some of his bills immediately, he would be ruined, bank-rupt. He needed just enough money to pay some of the most important bills and a little extra to tide him over and everything would be fine. But where was he going to get that kind of money?

"Suddenly he thought of Shimon, 'Yes, Shimon will help me!' So Reuven set out on the road to see his milk brother. When he arrived, exhausted, Shimon opened the door to him and immediately said, 'Shalom aleikhem! It's so good to see you.

How are you? I see by your face that you are disturbed. Tell me what's on your mind. No, wait—we'll prepare a good dinner for you, and you can rest, and we'll talk about it then.'

"After he had supped and rested, he told Shimon his problem. Shimon nodded his head slowly and said, 'Don't worry about it; go to sleep; have a good night's rest, and by tomorrow I'll be able to fix you up.'

"Reuven went to bed relieved, and Shimon went off to call on his bookkeeper. 'Tell me,' he said, 'what have we got liquid and what have we got invested? I'd like an entire list of each. If you can do it in the next couple of hours, there is a bonus in it for you.' Soon the bookkeeper came back with the list. Shimon took a look at the list, and he saw that he had a little bit more liquid than he had invested, so he took half of what he owned from the liquid portion and gave it to his milk brother, Reuven, in the morning, saying, 'Gezunterheit, my brother, and may this be helpful to you.'

"Reuven was overwhelmed, very grateful, and went back home triumphant.

"However, now Shimon's fortunes began to dip while Reuven's fortunes went up. And soon Shimon was in the very same situation as Reuven once found himself. He figured, 'Now I must go see my friend Reuven; he will help me out, especially since I helped him. He's my best friend, of course he'll help me.'

"Shimon went to Reuven that night, but Reuven seemed a little disturbed at the sight of him, and said, hesitantly, 'What can I do for you?' Shimon answered him without a worry, 'You remember when you came to me? Well, now I'm in the same situation and I need your help.'

"Then Reuven answered him just as he was answered when he made his own plea, 'Don't worry about it; go to sleep; have a good night's rest, and by tomorrow I'll be able to fix you up.' Shimon went happily off to bed, but Reuven immediately called his driver and told him to get his horse and his wagon ready, and he left in the middle of the night so that he didn't have to face Shimon in the morning."

People are often surprised at this turn of events in the story. After all, they are milk brothers and it seems so obvious that Reuven is going to return the favor. But I tend to think that a little wormlike fear had worked its way into Reuven's heart—perhaps an addiction to wealth and comfort—that wouldn't allow him to give up what he had once lost. Even though Shimon had saved him, proving that he had insurance through Shimon, he could never feel quite secure enough after that. It is likely that he began to fear the possibility of falling into such desperate circumstances again and began to build walls around his fortune and his heart, living in fear of the possibility that Shimon might ever require the same favor of him, which would leave him vulnerable to the same poverty that had almost enveloped him once before.

"SHIMON WAS BROKENHEARTED *in the morning when he found out what Reuven had done. He didn't know what to do with himself; he didn't even have the fare for a wagon to take him back home. He began to make his way home on foot as a beggar. Luckily, along the way, somebody offered him a little deal by which he could make some money, and before long, even on the way home, his fortunes began to rise, whereas Reuven's began to go down again.*

"Now, it was not long before Reuven was in the same situation as before and was more desperate and upset than ever. 'I don't know what to do,' he cried aloud, 'I couldn't possibly face Shimon, but there is nobody else I can go to.'

"So he traveled to see Shimon again, knowing that Shimon's fortunes had fully recovered. He knocked as a homeless criminal would knock on the door of the town constable, hoping to confess his crimes and be given food and a bed in jail. Shimon opened the door and was astonished to see Reuven standing stooped before him, but then, with deep sadness, he asked, 'What happened, Reuven?'

"Reuven could not even look up at him, but said, 'I simply couldn't part with my money; something had eaten at my heart, and I just fled. I got so anxious, and I just couldn't handle it. It was a hard time for me when I was in that down-and-out situation, and I just couldn't . . . I just had to leave. Please forgive me. . . . But Shimon . . . now I am in the same situation again.'

"And with that Reuven began to cry.

"Shimon took pity on his old friend, but spoke to him like a businessman this time, saying, 'I'll do the same thing for you that I did before. However, this time, you have to give me an IOU for the money I'll give you. Then, should I ever be in that position again, I'll know I can come and collect from you.'

"So he did the same thing again—gave Reuven the money, wrote out an IOU that Reuven signed, and got it witnessed—and Reuven departed with the money.

"Again the seesaw of fortune took them both; Reuven's fortunes rose while Shimon's began to dip. Now, Shimon was at Reuven's great, solid, and richly carved door with the IOU in his hand. A servant answered his knock and announced his name to the master of the house, but Reuven refused to see him! Shimon was astounded; he would really be ruined this time! He ran to the rabbi and said, 'This is what this man owes me; here is the IOU signed by him, showing the debt. Please make him honor it!'

"But the rabbi only replied, 'I won't be able to help you collect. This man is a very hard man, and he is a big boss in our community; if he doesn't want to give it to you out of his own goodwill, then there is nothing that I can do.'

"Twice heartbroken, Shimon turned to go home with heavy feet and a heavier heart. On the way he caught pneumonia and died before reaching his own door. He immediately came up before the court of the heavenly assembly, who said to him, 'Shimon ben Ya'akov, you have been twice good and you will go straight to Gan Eden (Paradise); and it has been decreed that Reuven ben Ya'akov, your milk brother, will be snuffed out immediately, going straight to Hell.'

"Shimon, to the surprise of all, spoke up, saying, 'How could I do that? What kind of Gan Eden will I have if my friend is suffering in Hell? No! I cannot agree to this; I'm not going to go along with that!'

"Faced with Shimon's holy defiance and great love, the heavenly assembly asked him what he suggested should be done with Reuven.

"Shimon answered after some thought, 'Let us be reincarnated. This time, Reuven should be a rich man right from the beginning. He should be fine with everything. He should be well off; have a good wife, good children, and good sons-in-law; good health; and a good house—everything that a man needs; he should not be in need of any kind of blessings. *I, on the other hand, will be born as a beggar. Thus when I come and ask him for a dole, he will be able to give me what I need without any concern, and the taint will be removed from him.'*

"The heavenly assembly looked kindly on Shimon and did as he requested; the two men were reincarnated and the 'new' Reuven was well off; had a good wife, good children, and good sons-in-law; good health; and a good house—everything that a man needs; he was not in need of any kind of blessings whatsoever. The 'new' Shimon, however, was a beggar. Just as Shimon had asked, the beggar in time crossed paths with the rich man. It was a cold day, and slippery, and he was coming for a hand out. But this rich man just couldn't stand seeing this poor man in front of him, nudging him, saying, 'You must help me! You really must! My family's need is so great! You can't do this! You must help me! You must help me!' The rich man pushed him and the beggar fell on the ice and later died from his injuries."

Then the rich man listening to the Ba'al Shem Tov's story, and who had been turning white and becoming increasingly rigid in appearance toward the end of the story, dissolved into tears. When he was finally able to speak, he said, *"Rebbe, what am I going to do about this?"*

The Ba'al Shem Tov answered him, *"You will do what you should have done all along; you will seek out the family of this beggar and give them half of what you own, and that's how you are finally going to fix this situation."*

There is something about hearing your own story from someone else's mouth that is transformative. Maybe it is just the simple fact of being outside of it that helps us to see it differently, without all of our rationalizations and justifications. My favorite story of this type is of King David, who is told a parable of his own life by Nathan the Prophet.

> In the Bible, we are told how God once sent Nathan the Prophet to King David, saying, "There were once two men in the same city, one rich and one poor. The rich man had great flocks and herds, while the poor man had but one small ewe lamb that he loved as his own child. One day, a traveler came to stay with the rich man, but instead of taking a lamb from his own flocks and herds to serve his guest, the rich man took and killed the poor man's beloved lamb." Hearing this, David was consumed with anger at that man, "As the Lord is living, that man deserves to die; he will pay for this four times over!" Then, with a quiet and deadly serious voice, Nathan the Prophet said, "You are the man." David fell back in amazement. "You have been given everything, and yet you contrived the death of Uriah the Hittite in order to take his wife to your bed, so I say again, you are the man" (2 Sam. 12:1–14)

A COMPASSIONATE JUDGMENT

The Ba'al Shem Tov was often dealing with these kinds of karmic situations, and dealing with them much in the same way as Nathan the Prophet. In the next *ma'aseh,* we have an interesting twist on the story of David and Nathan, in which the "David" of our story actually has to walk in the shoes of his "Uriah."

NEAR THE CITY *of Brod lived a simple Jew who made his living as a mover, carrying people's belongings from place to place and town to town in his simple wagon, drawn by a single nag.*

One Friday afternoon, he is delayed after a long journey to a neighboring town. Though he is trying very hard to get home in time for the arrival of Shabbat, *the roads are thick with mud from an afternoon rain, and, Oy!, his horse is already weary from a long day of work. As the time passes, an ache is steadily growing in his heart, an anxiety about arriving late for* Shabbat. *He begins to pray that he will make his way in time, but the sun is about to set and he still has several viorsts to go!*

Finally, the mover arrives home—it isn't quite dark yet—but he can already hear the people beginning to sing Lekha Dodi *in the synagogue! His heart begins to palpitate wildly. He puts the horse in the stable, makes certain it has some water and food, puts the wagon away, and washes up as quickly as he is able—fretting the whole time. He runs to the synagogue, coming just in time to hear them say,* "Barkhu." *He is crushed and feels horrible that he has desecrated the holy* Shabbat. *How could he have done it? Maybe he didn't plan his time well enough? And what did that imply? That he hadn't put God first!* "Oy! Oy! Oy!"

After Shabbat *is over, unable to stand his guilt and longing for expiation, he makes his way to Reb Mikeleh of Zlotchov, the son of Yitzhak of Drohobitch, a young disciple of the holy Ba'al Shem Tov known for his great piety.* "He will know what to do." *He recounts the whole ordeal to Reb Mikeleh and asks,* "What must I do to relieve myself of this burden and make amends with ha-Shem *(God, lit. "the name")?"*

Reb Mikeleh listens to the whole story with an increasingly furrowed brow. When the poor mover is finished, Reb Mikeleh sighs heavily, without unfurrowing his brow, and says, "You must fast both Mondays and Thursdays; you must also add an additional set of psalms to your daily prayer, and you must give tzedakah *(charity) in increments of seven, and every night you must pour out your heart and weep over the sin of arriving late for the* Shabbat!"

The poor mover leaves Reb Mikeleh even more burdened than before, though he is hopeful that through the penances that Reb Mikeleh suggests he will truly be able to make amends. But how is he going to do those things? Already he has to work hard, and there is little time for prayer as it is, and if he doesn't eat on those days, how is he going to have the strength to load and unload the wagon? And the tzedakah—*if only he were a rich man that he could give so much, it would be a pleasure—it is hard enough to feed himself and the horse! And just as he thought, all of this is too much for the mover. If he tries to do one of the penances, it only lessens his ability to do another, so soon he is failing at all of them and beginning to feel worse and more guilty than he had when he arrived late for the* Shabbat!

One day, the poor mover finds himself in Mezhbizh and determines to go and talk to the Ba'al Shem Tov about his problems. He is admitted to the Ba'al Shem Tov's study and begins to unfold his entire tale of woe. "Oy!," *he says,* "holy Rebbe, I know what I did was wrong, but now I am in an even worse place—how will ever dig myself out of this hole?"

The Ba'al Shem Tov looks at the mover with great pity, saying, "My friend, I can assure you and I want you to know that from this hour your sin has been totally and completely atoned for, the slate has been wiped clean. You may now leave off the penances that were prescribed for you.

"Now," the Ba'al Shem Tov continued, "I need you to do me a favor; when you return to Brod, please tell the holy Reb Mikeleh that I would like him to join me next Shabbat in Mezhbizh."

The mover is dumbfounded but relieved for the first time in weeks, and he does exactly as the Ba'al Shem Tov requested.

The next Friday afternoon, Reb Mikeleh is making his way to Mezhbizh to be with the holy Ba'al Shem Tov for Shabbat when the weather suddenly turns foul. The progress of the wagon is slowed considerably by the muddy roads. Soon he is beginning to get anxious as the wind and rain increase in ferocity and the sun is no longer even visible. Who knows what time it is? Then, just when it seemed it couldn't get any worse, the wagon wheel breaks! "Oy!" He jumps out of the wagon, frantic, heart pounding, not even thinking to help the driver, and begins to run in the direction of Mezhbizh. Heartbroken and road weary, he arrives just in time to hear the congregation say, "Barkhu."

Later he comes to the Ba'al Shem Tov and says, "Rebbe, how must I do penance for the sin that I have committed?"

The Ba'al Shem Tov turned and looked on him with pity and said, "Reb Mikeleh leben, how did you feel on the road as you struggled to make it to Mezhbizh in time for Shabbat?"

Reb Mikeleh exclaims, "Oy! Rebbe, I can't even tell you . . . I felt as if a fire were burning beneath me! I couldn't think of anything but the fact that I was about to desecrate the holy Shabbat! I was so upset and angry with myself. Why couldn't I have left earlier? I was so frustrated that my stomach was in knots and my chest was crushed by the weight of my guilt! I almost felt as if I were dying. Please Rebbe, tell me what I can do to purge myself of this guilt?"

The Ba'al Shem Tov sighed, "Reb Mikeleh, don't you think you have suffered enough? Didn't you long for nothing else than to be here in time to honor the Shabbat properly? And in that longing, with all the suffering you experienced because of it, didn't you feel all that would be required of you to feel in a penance?[20]

"No, Reb Mikeleh," the Ba'al Shem Tov continued, "that was your punishment . . . and twice over. For you have experienced this because of the harsh judgment with which you burdened the poor and holy mover who came to you for help. His sin was no greater than yours for which you have been judged kindly. Please remember this the next time someone comes to you in sincere repentance, because there is no greater atonement than the sincere distress of the heart."

———————

Sometimes a contrite and heavy heart is actually healing in itself. As we say, *Lev nishbar v'nidkeh, Elohim lo tivzeh,* "a broken and contrite heart, you God, will not despise" (Ps. 51:19).²¹ That is to say, one may be so contrite that intent can be lifted out of the act, until the act may become so emptied of intent that nothing remains.

REB MIKELEH'S *NIGGUN* OF GREAT LONGING AND THE PASSING OF THE BA'AL SHEM TOV

Reb Yehiel Mikeleh of Zlotchov (ca. 1731–1786) was one of the Ba'al Shem Tov's greatest and most devoted disciples, and he was also renowned as a singer and composer of *niggunim,* the holy melodies of Hasidic spirituality. Now, the *niggun* is a melody for tuning the soul, for creating a unique atmosphere, and for keeping it primed. If you want to drink in the Ba'al Shem Tov and be under the influence of his Torah, you sing "The Ba'al Shem Tov's *Niggun.*" Or if you want to have his presence in your prayer and celebration, you sing "The *Gagooim Niggun* of Reb Mikeleh of Zlotchov." It is like installing a "BeShT (Ba'al Shem Tov) Operating System" in your heart space. Why? Because there is a certain *kavanah,* a certain intentionality that goes into the composition of a *niggun,* and that quality can be invoked under the right circumstances.

I'll give you a story to illustrate what I mean. This is a *ma'aseh* I learned from my own Rebbe, Reb Yosef Yitzhak of Lubavitch . . .

———

WHEN REB MIKELEH of Zlotchov was a child, his father, Reb Yitzhak of Drohobitch, was a Hasid of the Ba'al Shem Tov and would often travel to see him.²² You can imagine what it must have been like for Mikeleh as a child to see his papa preparing for that journey, watching Reb Yitzhak's joy building as he did his inner and outer preparations, seeing how people would begin to give him messages and charity to take along to the Ba'al Shem Tov to be given to the tzaddikim nistarim (the hidden saints)! An air of expectancy would build and build in little Mikeleh as he watched his father, until finally it was deflated in disappointment as he was forced to stay behind, watching his father walk down the road alone, fading out of sight.

But when Papa came back, oh how his face was shinning; he was transformed! And the stories he brought with him—Oy! Oy! Oy! Finally Mikeleh said to his father, "Abba, when are you going to take me to see the Ba'al Shem Tov. I want to go with you next time."

Reb Yitzhak smiled almost imperceptibly and replied, "My child, I know you want to see the Ba'al Shem Tov, but I don't know if the Ba'al Shem Tov wants to see you yet; I will have to ask him first."

So when Reb Yitzhak made his next journey to the Ba'al Shem Tov, young

Mikeleh waited anxiously and composed the first part of his niggun, infusing it with all of his hopes.

When his father returned, he said to his son, "Mikeleh, the Rebbe says that I can bring you with me, but you will have to wait a whole year."

Mikeleh's heart leapt at the news, but Oy! a whole year of waiting!

During that seemingly endless year of longing, young Mikeleh composed the second part of his niggun.

Finally, the day of their departure came, and they set out on the road together. Then young Mikeleh began to compose the third and final part of his gagooim niggun (melody of great longing), which was so precious to the Ba'al Shem Tov.

You can well imagine how much complexity of feeling is embedded in this *niggun*, how much sadness, joy, longing, and anticipation are written into the very texture of the sound. And yet, it doesn't sing itself. It isn't living until it is *sung*. It isn't transformative until it is *heard* by an open and engaged heart. That is to say that the *niggun* is an interactive tuning instrument. Through it, the soul is tuned and transformed. But to effect this change or exchange, the singer must first be mindful and listen to what the *niggun* is trying to communicate, even as he or she is singing it.

MANY YEARS LATER, as the close disciples of the Ba'al Shem Tov gathered around his deathbed, he motioned to them to come nearer. They leaned in close to hear what he might need. Then he said to them, "Let me hear the niggun of Mikeleh of Zlotchov," which the Ba'al Shem Tov had named "The Melody That Stirs and Incites Divine Mercy."

They sang the niggun for him, slowly and beautifully.

When his disciples had finished singing, the Ba'al Shem Tov said to them, "I promise you, for all generations, no matter when or who shall sing this niggun with a stirring of teshuvah, wherever I am, I shall hear it—for there are angels that bring messages to souls—and I shall sing along, invoking divine compassion for the singer."

Once, when I was a young Hasid, I was in one of those *glatt kosher* hotels in the Catskill Mountains where various Hasidic Rebbes used to take their summer vacations. It was around Tisha b'Av, the fast day commemorating the destruction of the Temple, and all the Rebbes and Hasidim there were doing a lot of *davenen* and getting into longing. So we were all there *davenen* when one of these Rebbes turned to me, somewhat teasingly, and said, "Nu, young man, what have you got to say to us?" So I spoke up with this same story about Reb Mikeleh Zlotchover and the Ba'al Shem Tov I had learned from my Rebbe.

As I was finishing the story, I said, "As the Ba'al Shem Tov lay dying in his bed, he opened his eyes and asked his Hasidim, 'Please, sing for me once more the *niggun* of Reb Mikeleh Zlotchover.' Then they quieted themselves and began to sing that *niggun* beautifully and with deep longing for their master, and when they were done, he smiled a smile of satisfaction, and said, 'Whenever you will be together and will sing this *niggun* with an arousal of seeking *harmony* with the will of God (*hit'or'rut teshuvah*), I will join you and sing along, and pray for whatever you need.' "

When I had finished, the Rebbes and Hasidim listening were inspired and said, "Nu, nu, so sing the *niggun!*" I opened my mouth to sing . . . and drew a complete blank. I couldn't remember it! The Rebbe standing next to me said, "Oy! Oy! you've got such a good gun, and no bullets!"

It was a good admonition, and after that, I took it upon myself to really memorize that *niggun* so that I would have the bullets for bringing in the presence of the Ba'al Shem Tov whenever I needed it.

SHORTLY THEREAFTER, WITH *his family and disciples surrounding him, he comforted them, saying, "I do not lament my death; I know well that I shall go out through one door only to enter again by another." Then he said, " 'Let not the foot of pride overtake me' (Ps. 36:12)."*[23] *With these words, on the second day of Shavuot, in the year 1760, his soul departed from him, and he was gathered to his mothers and fathers.*

His body was buried in Mezhbizh.

Nevertheless, the Ba'al Shem Tov does not die. He only seems to grow larger. Even in life he was hard to hold, impossible to classify. He was something almost entirely belonging to Nature, more the element of Fire than the particular flame that was his manifestation. When he passed on, it was as if the elemental Fire were released from the flame, spreading through his disciples, in whom his living presence continued to manifest in myriad forms.

> **Once, after his passing, he appeared to his son, Tzvi, in a dream. The holy Ba'al Shem Tov took the shape of a fiery volcano, exploding with flame and raining sparks across the universe! His son asked him, "Why do you appear to me in this form?"**
>
> **He was answered, "Because this is how I served God."**[24]

PART II

The Circle of the Ba'al Shem and the Maggid of Mezritch

4

A Knowledge of Fire: Adel Ashkenazi, the Daughter of the Ba'al Shem Tov

AS WE BEGIN TO MOVE INTO THE NEXT generation of Hasidism, looking at the successors of the Ba'al Shem Tov, we would like to include someone whose place as a true heir of the Ba'al Shem Tov has long been overlooked.[1] Of course, we are talking about his daughter, Adel Ashkenazi (ca. 1720–ca. 1787). Often much is made of how the Ba'al Shem Tov's son, Tzvi Hirsh,[2] was unable to carry his mantle after his death, while little is said of Adel (pronounced *Uh-dl*), who was his close companion and confidante for many years as well as someone for whom he seems to have had a great love and respect.

For the most part, Adel is honored in the Hasidic tradition as the mother of the great *tzaddikim* Moshe Hayyim Efraim of Sudilkov (1748–1800) and Barukh of Mezhbizh (1753–1811) as well as for being the grandmother of Nahman of Bratzlav (1772–1810). This is a traditionally honored role and truly worthy of respect, but from the small hints and tangential references to her that remain in the sources, we feel that there is a person of greater complexity and significance yet to be revealed—someone who perhaps carried an alternate, some might say "feminine" lineage of the Ba'al Shem Tov. For while the "shamanic" dimension of the Ba'al Shem Tov's teaching becomes less and less emphasized by many of his male heirs from generation to generation (in favor of more acceptable textual learning), this lineage is very clearly passed on to Adel. Moreover, who among the *tzaddikim* inherited his role as a healer and herbalist? We don't hear of the Maggid of Mezritch dispensing herbs or dealing with *kamayot* (amulets), as the Ba'al Shem Tov did. But we do hear these things of Adel. So perhaps it is time to take a fresh look at Adel Ashkenazi, to revive what we can of the stories and teachings around her life, and to honor her as a true *tzaddeket*.

BRINGING HIM DOWN TO EARTH

When a daughter was born to the Ba'al Shem Tov and his wife, Hannah, around the year 1720, he named her Adel, claiming the verse *Aish Da'at Lamo* (a fiery knowledge unto them) (Deut. 33:2)[3] as his inspiration. It was a verse that spoke both of her character and her destiny as an important heir of her father, Yisra'el ben Eliezer, the Ba'al Shem Tov and keeper of the family traditions of holiness and healing.

The Ba'al Shem Tov was approximately 22 years old at the time of Adel's birth and was still living near the Carpathian Mountains. As we have already seen, these were years of intense spiritual practice for the Ba'al Shem Tov, years spent in study and meditation with his heavenly master, Ahiyah ha-Shiloni. And it is very much in this contemplative mood that we find him in the following gentle story.

DURING HIS HIDDEN years, it was the custom of the Ba'al Shem Tov to dwell in the solitude of the forest during the days of the week and to spend most of his time at home on Shabbat. Often, he fasted during these weekdays. It was not that he wished to discipline his body with ascetic exercises; but, being so absorbed in his prayers and meditations, he simply forgot to eat! Soon Hannah, his wife, noticed that he was looking rather pale and thin and realized what must be happening. She urged him to remember to eat, but what more could she do? When he was in the forest, either he would eat or he wouldn't.

But on Shabbat it was a different story.

After Hannah became aware of the fact that her husband was not eating during the week, she knew she would have to make certain that he ate on Shabbat. But, as often happened, when the Ba'al Shem Tov sat down at the table for his Shabbat meal, he was in such an awesome state of deveikut (adhering to the Divine) that after taking just one bite of the hallah his mind soared to the upper worlds! Hannah called to him, trying to draw his mind back down to the table but could not reach him. Then she had an idea. She put their infant daughter, Adel, in his lap, even as he sat lost in a deep trance; and the child began to pull at her father's holy beard, as children do. In this way, she drew the Ba'al Shem Tov back into his body, and he began to eat!

From then on, Hannah always placed Adel on her father's lap at the table, which immediately had the effect of drawing his mind down to attend to his daughter, because a child is made in the image of God.[4]

This is a wonderful introduction to Adel, for as much as she would prove to be a woman of sharp intelligence and contemplative depth, her concerns were very much grounded in *this* world. This shows itself through all of her stories. In a world dominated by male Hasidim, continually talking about and seeking to ascend to spiritual worlds—however holy they might have been—she provides us with a wonderfully warm and down-to-earth antidote to what can often feel like an overdose of spirituality.

THE SLEEPING CHILD

This *ma'aseh* is of the "out of the mouth of babes" variety. In it, a very young Adel provides her father with the wisdom he needs to intercede for the people of Yisra'el. It also shows us a very realistic image of a child's raw willfulness and cunning intelligence that will later be molded into great personal strength and a tool for healing others.

When Adel was little, she could be mischievous. But, being clever and bold, she was usually able to defend herself more than adequately to her parents.

One Rosh Hashanah, the Ba'al Shem Tov refused to sound the shofar because Adel was not present. He wanted to be sure that she would hear the shofar blasts with the congregation, according to halakhah. And because Adel was a high soul, the Ba'al Shem Tov was willing to delay the blowing of the shofar for her sake.

After some searching, they finally found her sound asleep in her bed. Now, to sleep during the day on Rosh Hashanah, when one is being judged in Heaven, is considered perilous. So when her father awakened Adel, he asked her, "You know that one is not supposed to sleep during the day on Rosh Hashanah, don't you?"

Adel replied, "Mama says—'When a child sleeps, they save the best portion for her.' " (This is something parents used to tell their children, encouraging them to nap before dinner, letting them know that the best portion of food would be kept for them until they awake.)

Hearing this, the Ba'al Shem Tov smiled inwardly and immediately took Adel to the synagogue and blew the shofar. Because one purpose of the shofar is to awaken the "sleeping" Children of Yisra'el and to call them to repentance, Adel's clever reply had given the Ba'al Shem Tov an answer to the heavenly accusations against the Jewish people for being "asleep." So the Ba'al Shem Tov blew the shofar to awaken them as a father would wake his children, whom he had encouraged to nap, promising them that the best portion had been saved for them.[5]

THE GATES OF DIVINE HELP

WHEN ADEL WAS a young woman, she once participated in a vigorous debate among the Ba'al Shem Tov's disciples about the recitation said at the end of the Shabbat: "May the blessed and holy One open for us the gates of light, the gates of long life, the gates of patience, the gates of blessing, the gates of understanding, the gates of joy" and so on, with a long list of many different gates. As the male disciples argued over which of the gates was the most important, each offering his opinion, Adel interrupted and said, "The gates of divine help are the greatest of all, and all others are included in them."

When they asked the Ba'al Shem Tov concerning this, he said, "Adel is right, for when a person attains any one of these gates—whether the gates of Torah, wisdom, and repentance or the gates of sustenance and livelihood—they should understand that it is entirely due to divine help. The gates of divine help include all the others, for without God's help, it is impossible to accomplish anything, even the smallest movement. Even the understanding that everything depends on God comes through the divine help of the blessed One."

Adel always used to say, "Heaven's help is better than anything."[6]

I love the image of this vivacious young girl of 16 or 18 years old debating with the Hasidim of the Ba'al Shem Tov. One is reminded of the 12-year-old Jesus debating among the teachers when his parents went up to Jerusalem for the Passover. It is an image that sets her apart. Women are so often on the periphery of Hasidic tales, only rarely coming into the foreground, and even more rarely providing the *ḥokhmah* (wisdom) of a *ma'aseh*. However, they do exist. Sometimes it is a situation in which a woman teaches a Rebbe to have compassion, as with the woman who reproves the Apter Rav, or when the wife of the Rebbe acts effectively in the Rebbe's place, as with Malkah of Belz or the

Chentsiner Rebbetzin, and rarest of all, the woman as Rebbe, as we have with the Maid of Ludmir.[7]

A WORTHY COMPANION

No one should be misled into thinking that one has to look very hard for Adel; her name is well known in Hasidic circles. Many stories of her are scattered and fragmented, but she also shows up and is featured prominently in *ma'a-siot* of the Ba'al Shem Tov that are so widely known that one cannot help but remember her name. Nowhere is that more true than in the following *ma'aseh*, which is a part of a cycle of tales about the Ba'al Shem Tov's ill-fated trip to the holy land in 1739–1740, a trip on which she accompanied him. There are various versions of this *ma'aseh*, in which different people play different roles, but this is one in which Adel features prominently.

ONCE, AFTER PESAH, *the Ba'al Shem Tov was inspired to fulfill his life-long dream of going to Eretz Yisra'el and he asked his holy daughter, Adel, to accompany him. Though she was only 19, she had already been with her father on many such journeys, but she couldn't help feeling that there was something different about this one. This was confirmed after they had set out on the road, for the farther they traveled, the more her father seemed to be looking over his shoulder. This concerned Adel terribly; nevertheless, she held her tongue, figuring that her father knew best, as always.*

Thank God, they reached the port at Istanbul safely. No troubles had overtaken them along the way. However, Adel noticed that her father also seemed relieved to have made it this far. She wondered again, "What was the matter? What could happen to her father, the holy Ba'al Shem Tov, who was so obviously in step with God?"

In Istanbul, they booked passage on a ship headed for Eretz Yisra'el. As they were boarding, Adel saw her father pause momentarily, as if wondering whether he should take another step. At that moment, a shiver went through her that she could not explain, but, only a few hours into their voyage, everything became clear . . . there was a judgment against their journey. A storm had arisen on the Aegean Sea and the waves began to crash against the sides of the ship. With each succeeding crash the walls seemed to creak louder and louder, threatening to break. The Ba'al Shem Tov then told Adel what he had known in his heart-of-hearts all along—he was not fated to make this trip to Eretz Yisra'el in this lifetime—but so great was his desire to see the Land that he had ignored all of the warnings.

Adel thought quickly and came to a decision: she would offer her own life in exchange for her father's, throwing herself overboard to satisfy the judgment!

This is a theme that will repeat itself two generations later in the life of Shneur Zalman of Liadi (1745–1812). At a time when the whole Hasidic movement was threatened by internal strife and seemed as if it might be destroyed from within, the pious daughter of Reb Shneur Zalman, Devorah Leah (d. 1790) perceived that her father's life was endangered by this holy drama. A person of great spiritual power like Adel, she determined to give her own life for that of her father and for the sake of the divine work of the Hasidic movement. Without telling her father, she bound three of his Hasidim by an oath of silence and spelled out to them her course. On the first night of Rosh Hashanah, the Rebbe called her to him and began to bless her to be inscribed for a good year, but Devorah Leah quickly interrupted him, and instead blessed *him* to be inscribed for a good year. She passed away on the Fast of Gedaliah and so too passed the threat to Reb Shneur Zalman's life and the Hasidic movement.[8]

IMMEDIATELY, HER SELFLESS *intention softened the decree—the ship ran aground on a tiny Aegean island. But the judgment was only softened, not annulled. For when they exited the ship, to his horror, the Ba'al Shem Tov discovered that he had lost part of his memory; he could not remember any of the Torah that he ever learned or taught!*

He began to walk the shores of the island with Adel at his side, desperately chanting the letters of the alef bet (the Hebrew alphabet), hoping that God would arrange the letters into prayers! Seeing that her father had become impotent in his prayer, Adel decided to say what he could not, praying his teshuvah, making clear his intention to turn from his course, to give up the attempt to reach the Holy Land in this lifetime. "Sovereign of the universe," she said, "please lift this decree and return my father to his proper place in the world; help him find the footprints you have laid before him once again; he knows he is outside of his destiny and your perfect will . . . please, return him to his place, my beloved!" At that moment, the Ba'al Shem Tov's teacher, Ahiyah ha-Shiloni, suddenly appeared before him and announced the lifting of the heavenly decree!

The Ba'al Shem Tov thanked and blessed his daughter, and they began the long trip back to Mezhbizh. The Ba'al Shem Tov would never seek to make the trip to Eretz Yisra'el again.[9]

In some versions of this story, it is the Ba'al Shem Tov's scribe, Reb Tzvi, who is the intercessor for his master, reciting the *alef bet*. But the story makes more sense to me with Adel in this role. For most Hasidim would likely be bewildered in a situation in which the Rebbe, who is seen as something more than human, is suddenly stricken dumb and impotent, saying, "How shall I intercede for the master? What could I do if he cannot do it?" Whereas, a daughter, like Adel, would not hesitate even for a moment to do whatever was necessary.

A SHOE FOR A *SHIDDUKH*

This was probably the last long journey Adel ever undertook with her father. At the time, she was still young and unmarried and therefore free to travel without difficulty. But now she was of an age to be married and to fulfill the traditional role of a woman in her time, to marry and bear children. If we are to believe the following story, it was Adel, and not her father, who pressed for a good match. This story is truly lovely, giving us a good picture of a strong-willed young woman who was the apple of her father's eye. Reb Leah Novick, who told me this story, was right in calling it a kind of "Hasidic Cinderella story," in which the shoe fits and everything works out well.

WHEN ADEL, THE daughter of the Ba'al Shem Tov, came of age, she anticipated that her father would soon make a good match for her. But several years passed, and still he had not even broached the subject with her. Thus she finally decided to confront him about this oversight. It was Simḥat Torah, and the house was full of young men, dancing and joyous, and she asked her father, "Abba, have you forgotten me? You take care of the whole world, and yet, you seem to have forgotten to make a match for me! Where is my bashert, Abba, the one who is destined for me?"

The Ba'al Shem Tov looked her in the eyes and said, "Alright, Adeleh leben, look around you tonight, because your bashert is here among these young men."

Adel began to look around the room, sizing up the various young men, but didn't see anything special in any of them. Then, suddenly, one disciple who was dancing wildly kicked up his leg, and off flew his ill-fitting shoe. It flew high over the entire room and landed right in Adel's hands! She looked over at the embarrassed young man and knew that he, Yehiel Ashkenazi, was her bashert.

Straight away, she went over to the little store she ran and took out a new pair of shoes. When she returned to the house, she presented the shoes to Reb Yehiel as

the contract price for their marriage. The surprised young man looked quickly at the
Ba'al Shem Tov, who only nodded and smiled knowingly at them both.[10]

People who were eager to condemn the Ba'al Shem Tov used the fact that
Adel was present on certain occasions to bring accusations against the entire
Hasidic movement, saying, "Those Hasidim dance with women on Simḥat
Torah!"[11] This was all one needed to say after the heretical antinomianism of
Shabbetai Tzvi (1626–1676) and Jacob Frank (1726–1791), when even the
appearance of impropriety could bring the wrath of the entire Jewish community down on one.[12] On the other hand, many people today might be
inclined to speculate about the great egalitarianism of the early Hasidic masters based on the same incident. However, I tend to think the truth is a little
more prosaic.

From what we know of the *beit midrash* (house of study) of the Ba'al Shem
Tov, it was basically one big room. There was no separate room for the
women; thus it is most likely that the women present (including Adel) stood
along the walls while the men danced in the center of the room. Nevertheless,
Adel does seem to have enjoyed a respect and freedom that was rare in her
day, participating in Torah discussions with her father and his disciples and
attending communal rituals with the standing of a community leader, and
this is to the credit of early Hasidism. We can be sure that while the Ba'al
Shem Tov yet lived, because of his unquestioned holiness, there was probably
a certain fluidity and ease in social situations that could not be maintained
after he was gone, but we should be careful not to impose too much of our
idealism onto the past. It was a different time, and the egalitarianism that we
would like to have seen there would have been extremely difficult to maintain.

A SHOE FOR A CHILD

The next tale is an interesting variation on a theme in which a flying shoe once
again serves to provide a clue to the identity of a desired person.

NOW ADEL, THE *daughter of the Ba'al Shem Tov, was married to Rabbi Yehiel*
Ashkenazi, a disciple of her father and a great scholar. In order that they might have
a living, she supervised the store she had owned from before her marriage to free
him for his studies, as many women did in those days. By this time she had already

given birth to two remarkable children who kept her busy, but she still felt a stirring in her body for one more child.

Thus one Simḥat Torah, while her father's house was yet again full of dancing and drinking, she comes to her father and says, "You know, I have a wonderful child, Moshe Hayyim Efraim, who is brilliant and studies Torah diligently like his father and grandfather, but I don't feel he is going to be a known Rebbe; clearly he will be a tzaddik nistar (hidden righteous person). Likewise, my daughter, Feiga, is inspired, and the ruaḥ ha-kodesh (spirit of holiness) sits on her face; but her options are limited, Abba, as you know. I am sure she is going to have amazing children, but I feel as if there is yet before me another child who will be a known tzaddik, like his grandfather. But Abba, the conception isn't happening. What am I to do?"

The Ba'al Shem Tov looks tenderly at her and says, "Adeleh leben, look around you tonight; somewhere here is a person who is capable of giving you the blessing necessary to allow you to conceive a son who will be a known Rebbe."

The issue regarding a blessing for children in this kind of a situation usually has two aspects. One, are you bringing down a new soul (*neshamah ḥadashah*) or an old one that has already accumulated a great deal of merit? Two, is the blessing to remove an obstacle or to create something completely new? Here's a little story to illustrate.

> During the hidden years of the Ba'al Shem Tov, there was a Ukrainian man who noticed how the Ba'al Shem Tov used to come to the river in the middle of winter to break the ice and dip in the water. Supposing him to be a very holy man, he decided that he would break the ice himself on the days that the Ba'al Shem Tov was known to come and to build him a little fire there as well.
>
> Years later, after the Ba'al Shem Tov was revealed, and many people came to seek his blessing, this Ukrainian and his wife also came to seek a blessing from him. When the Ba'al Shem Tov saw the Ukrainian, his face lit up and he greeted him with great kindness, saying, "What blessing can I give you, my friend—a house to live in or a child?"
>
> The Ukrainian looked at his wife and she looked back at him— how can they decide? He shrugged his shoulders and said to the Ba'al Shem Tov, "We want both."
>
> The Ba'al Shem Tov sighed and promised them both.
>
> The problem was that the Ba'al Shem Tov could see that there

was a heavenly decree saying that the Ukrainian was not fated to have a child. But since the holy Ba'al Shem Tov had made a promise to the Ukrainian, the heavenly assembly said, "We must keep his promise, but we are going to have to take away the Ba'al Shem Tov's part in the world to come."

For a moment, the Ba'al Shem Tov was shaken, but then a sudden smile came to his lips, and he thought, "Good! Now I can serve God purely, without any expectation of reward!"

Then Satan arose and spoke before the assembly, saying, "No, I can't allow this to happen! Give him back his part in the world to come; I'm not going to deal with him on these terms."

You see, this was a situation in which an obstacle needed to be removed (in this case, a very serious one). In Adel's case, the Ba'al Shem Tov is advising her to search the room for the person who has the perfect blessing, the particular key to unlock the door between her and the soul that will enter the child who will become a known Rebbe. For it is not only Rebbes who can give blessings; Hasidim can give blessings too.

———————

ADEL BEGINS TO look around the room, but she doesn't see anything special in any of the faces. Then she notices one disciple dancing more and more wildly, not unlike her husband had years before, until suddenly off came his shoe, and she reaches up and catches it! She looks at the state of the shoe; it was worn well beyond its own lifetime, so she knew what to do. Off she goes to her little store and gets a new pair of shoes. She returns and gives them to the poor young man as a gift. In gratitude, having no money to pay for them, he gives her a blessing!

Nine months later, Adel gave birth to a son who grew up in the house of the Ba'al Shem Tov and who later became the celebrated tzaddik Barukh of Mezhbizh, a Rebbe in his grandfather's own city.[13]

———————

Barukh of Mezhbizh was a famous and influential Rebbe in his day, but he could also be difficult and quarrelsome, having inherited his mother's fiery temperament. Nevertheless, even though other Rebbes objected, Reb Barukh was known to have his wife and daughters seated next to him at his *tish* (table), setting an example for his Hasidim. This is likely due to the strong influence of his mother, whom no man could fail to respect.[14]

A *KVITTEL* AND TWO LETTERS

In the Herson Genizah papers published by ḤaBaD Hasidim, we find a few small but interesting references to Adel, putting her squarely in her traditional context as a mother and daughter but also highlighting her unique place as the daughter-disciple of the Ba'al Shem Tov.[15] The first of these is a *kvittel*, a petition presented to the Rebbe on a small piece of paper.

FOR TZVI, THE son of *Hannah*,[16] *for all good things, and for his wife, Malkha, the daughter of Nehamah, and for Adel, the daughter of Hannah, to raise her sons to Torah, ḥuppah, ma'asim tovim, together with her husband, Yehiel ben Shifra, and their two sons, Barukh and Moshe Hayyim Efraim.*[17]

Obviously the Ba'al Shem Tov's Hasidim were making a gesture in giving this *kvittel* to him. First of all, it is a way in which they could give back to him in *kavanah*, expressing their own love for him by intentionally sacrificing the time in which he would ordinarily spend praying for their needs, allowing him to dedicate that time *instead* to prayer for his own family. It is a way of saying that what is important to him is also important to them. It also expresses a hope for continuity in leadership, that his son or grandchildren would succeed him.

The phrase "Torah, ḥuppah, ma'asim tovim" (Torah, the marital canopy, and good acts) means that they should be learned, marry well, and do good deeds in the world. But why is Feiga missing? It may be that Feiga was not the middle child, as the previous story suggests, and may not have been born yet.

The next piece is a short letter from the Ba'al Shem Tov to Adel, apparently written while he was traveling, right after Simḥat Torah.

TO MY DAUGHTER, *the God-fearing and chaste, Adeleh—*
I am prepared, im yirtzeh ha-Shem (God willing), to travel after Shabbat, and hope to come to your house for the next Shabbat, as I need to take with me the writings that are kept and hidden there. [Then, switching from Hebrew into Yiddish, he adds] These are the words of your father who wishes you a speedy recovery among all Jews.[18]

In this short letter, we find a touching intimacy as the Ba'al Shem Tov switches from the apparently formal communication in Hebrew to a more personal communication between father and daughter in Yiddish, praying for her recovery from some illness. We must also note his implicit trust in Adel, in as much as he has hidden various writings in her home that for some reason he did not feel were safe in his own. Were these the secret writings entrusted to him by his predecessor, Adam Ba'al Shem? We may never know, but we notice, without thinking ill of his son Tzvi, that it is not with him that these writings were hidden, but with Adel.

A second letter from the Ba'al Shem Tov to Adel continues to expand our understanding of her unique place as both daughter and disciple.

TO MY DAUGHTER, *the God-fearing and chaste, Adeleh* leben, *and to my dear grandchildren—*

Please receive these herbs from me through the man who carries these letters. Steep them for a half hour and drink the infusion of them—a half a glass every morning—and it will help you. Also, pass the word to my steward, Reb Nahman of Horodenka, that he should give the money for the week on Thursday, and not Friday morning so they can make Shabbat *preparations.*[19]

Once again, it seems that Adel was not well and because of it we are introduced to the Ba'al Shem Tov as herbalist and healer. But more significant for us in this letter is Adel's role as an emissary of her father, giving instructions from him to his right-hand-man, the venerable Nahman of Horodenka. Some might see this as no more than a simple errand, but in an environment in which gender roles were generally rigidly defined, we must take notice of any blurring of the lines, especially when we factor in the proud character of Nahman of Horodenka, who might otherwise have been affronted if any other young women had been sent with an order for him.

The "money for the week" in this letter refers to the various monies the Ba'al Shem Tov would distribute. For instance, the money for a *yoshev* (sitter) like Reb Hayyim,[20] was distributed on Tuesdays. But the money for others in need within the Hasidic community the Ba'al Shem Tov would distribute on Thursdays. Thus, in this letter, the Ba'al Shem Tov is simply reminding Reb Nahman not to let this wait until Friday, because there are many preparations to make; in those days it was not simply a matter of getting everything at the supermarket and cooking it in minutes, as we can do today.

ADEL AND THE BOOK OF REMEDIES

The following anecdotal information helps us fill out the dimensions of Adel's life.

ADEL, IT IS said, helped her mother, Hannah, in the running of the Ba'al Shem Tov's household, being in charge of the money and household expenses. She was the Ba'al Shem Tov's daughter but also his disciple. The Ba'al Shem Tov transmitted to her many of his kabbalistic secrets and the Holy Spirit was known to rest upon her. Adel's heart was on fire for God; she constantly yearned for God and never ceased to think of how she might serve God.

The Ba'al Shem Tov was known to keep a book of remedies and segullot (charms) for his own use as a healer. Once, when he was leaving Mezhbizh on a trip, he said to Adel, "My book of remedies is very precious to me. You have my permission to use it while I am away if someone cannot wait for my return. Nevertheless, do not let anyone else even touch the book or look into it; you speak to the sick person directly and not through an intermediary. If an amulet is required, you may ask one of my scribes to prepare it for you." Adel used the book of remedies on a number of occasions when her holy father was away and effected several miraculous healings.[21]

This anecdote, as much as any other story, gives us a wonderful picture of Adel's true vocation as a wise woman and healer. She is clearly the person the Ba'al Shem Tov has chosen and trained to follow him in the healing profession. But one wonders, who had trained *him* in herb lore and traditional medicine? A wise woman of the Carpathians?

GOOD TIMING

After the death of her mother, Hannah, Adel became indispensable to her father and was his private nurse during his last illness. Rabbi Leah Novick, with a practical eye, has pointed out that she must have been doing this while juggling her own children, running the store, and dealing with her own clients as an herbalist. Who else could have cared for her father as she? After all, she was trained by him personally. Thus she did healing on him and even prepared his food, because it was extremely important that his food be prepared with the right *kavanot* (intentions).

This story is of a genre in which the kabbalist gets close to bringing in the Messianic Era and just misses because the time is not yet ripe.

WHEN THE BA'AL *Shem Tov was on his deathbed, he made one last attempt to bring the era of the* Mashiaḥ *before his passing. To do this, he knew he would have to summon his master, Ahiyah ha-Shiloni. But as he prayed and meditated, Adel, who had taken care of him since her mother's passing, continually came in and out of the room with various foods, herbs, and medicines. Finally, he asked her to give him a little time alone, and he began his meditation again, uninterrupted.*

But Adel, after what she considered an appropriate time for a sick and elderly man to be alone, came in again to check on her father, and once again interrupted his prayer and meditation. The Ba'al Shem Tov opened his eyes slowly and said, "Ahh, I had finally contacted my master, but when you came in the room, he left. . . . So be it."[22]

Now, there are different ways in which this story can be read. In the past, many readers have said, "Oh, but for the fussing of his daughter, he might have brought the Messiah!" But this is short-sighted, for if we believe in *hashgaḥah pratit* (divine providence), we see that Adel is nothing more and nothing less than the tool of providence in this situation. Notice how Adel's role in this *ma'aseh* mirrors that of those told of her childhood in "Bringing Him Down to Earth" and "The Sleeping Child." And yet, another part of me is still unsatisfied with this story as it is. I am inclined to add something to the story, with ḥutzpah . . .

> Adel, after what she considered an appropriate time for a sick, elderly man to be alone, came in again to check on her father. The Ba'al Shem Tov opened his eyes slowly and said, "Ahh, Adel *leben*, I finally contacted my master, and just before you came into the room, he told me, 'Yisrolickel, do not be disturbed over your holy daughter's ministrations, for I tell you, the *Mashiaḥ* is waiting until there are more such daughters as yours in Yisra'el who can join in the leadership of our people,' and to this I will say amen, Adel *leben*."

THE WILL

The day before he died, the Ba'al Shem Tov called his personal scribe, Tzvi Hirsh, to make an amendment to his will, in which he mentioned Adel alongside his great disciple, the Maggid of Mezritch . . .

"MY BOOKS AND *manuscripts are to be given to my disciple and colleague, that Tall Tree and Prince of Torah, Rabbi Dov Baer, the son of Rabbi Avraham, except those books in Yiddish, which belong to my God-fearing daughter, Adel.*²³

In this amendment to his will, he also left books to Ya'akov Yosef of Polonoye. Now, Reb Dov Baer and Reb Ya'akov Yosef were considered his principal heirs,²⁴ and given that he left books to these two great heirs, it is reasonable to assume that the leaving of books to Adel also marks her as one of his heirs. She is clearly the heir to his healing ministry and even continued to act in a pastoral capacity for the extended family of the Ba'al Shem Tov and in Mezhbizh generally. In that period, it would have been nearly impossible for her to be a leader in the Hasidic movement in any official capacity, but we must not overlook her father's regard for her abilities. Here we see that she is given her father's books in Yiddish, perhaps even his precious "book of remedies," which no one else was even allowed to touch.

MATCHMAKING BETWEEN WORLDS

After the death of her father, Adel continued to be active in communal affairs, especially in its ritual life, receiving information from the Ba'al Shem Tov on high in her dreams and meditation. One such *ma'aseh* of Adel's role in the community has been preserved for us.

AFTER THE DEATH *of the Ba'al Shem Tov, there was not a wedding in the family, or in all of Mezhbizh for that matter, that took place without the approval and participation of his daughter, Adel. Everyone in Mezhbizh knew this and respected her authority.*

Thus on the day of a particular family wedding, Adel arrived as usual and secluded herself in a room, as was her custom before each ceremony. She sat down in the room, meditated, and waited for inspiration from her father. While she waited, everyone else waited as well—the bride, the groom—everyone! But this day was different; an hour goes by and still she doesn't come out. People start to get fidgety, and families are getting nervous. Two hours pass . . . three hours! Finally, the Ba'al Shem Tov appears to her, and she says, "Abba, what took you so long?"

The Ba'al Shem Tov answered, "Look Adeleh, this isn't just my responsibility; this has to do with your role too. I have always told you that you must be very careful about how you take people into the family. When there is a wedding, I travel around to all the worlds visiting the souls of the couple's ancestors, attempting to bring a tikkun (repair) to their negative actions and to those of the bride and groom. In this case, I have been to Geihinnom and back trying to repair that part of the ancestor that is connected to the groom, and it took a very long time. So I will tell you again; you have to be very careful about how you are going to bring people into the family."[25]

In a Jewish wedding, before the bride proceeds to the wedding canopy, she is first veiled. It is at this point that I usually gather all of the blood relatives together in one room and ask them each to forgive one other, because it is impossible to grow up in a family—with siblings, cousins, parents, aunts, and uncles—without having some secret anger. It is very important to relieve the bride and the groom of this karmic burden before they enter their next phase of life together. When the forgiveness work is done, then everyone is truly in a position to be able to bless the couple in a powerful way.

I also use this story when I counsel people who are thinking about getting married. I say to them, "Think of the impressions the marriages you have known have left upon you . . . your parent's marriage, your grandparent's marriage . . . what is there in the family DNA that you are bringing into your own marriage? I am sure you will find both positive and negative things, and now is the time to clean them up inside of yourself, to figure out what you want to reproduce, what you want to discard, and what you would like to create anew. It is important to do this *before* the wedding."

ADEL AND FEIGA AND THE LIGHT OF THE BA'AL SHEM TOV

A woman like Adel must have made a powerful impression on everyone around her, particularly the women. How significant it must have been for her daughter, Feiga, to have such a role model. From the little we know of her, it seems that Feiga was very much like Adel. According to the Bratzlaver Hasidim, Feiga, the mother of Nahman of Bratzlav, was also constantly in touch with the soul of her grandfather, the Ba'al Shem Tov. Through him, she was able reach the highest levels and was able to prophesy about all her relatives, in particular, her son, Reb Nahman, whose purpose was to prepare a path for the *Mashiaḥ*.

MANY YEARS BEFORE, *the Ba'al Shem Tov had made a match with his friend Nahman of Horodenka for the marriage of his son, Simhah, to the Ba'al Shem Tov's granddaughter, Feiga. Now Feiga was like her mother, a true inheritor of the Ba'al Shem Tov. Her brothers, who were themselves great tzaddikim, even called her Feiga ha-Naviah (the prophetess) and considered her to be a holy person. When she came of age, she was given in marriage to Simhah, who had likewise grown up in the house of the Ba'al Shem Tov and who was very pious and learned. And the match was a success, but sadly, they had no children.*

In the meantime, the Ba'al Shem Tov had passed away. As Feiga continued to be without children, her mother, Adel, began to be concerned for her and waited for a dream from her father. When the dream finally came, she cried to the Ba'al Shem Tov, "Abba, you do wonders for the whole world, can you not help my Feiga, who has no children?"

The Ba'al Shem Tov consoled her, "Don't cry, Adeleh, Feiga will soon give birth to a son whom I want you to name after me, 'Yisra'el.' Then Feiga will have another son who will illuminate the whole world."

A year later, Feiga gave birth to a boy, and seven days later, at his circumcision, the mohel proclaimed, "And his name will be called in Yisra'el" and Adel quickly called out, "Yisra'el!" Feiga fainted . . . Everyone in Mezhbizh knew that the children who were named after the Ba'al Shem Tov all died. Nothing could be done now, her mother had said it. On the third day after the circumcision, the infant died.

Why did the Ba'al Shem Tov need to have these three days in baby Yisra'el's body after the circumcision? Perhaps there was something still unfinished for the Ba'al Shem Tov . . .

> Once a woman came to the Ba'al Shem Tov after the death of her child, and she asked him, "Why, Rebbe? I had only just weaned him, and now he is gone!"
> The Ba'al Shem Tov responded, "There was a king who had a

son whom he wished to be educated. So he found a scholar of great reputation whom he brought to the court to teach his son. Immediately, the son took to the scholar, doing his lessons obediently and following him about the palace. He was curious about his teacher and wished to know everything about him. Most of all he wished to know where his teacher disappeared to every day after lessons. One day he decided to spy on him. He opened the door of his teacher's room ever so quietly, and there saw something that left him with an unmistakable sense of holiness. It turns out that the scholar was a secret Jew, and there he was *davenen* in tallit and tefillin! The boy opened the door wide now to make his presence known, and asked his teacher in amazement what he was doing. The teacher saw the innocent expression on his student's face and knew he would have to take him into his secret. But the young prince, remembering the sense of holiness he had felt, decided to make terms. He said, "If I am going to keep this secret, then I want you to teach me how to do what you were doing." Thus began a long apprenticeship for the prince, who wished to know everything about Judaism.

"In time, the prince became a man and knew that this was no idle fascination, but rather the true call of his heart. He wished to convert to Judaism in all sincerity; indeed, by this time he was already a Jew in his heart; this was his reality, and his other life merely the facade. He then told his father that he wished to study abroad and went with the scholar-rabbi to a land where he could undergo a full conversion and lose his previous identity. Over the years, the prince married a Jewish woman and became a great rabbi and *tzaddik,* exchanging every aspect of his old life as a prince for the life of the spirit as it is experienced in Judaism. At the end of his life, he had only one regret, that he had not been loved and nursed by a Jewish mother through the first years of his life."

Then the Ba'al Shem Tov said to the grieving woman, "I know you are hurting, but you must also know that you have also helped a great *tzaddik* to complete his journey home."[26]

Why the Ba'al Shem Tov needed this short incarnation we will never know for certain, but this story may help us to understand what is otherwise inexplicable.

BUT THE NEXT year, Feiga gave birth to another son who was called Nahman, after his grandfather, Nahman of Horodenka. He became Nahman of Bratzlav, and his light continues to illuminate the world.[27]

What is the moral here? Again we see that Adel can communicate with her father, and again we are told a little bit about her power in the community, but the story also seems to be about having faith in the divine wisdom that flows from the Ba'al Shem's predictions, because the one who dies makes room for the "consolation" that comes after. This must have been terrible both for Adel and Feiga, a difficult burden, and perhaps a strain on their relationship. We don't know, but it is hard to imagine that there was not healing over time in two such holy women.

This story also speaks of a divine inheritance from the Ba'al Shem Tov that was carried by his daughter, Adel, and his granddaughter, Feiga, and from her all the way to his great-grandson, Nahman of Bratzlav. But, as we know, Nahman of Bratzlav did not content himself with his inheritance; he sought his own light and became one of the greatest of all Hasidic Rebbes. And for all Bratzlaver Hasidim, he is still considered to be their living Rebbe.

Sadly, I know of no traditions concerning Adel's passing, or even of the date of her passing, which would allow us to celebrate her yahrzeit. However, one might still celebrate and honor her legacy on Rosh Ḥodesh with the New Moon or on one of the yahrzeits of the matriarchs. Let us remember her from now on as more than simply the daughter of her father but as a true *tzaddeket* and "a fiery knowledge unto us."[28]

5

Awake in the Dark of Night:
Pinhas of Koretz, the Silent Sage

ONE OF THE GREATEST OF THE BA'AL SHEM Tov's Hasidim and colleagues was Reb Pinhas of Koretz (1726–1791). Though little is known of his birth or childhood, we do know something about his grandfather, Pinhas Shapira, who lived a lifestyle consistent with that of the *tzaddikim nistarim*. It is said that the elder Pinhas was "neither a rabbi nor a communal leader, neither the author of books nor the head of a *yeshiva*" but would travel from town to town, admonishing and exhorting the children of Yisra'el. Yet he differed from other itinerant preachers in one significant way. Whenever he received payment, he would keep for himself only enough for his minimal needs, contributing the rest toward the maintenance of the synagogue."[1]

His grandson and namesake, Pinhas ben Avraham, with whom we are concerned here, was a brilliant student of Talmud in his youth who had also mastered a number of secular subjects, including grammar and geometry. However, the great love of his life was the Zohar. It is said that he studied the Zohar continuously and thanked God on numerous occasions that he had not been born before it was written. Later, he would say, "The Zohar helped me to be a Jew."[2] This suggests, as we shall soon see, that Reb Pinhas may have had doubts about the faith. It is possible that before discovering the Kabbalah of the Zohar, which opened up new horizons for him, he may have struggled to find himself in the limited paradigms of the Judaism taught to him in his youth.

DOUBTS ABOUT THE FAITH

Now, even though Reb Pinhas of Koretz is counted as one of the primary heirs of the Ba'al Shem Tov, he is thought to have visited the Ba'al Shem Tov on only three occasions. Little is known of these meetings—whether long or short—but their effect proved significant and powerful in the life of Reb Pinhas and for the whole history of Hasidism. For Reb Pinhas became one of the great luminaries of the Hasidic movement after the passing of the Ba'al Shem Tov and served as one of the twin beacons (along with the Maggid of Mezritch) of the movement as a whole.

Thus it is strange that there is so little in the literature of Hasidism to tell us about why the Ba'al Shem Tov was so important to him, not even a great story of their meeting as we have with the Maggid of Mezritch and Ya'akov Yosef of Polonoye. There are suggestions here and there about when and where they may have met, but little else. Nevertheless, in the early 1960s, I was privileged to hear a story of their first meeting that I have never read in any of the books, one that I believe to be authentic. It was told to me by Rabbi Abraham Joshua Heschel (1907–1972), who, at that time, was a professor of ethics and Jewish mysticism at the Jewish Theological Seminary in New York. Heschel was a mentor whom I admired greatly and who taught me several important stories (and much else that was vital to me at that time). As he was a direct descendent of Reb Pinhas on his mother's side, and since I have yet to find this same story anywhere else, I believe this story may be a family tradition. I am pleased to give it over now in English as I first heard it from Heschel in Yiddish.

THE SON OF Reb Pinhas came to him one day and said, "Rebbe (he was coming to him as a Rebbe at this time), what should I do? I have sefekot en emunah *(doubts about the faith), and I don't know if I really believe in God."*

This is likely Reb Pinhas's eldest son, Yehudah Meir, who later became the Rebbe of Shepetovka and who is also known to have been a Hasid of his father's friend and close associate of the Ba'al Shem Tov, Hayyim of Krasnoye. Regardless of which son it was, for a sincere seeker, it is very hard to have doubts about the faith and to have to live with that fact. This reminds me of a story of Reb Moshe Polier of Kobrin . . .

Once, a man came to Reb Moshe Kobriner and said, "Holy Rebbe, I don't know what to do; I cannot say the Ani Ma'amin, I can't say 'I believe.' "

Now, the Ani Ma'amin is based on Maimonides' "Thirteen Principles of Faith" as they are laid out in his Mishnah commentary, each one being introduced by the phrase "*Ani ma'amin be'emunah shelemah*" (I believe with perfect faith). So the Rebbe was astounded and said to him, "Why can't you say the Ani Ma'amin? You mean you cannot say, 'I believe with perfect faith that God is the Creator, I believe with perfect faith that the Torah was given to us' . . . all these things that you say in the Ani Ma'amin?"

The Hasid said, "Rebbe, if I really believed 'with perfect faith,' I would be a different person, so apparently I don't really believe!"

Reb Moshe asked, "Would you not *want* to say Ani Ma'amin?"

The Hasid answered, "*Holileh,* God forbid! If I don't say Ani Ma'amin, then I'm not even a Jew! How can I *not* say Ani Ma'amin?"

So the Rebbe said to him, "What do you propose to do then?"

The Hasid replied, "Rebbe, would it be okay if I were to say, '*Halevai* (would) that I believed with perfect faith'?"

The Rebbe smiled and said, "Yes, I think that would be just fine."

So you see that when a person deals with issues of this sort, and says, "If I really believed, I would be different," it is a far more difficult issue. What can they do about that?

REB PINHAS LOOKED at him and said, "Study the Sefer al-Kuzari of Yehudah Halevi, the Ikkarim of Yosef Albo, the Hovot ha-Levavot of Bahya ibn Pakuda, and the Moreh Nevukhim of the RaMBaM—you study all of this and it will be good."

Apart from his devotion to the Zohar, it is also said that Reb Pinhas studied both the Hovot ha-Levavot (*Duties of the Heart*) of Bahya ibn Pakuda and the *Moreh Nevukhim* (*Guide for the Perplexed*) of Maimonides over a thousand times each. Clearly, to study in this intense repetitive way was part of his spiritual practice.[3] It is even said that it was his deep study of these works that made him a great *tzaddik*. This has something to do with how a person trains his or her own consciousness. For consider, if your mind is always saturated with the kind of duties of the heart that are prescribed by ibn Pakuda, those thoughts will tend to keep on thinking themselves even when you have left your study! Much of ḤaBaD Hasidism is based on this idea.

Thus it is not surprising that he gives his son this kind of advice, which may, at first, seem very impersonal. In another *ma'aseh*, he gives similar advice to his chief disciple, Rafael of Bershad, who asked him how he might free himself from the lures of pride. To him, the Koretzer said, "Study the Zohar." When Reb Rafael persisted, "But I do study the Zohar," Reb Pinhas responded, "Then study it even more."[4]

But there is a difference *for some* between advising the disciple to study the Zohar and advising one to study these philosophical works, because depending on which Hasidic Rebbe you might be dealing with, these works might be considered either *kasher* or *treif.* The *Kuzari* and the *Moreh Nevukim* are part of a body of literature that in Judaism is called *ḥakirah.* *Ḥakirah* is the probing with the mind, or philosophy of religion (with reference to Judaism) if you will. The problem that many Rebbes had with *ḥakirah* was that it relied strongly on *sekhel enushi* (the human mind) and reason, as opposed, *they believed,* to revelation. As kabbalists, they quite naturally object- ed to the notion that reason was the greatest consciousness available to human beings, precisely because the Kabbalah had made available levels of knowing beyond those that were produced by reason. Thus many Rebbes, like Nahman of Bratzlav, objected to Hasidim spending time in the study of these works. The Tzanzer Rebbe, Reb Hayyim Halberstam, once admitted that he had read the *ḥakirah* literature but added that he had "read the answers before the questions" because he didn't want to doubt God for even a single moment!

So you were either on one side or another of this issue, and it is clear that Pinhas of Koretz was among those who found value in *ḥakirah,* feeling that this may be a necessary means of development for some souls. Actually, he prescribed the study of these things as being especially valuable during one's youth, but less so later.

A YEAR WENT by and his son read and worked with all of the books that his father suggested he study. He came back and said, "Tatte, I have read all those texts that you suggested, and I still have sefekot en emunah (doubts about the faith)."

Did you notice the switch from "Rebbe" to "*Tatte*"? It is an important switch, and with it comes a change in the way Reb Pinhas deals with his son, now no longer exactly as a Rebbe, but as a papa answers his beloved child.

REB PINHAS SAID, *"My child, I want to tell you, when I was your age, I came to my teacher with these same doubts, and he sent me to these books as well . . . and they didn't help me either. What was I to do? I remembered then the rumors I had heard about the Ba'al Shem Tov; and I thought, 'Perhaps if I go see this person, maybe he can help me.' But how was I, a poor* bokher, *a poor student, going to get to Mezhbizh? There was no way, it was too far. Then I heard that the Ba'al Shem Tov was coming to Zaslov, which was within walking distance! I felt that my fortunes were changing, and I began to prepare to make the coming trip.*

"When the time came, I set out on the road to Zaslov. However, it was the middle of winter, and I didn't have a good pair of shoes. In fact, they were so bad that I had to wrap shmattes *(rags) around them to keep my feet even remotely warm. That probably would have been alright had it not begun to snow that morning. By the afternoon, it was a blizzard already! So I trudged* viorst *after* viorst *to Zaslov through snowdrifts and biting winds, struggling to find my way. The road was lost under the snow, and my eyes were blinded by it. Pretty soon, my toes were so frozen and my feet so pained, my face and hands so bitten by the wind, that I began to despair, thinking, 'Oy! I don't know if I'm going make it. I don't even know if I'm going in the right direction!'*

"It was in this state that I began to pray, to cry out to God, 'Please, please God, You must *help me! You* must *help me! I need to get to Zaslov!' Then, within minutes, I saw in front of me a little bit of light burning in a window! I followed that light into town until I came at last to the* shtibl *where the Ba'al Shem Tov was to be* davenen!

"I entered the shtibl, *letting in a cold gust of wind and snow. Then the holy Ba'al Shem Tov, who had just finished* davenen Minḥah *and the silent* Amidah, *turned round and spoke directly to me . . . 'Pinhasel—if you pray and God helps—that is the best proof!' "*

So then Reb Pinhas looked directly at his son and said, *"My son, that is the best answer I can give you."*[5]

Philosophy can be helpful, especially when we are attempting to expand and mature our understanding of the simplistic religion we were taught as children. Reb Shneur Zalman of Liadi tells us that it is essential to use the tools of the intellect up to their very limits before we even dare to raise the question of faith. But ultimately, philosophy is still a concept system that cannot (for all of its brilliance) contain the complexities our basic life system; that is to say, in the moment of quiet contemplation, philosophy will not substitute for an experience of depth and knowing—not for a human being. We crave the bedrock testimony of experience. Sometimes we spend years searching for it, or as is often the case, trying to reconnect to it, because here and there along our individual timelines there have been moments when we prayed in desperation and were helped . . . and some part of us cannot forget this.

THE SILENT YOUTH

It is unclear when this first meeting between the Ba'al Shem Tov and Reb Pinhas of Koretz took place—or even how much time passed before they met again—but tradition suggests that Reb Pinhas probably did not declare himself a disciple of the Ba'al Shem Tov right away. It is likely that he returned to Koretz to resume the life of a hidden *tzaddik,* praying behind the stove where no one would notice him.[6] He seems to have been an extreme introvert, tending to hide his brilliance from those around him, a behavior that sometimes made his life difficult. To make matters worse, he also followed in the ascetic pattern of the Kabbalah of that era, actively denying his bodily needs in favor of long hours of prayer and study. When he was finally threatened with starvation, he was forced to find work and better sustenance, becoming a *melammed* (religious teacher) for children in a town near Polonoye. Still, his natural shyness and tendency to keep to himself earned him a reputation as being standoffish and brooding, and thus people called him "the black *melammed.*" Those who were more generous simply called him the *shtiller bokher* (the silent, or quiet, youth). Strangely enough, this is how he first began to earn a reputation as a known *tzaddik.*

———

IN POLONOYE, CLOSE *to where Reb Pinhas was teaching, was a man who had a dream that was troubling him. For such a dream he knew that he needed an interpretation from someone wise, but to whom was he going to go?*

He was smart enough to know that he needed help, but he was also a private man, so he didn't want to go to anyone who might talk to others about his dreams. Then he remembered that there were some people who thought that the shtiller bokher *in Koretz was actually a holy person, so he said to himself, "What can it hurt? If he is a holy person, then he will be able to help me with my dream, and if he isn't, then he still isn't going to talk to anyone about it!" Thus he went to the* shtiller bokher.

Reb Pinhas, it turned out, was able to interpret his dream, and this is how his reputation first began to spread.

If there is a true vocation, one cannot avoid it. Even though Reb Pinhas shunned attention and the spotlight—*davenen* and studying behind the stove in the *beit midrash*—this very behavior, his very mysteriousness and silence, began to draw the attention that he sought to avoid.

A BLESSING NO ONE ELSE WOULD GIVE—PART I

There is an important story of Reb Pinhas that begins in the period before he was fully revealed as a Rebbe but that does not end until nearly 50 years after his death. It is an important story, not only for our understanding of Reb Pinhas but also for our understanding of what it means to be a Hasidic Rebbe. The first half of the story is a good and pleasant Hasidic *ma'aseh* . . .

WHILE REB PINHAS *was yet hidden from the world, he lived in dire poverty and was in constant need when it came to the necessities of the hagim (the holy days). So it was that as Pesah neared, Reb Pinhas and his young family once again found themselves wanting. Around the same time that Reb Pinhas was praying for the means to make a seder, a businessman from a distant city was traveling around from Rebbe to Rebbe, brokenheartedly asking, "Please, can you bless me with children?" He had even offered donations, but they all refused to bless him. Finally, he came to a Rebbe in a town near Koretz who said to him, "Look, I cannot give you the blessing you want, but I'll tell you what . . . that shtiller bokher in Koretz isn't what he seems to be; he may not look like a tzaddik to you, but he can give you the blessing you desire.*

"Now," he continued, "he is a poor man, and Pesah is coming; if you will be his guest for Pesah and set the table for the seder, you will be able to ask him for a blessing, and your wife will have a child."

In the meantime, Pesah arrived in Koretz, and things looked bad for Reb Pinhas. He went to shul to pray as usual, not knowing what kind of a seder he'd be able to come home to that night. You can imagine his surprise as he returned home to find the candles lit and the table set in grand style! The businessman had arrived while Reb Pinhas was in shul, found out where the shtiller bokher lived, and had catered the whole meal. Reb Pinhas was so overwhelmed with joy and gratitude that he could celebrate yontif this way that he said, "My dear man, what can I bless you with?"

Of course, the businessman replied, "With children," and Reb Pinhas blessed him.

Still, the story is not yet finished, and we will return to it later in this chapter.

ETROGIM FOR THE HEIRS OF THE BA'AL SHEM TOV

It is said that Reb Pinhas of Koretz was present in Mezhbizh when the Ba'al Shem Tov first fell ill and stayed until his passing on Shavuot in 1760.[7] This seems likely as Reb Pinhas was on familiar terms with many of the disciples and colleagues of the Ba'al Shem Tov, especially Ya'akov Yosef of Polonoye and Dov Baer, the Maggid of Mezritch. Some have said that Reb Pinhas was not truly a disciple of the Ba'al Shem but more of a colleague. This may be true to some degree but certainly not entirely. For Reb Pinhas himself said, "From the day that I was with the BeShT, God helped me toward the truth. And I walk in the path of King David, may he rest in peace."[8] The Ba'al Shem Tov was known among the Hasidim to have been an incarnation of the soul of King David.

On the other hand, the Ba'al Shem Tov held Reb Pinhas Koretzer in such high regard that he did indeed seem to be his colleague. For when he was asked to describe the qualities of his disciples shortly before his death, he neglected to mention Reb Pinhas. But when his disciple Ya'akov of Anipol asked, "And what of Reb Pinhas?" The Ba'al Shem Tov replied, "About so great and holy a one as he, there is no need to ask."[9]

This brings us to our next story, which is the story of the succession of the Ba'al Shem Tov as it relates to Reb Pinhas of Koretz.

WHEN THE BA'AL Shem Tov was taken ill, his disciple, David of Ostrog asked him, "Rebbe, to whom shall I travel when you are no longer with us?" The Ba'al Shem Tov replied, "To the Maggid of Mezritch and Pinhas of Koretz."[10]

So it was that after the Ba'al Shem Tov had passed on, Reb David began to travel to the Maggid of Mezritch. This was not because he had chosen the Maggid over the Koretzer, but because Reb Pinhas did not preside over a court of Hasidim at that time, preferring to keep to his solitary ways.

Now, David of Ostrog was a wealthy man as well as a pious one, and it had been his custom for many years to send a choice etrog (citron) to the Ba'al Shem Tov each year for Sukkot. But since the Ba'al Shem Tov had passed away on Shavuot that year, and since he was now traveling to the Maggid of Mezritch, he decided that he would send that etrog to the Maggid. Then he thought, "The only reason I go to the Maggid exclusively is because Reb Pinhas does not hold court," so he decided that he would send a second etrog to Reb Pinhas because of what the holy Ba'al Shem had said to him.

Tradition tells us that it was also Reb David of Ostrog who asked the Ba'al Shem Tov, "What shall we do when you are gone?" To which he replied, "The Bear is in the forest and Pinhas is a sage."

Etrogim, being citrus fruit, had to be imported from the Mediterranean at that time, and thus were very costly. Often, only the wealthy could afford to have their own *etrog* for Sukkot. One version of this story adds that in this particular year a season of heavy rains had flooded and washed out many roads and made it even more difficult for merchants to bring in *etrogim* from the south.

THAT YEAR ETROGIM were particularly scarce in the Ukraine, and in Koretz there was not a single one. Thus, when Sukkot arrived, everyone was gathered in the beit midrash so that if they did happen to obtain an etrog, they could all fulfill the mitzvah together. But none arrived, and things were looking bad. They sent word to a neighboring town to send their etrog when they were finished with it. Finally, they decided that they must begin the liturgy without an etrog. Just then the shtiller bokher, Reb Pinhas, came out from behind the stove where he had been studying and said, "Wait! An etrog will come within the hour." Everyone turned to look at him in surprise, thinking, "Shtiller bokher—what does he know?"

But they waited.

Before the hour was up, Reb Pinhas signaled that they should begin. Just then, a gentile messenger arrived with an etrog and a letter from David of Ostrog to Pinhas of Koretz! A buzz ran through the beit midrash, for Reb David was known to be a wealthy and important man. "What could he want with the shtiller bokher?" The letter was addressed to "The Prince of Torah and Chief of the Children of Yisra'el in the Diaspora, Pinhas ben Avraham Abba of Koretz." The people were all struck dumb.

Then Reb Pinhas took the etrog and called for the lulav. The lulav was brought to him, and he proceeded to make the blessing and to lead the services. For in receiving this etrog, Reb Pinhas understood that the Ba'al Shem Tov was moving through the holy Reb David of Ostrog to tell him that it was time for him to leave his seclusion and to become a Rebbe presiding over a court of Hasidim. From that day he was no longer thought of as the shtiller bokher *but as Rabbi Pinhas of Koretz, one of the great leaders of the Hasidic movement.*

Popularity and Responsibility

Reb Pinhas may have acquiesced to his destiny at that time, but you could hardly say he was happy about it . . .

MUCH TO HIS *dismay, Reb Pinhas of Koretz had become popular. The time for his studies and meditation was cut short, and people of all kinds sought his advice for all the details of their lives, taking too little responsibility for their own spiritual practice. Soon he was feeling so overwhelmed that on Yom Kippur he prayed,* "Ribbono shel Olam, *I know I should be grateful for the gifts you have bestowed on me, for making your children like me so much, but now I have no time left for you! Please make them like me less!"*

God granted his wish.

Almost immediately, the visitors had ceased to come to him, and he breathed a sigh of relief. Peace at last. When Sukkot arrived, Reb Pinhas found that he had no guests to entertain in his sukkah; but that was fine with him, for he knew that the Seven Shepherds—Avraham, Yitzhak, Ya'akov, Moshe, Ahron, Yosef, and David— would be his guests. However, on the first day of Sukkot, Avraham stood in the doorway and refused to enter the sukkah! The patriarch said to Reb Pinhas, "If others must stay away, so must I. A Jew must stand with the people, as well as for the people." Chastised, Reb Pinhas resigned himself and prayed to God again in teshuvah.[II]

I once went to the Bobover Rebbe with a similar dilemma. Among the demands of my teaching career, lecturing around the country, and guiding individuals, it seemed to me that my own spirit was being depleted. There was no longer time for the deep contemplative practices I had once done to refresh my soul; what could I do for these people if I could not do the same for myself? So the Bobover Rebbe said to me, "They have asked you to tend their vineyard, but your own vineyard you have not kept. Nevertheless, because you have tended their vineyard dutifully, the *Shekhinah* will give you a double portion for your own."

THE WORDS OF A SAGE

Even though Reb Pinhas had assumed his place as Rebbe, some of the old *shtiller bokher* remained, for he was by nature an introvert and not accustomed to a lot of talking. Thus his teachings and answers to questions were often characteristically short, though still extremely original and evocative. Until recently, it was difficult to find anything other than *obiter dicta* (collected sayings) from him scattered throughout the greater body of Hasidic literature. Today, however, there are several anthologies available in which Hasidim have gathered his teachings together and arranged them in a logical order. The aphoristic fragments that I have translated here are all drawn from the book *Midrash Pinhas.*[12]

ONE CAN LIVE *in the same house with a* tzaddik *and still be stupid. What do you expect me to say? You hear one word and you think you know it all already?*[13]

This first aphorism reminds me of the reproof my Rebbe, Reb Menachem Mendel, the seventh Lubavitcher Rebbe, once wrote in a letter to his Hasidim (as my friend Reb Shlomo Carlebach quoted it): "I have so many unbelievable dreams, but I can't do them because your heads are so small."[14]

In this case, however, Reb Pinhas is talking about an age-old dilemma of teaching spirituality, a dilemma mirrored in Sherlock Holmes's own reluctance to give an account of how he solved his cases. On the one hand, Holmes wanted people to understand the fascinating mental gymnastics that were involved in his solutions, but on the other, he was reluctant to spell it out for them. For when they had heard it in an ordered and logical presentation, they were always saying, "Of course! How obvious." Well, the Rebbe has to deal with this problem too, except in the Rebbe's case, the disappointment doesn't have anything to do with ego.

A Rebbe is concerned with the transformation of the Hasid, but to stimulate that transformation, he or she must find a way to break through the shell of "knowing-ness" the Hasid has accumulated over the course of a lifetime, creating what Abraham Joshua Heschel called "radical amazement." For that is the place where transformation is truly possible. Unfortunately, the human mind has a short attention span and is delighted with something only momentarily, quickly filing the perceptions and experiences away as something "known." This sense of knowing then becomes a great barrier to spiritual progress and deep experience, because one has barely even begun to scratch the surface of *true knowing*. The true knowing would be to connect with the Divine in that moment of awareness.

So the complaint of Reb Pinhas is that his Hasidim don't stay open to un-knowing long enough to actually learn something in depth, actually com-muning with God in it. Thus they may "live in the same house with a *tzaddik* and still be stupid!"

THE BERAKHAH *(BLESSING) is not found in what is manifest to everyone's eyes. What is berakhah? The very mystery of the Shekhinah—that's what the Zohar calls the true blessing. Do you want to know when you have the berakhah? When all the chambers of the body vibrate with it.*

There are things on which the fate of half the planet depend; if I were to talk about it—even one word of it—it could all become spoiled and never bear fruit.[15]

This is connected with the last aphorism, but because of the Koretzer's admo-nition, I'll merely point out again that the *Shekhinah* is the Divine Presence and that a kind of equivalence is being suggested between true blessing and that presence. As it says in the Torah, "Thus shall you bless the children of Yisra'el; say unto them, 'May *Yah* bless you and keep you . . . And they shall put My Name on the children of Yisra'el, and I will bless them" (Num. 6:23–24,27).[16]

TO DISPERSE THE *clouds, you need wind. There are "clouds" that hover over the mind as well. The "wind" to disperse them comes from the movements of prayer, the in and out of the lungs. This is what the Zohar calls ruaḥ (spirit-breath). Oy! If I had talked about this years ago, people would have served God by breathing and all the "clouds" would have dispersed. Today I talk and no one takes it to heart.*[17]

Today, this seems like an obvious reference to breathing meditation, which creates tranquility and insight, but because he mentions "the movements of prayer," we also think of a more refined style of *davenen,* in which *shuckelen* (swaying in prayer) is linked to breath. This might be akin to the Sufi prac-tices of *zikr* (remembrance of God through the use of a sacred word or phrase) and *fikr* (putting the sacred word or phrase on the breath), both of which are often accompanied by bodily movement.

Again Reb Pinhas refers to the problem of those who "think they know it already." There are some Rebbes who even define Hasidism by the quality of the way Hasidim listen. For instance, the Sefat Emet, Reb Yehudah Leib of Ger says, "The Hasid is one who listens for God in every moment."[18]

When I must reprove someone, I tell them something gentle and wise. This helps them get in touch with their soul. The soul gives life to its owner, and so one begins to live the soul life. This is what Moshe Cordovero says in his Pardes Rimmonim. *Sometimes, I even help a person get in touch with their soul by telling them a joke. Still, there are those in this generation of ours who preach morals at people, urging them to repent. But the poor in spirit, to whom they preach, have no way to help themselves get to* teshuvah *if the preachers won't help them to get them in touch with their souls.*

This is very important. In fact, it is all new.[19]

This was the "all new" way of the Ba'al Shem Tov, who strove to overcome the detrimental effect the preacher-reprovers of the day were having on an already demoralized Jewish populace.[20] For British and American Christians of the same period, John Wesley and the Methodists provided a similar antidote to the "fire and brimstone" sermons exemplified by Jonathan Edwards' "Sinners in the Hands of Angry God." Both the Ba'al Shem Tov and Wesley were trying to deal with the potential unfolding of a person's soul and thus were careful not to make it cringe and retreat under threats from an "angry God." The Ba'al Shem Tov was especially concerned with finding something good to say, bending and reframing reality in such a way that the good was always emphasized and judgments were softened. Thus, on one occasion, Reb Pinhas, following in the footsteps of the Ba'al Shem Tov, spoke out when he heard someone putting Christianity down in his presence. Instead, he turned it into an opportunity to speak of Christianity as one "salvational option" available on the planet. This was a profound statement from a Jew in his time.

If you must reprove someone, the carrier-wave must be one of love; and if that love is palpable, then it will be very clear that you have not come to condemn the person and thus the words may be received. The traditional language for this is, "Reproof in the open; the love is hidden." In other words, the carrier-wave is love. When you come with a blast, and it is clear that you are venting your spleen and attacking the person, it is not likely to create anything but antipathy. Thus the Koretzer tells us to say it gently, perhaps even with a joke.

WHATEVER IS PRECIOUS in this world is also scarce. There are so few who know how to learn. Tzaddikim are even more scarce. Scarcer still are those who really know how to pray. The higher worlds just don't want to come down.[21]

In Hasidism, when the "higher worlds" won't come down, the *tzaddikim* ascend to them in their prayer, acting as advocates for the people with Heaven. When the situation is really serious and all else fails, they recite the great prayer of mercy, Judaism's *maha-mantra* (great mantra) . . .

Our almighty Sovereign, sitting upon the Throne of Mercy, acting with Benevolence, forgiving the missteps of Your people, removing every great sin, granting forgiveness to the accidental sinner and pardon to the willful transgressor; again and again You deal kindly with every living being, never judging them in accordance with their true wickedness.

Almighty One, You have taught us to recite the Thirteen [Attributes of Mercy]; remember the Covenant of Your Thirteen [Attributes of Mercy] on our behalf this day, as You have made them known to Moses, the humble one, long ago. As it is written . . . And God descended in the cloud and stood with Moses, and he invoked the Name of the God.[22]

IN THE TIKKUNEI Zohar, it says, "Hidden worlds that can be revealed, and hidden worlds that cannot be revealed." There are deep insights you ought not to reveal at all. For in talking about them, you cause God to die away from them.

Now, if a person, in talking about them, could say them with all the feelings of love and awareness alive in them, God would not die away from that insight. This is extremely difficult for those who have not learned to offer their feelings along with their speech. If you serve God with this insight for half a year, at least, you will have moved yourself, indeed, the whole world, further on the scale of merit. Then you will accumulate so much energy in it, that even if you talk about it, the divinity within the insight will not die away.

Try to understand this deeply.[23]

Martin Buber used to say, "God is not addressed in the third person." This is a wonderful statement. For in a very basic sense, God is simply not available to be talked about; it would be like an isolated cell of the human body attempting to discourse on what it is to be a human being! We might be able to reach penultimate categories of knowledge, but "knowing" in the sense of encompassing that knowledge is simply beyond our grasp. Deeper still, Buber is saying something very similar to Reb Pinhas, of whom he was an admirer: When God is talked *about*, without feeling, and without a deep investment in God's reality pervading and penetrating that very moment, then God is *not* present. And when God is not present, God is not addressed, and this is a kind of "mismeeting." From Buber's perspective, as well as that of Hasidism, to speak of God without at the same time *addressing* God is a kind of tragedy of constricted awareness. For we are always in the presence of God, and to live as if we were not is like talking about someone in the third person when he or she is right there in front of you. Thus Hasidism is nothing less than the attempt to do everything in the presence of God.

> Buber once described a moment of realization in 1914 when he was asked, "Do you believe in God?" He assured his questioner that he did, but after he began to walk home, he really began to consider whether he had spoken truly. Then, in a moment of clarity, it came to him—"If to believe in God means to be able to talk *about* him in the third person, then I do not believe in God. If to believe in him means to be able to talk *to* him, then I believe in God."[24] Later he would write, God is the "*Thou* that by its nature cannot become *It*."[25]

You see, this too is about the carrier-wave of love and the investment of *kavanah* (intentionality), the attempt to live as if we really believed what we claim to believe!

THE ZOHAR SAYS—*"Bitterness and irritation are the doors to Hell within; the gates to Heaven are the gazing eyes and the fountains of the heart."*
To the human being is given the power to discriminate between one and the other—to choose to embrace Heaven or Hell.[26]

Notice how often Reb Pinhas mentions the Zohar in these fragments; his consciousness is clearly absorbed in it, as you would expect after a thousand readings. You can see why he might be moved to answer a question with a simple, "Study the Zohar." Today, with Daniel Matt's enlightening Pritzker edition of the Zohar becoming widely available in English, this has become a

more accessible possibility for those who do not have access to the Aramaic of
the original.

SOMEONE ASKED REB Pinhas of Koretz, "How can we pray for someone else to
repent when that prayer, if granted, would curtail another person's freedom of
choice? Is it not said by the Rabbis that 'everything is in Heaven's hands, except the
fear of Heaven?' "27
    The Koretzer answered, "What is God? . . . The totality of souls. Whatever exists
in the whole can also be found in the part. Therefore, in any one soul, all souls are
contained. If I turn in teshuvah (in repentance), I already contain in me the friends
whom I wish to help; and, likewise, they contain me in them. My teshuvah makes
both the them-in-me better, and the me-in-them better. In this way, it is easier for
the them-in-them to become better as well.28

In this wonderful teaching, a great insight of Hasidism can be married seamlessly to one of Sufism. For, in it, I find a parallel to the great "Toward the
One" prayer of Hazrat Inayat Khan (1882–1927), who first introduced Sufism
into the West . . .

Toward the One,
the Perfection of Love, Harmony, and Beauty,
the Only Being, United with All the Illuminated Souls,
Who Form the Embodiment of the Master, the Spirit of Guidance.

When Reb Pinhas says that God is the "totality of souls," it is very close to
Inayat Khan's "the Only Being," who is "United with All the Illuminated
Souls," forming the "Embodiment of the Master, the Spirit of Guidance."
From this we come to understand from whence the Rebbes derive their
remarkable insight; for whatever insight we may receive (whether through the
outer Rebbe or from the inner Rebbe) can be understood to derive from "the
Spirit of Guidance," or the "Great Rebbe," if you will, a collective supercon-
scious of illuminated beings producing a greater awareness than any individual is able to contain in him- or herself alone.
    This Great Rebbe then filters this awareness into the right moments
through precisely the right people for that moment. Now, the local Rebbes,
who are able to make themselves especially transparent to the will of God,
become willing conduits of this grace and, therefore, are often thought to own
this territory because of their consistency in doing so. But the truth is, we are

all a part of that collective, and thus we are all contributors and conduits of that grace. As Murshid Samuel Lewis (1896–1971), a disciple of Inayat Khan, later wrote, "It is a mistake to assume there is any 'teacher.' The teacher is the positive pole of the cell, and as the pupil or pupils—the negative pole—show more aptitude, the electromagnetic field of the cell increases and knowledge comes through the teacher which would have otherwise been impossible."[29]

As great as this insight may be, we must not forget that it is meant to set up another point in the Koretzer's teaching, to explain why prayer is effective. For the Koretzer says that the best way to help someone else is to do our own spiritual work of *teshuvah*, turning ever back to God, thus creating a positive effect in the outer world for our friends but also healing the us-in-them in the inner world.

REB PINHAS OF Koretz says, "It is written, nishmat adam, telamdennu da'at, 'the soul of a human being teaches them knowledge.'[30] So why are we all so stupid? Because the soul is an indifferent teacher . . . it doesn't repeat anything twice!"

How many epiphanies have you had in your life? What happened to them? The Koretzer says, "The soul comes up with unique insights, but it doesn't repeat them, and thus we forget them before we have really gotten to know them." This is because the soul is not a good drillmaster. It never repeats itself. So the bright light of insight, if never repeated, vanishes and is lost. It is written, "And you shall teach your children diligently," repeating important truths until they become a part of life itself. We must anchor our insights with a name, ruminating on them, and eventually elaborating them in different ways that have meaning for our lives.

EAVESDROPPING ON A JOURNEY OUT-OF-BODY—PART I

In the following letter, we are introduced to Reb Pinhas as a true heir of the Ba'al Shem Tov with regard to his shamanic ascents of consciousness (described in Chapter 2).[31] In the letter of the Ba'al Shem Tov, it became clear that there is a multidimensional, multivalent awareness and presence available in out-of-body journeys. Here, Reb Pinhas describes just how real this can be and just how close two beings may be in prayer, bearing witness to what he says in the previous fragment when he asked the question, "What is God?" and answered, "*The totality of souls.*"

To MORENU (OUR teacher), the rav Yesha'ayahu—
My holy friend, beloved of my soul, who does all things only for the sake of the blessed name, may your light radiate for generations to come.
I write to you now with trembling in the all-seeing presence of the Holy One, and out of compassion for this troubled world, knowing its yearning for absorption in the Divine, and to guide you to a deeper love through the blessed assistance of the Holy One.
Recently, when I opened to the beholding, I sought to still all reflections of bodily sensation in my mind so that I might move with more alacrity and interior sensitivity in my imaginal faculty. For when the glorious influx rises and effects the mental organs (those faculties that are subtly linked to the body), the energy flow increases to overwhelm all bodily sensation completely. The subtle forms are thus freed and separated from their matrix. Then it is within the realm of possibility to adhere the mind's intellectual reverie to the sensible spiritual forms and thus to attain the true wholeness of one's essential humanity.

Notice how elegantly Reb Pinhas describes this process of blending the imaginal faculty (*ḥush ha-tziyur*) with the divine influx, allowing us to open the door to an interior world. If you have ever been involved in such shamanic-type imaginal journeys, you know that it is not simply a preprogrammed intellectual exercise; on the contrary, there is a great deal of surprise in it. You don't actually know what you are going to meet there; you may come upon a scene and decide to turn right and then find yourself confronted by something totally unexpected! So it is clearly not entirely dependent on will; there is something of an autonomous world there. As the Sufi scholar Henri Corbin (1903–1978) pointed out, "Who says it isn't a real world? Just because the criteria of *this* world says it isn't real, doesn't mean it is not real by the criteria of *that* world!"

What he is describing here is so important (and not simply because of its profound content), for this kind of direct experiential teaching about deep inner realities and spiritual techniques seems, by and large, to disappear from later generations of Hasidism, or at least becomes much less apparent. But here is a Rebbe teaching a senior Hasid real Rebbe-craft. When the Rebbes stop apprenticing their Hasidim, a great gulf grows between the Rebbe and Hasid, and they become locked in two unbridgeable roles.

In Hinduism, you have the ideal of the *sat guru* (the "being" teacher), who is on a pedestal (sometimes literally), and who tends to be declarative as the living embodiment of the teaching. But there is also the ideal of the *upa guru* (the "means" teacher), who comes off of the pedestal and draws you close in compassion, showing you how to get there. One is the archetypal model, and the other is the accessible model, and both are valid forms of teaching. The problem in Hasidism is that the accessible model fell away in most Hasidic lineages, and it is a shame. For a healthy spirituality needs both. Here, at least, we find Reb Pinhas being the *upa guru* for Reb Shaya, in the way the Ba'al Shem Tov was for Reb Gershon of Kittov.

ON MY BED *in the dark of night, when all other awareness was stilled, I let my consciousness soar. In that moment, my thought-form, now out of body, merged with your own, and I saw the difficulty you were having. Conscious and totally awake, I sensed that you had become entwined in a trap and could not find a way to set it straight. Because of my love for you, I cannot withhold the solution to the mystery that perplexed you.*

This is clearly not an isolated incident for Reb Pinhas to see and be aware of others in his journeys, as we see from a talk given by my Rebbe, Yosef Yitzhak of Lubavitch:

"Reb Pinhas, the holy Master of Koretz, writes (Sukkot Eve, 1761) to the Maggid of Mezritch, of blessed memory . . .
" 'Many thanks to your honored holiness, for you remembered me and raised me up in your holy thought on Yom Kippur. Be assured, my holy master, that I felt it here at that very moment. As a sign of truth to you, it was between *Minḥah* and *Ne'ilah*. . . .' "[32]

AT FIRST, YOU *questioned, "Why may a man legally marry his niece and yet not his aunt? For this being the case, should not a woman likewise be forbidden to marry her uncle?" (Lev. 18:12–13)[33] But the natural flowing is from above to below, from the masculine bestowing to the feminine receiving. In reverse, the order of creation would be disturbed, and thus we are bidden against obstructing the natural flow.*
Your second question, however, troubled you still more; you could not comprehend what you were shown in the vision, and then came to you an association with the sentence "You are altogether beautiful, my love, you have no blemish (mum) at all" (Sg. 4:7),[34] the significance of which escaped you. Well, my beloved, the delight of God and my own soul, allow me to share what my spirit discerned of your vision for you. You, my honored friend in Torah, were thinking of Bertinoro's[35] ques-

tion at the opening of the tractate of Shabbat,[36] where it is stated, "Yetzi'at ha-Shabbat shtayin sh'ḥem'arba' " (The emergings of the Shabbat are two which are four) and not Hoza'at ha-Shabbat (the carryings of the Shabbat are two which are four). The latter, no doubt would have been grammatically correct; but as I let my thoughts rise from that level to ascend to the realm of the solution, I realized that the tanna (the teacher of the Mishnah) wished to indicate at the beginning of the tractate the holy name Yah, and he sought to give an exegetical reason for this. You saw but through a glass darkly.

It is known that the prohibition against carrying objects from one domain to another on Shabbat points to the exalted mystery that, not even for one moment, is one to leave the domain of the One and to enter into the domain of plurality, the domain of Samael, God protect us. To do so would cause a puncture in the blessed name, Y-H-V-H. Therefore, the tanna pointed to this at the beginning of the tractate, for when the name YaH of two letters is filled (YUD He'), the numerical value is 26, just like the full name of four letters.[37] To this, the tanna points with Yetzi'at ha-Shabbat are two (YaH) which are four (Y-H-V-H); therefore, in this matter, one is to be extremely careful in order not to cause damage and puncture the name.

My holy friend, you began on the right track, but turned aside in the middle and got lost in the maze. Your mind, however, wished to bring you back to the right path and hinted, "Behold you are beautiful my lover," "for so you are in the beginning on this sequence, but there is no blemish (mum) in you now." "YaH MaLe' " (86),[38] the name of Yah in fullness, has the same numerical force as the word "mum" (86),[39] but this you did not understand clearly.

The third point that gave you trouble was the acceptance of the yoke of the sovereignty of Heaven. You lost sight of the difference between the mystery of the celestial union and the lower union. There are others, who, for this very reason, have fallen into perplexity, not understanding the Zoharic image of the melekh (the king) and the matronita (the matrix or Mother). However, this is a profound mystery, the very foundation (yesod) of the world, pointing to the secret of climbing Ya'akov's ladder. This is also further intended by "to you Shlomo the Alef," so sublime a mystery is this that it is intended for only a few singular individuals, who may share this treasure—but this is not given to be put into written script.

It seems clear to me that Reb Pinhas did not wish to detail in writing the mystery of the upper union, that of *yud* and *heh*, in which the merger is not completed by *vav* and *heh*. This is so that the Mother may return from that union with a seed spark that can grow and give itself birth as a word becomes flesh. This confusion is much in evidence today. In Hindu terms, the *jnani* (seeker of knowledge) can be *advaitin* (a nondualist), for the time of *samadhi* (one-pointed meditation), but upon returning to mundane consciousness, one needs the yoke of the divine sovereignty, the *yoga* of *bhakti* or *kriya,* devout God-loving or disinterested action.

Following the process in a functional manner, it seems that when Reb Shaya made his descent from the nondual realm of the one back into duality, he could not adjust himself to having to serve God as an other, as before. Having attained to the unitive level in his ascent to the atzilic consciousness, he encountered this difficulty in descent. This seems to be what Reb Pinhas is replying to.

BECAUSE MY LOVE for you is so great, I wish to share this mystery with you, and have put these words in the mouth of the bearer of this letter so that he might tell it to you by the word of mouth. However, first you must further refine your body substance by the purification and lustrations known in the hidden wisdom.

From me,

Pinhas Shapiro of Ostrog.[40]

Later in life, Reb Pinhas moved to Ostrog; nevertheless, he continued to be known among Hasidim as the Koretzer. It will be of interest to many lovers of Ḥasidut that the bearer of the letter and its oral instructions was none other than Reb Moshe Hayyim Efraim of Sudilkov, the grandson of the Ba'al Shem Tov.

EAVESDROPPING ON A JOURNEY OUT-OF-BODY—PART II

The following *ma'aseh* about Reb Shaya of Dynavitz is to be read in connection with the letter we just examined as a kind of postscript on that journey out-of-body.

REB YESHA'AYAHU OF Dynavitz, a disciple of the Maggid of Mezritch, was not a Rebbe leading a Hasidic congregation. Instead, he lived alone in a village and made his living from innkeeping and the sale of brandy. However, his great righteousness could not be disguised, and he became famous in the vicinity, even to the landlords and peasants. Everyone knew that any field in which he set foot would be blessed by great increase. Thus landlords contrived all manner of excuses for Reb Yesha'ayahu ("Shaya") to visit their property!

Late one evening, a landlord came to the inn of Reb Shaya of Dynavitz on just such an errand, intending to stay for the night. He entered the parlor and found Reb Shaya standing with his back to him. He then greeted him in order to get his attention. Nevertheless, Reb Shaya neither turned nor made a sound to respond to the greeting of the landlord! At this seeming insult, the temperamental landlord became furious, drew out his gun and shot at the wall Reb Shaya was facing, just missing his right ear! Still, Reb Shaya did not move. Astonished at this, the angry landlord realized that he must be praying and set to waiting, albeit impatiently.

When Reb Shaya concluded his prayers and meditation and began to stir, the landlord rebuked him, saying, "How dare you not respond to my greeting?"

Reb Shaya said, "The God who creates us both is witness that I knew nothing of your presence here."

"Weren't you scared that I might shoot you," said the landlord, pointing to the bullet hole.

"As God is my witness," answered Reb Shaya, "I heard nothing."

At that very time, it turns out, Reb Pinhas of Koretz was involved in his own "conscious ascent of the soul" and sensed Reb Yesha'ayahu's method was yet imperfect, for he had not yet divested himself completely from the appearances of this world and, therefore, wasn't able to break through to the divine realization awaiting him. Anyone who has cleared his or her body and natural soul will be able to understand the bright light of this letter.[41]

This story, taken together with the letter from Reb Pinhas, is a good example of what I like to call "transpersonal sociology," which to say, when souls do their together-ing.

THE MOURNING OF THE *SHEKHINAH*

Toward the end of his life, Reb Pinhas of Koretz was overtaken by a desire to travel to Eretz Yisra'el and soon set out on the road. He traveled first to the town of Shepetovka on the Russian frontier to say good-bye to his father-in-law but was taken with a fever there. When it became clear that he was dying, he sent for his beloved disciple Rafael of Bershad to comfort him. With Rafael at his side, he died and was buried in Shepetovka. He was 65 years old.

ON THE DAY *of Reb Pinhas's passing, Reb Ya'akov Shimshon of Shepetovka, who was at that time living in Eretz Yisra'el, had a dream in which he saw the Shekhinah (Divine Presence) in the form of a tall woman in a veil, weeping before the Wailing Wall of the Temple, as if mourning for a friend of her youth. Suddenly, he awoke with tears streaming down his face and declared aloud, "Pinhas of Koretz is dead!"*

When asked how he knew this, he replied, "There is only one tzaddik at this time for whom the Shekhinah would mourn in this way!" Then he arose and tore his garment in the traditional sign of grief and said, "Blessed be the true judge." And for seven days he sat shivah for his Rebbe.

Some wondered at his behavior; but, after some months, the news came to Eretz Yisra'el that Pinhas of Koretz had indeed died on the day Reb Ya'akov Shimshon had said.[42]

"There is only one *tzaddik* at this time for whom the *Shekhinah* would mourn in this way!" This is not meant to impune any other *tzaddik* alive at that time but to single Reb Pinhas out as one whom the *Shekhinah* mourned "like the friend of her youth," as a woman would mourn an ardent young lover of her youth with whom she had known deep intimacy.

A BLESSING NO ONE ELSE WOULD GIVE—PART II

At this point, nothing further need be said of Reb Pinhas's greatness or of his place in Hasidism. It remains only to complete the story we began earlier. It is not a happy story and is difficult to digest, but it is perhaps all the more true for being so. It takes place in 1838, 47 years after the death of Reb Pinhas of Koretz . . .

THE SECOND SON *of Reb Pinhas of Koretz was Reb Moshe Shapira, a rabbi in Slovita. The year after his father's death, he founded a printing press in Slovita to print new editions of the Talmud, Torah, and the works of various Hasidic masters. After 30 years in the business, as befitted a man of his age, he retired and turned the printing press over to his sons, Reb Shmuel Abba and Reb Pinhas Shapira.*

Now, the sons of Reb Moshe were both pious men and true grandchildren of Reb Pinhas of Koretz. So when the brothers took over the printing press from their father, it was not simply a matter of inheriting property for them or a means of

making money, God forbid, but a holy undertaking. After all, they would be print-
ing holy books and works of Ḥasidut. Therefore, they decided to invest in a new
press; and before they printed a single page, they carted the entire press to the
mikveh in Slovita and dipped each part of the press in the mikveh! After all, the
press was for the printing of holy books, and thus they felt it should be kashered. For
over 10 years the brothers ran the printing press in Slovita in holiness until fate final-
ly intervened.

In the month of Iyar, not long after Pesaḥ, when Jews were still vulnerable to
the blood libel, a gentile man was found hanging in the Tailor's Synagogue. His
widow had made it known that he suffered from depression, and it was very clear
that he had probably taken his own life. Nevertheless, troublemakers began to mur-
mur that the Jews had killed him. Before long, a man informed to the Russian gov-
ernment that Reb Shmuel Abba and Reb Pinhas Shapira, the holy printers, were
responsible!

Without a shred of reliable evidence, the two brothers were arrested and sent to
prison in Kiev. After two years they were tried, found guilty, and sentenced to a
humiliating punishment . . . they had to run a gauntlet of soldiers.

The soldiers lined up with sticks in their hands, waiting and ready for the two
brothers to come running through . . . but the brothers didn't run. They began a
niggun and started to walk slowly and with dignity through the gauntlet of soldiers.
I wish I could tell you that the soldiers were awed by their holy calm and the song
of these Hasidim, but they were not and beat them as they walked through. The
kippah (skull-cap) of one of the brothers was knocked off under the blows, but
instead of moving on, he turned round with the same solemn dignity and went back
to retrieve his kippah, enduring further violence because of it.

Now, what does all of this have to do with the blessing that no one else but Reb
Pinhas, the shtiller bokher, would give? Sadly, it was the son of the man he blessed
to have children who had informed against the brothers to the Russian government.
That is the reason all the other Rebbes refused to bless this man, because they knew
if he had a son, he would be the one who would wrong the children of Reb Pinhas.
But Reb Pinhas was so overwhelmed with gratitude, he refused to look into the
future before granting the blessing.[43]

I don't know of any *niggunim* sung by the Koretzer, but I remember just a
small part of the *niggun* sung by his grandchildren as they walked through
that gauntlet, and now I sing it to connect myself with the spirits of all three
of them, thus honoring their sacrifice for the sake of Heaven.

6

A Bear in the Forest: Dov Baer, the Maggid of Mezritch

AT LAST WE COME TO REB DOV BAER, the Maggid of Mezritch, the successor of the Ba'al Shem Tov and, in many ways, the architect of the Hasidic movement as we know it today. He was not like his Rebbe in education, in body, in temperament, or even in mind, but his master led him to the same well from which he himself had drunk, and in time, he became a *neshamah klalit*, an "aggregate soul" so great that he eventually encompassed the diversity of an entire generation of Hasidim.

THE FAMILY TREE

Little is told of the Maggid's childhood except that he was born in Lukatch, Volhynia, to Rabbi Avraham, a poor Hebrew teacher from a distinguished rabbinical family, and his wife, Havah. The earliest story that we have of the young Dov Baer comes from his fifth year when tragedy suddenly struck his family. You may remember that the Ba'al Shem Tov was also five years old when he lost his father, forever altering the course of his life.

ONE NIGHT, WHEN Dov Baer was only five years old, his parent's home caught fire and burned to the ground; the house and all of its contents were reduced to ashes.

*While the fire yet blazed and his father looked on, Dov Baer noticed that his moth-
er sat upon the ground crying. He approached her and said consolingly, "Imma, it's
only a house . . . we can get another house."*

*His mother looked up at him grief stricken and said, "Yes, Berel, we can get
another; God will provide. But that's not why I am crying."*

"Why do you cry then?" he asked.

*"Because," she answered, "in the house was our family tree, tracing our descent
all the way back to Rabbi Yohanan ha-Sandlar, who was himself a descendant of
David ha-Melekh."*

*Then, with a child's confidence, Dov Baer proudly proclaimed, "Don't worry,
Imma; we can start a new family tree from me!"[1]*

This is very interesting historically because in many ways, it is *not* the descen-
dants of the Ba'al Shem Tov (with few exceptions) who become the reigning
royal family of Hasidism, but the descendants of the Maggid—the great
Friedman dynasty.[2] Perhaps this is because Tzvi Hirsh, the son of the Ba'al
Shem Tov, played only a small part in the Hasidic movement, whereas the
Maggid's son Avraham the Malakh was a great *tzaddik* as we shall see in a
later chapter. Even though Avraham refused the succession, his son Shalom
Shakhna of Prohobitch (1771–1803) and his grandson Yisra'el of Rhyzhin
(1797–1851) were clearly treated as dynastic Rebbes and majestic personages
in their lifetimes. Indeed, many other Rebbes were known to visit the
Rhyzhiner to pay homage to him as the "king of Yisra'el."[3]

Dov Baer's father, Avraham, was too poor to have his son educated in a
yeshiva but managed to teach him on his own until the boy's prodigious intellectual gifts became general knowledge in the community. It was then that he
came to the attention of the rabbi of Lukatch, Shlomo Dov Baer, who agreed
to educate the young prodigy personally. But a time came when the young
man's gifts tested even the rabbi of Lukatch, and it became clear that he would
require a teacher who was equal to his prodigious talents.

At that time, one the greatest lights of Torah in all of Europe was Rabbi
Ya'akov Yehoshua Falk (1680–1756), the father-in-law of Rabbi Shlomo Dov
Baer and the author of the *P'nai Yehoshua* (Face of Joshua), a famous commentary on the Talmud. Thus young Dov Baer was sent to Lvov (Lemberg) to
study with this great Torah luminary.[4] During this time, he studied and mastered the entire Torah, Talmud, and halakhic codes of Judaism and probably
also became acquainted with the Kabbalah, the sources of which he would
master in the years to come.[5]

A SOJOURNER IN THE WORLD

After receiving his *smikhah* (ordination), Rabbi Dov Baer settled in the town of Torchin, where he married the daughter of Rabbi Shalom Shakhna. However, instead of seeking a post as a rabbi, he determined instead to make his living as a *maggid*. Now, a rabbi at that time was called on strictly as a halakhic or legal authority and rarely gave sermons as congregational rabbis do today. Sermons were usually given by *maggidim*, either one who was appointed by the *kehillah* (community) or an itinerant *maggid*. For a scholar of Dov Baer's distinction and poor health, a rabbinic post would seem to have been ideal. So why did he choose to become a *maggid*? One reason seems obvious: both the oral tradition and his recorded teachings show him to be an unusually skillful orator, weaving together elegant and effective homilies extemporaneously, as we shall see later. But perhaps we might also speculate that the young scholar was already feeling compelled to live outside of the ivory tower, to help uplift and comfort the people around him through sermons and stories, to bring the seekers among them to a deeper commitment to spiritual practice.

Before long, he acquired a reputation as one of the great *maggidim* of the time, preaching in Koretz, Dubno, and Rovno. Nevertheless, he seems to have remained poor, either because success as a *maggid* did not bring riches as much as reputation or because his ascetic spiritual values would not allow him to keep more money than was necessary for mere subsistence. There are a number of stories that speak of Dov Baer's poverty during this period, some describing the terrible conditions of the ramshackle shed occupied by him and his wife, and others depicting the couple's misery as they struggled to provide for their child.[6] One such tale gives us a vivid picture of the Maggid's life at this time, as seen through the eyes of one of the Ba'al Shem Tov's disciples . . .

ONCE, A DISCIPLE *of the Ba'al Shem Tov was sent as a* shaliah *(emissary) to Torchin to convey the Ba'al Shem Tov's regards to the renowned* maggid, *Dov Baer of Torchin. With difficulty, the emissary found the shack that served as the Maggid's home and was astounded at what he saw there: Before him sat Rabbi Dov Baer on a roughhewn wood block teaching pupils who, like him, sat on a plank of wood supported by other wood blocks at a table of the same construction! The rest of the room was empty of even the simplest furniture and comforts. It was clean, but to the eyes of the Ba'al Shem Tov's emissary, striking in the poverty it represented. As the Maggid was engaged in teaching at the moment, the emissary begged his pardon and promised to return later.*

After a few hours, he returned to find the Maggid sitting on the same wood block engaged in study while his wife set a meager dinner for their guest on the plank, which only hours before had accommodated the Maggid's pupils. The makeshift table had now been converted into a bed! Once again, the emissary was shocked at what he saw and could not contain himself, exclaiming, "Rabbi, how is it that you have come to such a state, living in such miserable conditions without even a chair to rest upon? Is there not a more suitable home available to you?"

The Maggid looked up at him unblinking and asked in return, "You have just come from a journey, yes? How do you take care of your needs when you are on the road?"

The emissary replied, "On the road I have to make do with what I have." So the Maggid said, "My friend, in this world, I am on the road."[7]

The implications of this statement are clear—for Dov Baer, the world was not a home. The poverty in which he lived and the ascetic practices of the Lurianic Kabbalah that he followed both supported this attitude. For the Maggid, the world was in *galut* (in exile) from the Divine, and so was he. It was an attitude that the Ba'al Shem Tov would work hard to change and one that the Maggid would later repudiate entirely, struggling to convince his own son of the error in this view. Nevertheless, the Maggid continued in these severe practices for many years before he met the Ba'al Shem Tov, and the toll they took on his already fragile health was permanent.

This little story also shows us that the Ba'al Shem Tov was actively courting the Maggid, but there is no indication that Dov Baer was inclined to respond to the Ba'al Shem Tov's overtures at that time. One version of the story has the Ba'al Shem Tov's disciple Reb Mendel of Bar passing through Torchin and visiting the renowned *maggid* purely for his own sake. Upon finding him lame and very sickly, he urged him to visit the Ba'al Shem Tov, who was famed as a healer. The Maggid refused. When Reb Mendel returned to Mezhbizh afterward, he went to the holy Ba'al Shem Tov to tell him of the holy soul he had encountered in Torchin. The Ba'al Shem Tov replied, "I've been aware of him for a number of years and long for his coming to Mezhbizh."[8]

WORDS AND REALITY

As we have already mentioned, the Maggid's health had been fragile for most of his life. He was lame in his left foot and walked always on crutches. Whether he was born lame or had a bout of polio in his youth, we do not know. Nevertheless, his disability was obviously the source of much discomfort and was perhaps related to the many episodes of illness in his life (exacerbated by his fasting and other privations). By the summer or fall of 1753, his illness had become critical and thus was the catalyst for his first extraordinary meeting with the Ba'al Shem Tov. What follows is the conversion story of Rabbi Dov Baer of Tochin, who would become the great Maggid of Mezritch.

RABBI DOV BAER, *the maggid, had often heard of the increasingly famous healer and teacher in Mezhbizh whom people called the Ba'al Shem Tov, how they traveled to see him from far and wide, and how he seemed to manifest a miraculous refu'ah (healing) and teshuvah (repentance) in them through means of his words and prayer. Nevertheless, Rabbi Dov Baer—a brilliant scholar, thoroughly versed in Talmud and halakhah as well as the most intricate teachings of the Kabbalah—was skeptical of this* ba'al mofet *(miracle worker). Moreover, the scattered reports of his highly unorthodox teachings made him more than a little suspect in the eyes of the famous* maggid.

However, it was not such a simple matter to dismiss this man from his thoughts. For the Ba'al Shem Tov had sent him regards through various disciples, and many of those disciples had impressed him by their character and learning. Still he was cautious. But there was also the matter of his continual illness. The pain in his leg and the general sickness of his body were getting worse, and now his body cried out to him, urging him to seek whatever help might be had—even from a miracle worker. But the disciplined Dov Baer was used to denying the demands of his body.

More difficult for him to ignore were the urgings of his wife, who, as his health deteriorated, began to exhort him to "seek a cure from the famous ba'al shem in Mezhbizh!" Nevertheless, he replied, "I have 100 questions about the Ba'al Shem Tov's behavior. When I receive explanations for all those questions, I'll consider visiting him." However, when his mentor, Rabbi Ya'akov Yehoshua Falk, also urged him to seek healing from the Ba'al Shem Tov, he could resist no longer. Surely if such a person as the P'nai Yehoshua would endorse this man, he could at least see if some help might come through him.

Now, the endorsement of the P'nai Yehoshua here for the Ba'al Shem Tov needs a little explaining. A *ma'aseh* to shed some light on this . . .

> There was a small town called Yazhlovitz not far from Lvov where the Ba'al Shem Tov once officiated as a *shohet* (a kosher slaughterer) and as a *hazzan* (cantor) on the High Holy Days during his hidden years. The Rabbi of Lvov at that time was the great *tzaddik* Ya'akov Yehoshua Falk, called the P'nai Yehoshua (after his book), whose fame we have already mentioned. During the P'nai Yehoshua's tenure there, he made a wise decree that all the Jews in the little villages surrounding Lvov were to assemble for the High Holy Days in that city to have services, to be instructed in the ways of God, and to pay their rightful share of the communal taxes. To his dismay, the P'nai Yehoshua heard that a young man was conducting services in the town of Yazhlovitz for the High Holy Days in spite of the decree!
>
> After Rosh Hashanah had passed, the P'nai Yehoshua sent a messenger of the court to Yazhlovitz to summon the congregation and their young leader to come to Lvov in their holiday garb and to repeat the service in full view of the entire congregation of Lvov. When the poor people of Yazhlovitz raised the point of obedience with their young leader, Yisra'el (the Ba'al Shem Tov, as we have said in his hidden years), he said only, "Of course, we must show our obedience to the venerable Rabbi of Lvov; we have nothing to fear." But the people of Yazhlovitz feared the ridicule more than censure. Nevertheless, upon their leader's agreement to be obedient to the *beit din* (religious court) of Lvov, they all traveled into town as they had been commanded.
>
> When the people of Yazhlovitz finally entered Lvov, they were mortified to see their worst fears realized; a tremendous crowd greeted them with jeers and condemnation. They were humiliated. Even the *heder* (school) children vied with one another in heaping abuses upon them! But the young Ba'al Shem Tov continued on unperturbed and, once in the synagogue, began his recital of the poetic portions of the prayers with the proper melodies. When he came to the recitation of the *Amidah*, the P'nai Yehoshua feared that soon the mocking of the crowd would turn from the mocking of a person and a disobedient community into the mocking of the sacred service, and he silenced the congregation with a glance and a simple gesture. Whereupon the

Ba'al Shem Tov said, "Now that I am about to continue with the poetry of the *Amidah,* only those who have fully atoned for the sins of their youth in *teshuvah* may remain."

Then he began.

It was the children who first felt the tremor of awe in the synagogue and left as soon as they could get out. Then their elders began to depart until only the P'nai Yehoshua remained of his congregation. Thus he walked over to the prayer desk and said to the Ba'al Shem Tov, "Young man, I commend you for your obedience. People who know how to conduct prayer like you have my permission to do so, even outside of Lvov."[9]

We can only assume that the P'nai Yehoshua learned the true identity of the "young man" in the ensuing years and thus was able to recommend him to the Maggid.

So Rabbi Dov Baer began the long journey to Mezhbizh, seeking healing for his leg and his poor health. But after two days on the road, he began to regret having left home as the travel was interfering with his accustomed patterns of study and spiritual practice. By the time he arrived in Mezhbizh, he was considerably disturbed and hoping that the journey would not prove a complete waste of his time. "Perhaps," he mused, "this ba'al shem will have some profound Torah to teach to make up for the disturbance of my studies."

Shortly after he was installed in his inn, having already sent a messenger to request a meeting with the ba'al shem, he was called to the study of the Ba'al Shem Tov, who greeted him disinterestedly and immediately began to tell him a common anecdote . . . "Once, I was traveling for several days through the wilderness and ran out of bread to feed my coachman. Then, as we traveled on, I met with a peasant on the road carrying a sack of bread."

That was it—a story of a coachman and he was dismissed!

The following evening, the Ba'al Shem Tov called for the Maggid again. "This time," the Maggid thought, "I am sure to hear something useful." But just as before, the Ba'al Shem Tov began yet another common anecdote, this time of how he had once run out of hay for the horses while out on the road. And just when he had given up hope, a farmer came along with hay that he was willing to give him.

"Horses!" the Maggid thought, "What is wrong with this man? Is he meshugge?"

Now, of course, all of these supposed anecdotes of the Ba'al Shem Tov were in truth mashalim (parables) of deep significance that were intelligible to those initi-

ated in his way. But to the Maggid, they seemed merely trivial and ridiculous. Disgusted by this ba'al shem's coarse tales of coachmen and horses, disgusted with himself for have made such a long journey to seek help from a peasant charlatan, he determined to leave as soon as possible. He returned to his inn and told the coachman, "We leave in the morning!" and he went about readying himself for the return journey.

Around midnight, there was a knock at the Maggid's door. The Ba'al Shem Tov had sent his gabbai to summon the Maggid to his study. Reluctantly, Rabbi Dov Baer answered the summons, perhaps thinking he might put this ba'al shem in his place before going home. But this time the unsophisticated veneer was gone from this strange ba'al shem and he looked shrewdly at the Maggid now, though he was oddly dressed in a coat of wolf fur turned inside out.

Up until this point, the Ba'al Shem Tov seems to have been preparing the Maggid for something, playing on the common notion that he was really just an unsophisticated peasant. Now the moment has apparently come to turn the Maggid's knowingness into unknowing, thus opening him to new dimensions of spiritual experience. This is all symbolized in the seemingly anachronistic detail of the coat made of "wolf fur turned inside out."

AFTER LOOKING AT him for several minutes, the Ba'al Shem Tov addressed a question to him for the first time, "Rabbi Dov Baer, are you well-versed in Torah?"

Receiving his reply in the affirmative, the Ba'al Shem Tov said, "Yes, truly, I have heard that you are a great scholar, but are you also versed in the Torat ha-emet (Torah of Truth—that is, the Kabbalah)?

Rabbi Dov Baer was taken aback for a moment; this was not what he had expected. He answered the Ba'al Shem, "Yes, I am."

The Ba'al Shem Tov then called for his gabbai to bring them a copy of the Etz Hayyim of the Ari ha-Kodesh. The gabbai returned with the volume, and the Ba'al Shem Tov asked the Maggid, "Are you familiar with this work?"

"Yes, of course," replied Rabbi Dov Baer, becoming more curious by the minute.

"And do you remember this passage?" asked the Ba'al Shem Tov, showing him a particular page of the text.

Rabbi Dov Baer scanned the page and said, "Yes."

"And can you explain it?"

"Yes," he answered and proceeded to recite it by heart. Then, summoning all the erudition he could muster, Rabbi Dov Baer began to explain the passage in all of its *intricacy, quoting source after source, demonstrating his profound knowledge of Kabbalah in a brilliant display of learning.*

But when he had finished, the Ba'al Shem Tov only shook his head.

Rabbi Dov Baer looked skeptically at him, reviewed the passage again, and said, "Oh, I see; you follow the minority opinion," and he explained this position also in all its detail.

Again, the Ba'al Shem Tov only shook his head disapprovingly.

Frustrated, Rabbi Dov Baer said, "So you explain it!"

The Ba'al Shem Tov asked him to stand, and Rabbi Dov Baer did as he was asked, holding the crutches under his arms.[10] Then the holy Ba'al Shem Tov slowly began to intone the Ma'aseh Merkavah (Work of the chariot, in Yehezkel) with deep kavanah, trembling as he read. A palpable vibration filled the room and stirred Rabbi Dov Baer in the core of his being. Then fear took him as the light from the candles began to take on strange forms and the angelic beings described in the passage began to flash and make their presence felt in all the dimensions described in the texts he had explained with such precise detail![11] It was all he could do not to faint in their holy presence!

As the Ba'al Shem Tov neared the end of his recitation, the light forms slowly retreated into the flickering candlelight, and the fullness of the holy presence in the room coalesced into just two beating hearts. The Maggid now looked with awakened eyes on the holy Ba'al Shem Tov.

The Ba'al Shem Tov then said to him, "The meaning of the passage is as you have explained, but there was no soul in your explanation."

Now the Maggid could see the depth of meaning in the deceptively simple wisdom the Ba'al Shem Tov had offered to him in his two previous interviews and was overwhelmed with possibilities he had never before considered. In the morning, he called his coachman and told him to return home without him . . . he would be staying in Mezhbizh.[12]

———

With this powerful and dramatic invocation of angelic presences, the Ba'al Shem Tov brought the Maggid into the fold and revealed to him what he had been missing through all the years of his seeking. While he may have mastered the words, he had not yet experienced the reality behind them. For the first time, he was truly experiencing what this text was referring to; he had never before understood its *life*.

I am reminded of a similar conversion story from the Tibetan Buddhist tradition of the scholar Naropa's meeting with a *dakini*, the feminine embodiment of wisdom that eliminates spiritual obstacles.

One day, Naropa, a brilliant scholar of Buddhism, was absorbed in his study when "a terrifying shadow" fell upon his books. He looked up with trepidation and saw the face of a profoundly ugly old woman. Before he could take his eyes off of her, she asked him, "What is it that you are studying?"

He replied, "Buddhist epistemology, logic, and other such things."

She then asked, "Do you understand what you are reading?"

When he replied in the affirmative, she asked him, "Is it the words or the meaning that you understand?"

Thinking about this for a moment, he said, "The words."

Then the strangest thing occurred—the ugly old woman began to laugh and dance in joy, amazingly, waving her walking stick in the air, which only a moment before she had been leaning on with all her weight!

Pleased with this strange reaction, Naropa added, "I also understand the meaning."

Immediately, the visage of the ugly old woman changed and she began to weep and threw her stick to the ground in grief.

Now the sense of the numinous that Naropa had briefly felt when her shadow fell across his books returned again, and he knew he was not dealing with an ordinary old crone. He asked cautiously, "Why were you elated with my first answer and grieved at my second?"

She answered him, "I was happy because you, a great scholar, did not lie and frankly admitted that you understood only the words. But when you lied, saying that you understood the sense—*which you do not*—I was grieved."

"And who, then, may I ask, understands the sense?"

"Tilopa."

"Please, will you introduce me to him?"

"Go yourself and beg him to help you to grasp the sense."

Then the *dakini* faded like a rainbow in the sky.[13]

Naropa made his way to his master Tilopa, and in time, became a great *siddha*, a being with a profound experiential attainment.

Both stories are dealing with the difference between studying a text and seeing it as a reality. This is the challenge that is always facing the student of Ḥasidut, to read the text and to study its concepts with a sense of the *mamash* (experiential) quality, the presence of spiritual reality behind the words, so that it is not a merely an idea, but a gateway to realization.

THE MAGIC CIRCLE OF THE BA'AL SHEM TOV AND THE MAGGID'S *TESHUVAH*

After his experience in the Ba'al Shem Tov's study, the Maggid became a fervent Hasid of the master and entered the inner circles of the great disciples. But there were many lessons yet to learn. He had surely found a new dimension to his relationship to God, but he was still new to the way of the Ba'al Shem Tov. Moreover, his relationship to God with regard to human beings was much as it had been before. However, he would soon find that the holy Ba'al Shem Tov felt quite different from the way he did about the simple Jews of the towns and villages.

The following story probably occurred in the year 1753 (5513) or 1755 (5515), for both the Maggid of Mezritch and the Maggid of Polonoye were present. My Rebbe, the sixth Lubavitcher Rebbe, Yosef Yitzhak Schneersohn, is the source for this story, which was preserved in his family for six generations. I give it over here much as he originally told it.

IT IS THE pashute Yidden *(the simple Jews) who excel in pure and uncomplicated faith, reciting* tehillim; *gathering in the shul to hear public lectures; and meeting one another in true joy, love, and fellowship—these people are the delight of Eden! The holy ones take pride in them.*

Our holy teacher, the Ba'al Shem Tov, loved these unassuming, God-respecting people and often kept company with them. Everyone knew how he felt about them, and it was a major factor in the great popular success he achieved in a very short time.

The idea of the *pashute Yid* or the simple Jew is often misunderstood. The *pashute Yid* is not an unlettered peasant or an unsophisticated person, but a Jew who has a simple, heart-centered approach to Judaism, unclouded by complex questions of theology and the minutiae of *halakhah*.[14] The *pashute Yid* simply *does* or *does not* with holy simplicity based on the light he or she is given.

When I think of American Jews today, I would say that there are a large number of *pashute Yidden* among them. They may be in business or college professors, brilliant people in their own fields, but the way in which they approach their Judaism is uncomplicated and simple. These people often have a difficult time because many synagogues and temples are not very accommodating to their open-heartedness and desire for a simple connection to God. There are always a few of them in every congregation, and often they feel trapped by the limited mind-set of the people around them—people who gossip or engage in congregational politics, rabbis who don't approach the liturgy as holy, busybody boards who constantly fuss about the budget or who stifle the creativity of the rabbi. The *pashute Yid* is not afraid of what will be preached about and does not care to control the spiritual life of the community, just to participate in it. *Pashute Yidden* are not afraid to get down on their knees and cry out to God for their needs, but neither are they forgetful of the needs of others in the community. To be a *pashute Yid* is to be spiritually rooted in a simple Jewish ethic.

MANY STORIES TELL *of the Ba'al Shem Tov's love for the* pashute Yidden.[15] *However, among his most brilliant disciples, there were those who had difficulty accepting his attitude. For the disciples, it was difficult to reproduce the same kind of intimacy the Ba'al Shem Tov had with some of the simple folk. Often, the Ba'al Shem Tov would send one of these disciples to learn a virtue like trust in divine providence, uncomplicated faith, or obedience from these people. Yet, it was very difficult for the disciples to structure these virtues of the simple folk into their own being.*

A story of the virtues of *pashute Yidden* comes to mind . . .

> Once, Reb Shneur Zalman of Liadi requested that one of his Hasidim give a certain amount of money that was needed for *tzedakah* (charity), and the Hasid brought him a little bag filled with coins. When Reb Shneur Zalman opened up the bag, he found that all the coins were shiny and bright—they had all been polished! It turned out that when the wife of the Hasid had learned of the Rebbe's request, she said, "If you're going to give the coins to the Rebbe, I will give the *shining!*" So she polished every coin. Reb Shneur Zalman was amazed at her virtue.

ONE SHABBAT IN the summertime, something happened that amazed and upset the ḥevraya kaddisha *(the holy fellowship)* of the Ba'al Shem Tov's disciples. Many guests had arrived for the Shabbat. It was the custom of the Ba'al Shem Tov that all guests could join him at the first and the last meals of the Shabbat, but everyone knew that the second meal was celebrated only with his close disciples. To this meal no one else was admitted. The majority of the guests were simple people who made their living from business, innkeeping, farming, handicrafts, tailoring, shoemaking, fruit and vegetable gardening, cattle and poultry raising, or from trading at fairs and markets; leading very full lives already, they had no more time to become experts in spiritual study and practice but still attended to holiness at every opportunity.

At this Friday night meal, the Ba'al Shem Tov simply beamed love and friendship to these people, the salt of the Earth. He gave the remains of his Kiddush *(sanctification)* wine to one and poured some wine into his own special cup and served it to another so that he might recite the Kiddush over it! To some he gave a piece of his ha-motzi *(bread over which he had made the blessing)*, and to others he gave some of the fish from his own plate! All of these intimacies and many more he showed to them. And these acts amazed and confounded the members of the holy fellowship, the close disciples.

Now, when the time of the second meal approached, the simple folk were aware that the second meal was a special meal for the Ba'al Shem Tov and his intimate disciples, and they went off to recite the holy words of the tehillim. They entered the beit midrash, and without anyone arranging it in a formal way, they each began to recite the tehillim.

Everything had its own order and system with the Ba'al Shem Tov, and the disciples sat down in the usual order. During the meal, the Ba'al Shem Tov gave a teaching, and the disciples soaked in divine bliss listening to it. They then sang many niggunim at the table, and when the disciples saw how delighted the Ba'al Shem Tov was, they too became filled with a holy naḥat *(enjoyment)*! Then, reflecting on this deep inner joy and the great privilege of being counted among the close disciples of the Ba'al Shem Tov, some of the disciples thought about how much better this holy intimacy of the second meal was when compared to the Shabbat evening meal, when all the unlearned simple folk were present. Why did the Ba'al Shem Tov favor these common people who were unable to understand all of the intricacies of his teachings? Why did he favor them with such great intimacies? His own wine in their cups! His own cup to drink from!

So preoccupied were they with their own thoughts that they did not notice how the visage of the Ba'al Shem Tov became clouded with a great earnestness, and out of great absorption he began to speak . . .

" 'Heartening, comforting words: it shall be well, well with the far and the near' (Isa. 57:19). Our Sages say that 'the perfectly righteous cannot reach and attain to the level on which the repentant stand.' "[16] He then explained that there were two ways of serving: the way of the tzaddikim (the righteous) and the way of the ba'alei teshuvah (the returning). The simple folk, due to their humility and their particular role in the world, walk the way of the ba'alei teshuvah. They partake of deep remorse over the past, and they firmly resolve to live a good life in the future.

The Ba'al Shem Tov stopped speaking, and his disciples meditated on their master's holy words while they chanted the melody of a well-known niggun. It was clear to all of them that their holy mentor had read their secret thoughts and had given them this discourse for that very reason. He had just explained the way of worship and service of simple people, and shown why it is so exalted—it partakes of and reaches the level of the penitent, a rung that many of the holiest are not able to attain.

Thus the Ba'al Shem Tov remained in deveikut (divine absorption) during the singing. When they had concluded the niggun, he opened his eyes and looked long and intently at each of his holy disciples, requesting them to place their hands upon the shoulder of their neighbors so that their intertwined hands might form a circle. The Ba'al Shem Tov sat at the head of the table and waited to place his holy hands on the shoulders of the disciples nearest to him. For in doing this he would complete the circle.

He then commanded them to sing a niggun and to keep their eyes closed, and not to open their eyes until he told them to do so. At this point, the Ba'al Shem Tov placed his hands on the shoulders of the disciples sitting next to him.

Suddenly, the disciples heard a delightfully tender and longing sound, a melody of great yearning intermingled with suppliant weeping—enough to shake a person's soul to the foundations. One voice was chanting and pouring out his soul, "Ribbono shel Olam, Master of the World! 'The words of Adonai are pure words, silver purged in an earthen crucible, refined sevenfold!'" (Ps. 12:7). Another was singing, "Ribbono shel Olam! 'Probe me, Adonai, and try me, test my heart and mind!' " (Ps. 26:2). Another was singing out, "Tatte hatziger! 'Have mercy on me, O God, have mercy on me, for I seek refuge in You, I seek refuge in the shadow of Your wings, until danger passes!' " (Ps. 57:2). Another cried out, "Oy! gevalt, zisser foter in himmel, Mercy, sweet heavenly Parent! 'God will arise, enemies shall be scattered, foes shall flee before God!' " (Ps. 68:2). Another was crying out, "Ty'erer tatte, precious Papa! 'Even the sparrow has found a home, and the swallow a nest for herself and her young, near Your altar, O God of hosts, my Sovereign and my God!' " (Ps. 84:4). And another pouring forth supplications, "Lieber foter, derbaramdiger tatte! Dear Father, compassionate Papa! 'Turn again, O God, our helper, revoke Your displeasure with us!' " (Ps. 85:5).

The holy fellowship, hearing the sound of this singing, flowing with the words of the tehillim, were deeply shaken. Though their eyes were closed, hot tears forced themselves through their eyelids, and their hearts were torn and shattered from the song of this supplication. Each and every one of the holy fellowship hoped fervently that the blessed name would help each of them to be worthy to worship on that level!

The Ba'al Shem Tov then raised his hands from the shoulders of those disciples who sat to his right and left, thus blocking their ears from hearing more of the song of lovely longing, the outpouring of the tehillim. Then the Ba'al Shem Tov told them to open their eyes, and they continued to sing those niggunim that he suggested.

The Maggid of Mezritch, in telling of this incident to his Hasid Shneur Zalman of Liadi said, "At that moment, when I heard the song and supplication through the words of the tehillim, that outpouring of the soul, an immense longing of delightful love, to which I myself had not yet attained—the slippers on my feet were wet from perspiration and tears, and an inner teshuvah welled up from the depths of my heart."

When the Ba'al Shem Tov concluded his singing and all of the holy fellowship were silent, the Ba'al Shem Tov remained in deveikut for a long time. Then he opened his eyes and said, "The song you just heard was the song of the simple people reciting the tehillim out of the elemental depths of their hearts and pure faith. Now, my beloved disciples, saints of the most high, look and see. Are we not merely on the edge of truth,[17] *for the body is not the truth—only the soul is truth. How much more so the blessed Holy One, who is the truth's truth, how much more does that One recognize the sincerity of the simple people, and their chanting of the tehillim!"*[18]

There is another story in which the holy Ba'al Shem Tov used this method of inducing shared telepathic experience by making a holy circuit with his disciples . . .

Once a disciple asked the Ba'al Shem Tov, "How are we to understand your teaching that says, Whatever a person puts their mind on, that is what they really are? Is this really so?" It happened to be *Shabbat,* and the Ba'al Shem Tov said, "Let us take a 'journey.' " He motioned for the small group of disciples to come near and they made a circle, laying their hands on one another's shoulders. When the Ba'al Shem Tov's hands came to rest on the disciples next to him, they all immediately found themselves looking in on the *Shabbat* of a proud-looking man in a beautiful *shtreimel* and *kappote* eating a splendid Shabbat dinner. But even as they looked at him, they saw that his face began to change, taking on a distinctly bovine appearance as he ravaged the meat in front of him! Then the vision shifted. They were now looking in on the Shabbat dinner of a poor man who didn't even have decent clothes for *Shabbat* and who was eating just a simple piece of hallah. But when his face began to change, it was pure fire!

It seems that the holy Ba'al Shem Tov could access what Sufis call the *alam al-mythal,* or the world of the imagination (in Hebrew, *olam ha-mashal*) at will. This is not a world of pure imagination, but a place where worlds or realities meet and coalesce.

———————

WHEN SHNEUR ZALMAN *of Liadi, the Alter Rebbe, told this to his grandson Menachem Mendel, called the Tzemah Tzedek, he further related that his teacher, the Maggid, had said that for a long time he had been in great grief over having thought with disdain of his master and had done many things to make amends. But he was unable to quiet himself for having permitted himself to think in this manner about his teacher regarding the simple folk. Then, one night, he saw a sublime vision. However, the Alter Rebbe did not tell the Tzemah Tzedek at the time what the Maggid had seen. This he revealed only a few weeks before his own death. He then continued to tell the story as he had heard it, "As I returned," said the Maggid to the Alter Rebbe, "through the Mansions of Gan Eden (the Garden of Eden), I passed through one of the mansions where the schoolchildren sat and studied the Humash (the five books of Moses), and Moshe Rabbeinu sat at the head of the class teaching the children.*

"All the children who were in that mansion studied the parsha Lekh Lekha. One of the children recited in a loud voice, 'Avraham threw himself on his face and laughed, as he said to himself, "Can a child be born to a man a hundred years old, or can Sarah bear a child at ninety?" ' (Gen. 17:17). Moshe Rabbeinu explained to the children that all the interpretations are true,[19] and yet the simple meaning of the sentence remains in force.[20] 'If one asks how is it possible that Avraham should have doubt concerning God's promise, you should know that this comes from the body, for even the most holy body is made of flesh.' It was then," the Alter Rebbe told the Tzemah Tzedek, "when my master and teacher heard that, due to inhabiting a body, such thoughts come as if of themselves, he found peace over having thought this after his master."

———————

Do you remember what the Ba'al Shem Tov said after his shared experience with the disciples? "[T]he body is not the truth—only the soul is truth." It is almost as if he were whispering a message to the Maggid.

NEEDLESS TO SAY *that from that time on until now, things have changed. Through the grace of the Most High God, through generations of our parents and masters, may their souls rest in the most high recesses and their merit protect us, the way was paved and made wider in which there occurred the development of the* Torat ha-Ḥasidut *(the teaching of Hasidism) and* darkei ha-Ḥasidut *(the ways of Hasidism). In our days, when minds have become smaller and hearts depressed and there is less intellection, understanding, and profundity, there is less effort in the service of the heart—*davenen*—and in the correction of impulses.*

Yet, pure faith and this beloved simplicity are still with us due to the grace of the Most High God and due to the merit of our mothers and fathers and our teachers, the saints of blessed memory; they are with us even now and with great strength, with a vital inner life, manifesting themselves in the observance of the mitzvot *and the acquisition of virtue.*[21]

This powerful *ma'aseh* is the perfect illustration of the teaching of the Ba'al Shem Tov called "The Heart Afire" (given in Chapter 2), and the two may be studied together to further enhance one's understanding of each.

A BEAR IN THE FOREST

Now we come to the accession of the Maggid to the throne of Hasidism. In many sources, this subject is treated fairly casually, as if it were obvious that the Maggid would succeed the Ba'al Shem Tov as the leader of the emerging movement, as if there were a clear and simple passing of the torch. But nothing could be further from the truth. It may have been obvious to some that the Maggid should succeed the master, but to many others it was far from obvious and was even considered a mistake. Of course, no one could deny that the Maggid was a giant among men, but to many in the Hasidic movement he seemed only a giant among giants. As to a clear passing of the torch from the Ba'al Shem Tov to the Maggid . . . it didn't happen. The Ba'al Shem Tov made no clear and public declaration of who should succeed him, though, as we shall see, he did hint and work behind the scenes.

To create a more complete picture of how this transition came about, we have brought together a number of sources to create a single narrative that we hope will answer these questions: How was the Maggid chosen? Who were the other candidates? What does it mean to talk about *the* successor of the Ba'al Shem Tov?

ON EREV SHABBAT ha-Gadol, *the eve of the Great* Shabbat *before Pesaḥ, in the spring of 1760 (5520), the Ba'al Shem Tov sat down to write his last will and testament, saying, "This I have written today because it was revealed to me last night by my master that this is to be the last* erev Shabbat ha-Gadol *that I will see in this lifetime."*²²

Then on erev Shavuot *the holy Ba'al Shem Tov called his personal scribe, Tzvi Hirsh, and dictated an amendment to this will: "My books and manuscripts are to be given to my disciple and colleague, that Tall Tree and Prince of Torah, Rabbi Dov Baer, the son of Rabbi Avraham, except those books in Yiddish, which belong to my God-fearing daughter, Adel. The commentaries of Gersonides on the TANAK, and the book* Neveh Shalom, *both containing my own marginal notes, are to be given to my disciple, who is as a son to me, the Pillar of Fire, Rabbi Ya'akov Yosef HaKohen."*²³

The will of the Ba'al Shem Tov referred to here does not name a successor, but it does speak of how that successor should be treated, as well as how the Hasidim should treat one another. The Ba'al Shem Tov wrote, "my successor is not to settle in Mezhbizh;" and then said, "treat him with even greater respect than you have shown me, for I know who will succeed me, and he is great even among the holy." He then spoke of the trouble to come for the Hasidim and the Hasidic movement but told them not to be troubled in their hearts, for the way of Hasidism is a true way. Then he added, "Above all, for God's sake, do not provoke others, and let peace reign among you!"²⁴

The amendment written the day before his death is more suggestive of whom the Ba'al Shem Tov regarded as his true successor. For it is impossible not to read significance into the fact that he gives the majority of his library and manuscripts to Dov Baer, the Maggid of Mezritch. In some ways, it would almost have made more sense to leave these to Reb Ya'akov Yosef of Polonoye, who would go on to write the first great works on the Ba'al Shem Tov's Torah. Nevertheless, he leaves these books and manuscripts to the Maggid, who would write nothing in his lifetime, giving Reb Ya'akov Yosef two specific works with his own annotations instead.

Another small detail of the amendment that may be significant has to do with the way Reb Dov Baer and Reb Ya'akov Yosef are referred to; both are called disciples, but Reb Dov Baer is called "colleague," whereas Reb Ya'akov Yosef is called "son." Of course, this can be read in favor of either Dov Baer or Ya'akov Yosef, but the Ba'al Shem Tov may be putting the Maggid on a par with himself to ease the transition. Likewise, he may be consoling Reb Ya'akov Yosef, letting him know how much he loves him by calling him "son."

This interpretation is supported by a tradition regarding the Maggid and a letter purported to be from the Ba'al Shem Tov to Reb Ya'akov Yosef. Once when the Maggid was set to depart from Mezhbizh, the Ba'al Shem Tov blessed him. Then the master lowered his head to be blessed by the Maggid. The Maggid hesitated, but the Ba'al Shem Tov took the Maggid's hands and placed them upon his head himself.[25] Even more straightforward is a letter (from the summer of 1759) to Reb Ya'akov Yosef in which the Ba'al Shem Tov says, "my place will be occupied by my holy disciple, the Prince of Torah, Rabbi Baer," but he adds with solemnity, "this is to remain hidden and concealed."[26] For this reason, I tend to see the reference to Ya'akov Yosef's being a "son" as consoling, knowing that he would hear the Ba'al Shem Tov's will read aloud, and it would be to him as a testimony of information that had been confided to him alone.

THE NEXT MORNING, *the holy Ba'al Shem Tov passed away with his disciples at his side. His will had not explicitly named a successor. Though his disciples mourned him deeply, they were also keenly aware that their movement was threatened by mitnagdim (opponents) on all sides, so they began to take counsel in smaller and larger groups among themselves as to who would succeed the master. Though there were many great Hasidim among them, three names continually floated to the surface in these conversations.[27]*

The first name mentioned was Rabbi Ya'akov Yosef of Polonoye, who was considered by many to be the foremost student of the Ba'al Shem Tov and the greatest exponent of his teachings. It was remembered by many that the holy Ba'al Shem had once said, "The blessed One will thank me that I have found for the blessed name a Yossele (Ya'akov Yosef) such as this!" and "If I would have nothing but this Yossele, it would be sufficient," and moreover, "All Ya'akov Yosef's works are pleasing to the creator, praised be the blessed name, and all his doings are in the name of God."[28]

As we have seen, Reb Ya'akov Yosef of Polonoye may already have known at this point that the Maggid would be the successor, and there is some sugges-tion that he may have felt slighted by this.[29] This is also pointed to as one rea-son he could not be the leader of the Hasidic movement—he had a temper, which is attested to in a number of tales.[30] But there is another reason that is far more significant. Reb Ya'akov Yosef was by temperament a *rav.*

In every Hasidic court there is a *rav* who is the *dayyan* or "judge" of the community, deciding what is halakhically appropriate and what is not. In the Ba'al Shem Tov's court, the *rav* was the Polonoyer. For him this wasn't mere-ly a function, but an expression of his very being. He saw himself as the judge of behavior for his community. Therefore, he wasn't a pastoral personality, looking compassionately on individual differences. This was the great differ-ence between he and the Maggid. For the Maggid, as we shall see, honored the individual differences of his disciples in such a beautiful way that each was allowed to fulfill their greatest potential, popularizing the movement and ensuring its survival through a difficult period. Likewise, the Polonoyer was a great scholar, but not an educator like the Maggid; he didn't want to have to bring the message down a level or lift the student up to it either. But the Maggid was continually talking about how to condense the message, to bring it down to a manageable size for his listeners.

Nevertheless, it would be a travesty against the Polonoyer if we were to see him only in the light of what disqualified him from the leadership of the movement. For he was a giant of the age, a passionate and holy *tzaddik,* whose *teshuvah* and holy tears were even more powerful than his wrath. It was the Ba'al Shem Tov who had first broken his heart open and shown him the error in the heavy judgments he had put upon himself and others. He was contin-ually occupied with his own *teshuvah,* opening himself to giving and receiving love as a balm for the excesses of temper in his youth. As he grew older he inspired great love and awe in others, especially Reb Pinhas of Koretz and a young Barukh of Mezhbizh, whom he befriended, and who were witnesses to his awesome *deveikut* (adherence to God) and occasions when his entire being seemed to be aflame before the Holy One.[31]

It is also fairly certain that had he indeed become the leader of the move-ment, he would not have made his most lasting contribution to it—his writings. The first and most important of his works, the *Toldot Ya'akov Yosef* published in 1780, is the first classic of Hasidism, and the work that garnered the most respect for the new movement in the eyes of the Jewish world. He followed this with *Ben Porat Yosef* in 1781, *Tzafnat Paneah* in 1782, and a posthumous volume, *Ketonet Passim* in 1866. These works, filled with origi-nal content, are also among the best sources of the Ba'al Shem Tov's teach-ings. In *Toldot Ya'akov Yosef* alone, he says a total of 249 times, "I heard from my master." It is thought by many that the Ba'al Shem Tov we know today would be far more mysterious and ephemeral if it were not for the teachings and information given in the works of Reb Ya'akov Yosef. Rabbi Aryeh Kaplan has suggested that it may have been providence that he did not become the leader of the movement, leaving him with "the time and leisure to produce the lasting works for which he is renowned."[32] It is out of respect for this work that we call him the Ba'al ha-Toldot, "Master of Results," after his classic text.[33]

OTHERS DEBATED WHETHER *it would be Dov Baer, the Maggid of Mezritch, or Pinhas of Koretz. Here they were on surer ground, as the Ba'al Shem Tov had actually made oblique indications that these two were his successors. For after the Ba'al Shem Tov had taken ill, his disciple David of Ostrog had asked him, "To whom should I travel when you are no longer with us, my master?" The Ba'al Shem Tov had answered him, "There is a bear in the forest and Pinhas is a sage."*[34]

We have discussed this tradition in Chapter 5 (*"Etrogim* for the Heirs of the Ba'al Shem Tov") on the Koretzer, but we should mention that Reb Pinhas did not think of himself as a candidate for this office. However, he was not necessarily a supporter of the Maggid either. He was very vocal in his belief that Reb Ya'akov Yosef of Polonoye should succeed the Ba'al Shem Tov. He was known to have said, "Even in the days of the sages who composed the Mishnah there was never such a mind as his."[35] He also held Reb Nahman of Horodenka in great esteem.[36] But this again was largely a matter of temperament.

Nevertheless, the Ba'al Shem Tov clearly expressed his appreciation for Reb Pinhas as a leader and teacher in this anecdote as well as others. Rabbi David of Ostrog, mentioned here, was also known to have asked the Ba'al Shem Tov's opinion "regarding all the noted figures of his generation," and Reb Pinhas seems to have been numbered "among the first four."[37] But the question, "To whom should I travel when you are no longer with us, my master?" *clever as it is,* is not the same question as, "Who will be your successor as the leader of the Hasidic movement?"

OF COURSE, NONE *of them put themselves forward as potential successors. What was most clear to all of the disciples was that the holy Ba'al Shem Tov had no intention of making an explicit declaration before he died, thus leaving the decision entirely up to the holy fellowship. Therefore, as one body they declared Rabbi Tzvi Hirsh, the son of the Ba'al Shem Tov,[38] to be the interim leader for the period of one year while other disciples took over various organizational functions. And this is how it was for an entire year.*

Even though the Ba'al Shem Tov appears to have made it known to Reb Ya'akov Yosef of Polonoye who his successor would be, this was a private communication and not meant to be revealed to anyone else. It was important to the Ba'al Shem Tov personally, and for the health of the movement also, not to seem to impose his will or unduly influence the process of who was chosen, even if many may have desired him to do so. This would only undermine the holistic integrity of the holy fellowship. More important, if he had, it may have seemed to many as if the Ba'al Shem Tov were *choosing* a successor, which he was not, at least not as he saw it. The fact that he seems to have *known* who it would be was not the result of choosing, but the recognition of who had been chosen by the heavenly assembly. The proof of this, which he clearly understood, was that he seems to have known ahead of time without making it known in any way that would influence the process on this side of the grave.

Although Reb Tzvi Hirsh (1730–ca. 1780) was made the interim leader, it is unlikely that he was ever a true candidate for the permanent leadership of the movement. There are some stories that have characterized him as a simpleton, but when one looks over the entire spectrum of stories regarding him, there is little reason to suppose this was true. These rumors and stories were probably started because Reb Tzvi was a very humble and introverted person and lived a quiet life outside of the more ecstatic Hasidic milieu. It seems he was not suited to be a *neshamah klalit* (general soul)—that is, a Rebbe—or a great Torah commentator, but that does not suggest in any way that he was not intelligent. After all, as we shall see, he was capable of delivering a discourse before the disciples of the Ba'al Shem Tov. Moreover, he was shown respect by the great *tzaddikim* among the Ba'al Shem Tov's disciples (as we saw in "A *Kvittel* and Two Letters" in Chapter 4). Even so, there is a letter (accepted as authentic by ḤaBaD Hasidim) written by the Ba'al Shem Tov to Reb Tzvi Hirsh two years before his passing in which he actually dissuades his son from seeking leadership of any kind: "for Heaven's sake, do not occupy yourself with *rabbanut* (leadership). Instead, you should pursue business, and in this you will thrive and succeed. Remember what I have told you; ever since that bitter day on which I was revealed, I have cried daily over my lot."[39] After his brief role in the succession, he seems to have taken his father's advice and retired to a quiet life in the house of his father-in-law in Pinsk, where he is buried.[40]

ON SHAVUOT 1761 (5521), *the disciples of the Ba'al Shem Tov gathered for the first yahrzeit of the master. On the second day of Shavuot, Rabbi Tzvi Hirsh sat in the place of honor among the holy fellowship and delivered a discourse* (ma'amar) *to them. After he had concluded the discourse, he arose and addressed a personal message to the hevra* (fellowship): *"Today my holy father appeared to me and said, 'The* Shekhinah *(the Divine Presence), and the accord of the* Pamalya Shelmala *(the heavenly assembly) that once dwelt with me have now passed on to Rabbi Baerenyu. Therefore, my son, pass on the leadership to him in the presence of the holy fellowship, and let him sit in my place, my son, while you go to sit in his.'" Then Rabbi Tzvi Hirsh walked over to the seat of Dov Baer, the Maggid of Mezritch, and removed his father's white* bekeshe (caftan), *asked the Maggid to stand, and placed the* bekeshe *upon him with a blessing for success.*[41]

The Maggid moved solemnly to the head of the table, looked out at the holy fellowship and delivered his first ma'amar *to them.*[42] *He discoursed on the* Ma'aseh Merkavah *(work of the chariot), on the verse from Yehezkel that says, "As for the appearance and structure of the wheels, they gleamed like beryl. All four had the same form; the appearance and structure of each was as of two wheels cutting through each other" (Ezek. 1:16).*[43]

It is important to understand the Maggid's silent acceptance at this moment. There is a funny story (probably a joke) told of how Sigmund Freud was once visited by a famous Reform rabbi from the United States that may help us with this . . .

A famous American rabbi had to come to Vienna for a rabbis' convention, and he figured, "As long as I am in Vienna, I might as well visit Dr. Freud." He went to see him at 22 Bergstrasse, where Freud lived, and they had a nice conversation. As the rabbi was about to leave, he said, "Dr. Freud, I want you to know I think everything that you have been teaching is really wonderful, but I have to say, the things about sexuality, 'slips,' and what you teach about the 'unconscious,' I can't quite accept." So Freud said to him, "Tell me, *Herr Rabbiner*, who do you think are the three greatest living Jews today?" The rabbi answered, "Einstein, You,

and Marx." And Freud says, "And how about yourself?" To which
he responded, "Oh no, no, no, no!" Then Freud said, "One 'no'
would have been sufficient."

You see there is something beautiful in the Maggid's silent acceptance. There
is no false modesty or hidden motive in it; he simply *is* a leader. He receives
the *bekeshe* and we don't hear him say, "Oh no, no, no, no!" He recognizes that
this is now his task to take on, and he is resigned to his fate. Can you understand what kind of responsibility it is to take over the leadership of a movement at its most critical hour? At the same time, we must appreciate Reb Tzvi
Hirsh's humility in yielding the leadership to Reb Dov Baer. For this reason
the fifth Lubavitcher Rebbe, Shalom Dov Baer of Lubavitch, speaks appreciatively of him, saying, "To act as Rabbi Tzvi did required great strength, for we
know that various sages of the past who in the beginning did not wish to
accept high offices, later found them difficult to relinquish once they had
accepted them." Reb Tzvi was truly humble and obedient to the will of his
father (even after his death) and thus he literally *divested* himself of the leadership and *invested* it in the Maggid of Mezritch by giving him the *bekeshe*.
This was the time-honored tradition of assuming leadership, "investiture"—
one is dressed (invested) in the garments (vestments) of the former owner.

Thus Reb Dov Baer became the new leader of the Hasidic movement. After
this, people no longer traveled to Mezhbizh but to Mezritch where the Maggid
set up his seat. As the Toldot, Reb Ya'akov Yosef of Polonoye is famous for
saying, "What can we do? When the holy Ba'al Shem Tov passed away, the
Shekhinah packed her bags and moved from Mezhbizh to Mezritch and we
must bow our heads in submission."

Succession is a complicated issue because people always want to say, "Who
is going to be *the* successor?" But this is the wrong question. The real question for a Hasid is, Who are the heirs, and with which of them is my *shoresh
ha-neshamah*? With which of them is "the root of my soul"? The truth is that
there were many heirs of the Ba'al Shem Tov, many disciples who became
Rebbes quietly doing their work in little towns throughout the region. Some
of these Rebbes were not even disciples in the precise sense but colleagues,
like Yitzhak of Drohobitch and Nahman of Horodenka, who were participating in the same *Zeitgeist* as the Ba'al Shem Tov. You see, a movement is
always far more diverse and complex than the later history paints it. The
Maggid's success has eclipsed most of the accounts of these other Rebbes, but
it has not lessened their impact as a whole. For although the Maggid was
training generals, these other Rebbes were training the army.

The important thing about being a Rebbe is to have a notion about whether the *talmid* (disciple) has their *shoresh ha-neshamah* with you. There have been some people who have asked me to serve them as Rebbe, and I have had to say, "No, I don't have your *shoresh ha-neshamah*." This is essential when you are dealing with someone who wants to work on a deeper level. There were people whose *shoresh ha-neshamah* drew them to the Maggid, but there were others who were drawn to Reb Pinhas of Koretz and to Reb Mikeleh of Zlotchov, and from them came other great Rebbes who were not of the Maggid's line. How else can one explain Rafael of Bershad (d. ca. 1825), Meshullam Feibush of Zbarazh (d. ca. 1795), Barukh of Mezhbizh (1753–1811), and Nahman of Bratzlav (1772–1810)? Thus the real issue of succession in regard to the Maggid of Mezritch had to do with the leadership of the movement at a vulnerable point in its development, not with his being the *one* true heir.

TRADITION TELLS US *that once, in the last year of his life (Hoshana Rabbah 5520), the Ba'al Shem Tov told a group of his youngest Hasidim that he would not survive the year, and that they should seek a new master. Hearing this, they suggested the name of a certain disciple to the Ba'al Shem Tov. He did not answer them directly but suggested, "Seek him out and ask him to show you the means to rid yourselves of the issue of pride. If he suggests a means of doing so, you will know then that he is not the one whom you seek. But if he says instead, "May God help you, for it is with God," then attach yourself to him."*[44]

Later, a group of these younger disciples approached the Maggid and asked him, "How can we rid ourselves of pride?"

The Maggid answered them, "Pride belongs to our blessed creator, as it is written, 'Y-H-V-H is sovereign and robed in grandeur (gey'ut, which may also mean "pride")' (Ps. 93:1).[45] *Thus there is no permanent way to uproot pride within us and we must struggle with it all of our lives, even until the last handful of earth is cast upon the grave!"*[46]

This is a wonderful teaching and it takes us back to the last moments of the Ba'al Shem Tov, when he says, "Let not the foot of pride overtake me."[47] Even in his last moments he was worried that pride might attempt to coopt his *kavanah* while he was dying! But it is also important with regard to our discussion of the succession, for while the leadership of the movement may have been settled decisively on the Maggid, that does not mean that the majority of the disciples moved on to Mezritch along with the *Shekhinah*. In fact, "only a handful of them accepted him as their leader."[48] The rest moved on to become Rebbes of small congregations and visited the Maggid only rarely, if at all.[49]

This handful of disciples is important, for they were probably the very disciples to whom the Ba'al Shem Tov said, "Seek him out and ask him to show you the means to rid yourselves of the issue of pride." As we have seen, the Maggid was the person who answered the question correctly for them, so we might ask now, "Who were the disciples?" We are told here that they are among the youngest disciples of the Ba'al Shem Tov, so it becomes clear that these disciples are probably Menachem Mendel of Horodok (later Vitebsk, 1730–1788) and Nahum of Chernobyl (1730–1798).[50] In a way, these Hasidim are unfinished; they have tasted the magic of the Ba'al Shem Tov but their own spiritual formation is not yet complete.

A NEW HOLY FELLOWSHIP

How did the Maggid look at his task?

The Maggid is now the leader of the Hasidic movement at a critical point in its evolution—there are clouds on the horizon: There would be persecution of his Hasidim in their communities and betrayal by other Jews to the authorities, and a clash with the Ga'on of Vilna, Eliyahu ben Shlomo Zalman (1720–1797) seemed inevitable. What is he to do? The Ba'al Shem Tov was a natural, a genius who took from the wellsprings of life to create a living organism called *Hasidut*. But the Maggid is a different kind of person dealing with a different phase in the life cycle of the Ba'al Shem Tov's creation. He has to find a way to make it grow and reproduce. He has to find a way to multiply this one seed, the essence of the Ba'al Shem.

The Ba'al Shem Tov's teachings were being brought together and prepared by the Ba'al ha-Toldot, Reb Ya'akov Yosef of Polonoye. So it was not the literary task that was left to the Maggid, but the task of cultivating this new life form, the Rebbe–Hasid relationship. This relationship was not about hierarchy or subservience, but about the hot-housing of spiritual transformation in Hasidim and the creation of *tzaddikim*. Thus the Maggid was actively seeking *talmidim* (students of the highest potential). People were mysteriously attracted to the Ba'al Shem Tov, and as far as we know, he courted only two specific disciples, Reb Ya'akov Yosef of Polonoye and the Maggid of Mezritch. While many would also be attracted to the Maggid, just as many were pursued by him, as we see in the following story . . .

ONE DAY, THE *Maggid called his* shaliaḥ *(his trusted emissary), Reb Ahron of Karlin, one of the first and greatest of his Hasidim, and said to him, "Arele, in Amdur is a* lamdan *(a great learner) named Hayyim Heikel. He should dwell among us. How you achieve that, I will leave up to you."*

Now Ahron was revered among the Hasidim and known for his tremendous charisma and quick mind. So soon after arriving in Amdur and after asking around about a young learner named Hayyim Heikel, he proceeded to the beit midrash, *where he saw a serious and ascetic-looking young man studying apart from the others. Instinctively, he sidled up to the table where the young man was studying and said, "What are you doing?"*

The young man, who was startled for a moment and then annoyed by such a pedestrian question, growled back, "Studying."

"Studying?" Reb Ahron said, "What are you studying?"

"Torah lishmah (for its own sake)!" he shot back, dismissively.

"Ah!" said Ahron, taking a more serious tone now and rocking back and forth slightly. "The Mishnah teaches in the name of Rabbi Meir that the mysteries of the Torah are revealed to those who pursue Torah lishmah.*"⁵¹*

Then Reb Ahron looked directly at the young man, who was obviously caught off guard by Reb Ahron's changed tone and words, and asked, "And have you experienced these mysteries yet?"

The young man thought for a moment about what Reb Ahron had asked, and how he had asked it . . . "experienced these mysteries." Then he said quietly, "No." He then added, as if to himself, "What am I to do?"

Ahron answered, "There is only one thing to do; find someone who has experienced these mysteries."

*In this way, Hayyim Heikel of Amdur came to the Maggid of Mezritch.*⁵²

It is said that Reb Hayyim Heikel of Amdur had been a disciple of the Ga'on of Vilna, as had other disciples of the Maggid like Yisra'el and Azrael of Polotzk, who actually tried to convince the Ga'on to visit and better acquaint himself with the Maggid before passing judgment. They were unsuccessful in this attempt, but it was a coup even to have acquired such learned *talmidim* from the stock of the Ga'on. The Maggid was collecting talent from near and far to become the next generation of Hasidic Rebbes, but also to shore up the defenses of the movement against charges of heterodoxy. It would not be so easy to accuse brilliant halakhists like Menachem Mendel of Vitebsk and Shneur Zalman of Liadi, who may have been on par with the Ga'on himself.

Some of his gifted disciples, like Reb Ahron of Karlin, were put in the service of the movement fairly quickly. Such was also the case with Reb Shmuel Shmelke and his brother Reb Pinhas, who were talmudic scholars of great distinction.

THE BROTHERS SHMELKE and Pinhas came to the Maggid and learned quickly, pouring over all the Maggid's teaching, soaking it up as though through their very skin. Within a very short time, the Maggid called them to his study and gave them directions as to where they should go next, and they departed soon after. Then some of the disciples approached the Maggid and asked, "Where have the brothers gone?" But what they really wanted to ask was, "Why have you given these brothers your endorsement so quickly?" Hearing their unspoken question, the Maggid answered, "The brothers Shmelke and Pinhas came to me like a store full of candles; all I needed to do was light one, and in no time, the entire store was on fire."

In other words, the preparation was already there for Reb Shmelke and Reb Pinhas. Before coming to the Rebbe, there were many disciples who had already done a great deal of inner work (like the Maggid before coming to the Ba'al Shem Tov), thus all that was necessary was to create a spark. It was a similar situation with the brothers Elimelekh of Lizhensk and Zushya of Anipol. Of course, there is always more work to be done, and Reb Shmelke and Reb Pinhas continued to return to Mezritch to deepen their understanding. Nevertheless, in this anecdote it was obvious to the Maggid that they were ready to begin their work right away. Later, they would each come to serve in very influential positions that helped to stabilize Hasidism in particular regions.

The Maggid's search for learned Hasidim was also practical; *Yiddishkeit* in eastern Europe was still in an impoverished state, and he needed to send his Hasidim out as missionaries to different communities who needed help. The following story is an illustration of this . . .

ONCE, REB AHRON of Karlin was about to depart on a short errand to a neighboring town when the Maggid took him aside and said, "Take along your Shabbat clothes." As it was early in the week and only a short errand, Ahron wondered at this, but did as he was instructed. After he arrived in that town, he found that the people had been exchanging spouses for years without proper divorces! Thus his errand was extended for a week so that he could facilitate and administer the necessary divorces and marriages according to halakhah!

The Maggid's every word and movement was of importance to the Hasidim, and they treasured every encounter with him, for he was often out of their presence. He usually did his *davenen* in a little room off of the shul by himself; his health (as well his temperament) required that he have ample time to himself to rest and recuperate.

ONCE, WHILE THE Maggid was resting and making his aliyat ha-neshamah *(ascent of the soul)* before Shabbat, several blocks away in the beit midrash Reb Ahron of Karlin was reciting Shir ha-Shirim *(the Song of Songs)*. Then, one of the disciples of the Maggid came into the beit midrash and said to Reb Ahron, "Reb Arele, the Rebbe says that he cannot sleep because you are reciting Shir ha-Shirim." Reb Ahron and the other disciples were amazed because his recitation hadn't risen above a whisper, but apparently in Heaven he had been loud, and because of this the Maggid couldn't sleep!

Can you imagine the power of a disciple who could say Shir ha-Shirim in such a way, and yet, the Maggid's sleep was even more important? Sadly, Reb Ahron would pass on before his master, the Maggid, and there is an important teaching story connected with this event . . .

ONE DAY, REB Ahron of Karlin was planning to depart from Mezritch and came to say good-bye to the Rebbe. The Rebbe looked at him tenderly, gave him a berakhah, and said, "Go in peace."

But before Reb Ahron could depart, the Rebbe told the other disciples, "Don't allow him to leave; don't let him go."

So just as Reb Ahron was about to depart, one of the Hasidim whispered to him, "Don't go, don't go; I don't think the Rebbe wants you to go." Hearing this, Reb Ahron went back to the Maggid's study to see if he was needed. But the Maggid only spoke to him as he had before.

In all, this happened three times, and finally Reb Ahron departed Mezritch. Not long after, he died.

So the talmidim came to the Maggid and said, "If you knew he was going to die, why didn't you say so, Rebbe?"

The Maggid answered, "Let me tell you something; it is written of Moshe that he was an eved ne'aman (a true servant of God). When someone is a servant, a secretary, they are to keep secrets, and a good servant keeps the master's secrets. In this case, I knew what I had seen, but I wasn't allowed to talk about it. So I did my best for my Arele."

This is difficult teaching, and one that occurs again and again in Hasidism. There are some divine judgments that cannot be annulled, and so the *tzaddik* attempts to "sweeten" or subvert them indirectly, as we see here. Nevertheless, it rarely works when a *tzaddik* like Reb Ahron is being called to his forebears on high.[53]

THE MAGGID'S *TISH* AND THE TRANSPARENCY OF THE TEACHER

As the Maggid's reputation grew, many rabbis and potential disciples desired to attend his now legendary *Shabbat tish* or table. Some came out of holy longing, some out of curiosity, and some came as if paying homage to a local potentate. Undoubtedly, it was a mixture of motives for many, but they all came. The Maggid's *tish* was one of the great wonders of eastern Europe, and it set a pattern in Hasidism that can still be seen to this day.

One Hasidic story tells of a legendary teacher who visited the Maggid's *tish*, someone who might potentially have become one of the Maggid's great *talmidim* but who somehow left untouched by the experience. His name was Rabbi Ya'akov Wolf Krantz, the Maggid of Dubno (d. 1804), and he was the most famous *maggid* of that period (apart from our own Maggid) and called by Moses Mendelssohn "The Jewish Aesop."

THE MAGGID OF Dubno had already come to the Vilna Ga'on and received great praise for his wonderful mashalim (creative parables) when he decided to visit the Maggid of Mezritch. He knew of course that the Maggid of Mezritch had been a famous maggid in his youth, so he especially hoped to impress him and gathered together all of his best material for his trip to Mezritch.

After the Dubno Maggid arrived, it was clear to the Maggid of Mezritch that this one was not going to become a Hasid, so he invited him to be a special guest at his tish *to communicate a point to his disciples. Now, the Maggid's* tish *had a very special form and structure, but he made an exception on this occasion for his honored guest to speak to the assembled Hasidim. So the Dubno Maggid began to weave his great tales, telling his classic of the bull's-eye and many others. All the while, the Maggid of Mezritch was nodding appreciatively with gentle indulgence, but his disciples were disturbed, whispering to one another while trying to seem attentive, "What's going on here?" In the end, the Dubno Maggid talked through most of the* tish. *He left the following Sunday, satisfied that he had impressed the Maggid of Mezritch and his disciples but unaware of the fact that he hadn't taken in or learned anything from his time in Mezritch. After he was gone, one of the holy fellowship said, "If only he could have stopped talking, he could have learned so much."*

The Maggid used this occasion to instruct his disciples through the example of the Dubno Maggid. The purpose was not to make the Dubno Maggid look like a buffoon, for he was truly gifted, and his illustrations brilliant. Nevertheless, by contrasting the teaching of the two *maggidim*, the Maggid of Mezritch and the Dubno Maggid, it became painfully apparent to the Hasidim that something was missing in the Dubno Maggid's sermon. Now they were certain that it was not the Rebbe's brilliance that had attracted them, for that was available that *Shabbat* from the Dubno Maggid, but the quality of the sacred, as communicated through one who is in touch with the source of holiness. When that is available, *wherever it is available,* one must keep quiet and strain one's ears to hear the message that wants to be communicated.

But the Dubno Maggid was not the only gifted individual to come to Mezritch and to leave without becoming a disciple. Often when you hear a *ma'aseh* told by Hasidim about their Rebbe, you can smell the hagiography a mile away. "Oy! the Rebbe, the exalted, amazing leader of our generation!" You can expect to hear them say amazing things, but it is hardly impartial. Thus we have chosen to include an eyewitness account of the Maggid and his Hasidim that comes from an outsider who, in the end, was not disposed to staying in Mezritch but who went on to become one of the great Jewish philosophers of the time. His name was Salomon Maimon (1753–1800).

Shlomo ben Yehoshua Heiman had been born in a small Lithuanian village near Mir and was given a traditional Jewish education. By the age of 11, according to his own account, the precocious boy was functioning as a rabbi in his village and supporting himself and his child-bride through teaching. But his true love he discovered was science and philosophy, especially as presented in Maimonides' *Guide for the Perplexed*. Eventually, in kinship with the great Jewish philosopher, he took the name "Maimon." Ever questing in search of greater knowledge and understanding, Maimon came into contact with a young disciple of the Maggid of Mezritch and what he called "the New Hasidism." This encounter, as we shall see, eventually led him to seek "membership" in this "secret sect." The following is drawn from Salomon Maimon's *Lebensgeschichte*, his autobiography.

I WAS UNABLE to form an accurate conception of the new sect and was unsure of what to think of it until I encountered a young man who had already been initiated into the society (Gesellschaft) and who had even enjoyed the good fortune of conversing with its superiors (Obern). This young man happened to be traveling through the place where I was living, and so I seized the opportunity to ask him about the internal structure of the society, the means of admission, etc.

It turned out that the young man was still at the lowest level of membership, and therefore knew little about the internal structure of the society. Thus he was unable to give me any real information on the subject; but as far as the means of admission were concerned, he assured me that it was the simplest thing in the world. Any person who felt a desire to perfect themselves and did not know how, or who wished to remove the obstacles to their doing so, had only to apply to the superiors of the society, and eo ipso (by that very act), they became a member (Mitglied).

It was not even required—as it is when applying to become a medical doctor— to say anything to the superiors about one's moral weakness and one's previous life, in that nothing was unknown to the superiors; they could see into the human heart and discern everything concealed in its innermost recesses; they could also foretell the future and bring near things that are far away. Their sermons and moral teachings were not, as these things usually are, considered and arranged in an orderly fashion beforehand. This method is appropriate only for people who regard themselves as existing and working apart from God. But the superiors of this sect hold that their teachings are divine and, therefore, infallible, but only when they are the result of self-annihilation (Selbstvernichtung) before God—that is, when the sermons are suggested to them ex tempore (extemporaneously) by the immediacy of circumstances, without their contributing anything themselves.

This is actually a fairly good description of how the Maggid of Mezritch approached teaching. The Maggid understood what it meant to be *m'zamtzem* (transparent to the divine will), and it was a firm principle with him that his teaching was never to be prepared beforehand but to proceed only from the moment, as it were. He believed that if he could get out of his own way, if he could remove the obstacle of the self, the divine will would make itself known.

I'll tell you a story about this teaching from my own life.

After I graduated from Yeshiva Tomhei T'mimim in Crown Heights, Brooklyn, my second job was as a congregational rabbi in Fall River, Massachusetts, for a small Orthodox shul. I was still pretty green then, and most of the time I was just trying to find my way with my congregation. One day, I got a call from the local Conservative rabbi in Fall River; it turned out that he had to be away for *Shabbat* and needed someone to "pinch hit" for him at their temple.

I said, "I'll have to get back to you."

I first called the people at my shul to make certain it was alright with them. Then I called Hayyim Lieberman, the Lubavitcher Rebbe's secretary, to clear it with the Rebbe (Yosef Yitzhak Schneersohn). My people from the shul called me back and said, "We consider it an honor that you are being called to speak there; you can go with our blessing." It turned out that their children were Conservative people, so they all planned to come to the temple Friday night as well! After this, the Rebbe's secretary called me back and said, "The Rebbe says, 'You can accept the invitation, but make sure that there will be some change [in the service].' The nature of the change we leave to you; you know the local situation and you will decide what you need to make different so that it will be clear that you are not Conservative. . . . And he also says, 'Do not prepare your sermon.' "

My stomach dropped and I hung up the phone. At that time I had it in my head that a Conservative congregation was full of college professors while all the simple *Yiddelakh* would *daven* in shul. I thought I could handle college professors, but without preparing? I wasn't so sure.

The whole week I was not preparing, but just in case—with those college professors there grading me—I was setting up a whole teaching in the back of my mind about predestination and freedom of choice, considering how the RaMBaM and the RaLBaG talk about it. With all those professors, I needed to be able to give them a learned sermon. But, God forbid, I wasn't preparing!

Come Friday night, the congregation agreed that there would be no organ, so that fulfilled the first of the Rebbe's requirements. Now, the choir was singing, and I was sitting there in the rabbi's chair in my Hasidic outfit, in my *kappote* and my Homburg hat, and the president was about to introduce me. I began to look around at the congregation, and I see these are just the people of Fall River. They were the same *Yiddelakh* that I saw at all the meetings of the United Jewish Appeal: Mr. Greenbaum the druggist and Mr. Abramson the barber! If I was to unload the RaMBaM and the RaLBaG on them, it would be a disaster! So as the president is introducing me I realize for the first time that I really don't have a sermon prepared! I'm standing at the pulpit without a sermon! Then, all of a sudden it hits me—"If someone were standing at Mount Sinai with a stop watch as the people received the Torah, how long would it have taken? It was probably just a few moments, but think of what impact those few moments had!" So out of that came an entire sermon about "moments of eternity in time." The quality moments that are available to us and how coming to shul on Friday night is our opportunity to reconnect with those eternal moments that give us values and direction. It simply came from the moment!

CAPTIVATED BY HIS *description, I begged the young man to give me an example of some of these divine teachings. He put his hand on his brow as if he were waiting for inspiration from the Holy Spirit and turned to me with a solemn expression. He moved his arms, which were half bared, somewhat in the manner of Corporal Trim,54 when he was reading the sermon* (Predigt). *Then he began:*

" 'Sing unto Y-H-V-H a new song, His praises in the congregation of the faithful' (Ps. 149:1). Our superiors explain this verse in the following way. The attributes of God, the most perfect being, surpass by far the attributes of every finite being, and thus 'His praises,' as the expression of His attributes, must likewise surpass the praise of any finite being. Until now, the praises of God consisted in ascribing to Him supernatural acts, such as the revealing of what is concealed, the foreseeing of the future, and the immediate manifestation of effects by His mere will. Now, the saints, our superiors, are able to perform these supernatural acts themselves, and thus God no longer has preeminence over them in this respect; therefore, it is necessary to find some 'new' praises, which are specific to God alone."

In the time of the Ba'al Shem Tov, hardly a disciple was not witness to one or another miracle of special insight, foreknowledge of events, manifestations of the Divine Presence, or the transcending of temporal or spatial boundaries. Thus they naturally came to see that if a person was capable of being the channel for these divine gifts, their praises of God must be elevated even higher! Once, Reb Shneur Zalman was asked about the miracles that occurred in Mezritch and he replied, "Miracles were so abundant in Mezritch that they fell upon the floor and rolled under the benches . . . but who would bother to pick them up when the Rebbe was alive and present in our midst?"

I WAS ENCHANTED by this ingenious method of interpreting the Holy Scripture, so I begged the young man for yet another example. He then continued in his inspired manner:

" 'As the musician played, the hand of the Y-H-V-H came upon him' (2 Kings 3:15). This is explained as follows. As long as one is actively aware of the self, one is incapable of receiving the influx of the Holy Spirit; thus one must be passive like an instrument in a self-effaced state. Therefore, the meaning of the passage is that when the musician (ham'naggeyn) becomes like the instrument (k'naggeyn), then the spirit of God comes upon him."

This is based on a wonderful passage in 2 Kings in which Elisha the Prophet is invited by the kings of Judah and Yisra'el to come and prophesy before they go out to fight with the king of Syria. Because, before you wage war, you need an oracle, you need to hear from a prophet how it is going to go. So Elisha the Prophet comes up alongside the kings and says, "I can't do prophesy cold; bring me a musician and let him make some music and then I will give you the prophecy." They send for a musician to give him a raising up of the *neshamah*, the soul. The musician comes, and it is written *vay'hi k'naggeyn ham'naggeyn vat'hi 'alav yad-Y-H-V-H*, "It was as the musician was playing, the spirit of God rested upon him" and he came through with a prophecy. Thus the Maggid of Mezritch teaches, "If one feels oneself as selfless as the violin, as an instrument in the hand of a great player, then the spirit dwells upon one."

Maimon wrote in a note that this interpretation is based on the fact that in Hebrew "*naggeyn*" may stand for "to play" as well as for a musical instrument, and that the prefixed letter "*kaf*" may be translated "as," in the sense of "when" or in the sense of "like." Then he added, "The superiors of this sect pull (literally, "rip") passages out of their context in the Holy Scripture—regarding them as mere vehicles of their teachings—selecting them according to a predetermined interpretation of the passage which suits their principle of self-annihilation before God."

"NOW," THE YOUNG man said, "listen to this interpretation of a passage from the Mishnah, which says, 'The honor of your friend should be as dear to you as your own.'[55] *Our teachers explain this in the following way: It is certain that no one will find pleasure in honoring themselves, for this would be ridiculous. But it would be*

just as ridiculous to make too much of honor received from another, as these honors add no more intrinsic worth to us than we already possess! Therefore, this passage simply means that 'The honor of your friend,' that is to say, the honor that your friend shows you, 'must be of as little value to you as the honor that you show yourself.' "

This last teaching finds a close parallel in the following story of the Maggid's disciple, Reb Shmelke of Nikolsburg . . .

When Reb Shmelke, whom we discussed earlier, first arrived in Nikolsburg to assume the post of chief rabbi, the Jewish community decided to hold a reception for him. But even though the people had already gathered, Reb Shmelke remained in his study while they waited. After a while, his disciple Reb Moshe Leib of Sassov heard a discussion going on inside and quietly approached the door of the study to listen, for he knew that his master was alone. From inside, he heard Reb Shmelke muttering to himself; so he put his eye up to the keyhole to have a look. There was Reb Shmelke walking up and down the room saying, "Welcome, Reb Shmelke! How do you do, Reb Shmelke? Reb Shmelke, we are so glad to have you here in Nikolsburg!" Finally, he says, "*Bah!* Enough!" He opens the door and says to Reb Moshe Leib, "Alright, let's go to the reception." As they walk, Reb Moshe Leib says to him, "Rebbe, what were you doing in your study?" Reb Shmelke answers him, "The Mishnah says, 'The honor of your friend should be as dear to you as your own.' This means, the honor that you get from other people should have the same taste as the honor that you give to yourself. Knowing that I was going to have all of these nice things said about me, I went through the whole ordeal in my study beforehand until finally I was sick of it."

I WAS ASTONISHED by the exquisite beauty of these thoughts and enchanted by the ingenious interpretations that supported them.

My imagination was stretched wide by what I heard from this young man and I now wanted nothing more than to have the pleasure of becoming a member of this honorable society. Thus I resolved to journey to M—— where the superior, B—— was living. I waited impatiently for the completion of my period of service, which lasted several weeks. But as soon as this was fulfilled, I started my pilgrimage at

once, not even bothering to go home (though I was only two miles away). The jour-
ney lasted some weeks.

In the period when Maimon wrote his autobiography, it was considered indis-
creet to mention names, even though it was clear that "M——" meant
"Mezritch," and "B——" meant "Baer," as in Dov Baer. The context and the
descriptions make it an undisputed conclusion that Maimon had come to visit
Rabbi Dov Baer, the Maggid of Mezritch and leader of the Hasidic movement.

FINALLY I ARRIVED in M——, and after I had rested from my journey, I went to the
house of the superior with the notion that I would be introduced to him at once. I
was told, however, that he could not speak to me at that time, but I was welcome
to attend his table on the Sabbath along with the others who had come, and then
I would have the pleasure of seeing the holy man face to face and of hearing his sub-
lime teachings from his own mouth. I was also told that even though this would be
a public audience, the individual references I would find made to myself by the supe-
rior would allow me to regard it as a private interview.

When the Sabbath came, I went to the solemn meal and found there a great
gathering of respectable men from far and wide. After a while, the great man
appeared, awe-inspiring and clothed wholly in white satin. Even his slippers and
snuffbox were white, this being the color symbolizing grace among the kabbalists.
He greeted every newcomer his shalom and we sat down to table. During the meal,
silence reigned. When the meal was over, the superior began a solemn but stirring
melody. Afterward, he put his hand on his brow for some time and then began to
call out, "Z—— of H——, M—— of R——," and so on. Every newcomer was
called by his own name and the name of his dwelling place, which caused great
astonishment.

Here we find the Maggid eating in solemn silence, for the Rebbe at a *tish* is
also doing his intentions (*kavanot*). Rarely does the Rebbe spell these intentions out to anyone and may even attempt to hide them. At the Bluzhover
Rebbe's *tish*, it was said that Reb Arele Roth was always close by watching his
Rebbe. Reb Tzvi Elimelekh of Bluzhov (1841–1924) was the Rebbe of Reb
Arele Roth (1894–1947), a Hungarian Hasid who later became a great Rebbe
himself in Hungary and Jerusalem. The Bluzhover Rebbe was always very
kind to Reb Arele at the *tish*, but the other Bluzhover Hasidim were from
Galicia and didn't much care for Hungarians and wanted to know, "Why is

the Rebbe so into that *Hungarisher bokher* (young Hungarian, i.e., Reb Arele)?" So the Rebbe said, "You all sit at the *tish* and watch me, but my Arele is the only one who notices my *kavanah* when I lift the spoon."

Some people can lose focus at the *tish* because there is a certain amount of relaxation when you sing and when the Rebbe tells a story, and sometimes they miss these moments and forget the liturgical ritual that is occurring at the table. In the time of the Second Temple, there were societies whose members would eat all their meals as if they were consuming sacrificial meat. It was called eating *al-tahrat ha-kodesh*, a meal eaten as if it were a sacrificial one, with the same sacred intention and detail. The Rabbis have said, "*Shulkhan domeh l'mizbe'ah*" (the table is like an altar).

This was very clear the first time I attended Reb Shlomo of Bobov's *tish*. I was in awe simply watching the solemn beauty with which he approached the table where the 12 hallot were arrayed. Next to him, he had containers full of myrtle leaves, and I could almost imagine him incensing the altar with them. The way he would make the *Kiddush,* the way in which the hallah was cut in seven big slices and distributed was all a reenactment of what happened around that altar. There was an awesome sense of ritual at the Bobover *tish*. I recall sitting at his table considering how I as a *kohen* (priest) would eat a portion of the sacrifice to help a sinner atone if I were serving in the Temple. With what intention would I consume that portion?

The mentioning of the names at the Maggid's *tish* also reminds me of the Bobover Rebbe. At his gatherings, whenever we gave beer or wine at the table and my name was mentioned, it was always "Zalman Zholkiever," because that is the town in Poland where I was born. You can just imagine hearing this today, "Richard from Oakland, Daniel Bostoner, Ruth from Jerusalem!"[56]

As he was called, each recited a verse from the Holy Scripture. Then the superior began to deliver a sermon, the foundation of which were the verses recited, so that although they were scattered verses taken from different parts of the Holy Scripture, they were combined with so much skill that they might be thought to form a cohesive whole. What was still more extraordinary was that every one of the newcomers believed that the part of the sermon that was based on his verse had some special reference to the facts of his own spiritual life! Of course, we were greatly astonished at this.

As the Maggid called each of those people by name, each one had to give him a *passuk,* a verse from Torah. Whatever verse occurred to them at that moment they were to give. All of these people were steeped in learning and probably had many favorites. Moreover, every child was given a *passuk* at the time of his bar mitzvah. Sometimes people would give these sentences and other times they might also give the sentences that were cooking in them. Based on these, the Maggid began to say a Torah.

Remember, this was not from a friendly witness, and thus it is remarkable what Maimon says (paraphrasing): "For every person who gave the Rebbe a verse, that sentence was woven seamlessly into the Torah that the Rebbe was teaching. As he gave an explanation of each verse, he also gave to each one an indication of what they needed to do in their work with God."

It was impossible for the Maggid to know beforehand what sentences the people were going to say. It wasn't that he was preparing anything. The deep teaching I get from that is that you don't come to a group that constitutes a new *group mind* and bring old Torah to it. The Maggid used to say, "*v'ha'karta v'darashta hetev*," check it out carefully on the inside. Is it for this moment? Is it for this group mind? Was it really prepared beforehand? For that is an abomination to the Maggid; one has to learn to speak without the self from the very source; there is a kind of speaking that happens in channeling, when the *Shekhinah* is using my mouth, as it were, and one has to have complete trust that the divine purpose will be served by it.

The Ba'al Shem Tov had embodied a means of catalyzing spiritual growth and intoxicating his Hasidim with a taste for deep spiritual experience, often transcending the boundaries of all that was thought possible to do so. But the Maggid had to find his own means of catalyzing growth and mediating spiritual experience for his disciples. Just as the Ba'al Shem Tov had taken him to the place of *mamash* (palpable) reality beneath the words, he had to do the same for his disciples. When the Ba'al Shem Tov showed him that numinous reality behind the words, the words made a different kind of sense afterward. If you don't feel love or are not in love, all the songs on the radio are kitsch. But if you *are* in love, they are all so true and speak directly to your condition. The words and all the concepts begin to serve the substance beneath. This is what I believe the Maggid is doing here; he is producing an enchanting awe in his *talmidim* that will catalyze their own spiritual growth, connecting them to the sacred dimension where the teaching can begin to take root.

Can you imagine the feeling this produced in the people who gave over the verses? After all, they had contributed to the Rebbe's Torah, and in the midst of his teaching he had given each of them an answer to take home and work with! Often they would work with this "answer" of the Rebbe for several years. That was their way of saying, "With this teaching of the Rebbe, I have to purify myself." Thus everybody who came to the Maggid found their own process opened up and their own situation clarified for them.

When I came to Israel for the first time, we arrived on Yud-Beit Tammuz, which was for ḤaBaD Hasidim a day for celebrating the Rebbe's freedom.⁵⁷ So instead of going to the hotel with the rest of my colleagues, I went on to Kfar Habad to celebrate. At that time, Zalman Shazar, the president of Israel (who was from a ḤaBaD family), was there celebrating as well, and we had a wonderful time. Then I hung out with some of the Hasidim at Lod, the station from which I got the train to Jerusalem to rejoin my colleagues. While on the train, I noticed three young Hasidim with a big demijohn of wine, and they were each looking intently into a different Hasidic *sefer* (book). I looked at their outfits trying to figure out what kind of Hasidim they were—it was not Belz, not Bobov—then I realized, it was Vizhnitz. But if they were Vizhnitzer Hasidim, what were they doing traveling to Jerusalem for *Shabbat,* when they should be going instead to B'nai Brak or Haifa where the Vizhnitzer Rebbes were? So I was looking at them and thinking about this when one of them said to me, "What are you puzzling about?" So I replied, "Your outfit is Vizhnitz, yes?"

"Yes," he answered.

"So why are you going to Jerusalem instead of to B'nai Brak or Haifa?" I asked.

They said, "The Rebbe has a son-in-law in Jerusalem (who became the Belzer Rebbe), and he has sent us up to keep him company for *Shabbat.*"

"So what are you doing with the *sefarim* (books)?"

They said, "We each look and find one piece of *Ḥasidishe* Torah that touches us, and at the table, he asks us to say it. Then, after all of us at the table have said our Torah, he weaves it all together into one teaching."

BEFORE LONG, I began to qualify the high opinion I had formed of this superior and the whole society. I observed that their ingenious interpretations were at bottom false and limited strictly to their own extravagant principles, especially their doctrine of self-annihilation. Once someone had learned these principles, there was nothing new for one to hear. Moreover, the so-called miracles could be explained quite naturally by means of spies and correspondence as well as by a knowledge of human nature, physiognomy, and skillful questioning. In this way, the superiors were able to elicit the secrets of the heart, and thus obtained a reputation among the simple for being inspired prophets.⁵⁸

Spoken like one the finest skeptical philosophers of his time. Maimon, who was still a very young man, would travel on to Berlin to meet Moses Mendelssohn and enter the circle of the *Haskalah* (the Jewish Enlightenment movement). In time, he would broaden his study of languages, science, and philosophy—publishing a textbook on Newtonian physics in Hebrew, a commentary on Maimonides' *Guide for the Perplexed,* a critique of Immanuel Kant's philosophy, works on logic and epistemology, and his famous autobiography.

Maimon does not dispute the Maggid's towering intellect or spectacular natural abilities, but as he points out, once one has become acquainted with some of the principles upon which the teachings of this "New Hasidism" are based, there is "nothing new for one to hear." His was a voracious critical mind, ever in search of new information. Within a few weeks in Mezritch, the young genius had probably indeed reached the threshold of new ideas and concepts, but while we might agree that there was nothing truly novel left to *hear,* it is not likely that there was nothing left to *learn.*

This of course is what we have been attempting to speak about throughout this chapter, the difference between the words and the reality, the surface and the depth. Much of this depends on how a Hasid listens, and the contemplative chewing that follows this listening. But it is not the critical mind with which the Hasid listens and contemplates. For the Hasid, that is the *mohin d'katnut,* the constricted mind, though perhaps it might be better to think of it as the limiting mind, or narrow awareness. For the critical mind is always focused on the isolation of details. But the Hasid cultivates an altogether different mind, which we call *mohin d'gadlut,* the mind of enlightenment, inclusion, or expanded awareness. It is inclusive rather than exclusive, harmonizing rather than separating, ever seeking pattern and relatedness.

When the Hasid listens to the Rebbe, it is not with the debate-oriented mind of the *yeshiva,* asking, "What is wrong with what has just been said?" Rather, the Hasid is involved in a process that is called "right-making," giving the benefit of the doubt and asking, "What is right with what has just been said? What would it take for my head to get into the place where I can understand this correctly?" Western education has taught us that we are not using our mind in the right way if we are not critical, that *mohin d'katnut* is intelligent while *mohin d'gadlut* is "airy-fairy," but this not so. Intelligence is functioning in both, the only difference is in how it is applied, whether toward separation or toward a holistic understanding. Thus we say, *punct farkehrt,* whatever it takes, meaning, "How can I tilt my mind to get the right perspective on this, to see the truth of what the Rebbe is saying?" For it is in this willingness to shift that we open ourselves up to the miraculous order.

This is how a Hasid approaches discipleship. The Rebbe may say something that sounds far-fetched or strange, but by saying, "I don't understand *yet*, but I trust that the Rebbe knows—*ruaḥ ha-kodesh* is coming through—so I must listen all the harder. Help me my God to 'awaken my heart and put my mind to this,' making it right, understanding its application for my own life!"

Of course this always raises the question of abuse, as it should, for one must be careful not to lose oneself in this process. Therefore, the Hasid can always ask, "Is the Rebbe asking me to fill out the unique dimensions of my being or to suppress them? Is the Rebbe gradually making me more independent or more dependent?" You see, it is a contract between a Rebbe and Hasid; the one says, "If you will agree to listen in this way and to do the work, then I promise that I will do the same on my end, and I will also do everything in my power to help you to become independent of me." Like a good doctor, the Rebbe's objective is to heal you and send you on your way, not to keep you just a little bit sick and hanging about the waiting room.

Thus the Hasid always tries to listen with an expanded awareness, trusting that the Rebbe is doing the same, knowing that the right-making mind sees possibilities where the critical mind does not. For possibility is precisely what the Rebbe is seeking: possibility for compassion in a world of harsh judgments and severe karma; possibility for reconciliation between the human and the divine, between the human being and the divine being within the human. The Hasid believes that the Rebbe is always seeking (on their behalf) to exploit some crack in the concreteness of reality, opening to the miraculous order, through which he or she might wiggle, opening onto unexpected vistas and new dimensions of consciousness and love of God. This is the secret of the Maggid's (and most Hasidic) Torah—the attempt to shift the frame on reality toward compassion and wholeness.

7

The Thirteenth Gate: The Great Maggid and the Voice of the *Shekhinah*

AS WE APPROACH THE TORAH OF THE MAGGID of Mezritch, we must remember to contemplate the teachings with an expanded awareness (*moḥin d'gadlut*) and a "right-making" mind-set. We have already seen in the teachings of the Ba'al Shem Tov and Pinhas of Koretz that Hasidic Torah does not often come with chapter headings or in a clear development of ideas. It is not a left-brain process. Hasidic Torah is in-sight, in-tuition, learning on the in-side and, therefore, oblique, something that leads to a surprise and an "Ah-ha!" moment. Nevertheless, the mouth is a serial instrument, allowing a person to say only one thing at a time, and so we must be aware of the Rebbe's tension throughout these teachings to convey a broad-spectrum message through the limitations of language and a serial instrument.

THE ANATOMY OF TORAH

As far as we know, the Maggid did not write down any of his Torah himself. Nevertheless, many of his *talmidim* dutifully memorized and recorded them for him. It is known that he approved of this activity and encouraged them to preserve these teachings for future generations. The collection we have trans-lated from is the *Maggid D'varav L'Ya'akov*, compiled and edited by Reb Shlomo of Lutzk (d. 1813), a disciple and relative of the Maggid's. Reb Shlomo, according to his own testimony, published these teachings with great reluctance. He felt that to commit these holy words to writing was nearly impossible, as it was difficult to convey in a serial way (as we have pointed out) what was actually being communicated by the Maggid. Even if one were to record the words faithfully, who would make the true dimensions of the teaching understood to the reader? In the end, Reb Shlomo only began to write these down at the urging of the Maggid himself, and after the Maggid's passing, he did not even think of publishing them until various corrupt versions began to circulate among the Hasidim. Seeing that it was inevitable that these teachings would reach people in one form or another, he finally resolved to publish the *Maggid D'varav L'Ya'akov* in 1781 based on reliable manuscripts from various disciples.[1]

TORAH IS LIKE the human body, having its own skin, muscle, sinews, and bone. The skin is the surface layer of Torah. The muscle is the body of Torah; "one who strains the muscles for the sake of Torah experiences the taste of flesh." The sinews and veins (giddim) are the admonitions (observances and abstinences) of the Torah.[2] Bone is the absolute inner being (etzem) and, as yet, undisclosed dimension of Torah.[3]

This is a wonderfully organic presentation of PaRDeS, the fourfold approach to interpretation of the Kabbalah. For we might look at the skin, "the surface layer," as the *peshat*, the "simple" reading of the text. The muscle of Torah may be seen as *remez*, the "hint," leading to a search for meaning by which our daily life is enhanced. And just as our muscles help us move us from place to place, so the muscle of Torah helps us derive substantial help from the text. The sinews are the *derash*, the allegorical "interpretation" that turns us away from the superficial and helps each of us live a more spiritually meaningful life. Finally, the bone is the deepest level of Torah, the *sod*, the "secret" marrow, hidden deep, and undisclosed.[4]

The Talmud says that after the destruction of the Temple, the taste that used to be in the flesh receded into the marrow of the bone.[5] So when the Maggid says that the *ta'am*, "one who strains the muscles for the sake of Torah [,] experiences the taste of flesh," this implies the taste that once was in the sacrificial meat.

Every letter of Torah has a "bone" in it—that is to say, something that cannot be assimilated easily and that will take time to reveal itself. In Hebrew, the word for "bone" is *etzem*. In the medieval period, when Jewish scholars wanted to find Hebrew words for Aristotelian concepts, they had to be creative with the existing language. If you wanted to talk about the "absolute essence" using biblical Hebrew, you had to use words that had reference to tangible life concepts. Thus for "essence" we say *muḥlat*, that which is left over after you have pressed the olives and cannot press any further. And to say something about the "absolute," you must speak of the *atzmiut*, the "bone-ness," that which is hidden within but provides the structure on which everything else hangs. In many ways these terms are interchangeable, but they help us get behind this teaching in a very direct way.

I think it is important to remember that this teaching comes from a time when western Europe was just on the cusp of the Age of Enlightenment and the Industrial Revolution. And with these will come mechanical models of the universe as well as mechanical models for Torah, like the Wellhausen Theory, in which Torah is seen as being cut and pasted together. There are of course historically valid reasons for approaching the text this way, but it treats human and divine phenomena like discrete parts manufactured in a tool-and-die shop. But however advanced mechanization might have seemed at the time, we now know it is but a crude imitation of an elegant organism within a holoarchical ecosystem. So for the Maggid to be affirming the value of an organismic model at this moment is simply wonderful.[6]

WE KNOW THAT *the Torah contains matter collected from the words of* tzaddikim *like Adam, our forebears (Avraham, Yitzhak, and Ya'akov), and Moshe, who, through their holy acts caused the* Shekhinah *(Divine Presence) to dwell in them. Such a life of holiness itself constitutes a perfect Torah, though Her absolute radiance is as yet undisclosed, as it will be until the coming of the* Mashiaḥ *when it will be made manifest. "And this is the* new *Torah which will proceed from Me . . . from My absolute innermost Being."*[7]

Here the Maggid makes a beautiful leap and the four-level teaching of the anatomy of Torah begins to take on a new dimension and meaning. For now we are told that a human life may be "a perfect Torah." Indeed, much of Torah is an account of lives, especially those of our forebears—Adam and Eve; Abraham and Sarah; Isaac and Rebecca; Jacob, Rachel, and Leah; Moses, Aaron, and Miriam. And if *their* human lives became Torah, then so might *our own;* the divine story continues in us, from the very substance of our lives, our very bodies!

Then he says, "And this is the *new* Torah which will proceed from Me."

Some people have a notion that Torah was given once at Sinai and that was it—everything else is not Torah. That is *Torah mi'Sinai*, "Torah from Sinai." But there is another idea that runs parallel to *Torah mi'Sinai* and this we call, *Torah min ha-Shamayim*, "Torah from Heaven." In other words, the Torah that God continues to send down to us. Even those who are *Torah mi'Sinai* people say, "It says, 'the voices have not yet stopped.'"[8] That is to say, the "voices" from Sinai are the background radiation that is still there, and from this we get the new Torah. Now there is a part of me that says everything was *not* there before, even as I affirm that it was there in potential. For true revelation continues to reveal, and this is true revelation. But how can I close the door on the Torah that God speaks through every vibration of existence? The Maggid seems to be allowing for this in his teaching, "And this is the *new* Torah (*Torah ḥadashah*) which will proceed from Me." In response to this verse, the sages say that a new dispensation will come with the *Mashiaḥ*, the Messiah.[9]

This is very important. You can imagine how sensitive many Jews might be on hearing that "the old Torah is abrogated and a new dispensation is coming in." After all, Christians and Muslims had said this to them as well, and the historical politics of power made this a very uncomfortable situation for Jews in many periods. The anxiety-producing word here is "abrogation." This is always the issue with renewal; "Can there be new Torah without abrogation?" So the Maggid is taking a position in between, affirming the continuity of the past, present, and future Torah, without separation or abrogation. Instead, he speaks of dimensions yet to be revealed![10]

WHEN THIS WAS *revealed to Yehezkel, he was amazed and said, "Will these bones yet live?" (Ezek. 37:3)*[11] *He was referring to the absolute inner essence of Torah within him.*

Now, connecting the beginning to the end, the Maggid reminds us of the well-known words from Ezekiel, "Will these bones yet live?" In the Maggid's context, we see that when Ezekiel learned that a *"new* Torah" and the "absolute inner essence of Torah" were within him, in his bones, as it were, he was amazed at the heretofore unknown dimensions of holiness that lay concealed and dormant within him. My Rebbe, Yosef Yitzhak Schneersohn, the sixth Lubavitcher Rebbe, often spoke of the need for the absolute hiddenness of the soul to become manifest. This "absolute hiddenness," of course, is the "bone." We must not forget that there are bones there. You can feel them inside of yourself, but often we forget what is under our skin. We must live with an awareness of what is beneath the skin if we are to lead healthy lives. Our muscles, inner organs, and bones cannot be neglected simply because they are not visible on the surface; in time the neglect of them will destroy the overall health of the body, and this is the Maggid's point.

SHORT SENTENCES, SHORT PRAYERS

In Chapter 6, "A Bear in the Forest," we spoke of how the Maggid of Mezritch was a true educator, always seeking to accommodate the student. The following teaching is a perfect illustration of that point.

"ONE SHOULD ALWAYS teach one's students in short sentences."
"He would pray a short prayer."[12]

When a teacher wishes to impart knowledge to his or her disciples and the disciples are unable to understand the teaching, then the teacher must make a tzimtzum, *condensing and contracting the ideas into words and letters that the student may readily grasp. One must do this in the same way as one would pour something from one vessel into another using a funnel to keep from spilling the liquid. In the funnel, the liquid becomes condensed and can thus enter into the second vessel without spilling. So it must be with the mind of the teacher, condensing the idea into words and letters communicable to the pupil. In this way, the pupil may be able to accept the vastness of the teacher's mind.*

If the teacher wants to make sure that the pupil will get the teaching, they have to pack it up in such a way that the pupil can receive it and unwrap it. So it is with every great insight or experience that we have; unless we make a *tzimtzum* (contraction) and funnel it down, it will not become anchored in our memory and our consciousness. Therefore, we have to go over it again and again, each time finding new ways to package the information that will allow us to access it whenever it is needed. This is connected with what we have said in Chapter 5 in "The Words of a Sage" regarding the indifferent teaching of the soul.

THE GLORY REVEALED TO THE WORLD

Now the Maggid moves from the human pedagogy of our last teaching to a divine pedagogy of the same pattern, wherein God, the Teacher, wishes to reveal and make divinity known to human beings and thus "must condense and contract" the overwhelming and all-pervasive divine radiance.

"MAY THE GLORY of God be revealed to the world;
God will rejoice in Creation" (Ps. 104:31).[13]

THE RADIANCE OF the blessed and Holy One is far greater than the worlds can bear. Thus the blessed One scales the radiance down through many tzimtzumim (contractions and condensations), until finally, we are able to bear it.

We are taught that "God will rejoice in creation," for God wishes to rejoice in this holy work like parents rejoice in their little child. When that child takes up a stick to use as a make-believe horse, it is as if the child leads the "horse," while in reality, it is the way of the horse to lead the human being. Still, the child derives a great pleasure from this play. So it is with the tzaddikim, for they wish to conduct the world, and thus the Holy One creates worlds for the tzaddikim so that they may derive delight through guiding them.

Here the Maggid uses his favorite analogy, that of the relationship between the parent and the child, especially as it parallels the relationship between God and the *tzaddikim*, the righteous ones. This is a relationship characterized by joy and indulgence. Joy in that the *tzaddikim* derive great pleasure from "conducting" the world, as a symphony conductor does with the baton— and seeing this, God also rejoices. And yet, it is also an indulgence on God's part, which is made clear by this analogy. For here we have a parent looking on and playing along as their child pretends to ride a horse. Now, a real horse would carry the burden, but in this situation, the child is riding the imaginary horse while also doing the horse's work. The implication by analogy is that that *tzaddikim* play at conducting the world while an indulgent God looks on. However, in divine actuality, there is no world to guide, only the imagination applied to an agreeable substrate, the "stick" that receives the "horse" projection of the imagination. Like the parent who plays along—though on another scale beyond reckoning—God's willing participation in the play of guiding the world makes the entire drama possible.

NOW THE GLORY *of the absolute being we are unable to attain. All that we may attain is the glory invested in the worlds. It is for this reason that God made a tzimtzum, contracting and condensing the Divine Self into these worlds, to derive pleasure from the delight of the tzaddikim who rejoice in them. This is the meaning of "God fulfills the will of those who respect God" (Ps. 145:19).*[14] *For God as* Ain Sof *(Infinite Nothing) is without "will" as we understand it. Therefore, everything done in this world is done by the will of the tzaddikim who respect God. As the sages have said, "With the Sovereign in council they sat."*[15] *With whom did the Sovereign (God) take counsel? With the souls of the tzaddikim.*[16]

There is so much packed into this little paragraph that we cannot avoid taking some time to look at it in depth. In the Kabbalah, God is spoken of as *Ain Sof,* "without limits" or "infinite nothing." *Ain Sof* is not the personal God of popular tradition but rather the *impersonal* or *suprapersonal* Godhead. Thus the Maggid tells us, "everything done in this world is done by the will of the *tzaddikim* who respect God" and not by the will of *Ain Sof,* which is without will. But then we must ask, "How did the world ever come into existence if God had no will with which to create a world?" To answer that, I have to make use of another famous *mashal* of the Maggid.

One day, a highly respected Torah scholar was expecting a visitor who was likewise a person of great distinction and dignity. But just before the visitor was anticipated to arrive, the child of the Torah scholar coaxed his father into a short play session. While they were yet playing, the distinguished visitor arrived to see the respected Torah scholar on his hands and knees, playing horse with the child on his back! Shocked at this ignominious display, he said, "How can you, a person of such dignity, degrade yourself like this playing on the floor with a child!"

The Torah scholar replied, "He wanted it."

"So," the visitor said, "children always want one thing or another; it doesn't mean we should give it to them."

Then the Torah scholar said softly, "No, you don't understand. He wanted it so badly, and asked with such joy and exuberance, that I began to want it too; you see, his will created a will in me."

So too, the will of the righteous to conduct the world created a will in *Ain Sof* where there was no will; thus "everything done in this world is done by the will of the *tzaddikim*." But how did God take counsel with the souls of the *tzaddikim* before they were even created? This question is better dealt with in the next teaching ("Ya'akov's Inheritance"), so it must suffice for now to say that God consulted with the primordial idea of the righteous in all their *potential*.

Now let's take a look at where we get hung up here. Often it is on the idea of the *tzaddikim*. To some, the will of the *tzaddikim* and their wish to conduct the world tends to sound elitist and ego driven. This is important to deal with now, because the notion of the *tzaddik* becomes very important to Hasidism from here on out.

First we must remember to see the reality beneath the word "*tzaddikim*," to remember that this is just another word for "the righteous" of the world. It is not some in-group above and beyond the rest of us. For at any given moment on the planet, who are the righteous of the world? Is it not those who are participating in righteousness at that moment? That is what we are talking about here, *the will directed toward righteousness in any given moment*. Those who participate in that "aggregate will" are the righteous for whom God created the world. We might also ask ourselves the most basic questions, "If *you* were God, in the activity of what group of people would *you* rejoice? Would *you* take pleasure in those who desire to hurt and harm others, creating separation? Or would you rather enjoy those who are compassionate and who desire to create harmony wherever they can? Think about which group of people would 'create a will' in *you* to make a world?"

Still we might wonder, "How can a desire to 'conduct the world' *not* be ego driven?" The simple answer is, "It cannot." By definition, as we have seen with regard to the *Ain Sof*, the one who is without ego is also without desire. But the concatenation that makes up the human persona is a bundle of competing desires; and as we saw with the Ba'al Shem Tov and the Maggid around the issue of pride and the impulses of the body, there are some desires that refuse to be quieted, even though we may choose not to engage or react to them.[7] It is this very struggle with competing desires—most being unhelpful or unhealthy—that prompts the *tzaddikim* to wish to conduct the world, to lead the "horse" of the body, rather than to be led by it!

That is not to say that there are not egoless moments, or even people who have more of them strung together than others (creating a kind of egoless continuity). But consider what an egoless moment really is in a practical situation.

Say you are happy in your current situation. You like your job, the time you get to spend with your children is good and well balanced with the time you get to spend on your own, and you are finally feeling a little contentment. Then, one day, you come home and your spouse tells you, "Honey, I think I want to go back to school and pursue my master's degree." In a half second, your stomach lurches, and your mind unleashes a tumult of thoughts, mostly having to do with the disturbance to your comfortable life. And right behind them are a host of "good reasons" for this not being a good time for going back to school. But somewhere amid the tumult, you hear a voice that says, "This is not about *you;* the person you love is trying to tell you about what they need." Somehow, you manage to take a breath, and then ask, "What are you going to need from me to do that?"

That is an egoless moment in practice, transcending one's own desires for the need of another. These are the moments and opportunities that we face every day—not running into a burning house or diving into the lake to save someone's life at the risk of our own. Nevertheless, you see, even if we do manage to transcend the ego, it is in the context of a world of needs and desires. Thus the desire to conduct the world—whether driven by not wanting to be led by unhealthy desires or selflessly motivated by the need or the desire of others—cannot escape the world of the ego. Not all ego is negative: ego is a good manager and can mind the store well enough; it just shouldn't get to thinking that it is the owner. The owner has to say what the rules are and determine what is good for the store. Thus when the store of the world, at varying levels, is run well, the *tzaddikim* are able to derive delight from guiding it.

So we see that the desire to conduct the world is unavoidably ego driven; thus the real questions are, "What motivates the desire to conduct the world?" and "What kind of ego is driving it?" For if the *tzaddikim* desire it, and, by definition, the *tzaddikim* are actually righteous, then there is no real problem with this desire. For who else would you want to conduct the world? The real problem we have with this is based on our all too frequent experience of those who merely pose as righteous to acquire power or those who are corrupted by the possession of power. This is not what the Maggid is talking about right now. In a later teaching ("Houses Bigger Than Synagogues"), we will see how he deals with the needs and necessary requirements of those who must lead in God's name, and how strict they must be with themselves.

Ya'akov's Inheritance

Here the Maggid explores the great "why's" of creation: Why did God create the world? Why did God create human beings? What is the purpose of creation? What is our purpose in the world?

"A LIMITLESS INHERITANCE was given unto Ya'akov."[18]

In the beginning, there arose in the divine will a desire for tzaddikim, and God derived great pleasure from their primeval presence. Thus the world of pleasure was created even before there was a creation, because the delight came solely from the primeval will as it desired tzaddikim and Yisra'el. However, because God wanted them to exist fully, and not simply in the primeval will, God drew forth the attribute of ayin (nothingness). For if this world was to have its own existence, and if God's great love and delight were to be drawn into this world, then the attribute of nothingness had to be created.

At first glance, this would seem to contradict what was said in the previous teaching about the *Ain Sof* not having a will, but if we remember the *mashal* of the child creating a will in the parent, things begin to make sense again. The Maggid is constantly trying to get at the source of sources, beyond time and space, where all things exist in *potentia,* including the *tzaddikim*. There, in the primordial pool of infinite possibility, the *tzaddikim* sought and discovered God; and with their discovery, God discovered delight, and thus the "world of pleasure" was created *before* creation.

Why should God be delighted by this above all other possibilities?

It is because God is an atheist; God does not have a God or the joy of discovery. God is the knowing, the knower, and the known. Nevertheless, in the divine play, Divinity may pull the wool over its own eyes and play the part of the *tzaddikim,* who are ignorant of the true dimensions of their own divine nature. When these *tzaddikim* in time discover God within themselves, as we saw with Ezekiel (in "The Anatomy of Torah"), the joy and surprise is immense as God finally looks upon God, as if for the first time! Thus it was the primeval idea of this joy, this delight that created the world of pleasure, which in turn created a divine will, or desire for the complete realization of *tzaddikim* and a world for them to inhabit! In the *tzaddikim,* the divine parent gives birth to children worthy of the parent, because they are capable of discovering their true nature, and this gives the parent joy.

But how is this all to come about?

As we have heard already, God's radiance filled all space, as it were, God being the *All-In-All*. Thus the divine light had to be scaled down so that the world would be able to bear it. "God drew forth the attribute of *ayin* (nothingness). For if this world was to have its own existence, and if God's great love and delight were to be drawn into this world, then the attribute of nothingness had to be created." In other words, it was necessary for God to create an obscuration of the divine reality that permeates and penetrates all, a concealing nothingness to make a separation, as it were, between us and God, thereby allowing us to exist. Thus the divine radiance contracted in on itself and withdrew, as it were, from a space within itself, creating a void that was, in a manner of speaking, *not-God*. There, in the seeming absence of God, the worlds were created and the *tzaddikim* play as if they guide the world.

This is such a deep teaching in so many ways, and the paradoxes are such that we might even call them *poignant*. Imagine the kind of deal that God made with the souls of the *tzaddikim*. The *tzaddikim* are consciously willing to play the game of falling into ignorance and discovering God within. But what happens after the game has begun? God has drawn forth the nothingness so that the *tzaddikim* may exist "fully" (and not simply in the primeval will), but a kind of amnesia now reigns in a portion of God where our consciousness will reside. It is as if 10 minutes before the Big Bang, God was dwelling on the idea of *tzaddikim* and then said, "Let's do it." Then God must go away from that delight for millions of years until human beings begin to come to consciousness; and when they finally do begin to achieve a primitive reflexive awareness, they do all manner of terrible things to each other, creating more separation in their selfishness. And all because they have no idea who they really are!

But the truth is the truth; to consummate a desire, you must go away from it in a sense before it can be consummated. If I love spending time with my family, simply enjoying one another, I have to go away from them and work in order to spend time with them later. It is a paradox in which the means seem to take you away from the end. Often we can't appreciate something from up close. When I look at a mountain from afar, it is so awe inspiring that I just want to get closer, but when I am finally on the mountain, it is more difficult to appreciate its majesty because I can't see it as I did before. It is this same paradox that exists between us and God.

Now the Maggid goes on to discuss the curtain of nothingness that has been drawn between the human and the divine and how this serves to help create the delight of which we have already spoken.

THE ATTRIBUTE OF *nothingness is the axial or universal joint of all paradox and opposing things. For each thing comes from another, like the chicken from the egg. When the nothing enters the thing, then the thing loses existence in the face of the Ain Sof. When it gains its existence again, it turns into something else. Thus we see that the nothing separates and yet joins the beginning of the thought to the end of the action. All has to pass through the Gate of Nothingness; it is for this reason that this "drawing down" is called the* pleroma, *and "limitless heritage,"*[19] *because it is so close to the nothing. This can be observed palpably in the fact that a parent loves their younger child more joyfully than their older child. This is because the younger child is closer in proximity to the delight that one had at the time of intercourse during which they were conceived. In the same way, the delight of God in* tzaddikim *is so much closer to the celestial will, for they partake of the nothing through which all further influence came. Therefore, the nothing is exalted and called the "inheritance without end." All this is quite profound and needs to be carefully understood.*

"All this is quite profound and needs to be carefully understood" is a fantastic understatement; this passage is nothing less than a verbal Möbius strip, without inside or outside, beginning or end. The Gate of Nothingness, as the Maggid describes it here, is a kind of black hole or singularity, a dimensionless point of infinite gravity—in other words, a physical paradox of the greatest and smallest "proportions." The closer one gets to its event horizon, the more one is sheered by the force of its gravitational pull. The Gate of Nothingness is the point at which the opposition of all opposites is canceled, the door through which all somethings become nothing. It is the screen between God and us, God and not-God, an obfuscating cloud through which we cannot pass without losing our individual existence.

The key to this Möbius strip is given when the Maggid says, "Thus we see that the nothing separates and yet joins the beginning of the thought to the end of the action." This points to what we have already discussed several times: the primeval idea (of *tzaddikim* who are able to discover divinity in themselves) and its consummation (when they actually discover the God within, canceling out their own existence). This, the *tzaddikim* do again and again through every means possible, continually returning to the nothing from which they were born, to the primeval pool in which their unique souls were conceived. Therefore, they are like the younger child in whom the parent delights, because they are always going back to the *fons vitae* (fountain of life) from which they were born and are constantly rejuvenated before God. Thus, with Reb Nahman of Bratzlav, we can say that the youngest knew most, for it was a knowledge of *that*, which once known, all things may be known in their essence.[20] This is the meaning of the phrase "inheritance without end," because the *Ain Sof*, which also means "without end," is our inheritance.[21]

After the Holocaust, many people began to ask, "Where was God?" My mentor and friend Abraham Joshua Heschel would take on a melancholy expression and say, "Where was man?" This is a beautiful answer, because many post-Holocaust theologians at that time were taking up Nietzsche's slogan of "God is dead!" I was part of the "God is dead" dialogue as well, but looking at it from the Hasidic point of view. Therefore, I said: All these years we have prayed for God to come down and dwell in us, to be immanent in us, and now that it has happened, we cry out, "Where is God?"—still expecting a great hand to swoop down from the Heavens! Thus we must embrace Heschel's reply, "Where was man?"

As children grow older, eventually reaching adulthood, they no longer need to have their parents hovering over them; the "parents" are now built into the children, and the children must be responsible for themselves and their own actions. Likewise, now that we have become more and more aware that God has poured divinity into us, as it were, we cannot expect to draw so heavily from the transcendent dimension for help. Just as a child grows up and is given more responsibility, we too, with our profound scientific and technical capability now have tremendous responsibility given to us, the likes of which we never had in the past. Before we were basically living off of what nature provided; now we have taken on the responsibility of meddling with nature, and we must look to ourselves for help with the karma we have created.

EGYPT, MATZAH, AND THE FREEING OF AWARENESS

In this Torah, the Maggid explains the exile in Egypt in the light of the cosmic drama of God and human beings.

IN MITZRAYIM, DA'AT (knowledge) was in exile, for they knew not that there was a God in the world.[22] Had they possessed knowledge, they would have known that God actually fills the worlds. As it is written, "With knowledge the rooms are filled" (Prov. 24:4).[23] "Rooms" refers to middot (divine attributes).

Now the Maggid begins to talk about the problems of existence, putting a helpful new frame around our troubles, past and present. Here he begins to juxtapose the concepts of knowledge and ignorance with the traditional Pesaḥ themes of freedom and exile. For *Mitzrayim* (otherwise known as Egypt) can be understood to mean "the narrows," the place where we were squeezed during our exile. The Maggid makes it clear that we were in "the narrows" of exile because we had lost the *da'at*, the intimate knowledge or awareness of our relationship to God as "the One Who fills all Worlds" (*m'malleh kol almin*). As it is written, "With knowledge the rooms are filled." These rooms refer to the *middot*, the emotional attributes of Divinity.

What is the connection between "rooms" and "emotional attributes"? There is a way in which people used to do memory exercises, learning a series of words and putting these words into the "rooms" of a "memory palace." Later, when they had to recall these words, they simply walked through the rooms and collected the words like keys left on the kitchen counter. When you are visualizing chakras within yourself, you are doing the same thing. So when the Maggid says, "With knowledge the rooms are filled," he is referring to how we may introspectively visit the "rooms" of the *middot*.

I once played a game in which the rules changed depending on what room you entered into, and in each room there was a different set of tools for you to make use of. So in the room of the *middah* called ḥesed, you have certain lovingkindness tools, in *gevurah*, tools of strength and discipline. So with knowledge you will see *what* the rooms are filled with. In the Christian New Testament it also says, "In my Father's house are many rooms" (John 14:2).[24] This was a part of the mystical language of the period, which said that in God's Heaven there are many *heikhalot*—rooms, mansions, or chambers— the mystical traveler could visit. The suggestion here is that God's knowledge fills every aspect of creation in multiple dimensions.

From the perspective of Jean Paul Sartre's existentialism, our exile has "no exit," and this, of course, leads to despair. When we are ignorant of the God within us, when we don't have this in our awareness, then it seems as if there really is no exit. This is what fills the mental landscape of a suicide; there is no exit from the situation while I am alive. So the Maggid says, What was going on in Egypt? *Da'at* (intimate knowledge) was in *galut* (exile), awareness was in exile.

This is connected to a teaching of Reb Shneur Zalman of Liadi, which was likely based on a teaching of the Maggid. He quotes, "Mighty waters cannot wash away love" (Sg. 8:7)[25] and then continues saying, the "mighty waters" are all the worries we have about survival, but they cannot wash away love because hidden deep within us is the love that we have for God, the *ahavah mesuteret* (the hidden love). Love remains whatever our situation might be. Nevertheless, if we want to survive that situation, we must remember the hidden love deep within us, and then no worries will be able to wash us away, and we will be freed from exile.

THUS IN MITZRAYIM, knowing waited to be redeemed and, with it, God, the known. For when a child calls to its parents, they respond, leaving their pleasures and interests to attend to the child, loving and pouring kisses upon it. This may not seem dignified in the eyes of others who may be watching, but the pleasure of playing with and giving delight to the child seems far more important at that moment. In the same way, God redeemed the middot (divine attributes) at the Exodus.

Eating matzah (the unleavened bread of Passover) was the beginning of our redemption, for matzah was given to us by God as a loving parent. Before we tasted matzah, we did not really know God as our parent. "Until Yisra'el ate matzah for the first time, they did not *know* how to call God, "Father."[26] This ignorance was the true exile for us, and this knowledge, the true freedom. For in the Zohar, matzah is called "the bread of faith."[27]

In Exodus, Pharaoh says, "The children of Yisra'el are lost in Egypt, the desert is locked off from them" (Exod. 14:3).[28] But *midbar* or "desert" also has to do with *meddaber,* "speaking," so this also meant that "speech was taken from them." When you go with the ideas of Werner Erhard (b. 1935), it means they were only doing "journalism;" they were not speaking the authentic word. So God gave them matzah, which is like the first grain that you feed the baby and which gives them reason to recognize you, saying, *"Abba"* (Father). When they were having matzah, they got into Pe-saḥ, which breaks down into "the mouth that speaks," which is to say, "Now we have a mouth that can speak," whereas before, they could not speak.[29] Now we could finally put words to God, to name God as our parent. And when we called out to God as children call out to a parent, the exile for both us and God began to fade away. For when a child calls to its parents, they respond in love, leaving their occupations, even pleasant ones, to attend to the child, loving the child and pouring kisses on him or her, as the Maggid says.

IN OTHER EXILES knowledge was also enslaved. We are told of the taunts of their captors, "Where are your God's mighty acts?"[30] Only later did they come to know that God was right there with them. When they left those exiles, the attributes (middot) became known, just as when they left Mitzrayim knowledge was liberated with them and it became known that there was a God in the world. This is the meaning of "God redeemed a nation and its God" (2 Sam. 7:23),[31] *for God then became a reality to them and the divine name was published in the world.*

The Ba'al Shem Tov is quoted in the *Toldot Ya'akov Yosef* as teaching that the exile in Egypt was caused by the ignorance of the Jews who lacked the knowledge of God.[32] The point is still the knowledge of God, how God was close the whole time, but we knew it not. This theme of exile and knowledge will continue in the next teaching and will be further explained there.

Notice the number of biblical verses the Maggid is quoting throughout these teachings. Remember the translation of Salomon Maimon in the last chapter ("The Maggid's *Tish*") and how the guests of the Maggid would call out their favorite verses and he would weave them all together? This is likely what is happening in these teachings, for as we have said before, the Maggid did not plan discourses ahead of time. This was the *ruah ha-kodesh* of the group mind, as it were, coming through the opened mouth of the Maggid, the *Shekhinah* speaking a message for everyone present on that occasion. This should constantly be in the back of your mind when reading the Torah of the Maggid.

THE WORKS OF THE *TZADDIKIM*

Now we return to the theme of the *tzaddikim* and their particular work in the world.

"THE WORKS OF the tzaddikim are greater than the works of the creation of Heaven and Earth."[33]

This is so because the creation of Heaven and Earth is the turning of ayin (nothing) into yesh (something), whereas the tzaddikim are able to take yesh and turn it into ayin. In all that the tzaddikim do, even in their involvement with material objects like food, they raise the holy sparks (nitzotzot) of the food upward. And so they do with all things in existence, turning them from something into nothing.

This teaching follows up on what we have already said about *tzaddikim* returning to nothing (in "Ya'akov's Inheritance"). Here the Maggid is showing how this is the specific work of the *tzaddikim:* to return all things to the source through *kavanah*, an intentional engagement with them. This he demonstrates is a work that is in some ways even greater than the creation of Heaven and Earth. For creation is the turning of nothing into something, making limited what was previously unlimited. But the *tzaddikim* turn the something into the nothing, freeing the limited from limitation. Which is the greater work?

In this way, the Maggid is once again putting a compassionate frame around human existence and answering the question, "What is it that we contribute?" or "How are we needed by God?" This is a Hasidic frame that Abraham Joshua Heschel brings together beautifully in his work on Jewish theology (or what he called "God's anthropology"), *God in Search of Man.*

When we get to the issue of "raising the sparks," we are now in the world of the Kabbalah of the Ari ha-Kodesh, Yitzhak Luria (1534–1572). The Ba'al Shem Tov tended to speak mostly from an inner wellspring and did not use the language of the Ari extensively, but the Maggid is an intellectually inclined kabbalist and makes of it a foundation stone for Hasidic thought. And because many of the young scholars whom he wished to attract to Hasidism were already firmly entrenched in the teachings of the Ari, he made brilliant and original use of the teachings to bring them into the fold.

Most powerful among these teachings was the Ari's great "cosmogonic myth" of creation and redemption. In the beginning, the light of Divinity fills all of existence, but then God chose to withdraw (*tzimtzum*) from a given point in Divinity, making a womb-space for creation. Into this void, God then sent a concentrated ray (*kav*) of divinity to inseminate the womb, as it were, with holiness. But the first "vessels" created to hold this infusion of light broke under the intensity of the light, sending sparks or shards of light throughout creation, which became embedded in the primordial matter. It is only through our recognition of these holy sparks in all material things that we may free them, raising them back to the source in holiness. This is what we call *tikkun olam*, the rectification of the world. This is the divine ecology of responsibly stewarding creation.

THIS IS THE *meaning of the words, "Set you a sovereign over you" (Deut. 17:15).*[34] *That is to say, set the attribute of sovereignty (*malkhut*) over you. And to this our sages have said, "Let awe (*yirah*) be upon you,"*[35] *meaning that your prayer should not be fixed by rote. One should not pray concerning one's own needs, but for the blessed Shekhinah, that She be redeemed from Her exile. Thus all prayer must "be mercy and supplication,"*[36] *meaning that one must always supplicate God for the sake of the Shekhinah, who is called ha-Makom (the Space), as is well known.*

What is the connection between *yesh* and *ayin* to *malkhut* (sovereignty) in this passage? The sovereignty and power of *malkhut* in this instance is based in its capacity, or receptivity, which allows it to accommodate both *yesh* and *ayin*, being and nothingness. Thus in *malkhut*, *yesh* is present, but its quality is *ayin*. And when *ayin* is present, its quality is *yesh*.

"Set the attribute of sovereignty (*malkhut*) over you," that is to say, remember the higher *tikkun* (reintegration) to be made with all things at all times as the service due to God as sovereign. Likewise, remembering the higher *tikkun*, the greater fixing of the spiritual world, do not pray in unmoved obedience or just because a scene in your personal drama has taken a turn, but pray for the liberation of the *Shekhinah*, the Divine Presence, from Her exile in the ignorance of the world. Thus, if your sister is ill, do not pray for her healing alone, but connect her in your prayer to the need of the *Shekhinah* for Her own *refu'ah shelemah* (complete healing). Again this goes back to the words and the reality, attempting to remember that there is a greater reality beneath this limited existence that we call "reality." My old friend, the Sufi master Pir Vilayat Inayat-Khan, of blessed memory, chose a wonderful title for one of his books: *That Which Transpires Behind What Appears*. The reality of that world is what the Maggid is trying to express here.

THUS THE ZOHAR *calls those who pray for themselves and not for the sake of* Shekhinah *"dogs with coarse souls."*[37] *For they are ever whining selfishly, "Give me! Give me!" And this is the intention of the sentence, "One thing have I asked from God, our Sustainer, only this/Her [OTaH, meaning the Shekhinah] do I seek" (Ps. 27:4).*[38] *Thus for the sake of the Shekhinah do I seek and pray before You to repair the injuries that have occurred through sin.*

Reb Levi Yitzhak of Berditchev gave a very similar teaching in the *Kedushat Levi*. Based on the Zohar, he teaches that those who pray only for themselves are like dogs with coarse souls, crying out "Give me! Give me!," thinking only of their own needs. Now, of course, we have needs, and our needs are important, but if we identify only with the body, with our lower self, and forget that the *Shekhinah* dwells within us, then we are like animals. Thus Reb Levi Yitzhak teaches that everyone should pray for their life and livelihood, but they should do so for the sake of Heaven, so that God will be able to delight in the fact that we receive sustenance solely from God. In this way, the receiver also becomes a giver—giving delight to God.[39]

Reb Zushya of Anipol always received everything as if it came directly from God. Moreover, he lived with a continual awareness of the *Shekhinah* dwelling within him; thus he would say, "*Shekhinah* are you hungry? I'll feed you. *Shekhinah* are you sad? I'll make you happy. *Shekhinah* do you need more light? I'll study Torah." That relationship was very real for him.[40]

EVEN THOSE WHO *do a mitzvah simply as a "commandment" create division in the world, because they have not done it l'shem shamayim (for the sake of Heaven). This is because the Torah and the blessed and Holy One are truly one. The person who engages in a mitzvah for the sake of Heaven affirms their unity and attaches the one to the other in deed. For all is one holiness and one spirituality. But those who do not do the mitzvot with this intentional kavanah cause a hardened shell, a kelippah, to encase the mitzvah so that it cannot become united with the holiness of the blessed and Holy One.*

As much as any teaching, this one shows the Maggid to be a spiritual radical. For to many, it is anathema to suggest that a mitzvah performed simply as a mitzvah could be the cause of division in the spiritual world! But for the Maggid, the unity of all being is paramount, and the *kavanah* behind a mitzvah is the glue that binds the material to the spiritual, creating harmony instead of separation. This goes for prayer as well. For according to the Ba'al Shem Tov and the Maggid, one's prayer lives or dies on the investment that is made in the words.

IN THE SAME *way, if anyone prays in a mechanical manner, the words do not live. For it is God, blessed be the name, who gives life to the words. Unless God, blessed be the name, is invited into the process, even saying, "Blessed are You, our God," can be lifeless. But one who prays according to the Kabbalah realizes that the words are also alive and contain in themselves the One who quickens the word.*

In studying someone's Torah, one becomes united with the mind of the author. For instance, reading the Zohar and coming upon the name (which is the very life) of Rabbi Shimon bar Yohai, the reader's life is tied to that name. Thus those who study Torah in awe (yirah) and love (ahavah) tie themselves to Rabbi Shimon and study as if at his feet.

So far the Maggid has dealt with the importance of bringing deep *kavanah* to mitzvot and *tefillah,* and now he gives us a way to connect our study to the reality beneath the words, to share the mind of the author. For when one studies with concentration the Torah of a particular author, he tells us that the student encompasses that Torah with the mind but is also encompassed by it. Thus two minds are connected through the same Torah, those of the student and the author. It is as if the resonance of the persona of the author were in direct communication with the learner. The Maggid wants to bring us to full awareness of this holy honor, helping us deepen our study as we open to new possibilities of connection to guidance in different dimensions.

My Rebbe, Reb Yosef Yitzhak of Lubavitch, was continually urging us to use our "imaginal faculty" (*hush ha-tziyur*) and, whenever possible, to see the author in front of us as we were studying their work. But I had an even more personal instruction in this teaching from the Bobover Rebbe, Reb Shlomo Halberstam. Once he quoted a passage from a book for me and then rose to find the book. I said, "I trust that you quote it correctly," so that he would know that he didn't have to prove it to me. Then he looked at me with something like pity and said, "Young man, when you quote such a teaching, the least you can do is take out the author's *sefer* (book) and kiss it," which he did before returning it to the shelf.[41]

In Mitzrayim, the "world of thought" (b'riyah) was revealed to Yisra'el. Those who enter the world of thought enter the place of understanding (binah). Here, all the kelippot fall away. This was the blessing of Rav Hamnuna Saba, "May the holy One open the divine eyes to you." This means that when the blessed and Holy One thinks of a person, then that person is raised to the place of understanding (binah) where all is goodwill and forgiveness; as it is written in the Zohar, "The blessed and Holy One was angry with Yisra'el and divorced them, but it is their understanding Mother who bestowed gifts upon them."

Now the Maggid takes the idea of sharing thought higher. When we put God in our thoughts, we are then seen by God. When we put our thoughts on God while we were in Egypt, God opened eyes upon us, and we were thought about and encompassed. Even though we were the ones being "read" at that moment by God, it was an open connection and God was revealed to us as well! We saw the divine process as it unfolded in our miraculous redemption from Egypt. Thus the Christian mystic Meister Eckhardt said, "The eye with which I see God is the same eye with which God sees me." We are raised to the level of understanding, because it is not only the content of the thought and the thinking that is happening, but at the same time, you realize that you are also God-ing! That vibratory level of awareness gets you to *binah* (understanding).

THE MEANING OF *this is that in the exile the attribute of* Havayah *(Y-H-V-H) does not become revealed, only the attribute* Adonai. *This can be understood in the miracles that happened according to the ways of nature in the days of Esther (in whose story God's name is not mentioned). It was Ahashverosh who raised Mordechai up, and through this power, Haman was hanged. While it was a miracle, it did not appear so because it occurred according to the way of nature. Because we are in exile, we are not worthy that the attribute of* Havayah *be revealed to us in a supernatural or miraculous way, so everything must occur according to the way of nature. This is the way of the attribute of* Adonai, *which is active in the worlds and gives them life.*

The Maggid describes two types of miracles: those of *Adonai* and of *Havayah*. The miracles that occurred while we were in exile were manifested through the attribute of *Adonai* (my lords). This name of God is connected with the attribute of *malkhut*, this world, and thus with "nature" (*teva*). Therefore, these miracles manifested according to the way of nature and had to do with the manifest world. But the greater miracle occurs through the attribute of the name *Havayah*.

Now *Havayah* is the way in which the divine name is rearranged and substituted in Hasidic texts so as to prevent its abuse. Thus we take the letters of the Tetragrammaton, *Y-H-V-H*, and make it *H-V-Y-H*, which is pronounced *Havayah*, meaning "existence."[42] So the Maggid tells us, the miracle according to the attribute of *Havayah* is the turning of a nothing (*ayin*) into a something (*yesh*) and, later, the turning of a something (*yesh*) into a nothing (*ayin*). Again, both of these miracles hinge on the equation of ignorance with exile (the miracles of *Adonai*) and the intimate knowledge (*da'at*) with freedom (the miracles of *Havayah*). Thus, as long as we are in exile (*galut*), ignorant of our true nature, we do not merit the greater miracle.[43]

The implication here is that we use the name *Adonai* and not *Y-H-V-H* because we are still in exile. This is one reason why we in Jewish Renewal went away from the use of *Adonai* in favor of the name *Yah* (Being). For *Yah* is a part of the divine name and participates in its power and immediacy, but the letters *yud-heh*, which are connected to *ḥokhmah* and *binah* in the highest worlds, cannot be injured by abuse in the lower worlds. However, the letters *vav-heh* are subject to injury because they are connected to the six lower *sefirot* and *malkhut* in the lower worlds, where there is emotion and action. *Yah* is also preferable because the divine name (*Y-H-V-H*) is connected to the attribute of mercy, while *Adonai* is akin to "the boss." This is an obstacle in prayer, because one must say, "Please, *Adonai,* attribute of boss-man-ship!" It doesn't make any sense; it is the wrong address if one is looking for mercy. You cannot pray to the boss-man as much as surrender to him. So I believe that the sense of being in exile is actually fostered by the extensive use of this name. Lastly, *Yah* is not an exclusively masculine patriarchal name but has both masculine and feminine attributes, making it even more palatable for use by both men and women today.

HOUSES BIGGER THAN SYNAGOGUES

In our commentary on the teaching "The Glory Revealed to the World" (earlier in this chapter), we talked at length about the *tzaddik*'s wish to guide the world, but deferred the discussion of what is required of the *tzaddik* who must lead in God's name until this point, because the Maggid spells it out for us in the following teaching.

"A CITY IN which there are houses whose roofs are higher than the synagogues will be brought low."[44]

In our world of palatial houses and skyscrapers, where churches and synagogues are more reminiscent of community recreation centers, it is not difficult to see that our societal values have changed. The great teacher of mythology Joseph Campbell (1904–1987) once gave a wonderful illustration of this situation, saying, "You can tell what's informing a society by what the tallest building is." He then went on to point out that in a medieval city, the cathedral is the tallest building. In an 18th-century city, "the political palace" is the tallest building. And when you approach a modern city, the citadels of economic power, the skyscrapers of commerce are the tallest buildings![45]

Nevertheless, the Maggid does not read this quotation literally. Instead, he sees in it a reference to putting the ego ahead of the in-dwelling *Shekhinah* (Divine Presence). Perhaps this is because, even in his own day, the large synagogue had already been replaced in many ways by the *shtibl* and *kloiz,* those little prayer houses where the *davenen* was intimate and intense. Thus it seems that while the quotation above may indeed be a valid comment on societal values, for genuine spirituality it is no hindrance. True spirituality is not afraid of being small and often tries to avoid great display. Even in Muslim countries where great mosques are still in abundance, Sufi mystics (with some exceptions) usually prefer to gather and pray in the *zawiyya*, the small alcove of the murshid's (Rebbe's) home.

THIS REFERS TO those who have an inflated idea of themselves, raising that idea, as it were, higher than the Shekhinah. As it is written, "All one's thought is that there is no God, always saying, 'Who is our God?' The Shekhinah is called Adonai, and also "the synagogue." [46] *This means that those who raise themselves higher than the synagogue—higher than the Shekhinah—will be brought low.*

Do you see how meaning is enhanced and given depth by the many layers of association in the tradition? For we see here that the divine in-dwelling (*Shekhinah*) is both the overseer (*Adonai*) of our lives and the place through which we commune with the Divine (the synagogue). The interesting thing about *Adonai* is that it is plural. Its not *adoni*, "my Lord," but *Adonai*, "my lords"! There is a sense of diversity and plurality to it that fits well with its association with nature and the *Shekhinah*.

OUR SAGES HAVE said, "Who is foolish? Those who lose all that (MaH) is given them." [47] *For the main principle of the human being is to be formed in the celestial image. As it says in the Zohar, "When a wild animal attacks a human being, it is because it seems to the animal that the human being is a beast."* [48] *This is because the divine image has faded from one due to the sins that one has committed. For the human being, "ADaM" has a numerical value of 45, which is the same as that or what (MaH). This is the meaning of "Who is foolish? Those who lose all that (MaH)," meaning, the celestial image, which numbers 45. For the celestial worlds imbue a person with the "mah," and if one loses this due to one's folly—for "No one commits a sin unless a spirit of folly has entered into them"* [49]*—then such a person deserves to be called a fool.*

"*Mah*" in this passage refers to the "essence" of the human being, which is Divinity itself. To throw that inheritance away is foolish beyond reckoning. In the following *mashal*, the Ba'al Shem Tov also talks about the divine image that is stamped on us and how we tend to mistreat that image . . .

> Once there was a peasant who in a burst of anger desecrated a statue of the king that stood in the city square. Nevertheless, the king did not punish the peasant but made him supervisor of servants in the palace. Slowly he promoted him to positions of greater responsibility until finally he was second only to the king himself. Each time the king blessed him in this way, he became more and more aware of the king's justice, and felt more and more ashamed of his crime—desecrating the statue of the king. But this was all according to the king's plan. For the king knew that had he killed the peasant, the man would have learned nothing, but in this way, the man would learn to prize the statue of the king, and the king himself, more highly than anyone else in the realm.[50]

The statue of the king in this *mashal* is our own image, for we are made in the image of God. Thus all the terrible things that we do to ourselves—the addictions, the foolishness, the anger, and the negative self-image—all of these besmirch the divine image stamped on our being. When that image is obscured, according to the Maggid, we are very much like an animal. Thus he quotes the Zohar, "When a wild animal attacks a human being, it is because it seems to the animal that the human being is a beast."

This also reminds me of an important little story of the Kotzker Rebbe . . .

> Once, Reb Menachem Mendel of Kotzk was walking with his friends when they were confronted by two vicious German Shepherds running toward them. The owner of the dogs had trained them to attack Jews and had let them loose when he saw Reb Menachem Mendel and his friends coming down the street. As soon as they saw the dogs, they turned and started to run as fast as they could; all of them, that is, except Reb Menachem Mendel. He stayed right where he was and stared at the dogs until they stopped and began to cower.
>
> Later his friends asked him in amazement, "How did you do that?"
>
> Reb Menachem Mendel answered, "When I saw the dogs coming toward me, I asked myself, 'Have I taken the dog-ness in me and put it in the service of God?' So I made an effort to do so, and

when my inner 'dog' began to serve God, these dogs could no longer attack me. But if your own 'dog' is not in the service of God, then you have to be afraid of dogs."

In doing this, he became human, and the true human being reflects the Divine.

THEREFORE, IT IS *said, "Say unto the priests who admonish the people"*[51] *for they (the priests—that is, the tzaddikim) are attached to the category of grace and forever cause an influx of grace by turning the world to good. It is for this reason that the sons of Ahron are called "the category of Grace."*[52] *Therefore, "Say unto them that they must not defile themselves before any soul" (Lev. 21:1).*[53] *This means that at the time when they stand up to admonish the world, they should have no pride or arrogance in themselves, nor should they have any extrinsic motivation, for this is how one would lose and defile one's soul.*

The "priests" in this passage refer to the *tzaddikim*, who as *neshamot klalit* (general souls) are responsible for ministering to the people. Thus he says that they must not defile themselves before the world by pride and arrogance, being especially careful to "admonish" their Hasidim with the attribute of grace. "Admonish" is an interesting word here, because the Maggid guides them to admonish from the side of grace (*ḥesed*), from the side of generous love, and not severity (*gevurah*). The manifestation of grace, grace in function (*hod*), is connected with Aaron the priest, who in dealing with the people's sins always chose to put a compassionate frame around their act, thus creating a channel for divine forgiveness.

"THEY MUST NOT defile themselves before a soul" means that they must not lose and defile themselves before a soul at the time when they are among their people admonishing them. This is the meaning of "to know Your ways on Earth" (Ps. 67:3).[54] *It is written, "And Adam knew his wife" (Gen. 4:1),*[55] *for knowledge (da'at) stands for sexual union. Thus we pray to God that the divine name should be intimately united with the Earth, so that the Earth will give birth to knowledge (da'at), which applies to the Shekhinah. This is made apparent by the use of the words "Your ways," for sexual union is also called "the way" (Prov. 30:19).*[56]

In this passage, it becomes clear that the *tzaddik* should not speak to the Hasidim unless the *tzaddik* has first connected to God experientially. To speak without this connection to God, the Maggid says, is to "defile" oneself before a soul, meaning that the *tzaddik* has fallen into "pride and arrogance." For to speak while in connection to God is to make the soul transparent to God; if it is not so, then one is in a situation of arrogant presumption admonishing the people regarding the service of God. This is then related to the sexual act (*zivug*) as a symbol of intimate knowledge (*da'at*) or connection (*deveikut*) with God as well as practical guidance for continuing to reestablish the connection while you are speaking, as one tends to lose contact intermittently.

OUTER AND INNER

In the next two teachings, the Maggid deals specifically with the issue of approaching sexual attraction and sexual intercourse in a spiritual way, showing how one may raise the sparks of holiness in these impulses (and the actual act) to a place of divine obedience and spiritual completion.

"Go out and see, O you daughters of Zion, the king, Shlomo" (Sg. 3:11).[57]

"Go out" of your materiality, always attempting to see the inner content of something, and not merely its physical substance. This is what is meant by "And you will see, O you daughters of Zion," for this is comparable to the beauty of a woman. The physical nature of this beauty is referred to by "daughters of Zion," for it is merely a Zion, a "sign" and symbol of a deeper and higher beauty residing in the sparks of beauty, which come from the world of beauty. No one ought to become attached to the lower beauty, but should always attach themselves to the celestial beauty, which is "the king, Shlomo," meaning the blessed and Holy One.

The Maggid begins with "'Go out' of your materiality," but I would want to say, "Let go of your covetous attitude." Most of the time we are dealing with the world in an I–It relationship, the lower levels of which usually have to do with "What will I do with it? I can't just appreciate and adore it as it is!" So the Maggid says, "Go out of your materiality" and attempt to see the inner content of a thing in the I–Thou relationship, and not merely its material substance. I would qualify this a little and say, if I could see the material substance with a good eye, that wouldn't be so bad, for that is still a part of the I–Thou relationship.[58] The problem around the physical substance really has to do with selfishness and greed, and seeing it only as utility. However, there is always a higher *tikkun* (fixing) to make, and this is to penetrate the surface and follow the beauty back to its source in the world of beauty.

THE BEAUTY OF RACHEL

Now the same teaching will be expanded and explored from different perspectives.

"RAHEL COMES WITH the flock" (Gen. 29:9).[59]

The Midrash says that Rahel came to be united with Ya'akov's beauty. This did not mean his physical appearance. The true interpretation is that seeing Rahel below stimulated Ya'akov to become united with the celestial Rahel, for all the beauty of Rahel below was derived from the celestial Rahel.

The basic teaching is that there was a charge that came from that encounter between Jacob and Rachel that he then invested in the source of beauty, as we have already discussed. But let's think about this a little differently. What do you get when someone smiles at you in a genuine way? Something is communicated very directly. So, when Rachel comes to Jacob (as we see them in their archetypes), I think there must have been a look or a smile that communicated so powerfully that Jacob simply came up and kissed her.

How does that relate to the celestial Rachel? Well, imagine the situation in which Jacob had begun to feel his loneliness keenly and to dream of an ideal partner with whom he could share his life and his visions. After this ideal was very clearly etched in his mind, he suddenly comes upon Rachel and a look of knowing passes between them. In that moment, it is not just the earthly Rachel he has seen, but the celestial Rachel as well!

THIS ALSO IS the meaning of "And Yosef came to do his work" (Gen. 39:11).[60] *Our sages have said concerning this, "He saw the image of his father's face."*[61] *This is because he knew that Potifar's wife had beautified herself to seduce him. As the Midrash says, "The garments she wore in the morning she did not wear in the evening."*[62] *This was in order to beguile Yosef the tzaddik. However, he did not desire this beauty but, seeing it, was inspired to behold the divine beauty, which is "the image of his father, Ya'akov," who is called the "beauty of Yisra'el" (Lam. 2:1);*[63] *"Seeing this, he fled outward" (Gen. 39:12).*[64] *This means that he fled from the lower beauty and was so ardent that he "fled outward," out of this world to become united with the celestial beauty.*

With Jacob and Rachel, the attraction had been one that could be consummated, but now the Maggid deals with a different situation where it cannot. For Joseph had come to do his work in the house of his master, Potiphar. And the woman in question (Zuleika in the Islamic tradition) is Potiphar's wife. Knowing this, Joseph the Righteous could not consummate the relationship. Instead, he looks upon her beauty and sees "the image of his father, Jacob." But the Maggid shows us that this is not exactly the forbidding image we might suppose, the father sternly warning his son about a forbidden relationship. There is something of that, of course, but Jacob is also associated with the attribute of beauty (*tiferet*) on the Tree of Life (*etz hayyim*). Thus Joseph sublimated the forbidden desire by taking it to its divine root.

This is the situation we face in prayer when desire arises but cannot be consummated. Thus the Ba'al Shem Tov teaches that when you are praying and a sexual image or thoughts of attraction to someone arise, this thought has arisen in order to give you an opportunity to raise the sparks of holiness in the thought back to their divine source. How do you do this? By saying, "Where does the beauty come from? From whence does the attraction originate? Am I not made by God? And did not God give me this body and these impulses? Surely God must have had a reason for doing this and allowing these thoughts to come to me outside of the moment of love-making. Obviously they come from the source of beauty! I must take them back to their divine root!"

THIS IS ALSO the meaning of "When you go out . . . to wage war" (Deut. 21:10).[65] *Those who "go out" from the union with the blessed name surely go "to wage war," God forbid, for they enter the world of separation in which war is waged. Furthermore, it says, "You will see among the captives a woman of beauty" (Deut. 21:11).*[66] *This is because the physical beauty of a woman is called "captivity," for it all derives from the shevirat ha-kelim (breaking of the vessels), after which the nitzotzot (sparks) become "captives."*

"And you will desire her" (Deut. 21:11). If your desire is aroused by her physical

beauty, you are not to take her beauty for your own sake or for your own enjoyment. Rather, when she comes to face you suddenly, you must return all to the woman *(isha) in fire (ishay), that is to say, through an offering of pleasant fragrance to God. In other words, to raise the sparks to which your thought has attached itself up to the source of beauty, the celestial attribute.*

Now the Maggid brings the teaching to the place of the physical consummation of the union, discussing the base desire and its result if left "unraised" as well as the ideal of spiritual love-making. This is brilliantly done, because this biblical passage is a difficult one, dealing with war and the desire for a woman among the captives taken in war. Thus two historically paired masculine preoccupations—violence and lust—are dealt with at once and connected. For when we are outside of the tryst with the Divine, the Maggid says, by necessity we end up in separation and divisiveness, which he calls "war," the activity of discord. In this place, sexual attraction is little more than libido attempting to discharge an urge. Thus the soldier takes a woman captive because of her beauty. Her beauty is called "captivity" because the soldier is enslaved by his lust. That captivating beauty is derived from the sparks of light imbedded and themselves captive in the shells of ignorance, exiled in the lower worlds.

Therefore, the soldier as an idealized peacekeeper must learn to use restraint. The Maggid tells the soldier, you are not "to take her beauty for your own sake or for your own enjoyment." This is a wonderful statement, for so often in matters of attraction and sexuality, we are involved in "stealing beauty," attempting to "own" the beauty that belongs to someone else. Again, it is the I–It utility, or mentality, of which we spoke before. To take it for your own sake or for your own enjoyment is to steal beauty. Thus the Maggid says, you must return all that you have taken to her, all that you have taken from her in your heart must be returned to her in life and in love-making. And not just to her, but to the *Shekhinah,* who is the source of the beauty held captive. So this is truly a teaching about the *kavanah* of holy loving, making a fire offering of sweet scent unto Heaven.

It is so important, especially today, to be able to see and use these sexual metaphors in a holy context, absent of the prurient attitudes that usually encase them. There is truly no better way of speaking about our most intimate relationship vis-à-vis God. Thus when the Talmud says that "a woman must not ask her husband to come to bed, but beautify herself" and create an invitation in this way, we see in this a way to approach prayer, our union with the Divine. As Reb Nahman of Bratzlav says, "Why are our prayers not accepted? Because they lack *ḥein* (charm)!" You see, if someone were to say, "Please come to bed!" whining and sobbing with a kvetchy face, it would be such a turn-off. So we cannot approach prayer and our tryst with God in this way either; we must beautify ourselves and let charm create a natural opening to union.

ONE WHO COMES TO BE PURIFIED

In this teaching, the Maggid deals with *mahshavot zarot,* disturbing thoughts during prayer.

"ONE WHO COMES to be purified will be helped."[67]

This needs to be understood clearly, for we see that when a person comes to be purified, they pray with great intention before God, who is blessed, and make great preparations. But even as they stand to pray in the heart of the prayer service (the Amidah), mahshavot zarot (diverting thoughts) begin to arise in their mind. Thus we are moved to ask, "Where is Heaven's help? Did they not prepare themselves thoroughly, clearing the mind in order to make it pure for prayer?"

There is the childish idea that if you are doing something with reference to God, God should make it easy on you. Thus if you are *davenen* or participating in a holy activity then you shouldn't have any distracting thoughts, as we saw in an earlier teaching of the Maggid during the Ba'al Shem Tov's *tish.*[68] Thus he got himself into a place of guilt and blame from which he was unable to free himself until he learned from Moses that these thoughts arise unbidden from the body.

But who gave us such a body?

In the Hindu pantheon, one of the most popular "masks of God" is the elephant-headed image of Ganesh, who is called "the Lord of obstacles, the remover of obstacles." Thus many devotees who are experiencing various troubles and obstacles in their own lives send their prayers, as it were, to the address of Ganesh so that they may be removed. But who gave them the obstacles? *Ganesh,* "the Lord of obstacles, the *giver* of obstacles"! Ganesh is ultimately "the Lord of the Threshold," both giving and taking away our obstacles.

Thus the Maggid continues with the following . . .

THE TRUTH IS that the diverting thought is the help that Heaven sends, as we will explain. For the blessed name sends such thoughts to us in order that we may raise them up and ourselves with them. Thus it is written, "The merit worthy receive the merit to do a meritorious act."[69] Therefore, such thoughts are not accidental, and it is our business to raise them to their root. For if the external thought comes from a negative attraction or a negative fear and we cast this thought aside, attaching ourselves to celestial love and celestial awe, finishing our prayer with greater ardor, then we will have managed to raise the sparks from the kelippah (shell of ignorance).

Now the raising of the sparks of base thoughts recommended by the Ba'al Shem Tov and by the Maggid elsewhere[70] is not what is recommended by the Maggid here. In this teaching, he takes the position that his disciple Reb Shneur Zalman of Liadi would later endorse for most people. For as we have seen, the Ba'al Shem Tov says that if you have an erotic thought during prayer, you can look at it and say, "Oh how beautiful is that which comes from the source of beauty!" and raise it up. But Reb Shneur Zalman says, "No, don't try to do that; the likelihood is that you will only drag your mind deeper into external thoughts and out of the prayer." Being that he was dealing with a diverse group of Hasidim and putting his teachings in writing, he didn't feel that he could recommend the Ba'al Shem Tov's approach to everyone for whom he wrote, an approach that might fail without the proper spiritual depth, training, and support. Thus he recommended that one should *push off* from *it* toward God, instead of *going through it* toward God. This is what the Maggid is talking about here, for sometimes when you reject something, that too is a way to raise its sparks and to propel you toward God.

THIS IS THE HELP that is granted to us in prayer. And this is the meaning of "the sun rose and the sun set." In other words, we begin to pray with great ardor and "the sun rises," illuminating us. Then suddenly "the sun sets," for all our ardor is taken from us by a diverting thought. Why is this? Because "Unto its place does it long" (Eccles. 1:5).[71] In other words, the sparks within this thought desire to be raised, so we must kindle all of our longing and return it to the place and root of holiness.

Why does a diverting thought raised to its source have greater spiritual effect than a purely spiritual thought? Hasidic teaching puts it the following way . . .

Why should God have desired a cow for a sacrifice? Because the angels who surround God's throne are continually saying, "Holy, Holy, Holy!" But there is nothing special about an angel saying "Holy!" However, when a cow that has been offered as a sacrifice ascends to Heaven and says, "Holy!" before God's throne, that is really something special!"

FAITH-ING

People say "You have to have faith," which is a strange statement, as if you could go out and buy faith at the supermarket. Faith is not a commodity, nor is it something that you can *have*—faith is something that you *do*. This is why I like to speak of *faith-ing*.

EACH OF US must apply faith to all that that we do, whether it be a mitzvah, the study of Torah, or prayer arousing great delight above. We must not say to ourselves, "How am I worthy of bringing joy to God, who is blessed?" It is for this reason that applying faith, or faith-ing, is called emunah, *which is related to the word* "oman," *for it is a craft. In the performance of all mitzvot one must intend to give great delight unto Heaven; thus one brings all matter to the world of delight, for in the world of delight the* shevirat ha-kelim *(breaking of the vessels) never occurred, and* hokhmah *gives life to its owner. But if we think that we are special because Heaven derives pleasure from us, we come only to pride and arrogance, and then we will have to realize that we stand naked. For the power to give pleasure above is not gained by us. It is only when we, in the ardor of our ecstasy* (hitlahavut), *arouse the celestial delight that we enter into the world of delight. Thus are we capable of doing the will of our blessed creator.*[72]

Martin Buber wrote a book called *Two Types of Faith* in which he talks about how faith is seen in Judaism and Christianity. In the Greek of the New Testament, he points out, the word that is being used for faith is *"pistis."* This can be seen in the philosophical term "epistemology," which has to do with how we know what we know. With *pistis*, you can talk about *"having faith,"* because there is a cognitive element of knowing to the word. On the other hand, the Hebrew word for faith is *"emunah,"* which is related to the same word that you use for piano practice, *"imunim,"* as well as *"ameyn,"* "so be it," and the word *"oman,"* "an artist." Do you see? *"Emunah"* is a functional word, a process word. So while in English I may say, "I have faith," in Hebrew it comes out as "I am doing my faith-ing!" This also has the sense of something I do in service to my God—it is faithfulness, loyalty. So *pistis* is faith in the mental world, where "all is clear"; but when I say, "you are loved," this is something I cannot prove. How can I prove to you that you are loved? You either feel it or you don't, and this is the terrain of *emunah*.

EVERYTHING THAT WE *see or hear, everything that happens to us, comes to awaken us, whether it pertains to love (ḥesed), awe (gevurah), beauty (tiferet), victory (netzaḥ), glory (hod), relatedness (yesod), or sovereignty (malkhut). For it can happen that all the negative deeds that you have done will occur to you in prayer, and, of course, they come up so you may correct and raise them up. This is the same as with one who sees oneself in a mirror.*

When the Maggid says, "Everything that we see or hear . . . whether it pertains to love (*ḥesed*), awe (*gevurah*), beauty (*tiferet*), victory (*netzaḥ*), glory (*hod*), relatedness (*yesod*), or sovereignty (*malkhut*)," he means that they have their origin in the *sefirot* (divine attributes), that these are the roots of all things in the material world and the place to which all things must be returned. Thus the fear that enters our heart must be returned to *gevurah*, just as lust is sent back to *ḥesed*. For these enter our consciousness in order to be redeemed at their roots in the *sefirot*. When the Maggid says, "For it can happen that all the negative deeds that you have done will occur to you in prayer, and, of course, they come up so you may correct and raise them up," he is saying that moments of guilt and other difficult feelings will come, but we must greet them with a sigh, turning to God, and returning the feeling to its source, saying, "I wish I hadn't done that; I see now the origin of the impulse for this deed, and I return the original and pure impulse to you in love." "This is the same as with one who sees oneself in a mirror," meaning that when the thought comes up, it gives you a chance to look at who you really are.

THUS OUR DEEDS *appear in the mirror of the mind. There are letters and words that derive from our breath, and we must be careful to make certain that these are letters of love (ahavah) or awe (yirah), or if of any other emotion, that we raise them to their source. For there are situations in which we are overcome by fear, but this is only "that we may raise up the fear."*[73] *This is what was said of Shlomo ha-Melekh, peace be upon him; "he spoke of trees" (1 Kings 5:13).*[74] *This means that* everything Shlomo ha-Melekh saw (including trees) provided him with reasons for serving God, who is blessed. This is the meaning of "Y-H-V-H desires those who fear God, and who seek divine grace" (Ps. 147:11).[75]

One can also raise a fear up and by that act come to love of the creator. Imagine a soldier has come to call a man to the presence of the sovereign. This soldier is dressed in a magnificent uniform and approaches this man with all the haughtier and command of his office. Naturally, the man will be seized by worry and anxiety before such a presence. But in truth, all this fear is all for nothing, for he need not fear the soldier at all; the soldier is but a symbol, and his uniform only a badge of the sovereign, representing the awe of sovereignty.

If the man is wise, he will not even bother to fear or speak to the soldier, but will hasten to come to the sovereign. If perhaps a messenger of the sovereign comes with love and attentiveness, only a fool will spend time with the messenger of the sovereign, thinking that it is in the messenger that the love originates. One who is wise will see that the love originates in the sovereign, so why spend and seek delight with the messenger? Thus all the delight and love belongs to the sovereign and not to the messenger, and one should treat messengers as messengers of our blessed and holy sovereign and raise the impulses upward.

If any external fear or financial crisis appears, or if any joy or delight arises, all this must be raised up to the celestial sovereign. You must not be a fool and take delight, eating and drinking with the messenger who has been sent to you from the sovereign. It would be an awful folly to spend all one's time in eating and drinking with the messenger and not to appear before the sovereign who sent for you. For when you eventually came before the sovereign, the meeting would be full of disappointment and regret. One who is wise, having eyes to see, will realize this and say, "Why should I spend time conversing with the messenger? Is it not better for me to appear before the sovereign to do the divine will?" Therefore, a person must consider well the service of the blessed name and take heed in everything that arises as an opportunity.[76]

While this is obviously a teaching about our impulses, the Maggid may also be seeking to undermine any hierarchy that has been built up around him, saying, "Don't focus on me as Rebbe, don't be content with me, but move on to God for whom I am merely a messenger." In this case, the Maggid is like the friendly messenger, inspiring love and awe. But he is saying, "This love and awe is but the uniform in which God has clothed me! Follow me back to God, the sovereign; don't sit around admiring me!"

THE WOUNDED *TZADDIK* AND
THE PASSING OF THE MAGGID

Nevertheless, the Maggid was adored by his disciples, who, on occasion, fell into discussing his place and significance in the world, as Hasidim sometimes do. In this *ma'aseh*, we are allowed to eavesdrop on one of those occasions.

ONE EVENING, SOME *of the younger talmidim of the Maggid of Mezritch are sitting around and speculating about the tzaddik ha-dor, wondering who might be the real tzaddik of the generation. Various names are mentioned, but curiously, no one mentions the Rebbe. Most agree that it is the Rebbe of Alik. But Reb Shneur Zalman of Liadi, who came into the conversation late, asks the question that no one else had dared to utter, "Why don't you nominate the Rebbe?"*

One of the Hasidim answers, lowering his head and whispering, almost as if in shame, "You know the Rebbe is lame, *and you yourself have heard him teach about 'a small defect in the body' . . . he can't be the tzaddik ha-dor. It must be the Aliker Rebbe."*

But Reb Shneur Zalman replied, "The Rebbe is a tzinor, a channel through which divinity comes down to us. When he moves his head to the right, it is hokhmah (wisdom), to the left it is binah (understanding); when he moves his right hand, it is hesed (lovingkindness), his left, it is gevurah (discipline). But it is through the legs that it descends into our world: the right leg is netzah (victory), and it delivers the hesed; the left leg is hod (glory), and it delivers the gevurah. Now, our Rebbe wishes to limit the amount of gevurah that comes down to us, thus he is lame in his left leg! Therefore, he is the tzaddik ha-dor."[77]

It was for healing in his body that the Maggid originally came to the Ba'al Shem Tov, but what came of it?[78] As far as we know, not very much. Hasidim say, "If the holy Ba'al Shem Tov thought it would have been good for him, he would have healed him." But he didn't. Instead, he seems to have wrought a miracle in the Maggid's consciousness and left his body much as it was.[79]

One of the Maggid's Hasidim was a doctor; his name was Dr. Gordon. He was originally brought to the Maggid in his capacity as a doctor, but soon became a disciple. Dr. Gordon was puzzled by the Maggid's illness; after all, here was a person with amazing control over his body, from whose fingertips miracles fell and rolled under the benches, and yet he was sick. The doctor simply couldn't understand it! Finally, he was forced to conclude that there was something about the way in which the Rebbe wanted to teach, or about the way in which God needed him to teach, that required him to have such a vessel.

That the Maggid's health was somehow connected with the Hasidic movement and his disciples is borne out in this last *ma'aseh*, which immediately precedes his death.

AFTER MUCH PERSECUTION *from the* mitnagdim, *the disciples of the Maggid decided that they could no longer bear it in silence—they would put the* mitnagdim *in* herem, *pronouncing a ban on them.*

Reb Shneur Zalman objected, feeling that it was too strong a measure. He said, "Listen, if you put someone in herem, *you endanger their soul; they may even be cut off from God, and it is possible that they will turn to another religion. Do you understand? This may lead to a desecration of the name; don't do this."*

But the die was already cast.

The mitnagdim *had recently taken the family of Reb Levi Yitzhak and forcibly thrown them on a garbage cart, driving them out of town just a few hours before Shabbat! Such behavior was unthinkable; they had to fight back! They put the* mitnagdim *in* herem *that very night.*

The next morning, the Maggid entered the beit midrash *on his crutches and said to the assembled* talmidim, *"You have now lost your head; this will be the year of my passing. Nevertheless, you have achieved something—for whenever there will be an argument between Hasidim and* mitnagdim *from now on, the Hasidim will triumph."*[80]

The Maggid passed away quietly in his home in Anipol on the 19th day of Kislev, 1772, surrounded by his disciples. On his tombstone were written these words:

Concealed here is our master, guide, and teacher, the teacher of the whole Diaspora, the great luminary and *ga'on* of both *nigleh* and *nistar*; no secret was hidden from him, the Divine eagle and holy light, the man of wonders, our teacher and master, Rabbi Dov Baer, the son of Rabbi Avraham, may his memory be a blessing for life in the World-to-Come.

THE THIRTEENTH GATE

While most of the teachings in this chapter were chosen to give the reader a sense of *what* the Maggid taught, we feel that this last teaching actually says something about *who* the Maggid was as a Rebbe, and *how* he functioned in his role as the successor of the Ba'al Shem Tov.

ONE OF THE disciples asked which liturgy to employ.

It is well-known that there were thirteen stations of genuflection in the holy Temple. These thirteen, of course, correspond to the thirteen gates, which were alluded to by Yehezkel when he said, "In the future, there will be a gate for the tribe of Reuven" (Ezek. 48:31). For then the holiness of the entire city of Yerushalayim will be equal in holiness to the Temple of days past.[81]

It is taught that thirteen times the *kohanim* (priests) bowed during the service in the holy Temple, and the Maggid is saying that these thirteen genuflections correspond to the thirteen gates of which Ezekiel spoke when he said that in the future there will be a gate for all tribes. For in the days to come, the holiness of Jerusalem will equal the holiness imbued in the Temple in the days of old. This is a wonderful promise of the future that we should all take to heart, for the Temple will no longer be the focus of Jerusalem's holiness, but Jerusalem itself will be as holy as the Temple, including its churches and mosques, and the entire city will then be "a house of prayer for all peoples." Jerusalem will become a Thirteenth Gate through which all may ascend.

NOW, EACH OF the twelve tribes has a gate assigned to them, and as is well known, the Temple below corresponds to the Temple above.[82] *Thus the Temple above also has thirteen gates, one for each of the tribes, as it is further explained in the writings of Rabbi Yitzhak Luria, the Ari.*[83] *Thus the genuflections most truly correspond to the heavenly gates through which all influx comes to the worlds, as is well known to those who have entered the gates of the writings of the Ari.*[84]

The intent of prayer is that through it each one should be able to enter through their own gate, for prayer is "the ladder which stands below and whose head reaches the heavens" (Gen. 28:12).[85] *But each gate has a different combination; it is for this reason that there are different orders of the liturgy. However, the Thirteenth*

Gate is for those who do not remember the tribe from which they come. Thus even though they know not how to come before our sovereign through the gate of their own tribe, still they may enter by the Thirteenth Gate, which corresponds to the thirteenth attribute of mercy, which is called v'nakeh' (and cleanses), for it receives in itself the other twelve attributes. Thus, the holy Ari, to whom the ways of Heaven were clear, taught for those who did not know from which tribe they came and created for them a liturgy which was derived from various other orders of liturgy.[86]

This teaching is of course a justification for the use the Sephardic liturgical rite (with the *kavanot* of the Ari) by the Hasidim over that of the Ashkenazic rite of the region, but for us, it also has something very important to say about the Maggid himself and of his approach to spiritual guidance.

There is a Hasidic melody known as "The Maggid's *Niggun*," which has been preserved in many different Hasidic lineages—in Belz and Bobov, Satmar and Lubavitch—but each Hasidic group sings it differently, in the spiritual style of the group. I think that there is something significant to this, because this individuality is something that the Maggid seems to have encouraged in his disciples and that can be seen in various other Hasidic customs that derive from his time. Somehow, the Maggid seems to have made it clear that the way in which he was doing things was a way that fitted *his* personality, but that his disciples were welcome to do these things in ways that were more suitable to their own personalities. Thus the ecstatic *tish* and the *niggunim* of Reb Levi Yitzhak of Berditchev were very different from the deeply contemplative *tish* and *niggunim* of Reb Shneur Zalman of Liadi.

According to the Ari ha-Kodesh, in the higher worlds there is a level called *akudim* (banded), another called *nekudim* (spotted), and a third called *berudim* (streaked). These correspond to the different markings on the sheep that were born to those that Jacob had trained in the Bible (Gen. 31:10–13). *Akudim* means "tied together," which is to say, prior to any differentiation. *Nekudim* refers to separate black spots on a white field. And *berudim* refers to white spots or streaks on a black field, meaning that the black spots have come together and become interactive with each other.[87] When I think of the Ba'al Shem Tov, I think of his teaching as *akudim*, undifferentiated. But when we come to the Maggid, there is a recognition of the *nekudim*, the unique and separate points that need to develop and differentiate in their own way. One does not shift them from their path.

The Maggid recognized that there were indeed many paths to God and thus never attempted to change the basic pattern of his disciples. One can hardly imagine more different individuals than Ahron of Karlin, Elimelekh of

Lizhensk, Zushya of Anipol, Shneur Zalman of Liadi, Levi Yitzhak of Berditchev, and the Maggid's own son, Avraham the Malakh. It is said that the Maggid had 40 close disciples and not one of them was the same. This is a testimony of the Maggid's true greatness, that he recognized and cultivated the uniqueness of his disciples, never seeking to alter their life-path or to make clones in his own image. That image was so transparent to the Divine that each disciple was able to take from it only that which suited his own style. Thus everyone who came to the Maggid found their own process opened up and their own situation clarified for them.

In this teaching, we are told that holy Temple had thirteen gates through which one might enter. Depending on the tribe to which you belonged, you would go through one of twelve gates that corresponded to the twelve tribes. But the Thirteenth Gate was for those who did not know which tribe they belonged to and thus could accommodate all types. It was called the *sha'ar ha-kolel* (the gate of all).

Some have asked, "If there is a Thirteenth Gate to the temple, then why shouldn't everybody simply go through it? Why should you have to go into the gate of your own tribe at all?" Reb Menachem Mendel of Lubavitch I, the Tzemah Tzedek, once asked this with regard to the *kavanot* (mystical intentions) of the *Amidah*, saying,[88] "Why should you pray for healing with *tiferet*? Why should you ask for abundance in *netzah*? Isn't it easier just to go through the Thirteenth Gate?" He then answered that while the Thirteenth Gate yields to you, it is not a perfect fit. In other words, its vibration is not perfectly tuned to yours so that all of the fibers of your being vibrate with its holiness. Thus there is a gate for each person.

Whereas other Rebbes could accommodate only certain types of Hasidim, corresponding to their own particular tribes, the Maggid was the *sha'ar ha-kolel* of Hasidism in his time, a Thirteenth Gate accommodating of all types of uniqueness. What then of the Tzemah Tzedek's teaching that the Thirteenth Gate could not create a perfect resonance in all the fibers of one's being?

Perhaps the Maggid would embrace this answer, saying, "Of course not; that was not my job. Mine was not to complete them; mine was only to set them vibrating with the universal sound and to send them on to their individual gates with the means of attuning to the frequency of their own souls!" Or perhaps we might think of the Maggid as a kind of "locator" of individuals and their tribes. For if one is looking for a folder called "Judah" on the computer, it is simple enough if it is sitting on the desktop. But what if it is buried somewhere deep, in a folder within a folder within a folder? To find that "Judah," one is going to have to use the search function, a finder. Still, it's not going to be easy; the finder will have to search the entire computer, going through circuitous routes to come up with the folder called "Judah." It may be that a *sha'ar ha-kolel,* a Thirteenth Gate, can do what the other gates can do, only it must work much harder to locate the tribe of the individual who wishes to pass into the holy Temple . . . but it is all the more holy for having to do so.

PART III

The Circle of the Maggid and the Rebbe King

8

The Heavens of the Angel: The Lonely Path of Avraham the Malakh

AFTER THE PASSING OF THE MAGGID, THERE WERE some who looked to his son, Avraham, to lead them, for he was truly great even among the inner circle of his father. Nevertheless, he had no desire to become the leader of the Hasidic movement or even of a single Hasid.[1] It is difficult to express what this means in Hasidism without borrowing from the language of Hinduism, for Hasidism has little experience of this situation, whereas Hinduism is full of such individuals. Thus the Hindu tradition makes two very useful distinctions that will be helpful to us in our understanding of Reb Avraham the Malakh's place in Hasidism.

The first distinction is between the "guru" and the "pandit." In the Hindu tradition, the guru teaches the disciple, while the pandit teaches the idea. In this sense, Reb Avraham is clearly a pandit. But the pandit can also be quite divorced from the experience of spiritual realities, a "talking head," if you will, and this was not at all the case with Avraham the Malakh. Thus we might appeal to another distinction in the Hindu tradition, that between the *upa* guru ("means" teacher) and the *sat* guru ("truth" teacher). Now, the *upa* guru draws the disciple close and teaches them how to experience the spiritual realities themselves, but the *sat* guru may not speak at all, being a walking archetype of the effects of spiritual realities who is studied as a lesson in piety. If they do speak, they speak the teaching directly into the universe, and those who can must reach up and grasp of it what they may.[2]

This model is much closer to what Avraham the Malakh was; he was studied and admired by his fellow Hasidim, and when he spoke Torah, all who were present sought to hold some small measure of its profundity. But he did not bend down to teach them as his father had. Later, Hasidism would assimilate this type of individual into the role of Rebbe, making accommodations for them, as one would a *sat* guru, but in Reb Avraham's time there was no true precedent for this, and he became a Hasidic enigma.[3]

Reb Avraham's Torah is from the upper *Gan Eden* and difficult to grasp; he was perhaps the most abstract monist in all of Hasidism. Nevertheless, we feel that his Torah is unique in Hasidism and has much to teach us still. In his own time, he was a *tzaddik* and not a Rebbe, but through his Torah he may yet be a Rebbe to us today.

THE *MIKVEH*

This *ma'aseh* comes from the years when Reb Dov Baer was still an itinerant *maggid* traveling from town to town preaching sermons, perhaps 10 to 15 years before his meeting with the Ba'al Shem Tov.

IN THE YEARS *when the Maggid still lived in poverty, he often traveled the region in search of* parnasa *(livelihood) as a preacher. One night, he returned unexpectedly after a long journey, and his wife immediately set off for the* mikveh *(ritual bath). It was the time for her purification, and even though it was the middle of the night—as well as the middle of winter—she was determined to go. She had a sense that this was to be a night of conception. After a long cold walk, she knocked at the door of the* mikveh *and told the* mikveh *keeper her name.*

He refused to open.

You see, the mikveh *keeper in Rovno despised the poor and refused to go out of his way for them, especially on cold nights such as this. After all, they could not pay him what the wealthy could, so why should he trouble himself?*

She begged and pleaded, but he would not open.

Then, just as she was ready to give up, a carriage pulled up to the mikveh *carrying four ladies. The driver descended from the carriage and banged hard on the door of the* mikveh, *saying, "For these noble ladies, would you open the* mikveh?" *The* mikveh *keeper opened the door without delay (as he expected to be well paid), and thus the wife of Dov Baer was able to go in as well!*

Later, when the Maggid spoke of this to his son, Avraham, he said, "That night, Sarah, Rivka, Rahel, and Leah put on bodies and came to your mother's rescue, and they even persuaded Eliezer to be the coachman."[4]

It is said that this was the night his son, Avraham "the Angel," was conceived. Other *ma'asiot* remind us that the Maggid was strictly observing the ascetic practices of the Lurianic Kabbalah during this period and had purified his body to such a degree that "his body was as his spirit, and his spirit was as his body." Thus in the hour that Avraham was conceived, "a pure spirit from the world of the angels" entered his mother's womb to live for a brief time in the world of human beings.[5]

A FATHER'S LOVE

What can we say about his childhood? Of course there is what we know of the Maggid's life during these years—the terrible poverty, the ramshackle house in which he taught children, his travels, his deep study and spiritual practice, and his frequent illness—and his son must have shared or been witness to nearly all of this. Admittedly, it doesn't paint the picture of a rosy childhood; but who can say for certain? The eyes of children are wide open and look on the world differently than adults. Some who have experienced such childhoods have described them in terms of pure misery, whereas others in similar circumstances speak with wonder of those years with nothing! More often than not, the child sees and feels both pain and wonder, for it is the nature of children to look with awe on the terrain of their childhood.

Somehow, I suspect that Avraham's childhood was probably filled with this mixture of joy and pain. For as we look around for hints that might tell us something more about his childhood, little remembrances of *ma'asiot* and Torah arise to balance out the picture. It is difficult to imagine that the Maggid would so frequently use the analogy of the father's love for his child—the delight in the child, bending down to the child, scaling down the mind for the child, and playing games with the child—if he had not done so with his own son, Avraham. And, as we shall see, Avraham also uses this *mashal* in his own Torah. Might we suspect then that the Maggid's famous parable of playing with the child is really a remembrance of a moment with his son, Avraham?[6]

One day, Reb Dov Baer, who was greatly respected as a Torah scholar, was expecting a visitor who was likewise a person of great distinction and dignity. Nevertheless, just before the visitor was anticipated, his son, Avraham, who was only a small child then, coaxed Reb Dov Baer into a short play session. While they were yet playing, the distinguished visitor arrived to find the noble Rabbi Dov Baer of Rovno on his hands and knees playing horsy with a child on his back! Shocked at this ignominious display, he said, "How can you, a person of such dignity, degrade yourself like this playing on the floor with a child!"

Reb Dov Baer replied, "He wanted it."

"So?" the visitor said, "Children always want one thing or another; it doesn't mean we should give it to them."

Then Reb Dov Baer said softly, "No, you don't understand . . . He wanted it so badly, and asked with such joy and exuberance, that I began to want it too; his desire created a will in me to play as well."

The teaching in the *mashal* remains, but the situation suggests a basis in reality, of something that could actually have happened in the Maggid's own life—and probably did. In any event, this is how I choose to see it. A father who played with his child with such obvious love must have brought some joy to the child's life.

Nevertheless, Avraham is stamped with some other impression as well. Is it the imprint of his father's asceticism, his awesome prayer, or his illness? Or was it the cold dirt floors of their shack and a continually empty belly that made Avraham the Angel ascend so far above the world? Was the impression of that difficult time and his father's own disposition in those years the definitive impression of his life? Remember what the Maggid said to the Ba'al Shem Tov's emissary when questioned about his extreme poverty, "My friend, in this world, I am on the road."[7] That changed for the Maggid, but for Reb Avraham, it would be a road he would follow to the end.

By the time the Maggid first encountered the holy Ba'al Shem Tov, his son, Avraham, was probably bar mitzvah, and by the time he himself ascended to the leadership of the Hasidic movement, Avraham may have been 20 years old. Whatever change may have come over the Maggid in that seven-year period, the die was probably cast for Avraham by the time he was 13, if not from the time of his birth.

THE FACE OF AN ANGEL

It is in Mezritch that Avraham seems to have picked up the name by which he would be forever known—*ha-Malakh* (the Angel). This was almost certainly given to him by the Maggid's disciples, and one can only imagine the kind of physical and spiritual impression that might have evoked such a holy and ethereal description from these men of the *ḥevraya kaddisha* (holy fellowship), who were themselves the delight of Heaven. But we need not be contented with simple speculation, for more than one *ma'aseh* speaks of his awesome appearance, which may have suggested the name "Angel" to people.

> Once, the young grandsons of the Ba'al Shem Tov, Moshe Hayyim Efraim and Barukh asked themselves, "Why do people call the Maggid's son 'the Malakh'?" So they went to see if they could get a look at him for themselves. When they reached the street on which the Malakh lived and approached his house, they spotted a young man through the window. They crept forward and saw that he was placing his tefillin. The young man then turned his face toward the window and the boys were so shaken by his awesome appearance, that they turned and ran as fast as they could.[8]

Clearly it was no baby-faced cherub that they saw, but an angel of fire. A story from the Malakh's wedding night sheds a little more light.

ON THE NIGHT *of his wedding, Reb Avraham the Malakh entered the bedroom with trembling awe, chanting words of Torah, his face on fire. Seeing his face illuminated with divine passion, his young wife fell back in terror and fainted. For the rest of the night, she lay in a fever.*

The next night he entered the room as before, but this time his wife took heart and endured the awesome visage of her husband and conceived a son.

The following night, he retired to a separate room.[9]

Such stories are not unique to the Malakh; similar stories are also told of his father. Reb Levi Yitzhak of Berditchev once described the Maggid's face during the *Minḥah* prayer as so awesome that he fell back in surprise. But even more famous, the Maggid once appeared at the door of his study with a face so radiant that it struck terror into his disciples, sending some under the tables and others jumping out of the windows!

But Avraham was not called the Malakh solely for these moments of radiant appearance. At the end of this wedding night *ma'aseh*, we are told that the Malakh retired to "a separate room." Apart from the obligation to go in to his wife for the purpose of begetting children, he lived apart from her. In fact, he lived in the world as little as possible. Anything of the flesh that would bind and tether him to the Earth—food, sex, sleep, warmth—he fasted from almost continually. Thus what was said of his father on the night of his conception could also be said of the Malakh, "his body was as his spirit, and his spirit was as his body." Reb Levi Yitzhak of Berditchev would add, "Not in vain did they call him 'the Angel,' for he is as pure as his deeds."[10]

FRIENDS AND MENTORS

In 1765 (5525), when the Malakh was about 24 years old, a 20-year-old Lithuanian genius arrived in Mezritch to learn from his father. This was Reb Shneur Zalman (later of Liadi), and the two would become inseparable. In fact, the Malakh's father even made the *shiddukh* (match) between them. Seeing that the young Litvak (Lithuanian), even at 20 years old, had an almost unparalleled knowledge and comprehension of *halakhah* and codes, he called the two together and addressed them intimately: "I would like the two of you to have a special *ḥevruta* (study partnership); for one hour Zalmina, you will instruct Avramenyu in Gemara, and for one hour Avramenyu, you will instruct Zalmina in Kabbalah."

Later, the Maggid took Zalman the Litvak aside and said to him: "Let my son go his own way. Explain the Torah to him as you understand it, and he will interpret it according to his own conception. Show him the Talmud according to the letter, and he will explain its meaning to you according to the spirit."[11] In this way they developed a deep love and friendship.

Still, each was a *mashpiyya* (mentor) for the other. There are two *etzot* (spiritual suggestions) that the Malakh gave to Reb Shneur Zalman that are remembered in the HaBaD tradition.

ONCE, WHEN REB Shneur Zalman was preparing to leave Mezritch, his friend

Avraham the Malakh walked him to the wagon and said to the driver, "Discipline the horses so that they know they are horses." Reb Shneur Zalman stopped and was thoughtful for a moment—then he took his bags from off of the wagon and stayed in Mezritch a while longer.

It was obvious to Reb Shneur Zalman that the Malakh was not talking about horses. "Discipline the horses so that they know they are horses" means that when the body knows its place in life and does not arrogate itself to the place of the soul, then all is in its proper order. One has to discipline the body in order for it to know that it is a body, which is to say, a vehicle for the soul. Hearing this, Reb Shneur Zalman must have felt that he had not yet sufficiently disciplined his body, at least not enough to go home, where he would not have the support of the *ḥevraya kaddisha*.

YEARS LATER, WHEN Reb Shneur Zalman was preparing to depart Mezritch after the passing of the Maggid, he was once again accompanied to the wagon by his friend the Malakh. This time the Malakh said to the driver, "Urge the horses on, and let them run until they are no longer horses." Reb Shneur Zalman looked his friend in the eyes, shook his head in comprehension, and departed for home.[12]

This latter *etzah* (counsel) is not about disciplining the body but about transcending it. That is to say, when you already have a disciplined body and you know the true nature of the soul, then you can really let the body "run" until it is no longer bound by its physical limitations. It was an exhortation to Reb Shneur Zalman, as if to say, "The Maggid is gone, and you are now ready for your task in the world; just remember that you are a divine being having a human experience, and not the other way around."[13]

Theirs was one of the great friendships of Hasidism and one of the most mutually beneficial. For Reb Shneur Zalman would in time become one of the greatest kabbalists of the age, seen as the contemplative par excellence, and this had its true beginnings in his *ḥevruta* with the Malakh. From Reb Shneur Zalman, Reb Avraham gained a deep grounding in *halakhah* that no doubt added dimension to his Torah and probably even kept the Malakh in the world longer than he would have been otherwise. After his father's death, he would take up a rabbinic post in Fastov for a several years. But the grounding of Reb Shneur Zalman was also responsible for actually saving his life on one occasion . . .

Once, the Malakh and Reb Shneur Zalman got very deeply involved in a meditation, eventually reaching the place of *atzilut* (nearness). Suddenly, Reb Shneur Zalman became aware that his friend did not wish to come back. He shook himself from his own meditation and ran into the kitchen and came back with a bagel and beer. He tore a piece of the bagel off and put it into the Malakh's mouth, forcing him to chew, and then poured some of the beer down his throat, bringing him back to consciousness! The next morning, the Maggid called Reb Shneur Zalman over to him and said: "Zalmina, I want to thank you; in the place where I was in my own *davenen,* I was powerless to do anything about Avraham's situation. I am so glad that you were there with him at that time and able to save my son's life—*yasher koaḥ.* But one thing I don't understand—where did you find a bagel in *atzilut?*"

TWELVE MORE YEARS

Reb Shneur Zalman was not the only person to draw the Malakh back into the world. We can well imagine his father's gentle efforts and admonishments to be careful, even as he recognized his son's right to go his own way. But still more important, it seems, were the efforts of his faithful wife . . .

ONE NIGHT, AVRAHAM the Malakh's wife had a dream in which she saw a great hall filled with a circle of thrones, each of which was occupied by a sage of noble mien. She heard one of them say, "Let us summon him home." Then she understood that they were referring to her husband, the Malakh. Gathering her courage, she entered the circle and began to plead for the life of her husband: "Just let him dwell among us for a little while longer," she ended. All the sages had listened in silence, but now one of them spoke, "Let us give him to her for 12 more years." The rest of the sages nodded their assent and the dream was ended. The next morning, her father-in-law, the Maggid of Mezritch laid his hands on her head and blessed her.[14]

This would have been in 1764 or 1765, around the time Reb Shneur Zalman came to Mezritch, about seven years before his father's passing. Whatever the Malakh's relationship with his wife might have been, and whatever her reasons for preserving his life, it was enough for the heavenly assembly, and the Maggid blessed her as he had done Reb Shneur Zalman. One is even tempted to see her dream and Reb Shneur Zalman's quick-thinking act to save the Malakh's life as somehow related. Who can say for certain? These are the stories we are given, and these are the dates that link them; it is for us as individuals to decide.

NOAH AND THE HOT WATER

As we have seen, the tradition tells us that the Malakh was granted a temporary reprieve. And we are all grateful to his wife and Reb Shneur Zalman for their efforts to save him. For his great and unique legacy of Torah almost certainly comes from the last 12 years of his life. It may have even benefited from his *ḥevruta* with Reb Shneur Zalman, as it certainly did the latter.

His Torah was later gathered and published in a volume called *Ḥesed L'Avraham* in Chernovitz in 1851. Though it contains the Torah of other *tzaddikim,* such as Reb Avraham of Kalisk (1741–1810) and even the famous letter of Reb Pinhas of Koretz to Reb Shaya of Dynovitz, it is predominantly the work of the Malakh.[15] And what a work it is. There is no mistaking the Malakh's Torah with that of anyone else in *Ḥesed L'Avraham,* or even with anyone else in all of *Ḥasidut.* If most of the other books of *Ḥasidut* are golden, then the Malakh's book is certainly platinum. Not because he was a greater *tzaddik* than the others, but because of the rarified atmospheres and subtle spiritual maneuvers he was attempting to describe there.

The following piece on the *parsha* (Torah portion) of Noah is an example of his Torah interpretation, though a later teaching will take us into much more challenging realms.

"THE DOVE CAME back toward evening bearing an olive-leaf" (Gen. 8:11).[16]

NOW IT IS KNOWN that prayer must come from the depths and chambers of the heart, which means that one must raise speech to its root in binah, the divine attribute of understanding, from which arises judgments, as is spoken of in the Zohar.[17] *And this why we speak of the chambers of the heart, for the introduction to the Tikkunei Zohar (17a) says that binah is the heart, and this is also what is called "gathering," meaning the synagogue. For there, in that heart place of the synagogue, are gathered all the middot (the modes of being, investment, attitude, and affect), like congregants. This means that our love (ahavah) and awe (yirah) are bound together in unison, and one's prayer is heard, and all the resident middot in the heart are raised upward.*

Middot are the holographic fragments of the sefirot, the divine archetypes or forms, or perhaps even models for every particular action or substance in creation, in existence. From our perspective, they are seen as modes of being, forms in which we invest attitude and emotion either positively or negatively. If negatively, then the divine spark (nitzotz) of the middah is encased in a shell (kelippah), and if positively, then the spark is released to ascend upward to its root source.

Now love (ahavah) and awe (yirah) are often depicted in the tradition like two angelic wings; thus when they are bound together in prayer, as the Malakh suggests, they are able to fly and raise speech (and the middah contained in it) up to its roots in binah, the place of the first divine articulation.

THIS IS WHY the psalmist says, "I long, I yearn for the courts of Y-H-V-H" (Ps. 84:3), meaning that speech desires to rise upward to its root. What is the root of speech? The maskilim (the primal causes of awareness), hokhmah (the divine attribute of wisdom), and binah (the divine attribute of understanding), which are called "the courts of the Y-H-V-H." For this is where the blessed and Holy One may be encountered, as is says, "Y-H-V-H, in hokhmah founded the Earth" (Prov. 3:19).[18]

It should be understood that "maskilim" is a term that the Malakh uses in his own particular way. No one else that I am aware of uses the word "maskil" in quite the same sense. We will deal with this at length later on, but for now, it is sufficient to say that "maskil" translates as "the cause of awareness" and has the sense of being the one who causes mind or effects the possibility of knowing.[19]

What the Malakh is trying to express in this passage is the notion that Earth, though being at the lowest level, is nevertheless connected to hokhmah in the highest realms. This is because hokhmah was created first, and like a seed that contains an entire tree, hokhmah contains the entire plan of creation in seed form. For "Y-H-V-H, in hokhmah (wisdom) founded the Earth." In hokhmah the Earth is just a nekudah, a tiny "point"; nevertheless, it is there in the most subtle and compressed way.

THUS, THE MIDDOT, the modes of being of the lower strata, become clarified as they enter into hokhmah, their holy sparks (nitzotzot) rising upward, and the shells (kelippot) of negativity falling away (Zohar, Va-yikra' 10b). And this is the meaning of the sentence "My heart and my flesh sing to the living God" (Ps. 84:3).[20] For *even "my flesh," meaning the substance of the lower strata, begins to "sing to the living God," meaning that it rises upward, as we have shown.*

In other words, the Malakh is talking about taking the words up to such a refined and rarified atmosphere that everything coarse and unspiritual simply falls away. This process he likens to musical resonance. For when we attune to the divine "note" by taking the words back to their root in the *maskilim*, the body is somehow righted, recalibrated, and begins to vibrate, or sing—God is in the heavens and all is right with the world again.

THIS IS THE *meaning of "And God caused a wind to blow across the Earth" (Gen. 8:1), for the mercies having to do with the mode of Ya'akov were aroused, which in turn is understood by the sentence "And the spirit of Ya'akov, their father, was revived" (Gen. 45:27), meaning that all the constituents of the lower strata involved in physical life on the Earth were uplifted, because it is the divine intention that nothing and no one should be pushed away or rejected, as it is written in 2 Samuel 14:14.*[21]

In the Kabbalah, Jacob is associated with the *sefirah* (attribute) of *tiferet* (beauty) on the Tree of Life (*etz ḥayyim*) and thus also, by further correspondence, to the divine name, Y-H-V-H, representing mercy. Thus "the mercies having to do with the mode of Ya'akov were aroused." And when the Torah says that "And the spirit of Ya'akov, their father, was revived" it means that Jacob's body had been dull and heavy up to this point, like the shells (*kelippot*) encasing the sparks (*nitzotzot*) of holiness, but when divine mercy was activated in Jacob, the sparks hidden within were released and he was revived and healed.

THUS, WHEN THE *wind-spirit passed over the Earth, the waters settled. For it says in the Gemara that the waters of the flood were boiling hot,*[22] *and because water ordinarily represents ḥesed (lovingkindness), it is clear that the generation of the flood saw the cool and calm waters of ḥesed turned into the boiling hot waters of gevurah (judgment). Therefore, it was no longer possible for them to receive life from it; they did not have the proper vessels and they expired. Later, mercy was aroused through Noah, a tzaddik from the foundation of the world, who raised everything up to its root in ḥokhmah.*

The Malakh is trying to say that water should be "grace" (*hesed*), but through the actions of the generation of the flood, the waters were heated to the point at which they began to boil, and thus they turned grace into rigor and judgment (*gevurah* and *din*); water was no longer a giver of life, but the means of their destruction. Who can hear this today and not find in it an admonition regarding our own ecological abuses as well as startling parallels between the boiling waters and the heating up of our oceans through global warming?

Ḥokhmah *represents* koaḥ mah, *the potential for what-ness,*[23] *meaning that Noah was able to raise the 28 times (mentioned in Ecclesiastes 3:1–8) to their root.*[24] *How did he raise those* koaḥ *"twenty-eight"? Through* mah, *"what-ness,"* koaḥ mah, ḥokhmah, *he raised them upward to* malkhut *(the divine attribute of sovereignty), which has nothing of its own, as David ha-Melekh has said, "Yours, Y-H-V-H, are largesse (hesed), might (gevurah), splendor (tiferet), triumph (netzaḥ), and majesty (hod)—yes, all that is in Heaven and on Earth; to You, Y-H-V-H, belong sovereignty (malkhut) and preeminence above all" (1 Chron. 29:11). When one manages to bring those middot (modes) back to their root, then one brings an abundant awareness of divinity into the world.*

This passage will no doubt raise a number of questions for those who are not fluent in the language of Kabbalah. For instance, what are the "28 times" that the Malakh mentions? What is this *koaḥ mah*, "the potential for what-ness"? And what does *malkhut* have to do with *ḥokhmah*?

First let's deal with the business of the "28 times." This is a reference to the famous verses of Ecclesiastes 3:1–8:

A season is set for everything, a time for every experience under
  Heaven:
A time for being born and a time for dying,
A time for planting and a time for uprooting the planted;
A time for slaying and a time for healing,
A time for tearing down and a time for building up;
A time for weeping and a time for laughing,
A time for wailing and a time for dancing;
A time for throwing stones and a time for gathering stones,
A time for embracing and a time for shunning embraces;
A time for seeking and a time for losing,
A time for keeping and a time for discarding;

A time for ripping and a time for sewing,
A time for silence and a time for speaking;
A time for loving and a time for hating;
A time for war and a time for peace.[25]

In this list are 14 positive activities and 14 negative correspondences, making a total of 28 "times," which Noah raised to their root, meaning that he lived his entire life in righteousness.

Now *koah mah* (the potential for what-ness) goes a bit deeper. For the kabbalists have noted that the letters of the word "*hokhmah*" (wisdom) may be rearranged to spell *koah mah*, and thus it is felt that *hokhmah* may also be understood to mean "the potential for what-ness." And what is that, you may ask? It is the divine conceptualizer; it is that which says, "What kind of a conceptual form can I give to that which is not yet in substance?"

The relationship between *malkhut* and *hokhmah* here requires a leap. Think of Pallas Athene in Greek mythology, who jumps out of the head of her father, Zeus. As it says in the Jewish tradition, "The Father founds the daughter."[26] In the same way, *malkhut* (which is conceived of as a divine "daughter") is born from *hokhmah* (which is seen as a divine "father"). Thus *malkhut* is also called *hokhmah tata'ah*, the "lower *hokhmah*," just as Pallas Athene is a daughter-goddess of wisdom. And because it is written, "The end of action comes first," the first thought is what you want to achieve, which is to say, the end product is already found in potential in *hokhmah*, as we have said before. But just as *malkhut* is present as a seed within *hokhmah*, *hokhmah* is also present as a seed within *malkhut*—thus the finite lower world has an innate attraction for the infinite higher worlds.

CONCERNING THIS IT *is said, "Fire is God's vanguard" (Ps. 97:3), meaning that all the sparks (nitzotzot) are raised up and made sweet in their root. As it says, "God passed that window with him,"[27] meaning that all the judgments that had caused the flood fell away through that ruah spirit that aroused mercy on the Earth through Noah. In this way, divinity became manifest in the world. And the fire that was God's vanguard also brought a manifestation of divinity in the world. Thus "There are ten generations from Adam to Noah"[28] refers to the fact that the generation of the flood had turned the 10 beautiful modes of being (middot, sefirot) into judgment (din, gevurah) through their evil deeds and, therefore, were no longer able to receive life. But Noah in the end rectified this situation and brought it to wholeness and completion.*

Again, the Malakh is saying that the flood was not so much a punishment as a natural consequence of that generation's deeds; they had cut themselves off from the divine source of life and thus transformed the waters of kindness into the turbulent waters of judgment and death. They had abused all the divine attributes at their disposal and thus, without knowing it, turned them all into judgment and their own destruction.

THIS IS WHY *it says, "Make yourself an ark of gopher wood with compartments . . . make in it an opening for light . . . make an entrance in the ark; make it with lower, middle, and upper decks" (Gen. 6:14–16). This too refers to our taking speech to its root, for to "come into the ark (tevah)" (Gen. 7:1) is to enter into the word (tevah). And within that word, you will find a lower level, a middle level, and an upper level, meaning that there are three types of speech. The lower level is made up of foul and negative speech, as the lower level of the ark was for the dung of the animals. The middle level is composed of the ordinary speech of life, as this is where the animals lived. But there is also the speech of mitzvah, which is spoken with love (ahavah) and awe (yirah), upon the two wings of which speech is raised to its root. This is why it is said that the upper level of the ark was for human beings. For Noah caused speech to rise on these wings to hokhmah, which is also koah mah, meaning that he caused the KoaH (potential-28, as in the "28 times") to enter into the MaH (what-ness-45), which has the same numerical value as "Adam," a human being. Now there also has to be a way of raising the lower levels of speech containing the seven holy middot that have fallen and been encased in shells (kelippot). This is brought about by the tzaddik who causes the middot within the shells to yearn for God and the shells to surrender; thus the middot are raised from the lower rungs up to God. This is the meaning of the lower, middle, and upper levels of the ark and what must be done with them. Noah did all this as God commanded, and "the ark rose above the Earth" (Gen. 7:17), meaning that speech was no longer earth-bound and was raised upward.*

You can see that the Malakh is returning to the Ba'al Shem Tov's reading of this passage in the *parsha* of Noah and is putting his own interpretation on it.[29] As discussed in Chapter 2, the interpretation hinges on the biblical word for ark, "*tevah*," which in Hebrew means a "box" but that may also refer to a "word," as when we speak of *rashei tevot* "the heads of words," meaning initials. It is also relevant to this reading that God says, *bo el ha-tevah*, "*come* into the ark,"[30] and not "*go* into the ark," for God is actually inside the ark, inside of the word.

What he says here about the potential for words to exist on three levels is so true. Just take an ordinary word like "dance." Now a dance can be everything from a pole dance on the lowest level, to a prom dance on the middle level, to a Hasidic dance on the upper level, right? And when I talk about dance in a holy context, and say the word with *kavanah* in an ecstatic tone, putting my love and my awe into it, all the other negative and neutral meanings fall away; those associations are the shells (*kelippot*).

AND THIS IS *the meaning of "And these are the begettings of Noah" (Gen. 6:9), for what do tzaddikim really beget? Good deeds (gemilut hasadim), as it says in the Midrash.*[31] *And what has he accomplished for those* middot? *Rest. For the name Noah has a sense of "rest," and thus Noah brought rest and completion to those* middot *by raising them up to their root; no longer will they have to yearn to rise upward; they are at home in the place of rest and completion where there are no judgments, where all decrees are sweetened in their root, where sparks rise and evil falls away, as was said before. This is the reason Noah is called a tzaddik and a complete one, for he was able to help all the* middot *to come to completion.*

In this way, a tzaddik *creates connection (yesod) and completion (tammim) for the* middot *in the lower levels, turning judgment into compassion. This is the meaning of* E"T *in et ha-Elohim hit'halekh Noah, "And Noah walked with God" (Gen. 6:9)—all of speech, from E (alef, the first letter of the Hebrew alphabet) to T (tav, the last letter), and the judgments that surrounded it (the divine name, Elohim, representing gevurah and dinim), were turned into mercy as "Noah walked." But what does "walking" mean? This is the process of drawing down mercy, which is accomplished by bringing the troubled and yearning* middot *to "rest." This is the meaning of "And Noah walked with God," for he raised the* middot *to their root, unto rest and fulfillment, and mercy descended into the world once again. And this is the meaning of "The dove came back toward evening bearing an olive leaf" (Gen. 8:11), for speech, which is called "the dove," had been raised and when it returned, it brought with it a response.*[32]

In all of this, the Malakh has been attempting to describe a process that liberates the *middot* that are buried in the substance of the world.[33] And this is the point he is making with "And Noah walked with God." For as Reb Shneur Zalman of Liadi teaches, "The *tzaddik* is called 'one who walks,' for in walking one bobs up and down and does not stand still." That is to say, walking for the *tzaddik* is a process of going up and coming down, raising the sparks upward and bringing down mercy. Noah raised the sparks to Heaven to release the flow of mercy, to sweeten the judgments, which were like a sluice restricting the flow that wanted to descend.

How exactly did he cause the shells (*kelippot*) to surrender the sparks (*nitzotzot*)? Imagine I have a lightbulb screwed into a socket that is surrounded by a frosted glass fixture. The light switch is off and no power is flowing to the bulb. This is like the dormant spark within the shell. But if I turn the switch on, the bulb lights up and so does the fixture, which, instead of concealing the bulb within, now reveals an inner light source and diffuses the light in a helpful way. This is how I see the shells surrendering the sparks.

GROUNDING THE ANGEL

As we have seen, the Malakh was capable of producing deep and holy Torah like his father; but his father, the Maggid of Mezritch, remained concerned for him, fearing that his son might not return from his "flights" to the highest worlds when he was no longer around to plead for his son's life on this plane. Therefore, two months before his own death, the Maggid composed a special will that was addressed only to his son, Avraham the Malakh. In this will he wrote the following:

YOU SHOULD RECITE Minḥah and Ma'ariv (midday and evening prayers) daily with a minyan.

Every day, you are to learn one halakhah (law) from Yad ha-Ḥazaka (the Mishneh Torah of Maimonides).

You are to have something to eat between donning the tefillin of Rashi and those of Rabbeinu Tam, and this is to be followed by Torah study.

Every day, you are to recite at least four chapters of tehillim with great fervor, just as when reciting the four chapters on the night of Yom Kippur.[34]

For Heaven's sake, do not seclude yourself in solitary meditation for more than one day a month, but on that day, you should not even speak with members of your household.

Do not be excessively frugal, but from what is left over after meeting your needs, give to charity.

Every day, you should study what I have recorded of the teachings that I was privileged to hear personally from our master, guide, and teacher, the holy Ba'al Shem Tov, may his merit protect us.

On the anniversary of my death, do not fast; rather, you should make a festive meal and give charity beyond that which you would ordinarily give.

You are to pray with the tallit I received as a present from the holy Ba'al Shem Tov, may his merit protect us, only on Yom Kippur.

Pray from a simple siddur *(prayer book) that does not contain any commentaries.*

You are to visit my grave site only once a year, on my yahrzeit *(the anniversary of my death).*

When the mitnagdim *(opponents of Hasidism) provoke strife, remain silent and let God deal with them.*

Listen to the counsel of Reb [Menachem] Mendele [of Vitebsk] and adhere to the holy virtues of Reb Yehudah Leib HaKohen and the humility of Reb Zushya [of Anipol]. Know that the first thought of my circumspect talmid Reb [Shneur] Zalman [of Liadi] is a minor form of prophecy. Do whatever he says, for even in the generation of the Ba'al Shem Tov he would have shone—a word to the wise is sufficient. Listen to him in all matters, for his wisdom (ḥokhmah), understanding (binah), and knowledge (da'at) are immeasurable.

Do not push my talmid Reb Zushya to assume any mantle of pastoral leadership, for this holy man has already transcended this possibility—a word to the wise is sufficient.[35]

This will tells us a great deal about the Maggid's concern for his son's health and well-being, but you will no doubt have noticed that there is nothing especially esoteric about the advice he gives—on the contrary, most of it is extremely practical. Of course, there was little necessity to speak to his son about abstruse aspects of Kabbalah of which he was likely already aware. My own sense is that this was not what the early Hasidic masters spent their time on. After all, the great insight of the Ba'al Shem Tov was to find a way around all of the hurdles and complexities that barred the way to spiritual experience for ordinary people, opening the gates of direct access. Even if these brilliant *tzaddikim* were aware and fully capable of the mental gymnastics various systems of Kabbalah required, they had learned that the great door of myriad locks could also be shattered by the force of deep and simple *kavanah*.

Whatever the reasons behind the simple advice, I don't want to stray too far from the primary point of the will: a father's concern for his son whom he is about to leave on his own. This is why the latter part of the will is concerned with those whom the Malakh, who was still a young man, could turn after his father's passing, and who the Maggid was also leaving as guardians of his son's well-being. We know that these were all disciples who were especially close to the Maggid, but we suspect they were individuals to whom the Malakh also felt close. Otherwise, other great disciples of the Maggid might have been mentioned. It is the same group who is present with the Malakh at his father's bedside two months later, just before the Maggid's passing, when he reiterates his advice to his son in brief . . .

AVRAMENYU, CONDUCT YOURSELF as you have always done; listen to Zalmenyu and all will be well with you. Please do not afflict yourself, for I tell you, a small hole in the body causes a large hole in the soul[36]—and your soul is something altogether unique.[37]

I have quoted this teaching time and time again—"a small hole in the body causes a large hole in the soul." We must take care of our physical bodies as if it were care for the soul. And one can hear in this the regret the Maggid must have felt about the damage he had done to his own body over the years through rigorous asceticism, and his fear that his son might do the same, perhaps shortening his life.

THE MAGGID'S SUCCESSOR?

After the passing of the Maggid, three of the four "guardians" of the Malakh submitted a *k'tav hitkashrut,* a letter of commitment to him as a Rebbe that read as follows . . .

WE, THE UNDERSIGNED, desire to link our spirits and souls to the One whose name is a blessing, and for this purpose we submit to the authority of our teacher and master, Rabbi Avraham—may he be blessed with life—the son of our master and teacher, the head of all those in exile, the Maggid of Rovno—may he abide in peace—with love and respect. We pledge to obey his words faithfully, and thereby to climb the divine ladder together with him. And thus we ask that our teacher and guide may, upon receiving this letter, consent to inspire us with ruaḥ ha-kodesh and penetrate us with ḥokhmah and binah, granting us his good counsel.
—Anipol, Hanukkah, 1772 (approximately seven days after the Maggid's passing).
Rabbi Yehudah Leib HaKohen
Rabbi Meshullam Zushya [of Anipol]
Rabbi Shneur Zalman [later of Liadi][38]

This was a beautiful gesture, but it clearly wasn't something that Reb Avraham desired. He did not become a Rebbe to these already accomplished masters, nor to anyone else. It is likely that Reb Yehudah Leib, Reb Zushya, and Reb Shneur Zalman knew that he would not accept this letter of *hitkashrut,* and that it was really intended in another privately understood sense. *"Hitkashrut"* literally means "self-binding," and it is possible that these three devoted disciples of the Maggid were doing the will of their Rebbe, "binding" themselves in a contract to protect the Malakh, and through their devotion, to keep him in the world as long as possible.

It seems that it was too early in the Hasidic experiment for dynastic succession. Was this by design? If so, whose design? Looking at Reb Tzvi Hirsh, the son of the Ba'al Shem Tov, we see that he was not charismatically or temperamentally suited to leadership and did not succeed his father. And while the Malakh was infinitely more suited in ability and charisma, he did not desire the succession either, and even followed a path that ran somewhat against the grain of Hasidism. For me, it is difficult not to see a teleological wisdom at work here, an "intelligent design," if you will, in which neither of the sons of the two most influential figures in the whole Hasidic movement were capable, for various reasons, of becoming dynastic successors. Was it because it was not healthy at this early stage in the movement's development? I think there is much that can be said for this view. For if Hasidism would have succumbed to a strictly dynastic succession at that early stage, the development of truly dynamic individuals would likely have been stifled, while at the same time, other less qualified sons might have been pushed into a position of leadership that they were never suited for; both situations would have weakened the movement considerably when it most needed to expand with new life.

THE MOUNTAIN

An anecdote that is still told among Hasidim gives us an example of Reb Avraham the Malakh's abandonment of any status based on his father's reputation and his refusal to receive people in the manner of a Rebbe.

ONCE, WHILE REB Avraham the Malakh was visiting his father-in-law in Kremenitz, the leaders of the community sought to honor the son of the famous Maggid of Mezritch, but found him uncommunicative and aloof. Eventually, he walked over to the window to look out at a nearby mountain. Seeing him move toward the window, a prominent young scholar in the community saw his opportunity to approach the Malakh and impress him with his own Torah. He had expected the Malakh to turn and greet him, but he didn't. The Malakh simply continued looking out at the mountain. So the young rabbi sidled up to him and said, "What's so special about that lump of stone?" The Malakh replied without turning, "I am contemplating the mystery before me . . . how one can be in the presence of such a majestic mountain and still fail to see its glory, thinking it only a lump of stone."[39]

In some tellings, the Malakh replies with a strong rebuke, "See how you can seem to be tall and high and still be nothing more than a lump of stone." And elsewhere, "I look and I am amazed to see how such a lump of earth made much of itself until it grew into a tall mountain."[40] In both, he sets the self-important young rabbi low, and this seems to be the point of the *ma'aseh*. But I tend to see the point elsewhere—not in his quip, but in the situation itself. He stands aloof from everyone, and even when approached directly, he does not turn from his meditation on the mountain to acknowledge the young man. In the telling we give here, what he says aloud may be an admonition to the self-important young scholar, and even instructive, but it is not exactly delivered in the manner of a Rebbe. There is still something of the brush-off, or at least the single-minded absorption that does not have time for a potential Hasid. For Reb Avrahm, there is only the mountain. It is always the mountain.

THE FIFTIETH GATE

This mountain of the Malakh's meditation is significant, for in many ways it is symbolic of the heights to which he constantly wishes to attain or at least the jumping off place to still higher regions. It is in this sense that he is most appropriately called "the Angel," for Reb Avraham is seeking nothing less than to ascend to regions where no ordinary human being can hope to exist. He is like a spiritual cosmonaut attempting to launch himself ever higher through the atmospheric strata—passing well beyond the barriers of the stratosphere in a perilous struggle to maintain life and, more important, consciousness, as he searches for a kind of Karman line between the Earth's atmosphere and outer space. The end of his existence is the necessary outcome of such a journey and is even the goal in some sense, but he wants to maintain awareness for as long as possible, to bring back the secrets of the heavens, where all opposing things are reabsorbed into harmony and all rends in the fabric of the universe are healed.

This brings us to what I believe is the most important of the Malakh's teachings, brought back from his own explorations of the nether regions of existence and nonexistence. It is found in the introduction to the *Ḥesed L'Avraham* and sets the tone for everything else he teaches.[41]

Before we begin to look at this teaching, it should be remembered that Kabbalah is a language, and whenever we speak of anything that has subtle differentiation, we need a lot of vocabulary. Just as a mountain climber needs to distinguish terrain with great subtlety, so does a spiritual climber. For it isn't just "spiritual," it is spiritual on the material level, the effective level, the cognitive level, and also on the numinous level. By the Malakh's time, there was already a wealth of kabbalistic vocabulary to cover various parts of this terrain, though not all of it equally. But the Malakh does not want to use the old vocabulary that everybody else uses. For he believes that the territories he wishes to explore have not been adequately described. Even more important, he believes that if he were to use that language, then everybody would say, "Ah-ha! I know what he is talking about!" before they have really taken it in and digested the profound holiness and subtleties of these celestial realms. He is aware, even if they are not, that what he is talking about is what the vocabulary is trying to say. When people become inured to the sound of the words of the vocabulary, they can no longer know what the essence is that is being talked about, just as we saw with the Maggid in his encounter with the Ba'al Shem Tov.[42] So the Malakh in this teaching is using his own terminology to describe these regions in such a way that people will be forced to look on them with new eyes, eyes de-conditioned and prepared for wonder, allowing a new understanding to begin to take hold. So if you are able, try to look on this teaching with a beginner's mind.

Please be patient in the reading of this material and its accompanying introductions. The truth is, we are almost ashamed to lead most readers into the Malakh's highly abstruse Torah without these extended *hakdamot* (introductions), which was also true in the Maggid's case. It was difficult to decide whether we should even to attempt a translation of it, not knowing who would be able to appreciate what he is trying to say. But for those who were willing to strain at the edge of awareness, like the Malakh himself, we finally decided to do this.

BEHOLD, THE VERY *emergence of the manifest essence of the blessed One, whose name is blessed—the same One who has granted permission to reveal a little of the Torah of Truth here, which is called the Kabbalah, to those on this lower stratum, to those who hasten toward the great darkening conflagration, the fire that has been darkened due to our sins and the extension of the exile in which the people of God suffer from generation to generation. However, the truth is that our Torah (already in our possession) is in fact that very truth (of the Kabbalah), but it has been darkened, obscured, and materially concretized through our sins. If someone in arrogance thinks that they can stretch forth their hand and encompass with it our sovereign God, then all they will find in the words of Torah are thorns and thistles, and not the Torah of Truth.*

———————————

The Malakh opens his book with a parallel to the opening lines of the Torah, "In the beginning, God created Heaven and Earth" (Gen. 1:1), saying instead, "Behold the very emergence of the manifest essence of the blessed One, whose name is blessed." Like every good kabbalist before him, the Malakh wants to know: What came before that "beginning"? How did the process of the divine unfolding begin, from its most subtle emergence in the primeval desire to the gross material manifestation of which we are currently a part? How did the Godhead give birth to the God that we can even begin to conceive, the name of God, which unfolded through infinite degrees of concretization until we came into existence in such a way that we saw ourselves as somehow separate from God? How did that happen, and how can we follow the trail back to the source beyond manifestation?

To whom is this truth to be revealed? To those of us who still see ourselves as separate from God, who in our confusion run toward "the great darkening conflagration" of ignorance, toward the obscuring fire, which is fed and continues to grow because of our sins. Can we really be blamed for acting according to a divinely ordained irony? Perhaps not; it is, after all, the nature of the universe God created, or unfolded. Nevertheless, another aspect of the universe is truth and knowledge. The Torah is an example of the truth that leads us back to the beginning and away from the "dark fire." We see this notion of the twin principles of the universe everywhere, from the Hindu Vedanta to the American philosopher Charles Sanders Peirce—one evolutionary principle making order, and a second parallel involutional principle making chaos.[43] Indeed, so paradoxical are they that one could easily switch the definition of the other, seeing evolutionary unfolding as the chaos maker and the involutional collapsing as the return to primordial oneness! This is the place to which the Malakh brings us with just a few potent words. Fortunately, he immediately he throws us a lifeline, the Torah of truth, the Kabbalah.

Now, the phrase "Torah of Truth," *Torat ha-Emet*, is well known in Kabbalah, and kabbalists are often referred to in the literature as the *ḥakhmei ha-emet*, the "wise ones of truth." But the very phrase "Torah of Truth" suggests that there is a Torah that may not be true, that the Torah may be misunderstood, and thus the Kabbalah, the *Torat ha-Emet*, acts as a kind of skeleton key to unlock the levels of truth inherent in the *Torah mi'Sinai*, the Torah that was given at Sinai. Even more interesting, the Malakh suggests that the Torah of Truth in its ideal state is not concretized into letters and words but is only in such a state due to our ignorance and sin. Thus when he talks about those who will find in the words of Torah "thorns and thistles," he means that you have to know what those words are referring to; if you only know the words and not the reference, you haven't got it.

BEHOLD, "GOD HAS said, 'Let there be light' " (Gen. 1:3), and light flowed unto God's servants, our great teachers, and especially to my Rebbe [the Maggid of Mezritch], and the teacher of my Rebbe [the Ba'al Shem Tov], the light of my eyes. Even that teaching that we have received from them [the Maggid of Mezritch and the Ba'al Shem Tov] has become grosser and more concretized.

There are some *ma'asiot* that have emphasized Reb Avraham's apparent rebelliousness and spurning of his father's advice regarding asceticism, but here we see so clearly how he speaks of his father with love as "the light of my eyes" and honors his teaching, which he believes is becoming "grosser and more concretized."[44] But what does this mean, "grosser and more concretized"? There is a wonderful teaching by Reb Kalonymous Kalmish of Piasetzno, where he says, "How can we speak of Kabbalah as being *nistar* (hidden) anymore? After all, there are so many books written about the Kabbalah now—nothing is 'hidden'—it is actually *nigleh*, 'revealed.' What is 'hidden' is the move from the words to the inner experience; that is what is called *nistar*." Over and over again we see this teaching in different forms—the *nistar* is the inner dimension, the inner application of the teaching, the realization or actualization of it—thus what the Ba'al Shem Tov actually showed the Maggid was the *nistar* of the *nistar* behind the *nigleh* of the *nistar!* This is likely what the Malakh means to say. For he could see, even at that time, a degradation in the teaching, getting farther and farther away from the source—the primordial *shefa* or flow from which the Ba'al Shem Tov and Maggid of Mezritch drew—becoming petrified into dogma and spurious techniques. Thus the Malakh is saying that he is going to that same source.

However, if we are to truly understand the significance of the Malakh's Torah, we should consider the evolutional progression from the Ba'al Shem Tov through the Maggid and eventually imparted to the Malakh. Here we are not talking about diminishment and degradation, but a refinement of ideas. For with the Ba'al Shem Tov, it was all one great organic process; he is the spiritual genius who lives in the moment and does not ask so much about "how," but the Maggid is more the intellectual and begins to analyze the process. The Maggid seems to be more aware that he is reaching into a divine place, which he called *kadmut ha-sekhel* (the beginning of awareness), analogous to preverbal awareness for us, which is even prior to thinking in words. This is a very important move in Hasidism. I don't think "analyze" is even the right word for what he was doing, because this is already a *binah* word; he is trying to catch this "something" before it even comes into *ḥokhmah*. That is *kadmut ha-sekhel*.

It is no accident that the Torah of the Maggid of Mezritch and his son, Avraham the Malakh, are the most difficult teachings in this volume, for they are both of similar mind, and both are attempting to explore the same territory. Indeed, the Malakh takes over his father's exploration of *kadmut ha-sekhel* (the beginning of awareness), and begins to talk about it as the *maskil*, the "*cause* of awareness." In some sense, we might even say that the Maggid was the one who discovered this territory for us. That is not to say that no one discovered that territory before him; they certainly did, but he discovered it *for us* in Hasidism and began to put it to practical use in his teaching. Upon this foundation, we begin to build everything that we know of the cause and use of awareness. But if he was the one who discovered that territory for us, Avraham the Malakh was the one who went back, exploring and mapping it in a thorough way, making a bridge between the Maggid of Mezritch and the teachings of Shneur Zalman of Liadi.[45]

In a way, this progression from the Ba'al Shem Tov to the Malakh could be seen as a process of something becoming both grosser and more subtle. In one sense it is an advance, and in another a retreat. For with differentiation, you always go farther away, and yet . . . how far is it from my fingernail to my stem cells? Very far away, right? You can't expect that fingernail to have the same capacity that the stem cells had to become a fingernail. Nevertheless, you can read my DNA from my fingernail. So there is a narrowing of teaching that happens simply because you cannot go down all roads at once; nevertheless, it is still connected to the source.

NOW LET US *begin with God's help, and through their [the Maggid's and the Ba'al Shem Tov's] merit as well as that of our other teachers and masters who served God and revealed the Torah of Truth (Kabbalah) to us in dark places. For it is indeed a Torah of the truthfulness of Truth that is revealed to us (a little at a time) from its essence, intending to guide us on the path back to God. It is this that saves us from the great darkening conflagration and transgression against God, and the Thirteen Principles constellating the true faith of Yisra'el, which we have received from our ancestors, the* tannaim *and the* nevi'im rishonim, *and those who came later, as our teacher Nahmanides has taught us, and as we can also find in the introduction to the* Tikkunei Zohar.

It is written, "Yours, Y-H-V-H, are greatness, might, splendor, triumph and majesty—yes, all that is in Heaven and Earth" (1 Chron. 29:11) (referring to the lower seven sefirot, *which are here called* sikhliyot). *Now, a human being has seven kinds of* sikhliyot, *ideating, or causative modes of awareness [. . .]*

In modern parlance, *sekhel* (the singular form of *sikhliyot*) has come to mean "common sense." Thus we have the wonderful anecdote about the ḤaBaD Hasid who is sitting around with the other Hasidim having a bottle of vodka. He sighs and says, "Isn't it wonderful that we have so much *hokhmah, binah,* and *da'at*? (ḤaBaD stands for *hokhmah,* "wisdom," *binah,* "understanding," and *da'at,* "knowledge.") If only we had a little more *sekhel,* we might start to make use of them!" That is to say, it is common sense that puts it all together.

Now if you take that to be the colloquial meaning of *sekhel,* you can see that it also has something to do with the "creative conceptualizer" within. It isn't yet a concept, but it is endeavoring to find a concept that can hold it. The *sekhel* is that which transforms the abstract into the concrete concept, and later, it is also that which tries to abstract from the concrete model (that I already have and understand) a gestalt that would fit the abstraction, and therefore bring a sense of understanding to it.

[. . .] THAT HAVE SEVEN divine counterparts, as it is written, "And one against the other has God arrayed them" (Eccles. 7:14).[46] *If one wishes to magnify the name of the creator and elevate oneself, having the power to overcome the enemies of God and one's own enemies, to make God and oneself beautiful, as it is expressed elsewhere, one must bind these seven kinds of* sikhliyot *to the seven* sikhliyot *of holiness, purifying the lower with the higher, according to God's design.*

"And one against the other has God arrayed them" refers to polarities of the same energy, positive and negative valences, neither God nor oneself but the vis-à-vis connection *between*. Though the higher causative modes of awareness (*sikhliyot*) are parallel to and even connected with those in the lower world, the seven basic causative modes of awareness below are so often used in the service of ignominious ends that they appear to be on opposite ends of the spectrum. Thus, the lower *sikhliyot* must be *intentionally* bound to the higher *sikhliyot* to bring about the divinization of our consciousness and our world. In other words, one should do all the things that one does in this world for the sake of Heaven, so that even the part that is secular will also be done in the purity of holiness.

In many ways, one can find much greater precision about the *sikhliyot*, or *sefirot* in the teachings of the Malakh's friend Reb Shneur Zalman of Liadi, but we must not forget the fantastic contraction and descent from the subtle vibration that the Malakh has made even to talk about them in this way. For this reason, I always wanted to gather a group of students to study this text with a parallel piece by Reb Shneur Zalman on the *sefirot* that is appended to the *Hesed L'Avraham*.[47]

EACH OF THESE seven sikhliyot *(causative modes) contain in themselves seven more (as it is explained in many places), so that really we must speak of forty-nine* sikhliyot. *When these holy forty-nine (from* hesed *of* hesed *to* malkhut *of* malkhut) *are gathered together, there rests upon them a Fiftieth Gate of Understanding, which is beyond human conceptualization.*

When the Malakh says, "Each of these seven *sikhliyot* contain in themselves seven more (as it is explained in many places), so that really we must speak of forty-nine *sikhliyot*," he means that each of the seven *sikhliyot* (*sefirot*) has a fractal of the Tree of Life (*etz hayyim*) within itself; that is to say, versions of each of the *sikhliyot* that are "colored," as it were, by that particular divine attribute. Thus within the *sekhel* of *hesed* alone, we have seven distinct permutations: (1) *hesed* of *hesed*; (2) *gevurah* of *hesed*; (3) *tiferet* of *hesed*; (4) *netzah* of *hesed*; (5) *hod* of *hesed*; (6) *yesod* of *hesed*; and (7) *malkhut* of *hesed*. Together these make up the dimensions of this one *sekhel*.[48] If we consider that a similar pattern is repeated in each of the other *sikhliyot*, we come up with forty-nine distinct permutations of these causative modes.

In the kabbalistic tradition, it is these permutations we attune ourselves to as we "count" the Omer from the second night of Pesah to the night before Shavuot. Originally, this period of forty-nine days was a way to punctuate the ripening barley's daily growth, until the Omer of ripened barley was brought as a sacrifice to the Temple in gratitude for the harvest. After we were no longer involved in farming, the sages ordered us to count, and this counting became a moral preparation for the receiving of the Torah at Sinai on Shavuot. Later, these ideas are further refined in the Zohar as a movement from the Forty-Nine Gates of Defilement to the Forty-Nine Gates of Understanding, as the Malakh is speaking about here. Thus this pattern of seven times seven has both a cosmic and a personal significance for us. The kabbalists taught us that the seven weeks represent the periods in which one or another of the seven holy attributes represented by the seven names not to be erased appear in forty-nine different combinations.

So now, the Malakh will most often speak of the forty-nine *sikhliyot* to continue to make his point about the Fiftieth Gate, which also participates in the same symbolism of the Omer counting, as well as the Jubilee (*yovel*) year. In the counting of the Omer, "fifty" corresponds to Shavuot, meaning that we have traveled fifty days from the slavery of Egypt in Pesaḥ to the freedom of receiving the Torah as God's people. Likewise, the Jubilee year represents the year in which all things return to their source, or former owners, and the captives are set free. In the Fiftieth Gate, all things return to their primeval origin, and all ideas of separation and bondage begin to break down.

Freedom will become a theme as the passage progresses.

THIS IS THE *beginning of* binah *(understanding), from which arises judgments, as it says in the Zohar.*[49] *These forty-nine* sikhliyot *are called* Ma"T *[the Hebrew letters* mem *and* tet, *which equal forty-nine, and also form the word] "stumbling-block," meaning that they are mixed with good and evil, arrayed forty-nine* sikhliyot *against forty-nine [another reference to positive and negative valences].*

This is the way they stand at the beginning when they have not yet been assimilated in holiness, concerning which it was said, "God will not give the tzaddik *a stumbling block (*Ma"T*)" (Ps. 119:165).*[50] *Thus there rests upon them the Fiftieth Gate of celestial holiness, and therefore we speak of Fifty Gates of Understanding (*binah*), the world of total freedom [*herut*].*

There is an understanding that God creates good as well as evil, one array against another, seven against seven; in the literature (the Zohar and elsewhere), the negative seven are the "seven nations of Cana'an" (Deut. 7:1) that have to be removed. But we must also understand that the Malakh is not talking about it from a place where it becomes real evil; it is only a fragment of a fragment of *potential* for evil. It is so subtle on this level and likewise so easy on this high level to bring it into harmony, and that is what the Malakh wants to do with this teaching: to fix evil at the place where it is only the slightest potential for evil, and to harmonize the manifestation with its holy matrix of potential in *binah*.

NOW, THAT FIFTIETH Gate (which is the nun of ayin, "nothingness"), which is beyond the awareness, is also beyond the effect of any evil, and the mind is not able to comprehend it, for if it were, one would cease to exist. Thus it is called maskil (cause of awareness), that which effects the possibility of knowing.

So how do we understand *maskil* vis-à-vis the *sekhel?* The *maskil* causes the *sekhel*. The prefix *"ma-"* in *"maskil"* is a causative; it is the ma, matrix, mother that gives birth to the *sikhliyot,* the ideating or causative modes of awareness, its children. In a sense, they are just subtle concretizations, or little versions of the *maskil.* They are also in a reciprocal relationship to the *maskil,* for what the *maskil* wants you to know is *sekhel,* and what *sekhel* wants you to know is how to put it all together in such a way that it creates an awareness of the *maskil!*

ABOVE THIS IS yet another maskil, the yud of ayin. In all the books this is called ḥokhmah (wisdom). Concerning that Fiftieth Gate, one cannot attain it, and anyone who would attain it, would become annihilated, as we have said before. Above this second maskil is the beginning point of another maskil, the alef of ayin. Above that very first maskil, the alef of ayin, there are still further maskilim, but they are such that you cannot even assign names to them. This very beginning of a maskil, called "alef" (which makes no sound), one cannot attain to, even though it is pointed to in the alef, because that maskil is like a garment over the second maskil, which is beyond it. And one above the other, each one cannot attain to the other; each one finds that the other is beyond, and although there is life in them, this maskil has been called alef, even though that highest maskil is still nothing but a garment for the maskil below it.

Now, there are things that can be explained here, and things that can only be contemplated, as more words will not necessarily untangle this paradox and create awareness.

What is clear is that he is now discussing the upper three *sefirot*—keter, ḥokhmah, and *binah*—which are often seen as aspects of the divine mind.

Together, he describes these as *maskilim* (causes of awareness), and as *ayin* (nothingness). Separately, each is a *maskil*—*keter* the first, *ḥokhmah* the second, and *binah* the third and closest to the forty-nine *sikhliyot*. Thus when one ascends through the Forty-Nine Gates, one reaches *binah*, the Fiftieth Gate. The Malakh likewise distinguishes each of these three *maskilim* with the three letters of the Hebrew word *ayin* (nothingness). Thus *keter* is the "*alef* of *ayin*"; *ḥokhmah*, the "*yud* of *ayin*"; and *binah*, the "*nun* of *ayin*." All together, they comprise aspects of the unknowable nothingness.

The Malakh also tells us that there are *maskilim* "above" the "first *maskil*" of *keter*, or the "*alef* of *ayin*," which is only the "very beginning" of a *maskil*. That is to say, *keter* is like an hourglass, narrow at its center with an opening above and below the center. In kabbalistic parlance, the opening above is *Atik Yomin* (Ancient of Days), the impersonal or supra-personal Divine, and below is *Arik Anpin* (Long Face), the very beginnings of the personal God who is "slow to anger" and compassionate.[51] Thus the *maskilim* above refers to the most transcendent impersonal Godhead, utterly beyond even our attempts at conceptualization. Earlier we spoke of *keter* and *ayin* as a kind of "black hole" or "singularity," and it may be well for one to compare the teachings of the Maggid and the Malakh on these matters.[52]

When the Malakh says, "the mind is not able to comprehend it, for if it were, one would cease to exist," he is saying that we cannot put our mind around it, we cannot encompass it in the sense of "grasping," as one would grasp something within one's hand; it may "comprehend" us, but not we it, for we are encompassed and surrounded by its greater reality. Because this idea transcends mentation and takes us out of our discursive mind, the ego structure is annihilated, and thus we "cease to exist."

The way in which he speaks of "garments" here goes nicely with the language of holarchy, as Ken Wilber has elaborated it.[53] Therefore, every layer "transcends and includes" the layer beneath. Nevertheless, the Malakh is also describing a paradox here, for the garments (*levushim*) have both *makif* (transcending, enveloping) and *penimi* (inwardly penetrating, influencing) qualities.

As we saw with his father, the Maggid, he isn't trying to tell you about mind, but the cause of mind, the ultimate reality behind mentation, and this is necessarily paradoxical. Can you imagine Reb Avraham trying to write this out, trying to put a pen and ink to such thoughts that are nearly beyond thought? When he is speaking here, I have the feeling that he is in touch with that place and cannot help but stammer. Thus we have to remember that we are looking at material that was written by a person of expanded consciousness, for whom his hand and the pen were not suitable vessels for condensing what he wished to put into words. However, he writes in telegraphic style, and if we want even to begin to understand him, it pays to go over the material several times with a contemplative mind, allowing the *maskil* in us to try and make sense of it.

IN THAT VERY first maskil *(keter), of which we have already spoken, there is a hint, a spark* (nitzotz) *of the blessed holiness of the* Ain Sof *(the Infinite Nothing), which is above all. It is even beyond the* maskilim, *and certainly beyond the* sikhliyot *that the* maskilim *have produced. For all these are emanations of the One emanator— all the* maskilim *and* sikhliyot—*invigorated with life, sanctified, and brought into being in every moment, because the One desires to have them in existence. All of these are like the clay in the hand of a potter who is far beyond the clay, a nothing in a nothing, and there is no possibility to estimate it as something and give it a place. In* Ain Sof *they are all annihilated completely, as if they didn't exist. They all become what they were before they became, a dimensionless point of desire to be brought into life, still hidden in the divine will.*

In the Kabbalah, God is often referred to as *Ain Sof*, "Infinite Nothing," which is a way to preserve God's transcendence. Another good translation might be, "Without Limits." Both are concepts of what cannot be conceived, at least not completely. Nothing, not-a-thing, not divided, not separate, by itself can almost be conceived; but then we qualify it with the notion of infinity, and we simply fade out of existence. For we can easily imagine a blank white or black piece of paper, for instance, containing nothing, but when we remove the concept of borders on that paper and begin to watch it spread to encompass all that there is, there is no longer a point of reference, even for our own existence!

For the philosophers of the medieval Kabbalah who were inspired by Maimonides (1135–1204), *Ain Sof* refers to God as the absolute. Now, an absolute is not limited by any attributes or parts; it is beyond perception and transcendent of all our concepts, especially temporal and spatial concepts. This is the axiom around which all kabbalistic ideas of God must conform; they must preserve God's transcendence. For it says in the Torah, "I am *Y-H-V-H*—I have not changed" (Mal. 3:6). That is to say, God is not changeable, or subject to change; therefore, God must be transcendent of all our concepts.

Here the Malakh tries to give us just the barest hint of how this must be, comparing the *Ain Sof* to a potter, and the *maskilim* to clay in the potter's hand. Now, the level of our perceptual awareness is of a world of pottery, as it were, but the levels of the *maskilim* and *sikhliyot*, in comparison, are still in a world of clay, being very plastic and malleable. Even so, by using the example of the potter, the Malakh seems to be asking, "What substantive relationship exists between clay and the potter's hand?" Moreover, "What relationship exists between the clay and the idea of a particular pot in the potter's mind?" Beyond even that, "What relationship exists between the clay and the desire to make a vessel of some sort, or even to make something at all?" The distance between the mental origin and the physical substance is so great that there is almost no relationship, and where it does exist in the mind is only a dimensionless point, a "nothing in a nothing" that cannot be estimated or evaluated in any way. Its life is but *possibility* until gradually it is invested with life as the potter entertains the idea, muses on it, and begins to form it into a something.

NOW THE SIKHLIYOT *of the* maskilim *receive general and specific tikkun or refinement as they pass through the seven forms, so that all forty-nine* sikhliyot *are gathered together, and the Fiftieth Gate hovers over them, as we have said. From the creation of the world until the coming of the* Mashiaḥ *in the future, this hasn't been fully accomplished by anyone except Moshe Rabbeinu at the time that the Torah was given to him and in that moment before he died, concerning which it was said, "there is a portion of the legislator hidden" (asher sham helkas m'holki tzafun) (Deut. 33:21),[54] meaning that he had completed the tikkun of the sikhliyot until the Fiftieth Gate hovered over them, allowing him to legislate and to teach us so that we too might be able to reach the awareness of those seven* sikhliyot *with our minds.*

Thus we shall make connections and integrations of letters and thought, constructing an alphabet and a language concerning the Fiftieth Gate, making our own engravings and impressions of the sikhliyot, *which are hinted at in general and in detail to each person according to the root of their soul. This will not comprise the entire Fiftieth Gate, but will merely be a fractal of a fractal (mahshehu) of the forty-nine for which he (Moshe) made a tikkun, so that we should be able to bear that awareness and not be annihilated by it. For again, we cannot fully attain to them with our minds, not even a fractal of the hovering* maskil *(Fiftieth Gate) and certainly not the higher levels, because we would certainly become annihilated in them. Therefore, that Fiftieth Gate does not hover in total for us, but only a portion of it. This even applies to Moshe Rabbeinu, concerning which we have spoken before.*

In the beginning of this passage, the Malakh uses the word *"tikkun"* (fixing) to describe a process through which the Forty-Nine Gates are opened. But *tikkun* is a very difficult word to translate because of the broad range of meanings that may be given to it; it is not as simple as the colloquial meaning of the English word "fix" would suggest. For on the one hand, we could say that the devolution of the *sikhliyot* as they emerge from the *maskilim* is also a process of *tikkun*, whereby the *sikhilyot* are progressively "molded" and "fixed" into reified forms. Nevertheless, the Malakh is talking about the reversal of this process, taking the *tikkun* in the opposite direction. Here the *tikkun* is no longer to "mold," "refine," and "fix" into form, but to "realign" these modes and patterns with their original intentions, making careful "adjustments" to them, chipping away the coarse materiality to reveal those angelic and gossamer energies within, which are by nature light and ascendant.

Now, according to the Malakh, *only* Moses, our teacher, has accomplished the opening of the Fiftieth Gate, and even then, it was only twice, and not even a complete opening. For he names the two occasions—"at the time that the Torah was given to him and in that moment before he died"—and in the end of the passage, he says, "This even applies to Moshe Rabbeinu," meaning that he did not open the Fiftieth Gate fully. This latter point we will return to, but first we need to consider what it means that Moses was able to open the Fiftieth Gate at all, and how this is connected with his function as a "legislator," as the Malakh suggests it is.

The opening of the Fiftieth Gate by Moses meant that he was able to be a channel for the people, bringing an "understanding" of a "fractal of a fractal" of the holy *sikhliyot* into the minds of the people. This channeling and scaling-down of divinity is identical with his work as a legislator, as a lawgiver, meaning that the sacred technology that will allow one to open the Forty-Nine Gates is embedded in the Torah that came down at Sinai. This we may understand in varying degrees, according to the "root" of our "souls"—that is, according to the light we are given.

The "legislator" is the one who causes the statutes to be made, setting down and making static what was previously dynamic. Most of Deuteronomy is trying to nail down that which cannot be nailed down, and so you can see what a struggle it is to bring divinity into manifestation and somehow still allow it maintain its divine character. This is one *tikkun* that Moses made for the people. But you see how it brings us back to the open-ended nature of the process of *tikkun*? For Moses first had to make the *tikkun* "upward," as it were, through all the Forty-Nine Gates, to open the Fiftieth Gate, and then become the channel for a new *tikkun*, "downward," putting divinity once again into form, but this time a form that could be read like a map by the people, taking them back to the source!

He tells us that the map is clearly not the territory, but slowly we may be able to use it to put a message together, to construct a language of understanding, scratching together clues ("engravings and impressions") even as the Malakh is doing in the very moment of his writing this for us. Even so, this will not allow us to open the Fiftieth Gate fully, for that would cause the end of our existence. Nevertheless, we may be able to attain a "fractal of a fractal" of the great pattern, or a "smidgeon of the smidgeon." That is what the word he uses means, for *mahshahu* is barely there, barely in existence. Nevertheless, we may begin to see a branch of a branch of the greater pattern, transforming our awareness, and yet still preserving our life! After all, the transformation is best used in this world. Thus he teaches that Moses was able to do this only twice: once at the Revelation at Sinai, and once at the moment of his death.

FROM THE TIME *that he [Moshe] spoke his prophecy as the legislator for the people until the end of the writing of the Torah, he ascended through higher and higher levels until a spark (nitzotz) from the very mouth of God was finally revealed to him, a spark of the Ain Sof, of which we have already spoken. It flashed on him and the* maskilim *were made manifest and attained one by the other until the Fiftieth Gate of the last* maskil *(binah) was opened above the forty-nine* sikhliyot, *which were all annihilated in that Fiftieth Gate, their root. For this is the way of nature, that everything rushes to its root. It is the same when a candle is brought to a larger flame—the fire desires to merge—and so, that which is below wishes to be annihilated and incorporated in its root. Concerning this it was said, "no one knows his [Moshe's] burial place" (Deut. 34:6). The angels said he was buried "below," and the humans said "above," all of which is to say that he entered into the Fiftieth Gate, which is called* hi'uly *(unknown).*

We see now that Moses was able to open the door "just a smidgeon" at Sinai, allowing a "smidgeon of a smidgeon" of the light to flow down to us on the level of our existence. We know that it was "just a smidgeon" because he did not die in the effort. Nevertheless, he obviously saw more in the moment before he died, having been kissed, as it were, by "a spark from the very mouth of God." That is to say, a fragment of the *Ain Sof* was revealed to him at that time.

How can this be if he had only just attained to the opening of the Fiftieth Gate, which is so far below the *Ain Sof?*

Imagine if you will, Moses' ascending through the Forty-Nine Gates to knock on the Fiftieth Gate. The Fiftieth Gate is closed, of course, but the knock will surely be heard within by the master of house. The intensity of the knock will convey the urgency of the message to the master. Thus we learn from the Malakh's description that it was *as if* the *Ain Sof* "heard the knock" of Moses and commanded the chamberlains of the house (the *maskilim*) to open one door after another until the Fiftieth Gate was opened before Moses and he saw then a small shaft of light issuing from the innermost rooms, but whose intensity eclipsed his very existence. So we see that the inability to bear the fullness of the light applied even to Moses, because nobody can reach that level and still be a "somebody." Therefore, the consciousness that was Moses was reabsorbed into "the body of the sovereign."

Thus the Malakh connects this beautifully to the question of Moses' unknown burial place. He quotes the teaching that the angels said it was "below," while the people said it was "above." Both are correct, for it was between the celestial mansions and this Earth in the region called *hi'uly*, meaning "unspecified" or "unknown." "*Hi'uly*" comes from the Greek term "*hyle*," the *prima materia*, the "primordial matter" of the universe,[55] the place where potentiality may become materiality between the last *maskil* and the first of the *sikhliyot*.

THOSE WHO WERE *below said, "It is beyond our understanding," meaning the Fiftieth Gate, the beginning of the* maskil. *The* maskilim *couldn't understand either and said it was below. This occurred at the time of Moshe's passing. But at the time of the giving of the Torah, the Fiftieth Gate was also manifested to the* sikhliyot *that had made a tikkun for the forty-nine unaligned* sikhliyot *(causing the Fiftieth Gate to rest on them), and created a situation in which the Fiftieth Gate should rest upon them in general, especially regarding the details of the details, until it contained every means of correcting Yisra'el through deeds.*

This was accomplished through the compassion of the emanator, concerning whom it is said, "your breasts are prepared, your hair grown long, and you are naked" (Ezek. 16:7). What is meant by "your breasts are prepared"? There is a desire greater than that of the calf's desire to suckle, and that is of the cow to give sustenance. Therefore, through great compassion God wishes to be mashpiyya, *to channel and condense the flow of divine energy, so that one should be able to attain the good by deeds, for oneself and for all of Yisra'el, as it is written, "the children of*

Yisra'el went out of Mitzrayim (Egypt) well armed" (Exod. 13:18), meaning that all of Yisra'el came to the Fiftieth Gate.[56] *Thus they attained the life of the world of freedom after their slavery in Mitzrayim; they were redeemed from the exile and came to full redemption. But it's not that the entire Fiftieth Gate was made manifest to them in detail as with Moshe, for they received only a compression (tzimtzum) of that Fiftieth Gate, in order that they should be able to bear it and live.*[57]

This is the last major point the Malakh makes before going off on a long digression that we will not translate here. Nevertheless, this is a nice conclusion to the teaching. For he says that "at the time of the giving of the Torah," the forty-nine *sikhliyot* became aligned and adjusted in such a way that "the Fiftieth Gate should rest upon them in general," and thus the Torah contains in itself "every means of correcting Yisra'el through deeds." That is to say, the forty-nine modes became concretized and encoded in the prescriptions of Torah, so that they are now embodied in deeds. In the Torah, a fractal of a fractal of the Fiftieth Gate is contained and remains open "just a smidgeon" for those who can engage the mitzvot (the God-connections) with the proper *kavanah*.

This is a wonderful teaching and goes beautifully with a *mashal* that Maggid Michael Kagan tells of a king who needed to get an urgent message to his general across enemy lines, a message that would end the war and bring about peace in the realm. He tells the entire court of his need and asks for a volunteer, but only a simple servant steps forward to answer the king's call . . .

> The king began relaying to him the message that he would carry to the general. It was a complicated message, much of which the servant had trouble understanding. After a while the king realized that this was perhaps not the best way to impart such a crucial message. What if the messenger forgot parts of it or confused this with that? The message had to remain intact, otherwise the battle would be lost. So the king began to write the message down. And as he wrote he explained the connection between the oral message and the written message so as to increase the probability of the message getting through. But then the king began to worry about the possibility of the scroll getting lost, damaged, or copied with errors. What would happen then? All would be lost. Then the

king had an idea. He would encode the message into a practice, a discipline that the messenger would embody. Thus, the messenger himself would become a living message!

So he started teaching the messenger the form that contained the hidden message. From the moment the messenger awoke to the moment the messenger slept he would be involved with the practice. In the way that he dressed, in the way that he ate, in the way that he spoke, in the way that he related to others. In fact, every aspect of his life was touched by the discipline passed to him by the king. He learned diligently with all his heart, with all his spirit, and with all his strength. He was determined not to fail the trust that the king had bestowed upon him.

When the king was sure that the messenger was ready, he blessed him and reminded him how important was the task, how critical it was for him to succeed and to reach the general with the message fully intact, and finally, how precious he was in the eyes of the king.[58]

The *mashal* goes on to tell of how the servant traveled so long that he actually forgot that he was carrying a message, but continued the practices without an understanding of the message encoded within them. This is what the Malakh's teaching is trying to express. For he says, "There is a desire greater than that of the calf's desire to suckle, and that is of the cow to give sustenance," and thus God has condensed the holy forty-nine *sikhliyot* into a special form that may lead us out of exile and into the world of freedom, where the Fiftieth Gate rests on us in a general way. The specific way is much too complicated for most of us, taking us dangerously close to the annihilation of our existence. Thus God in compassion has generalized the holy forty-nine *sikhliyot* into a pattern of deeds whose message will bring us peace. Just as in homeopathy, when you have a substance that is only a memory of the substance of the substance, very highly refined, it somehow turns out to be more and more efficacious, so we can see God's compassion in this condensing of the divine *sikhliyot*.

The Torah of the Fiftieth Gate, or the *maskilim*, is the quintessential Torah of Reb Avraham the Malakh and represents, as I said before, a continuation of his father's exploration of *kadmut ha-sekhel* (the causative source), for *maskil* is only another way of saying *kadmut ha-sekhel*. These higher regions are where the Malakh wishes to spend most of his time. So when he speaks about the *maskilim* and the *sikhliyot*, it is always from the perspective of the highest of the four worlds, *atzilut* (the realm of "nearness"). That is why he needs a bagel there, as we saw earlier in the *ma'aseh* with Reb Shneur Zalman.[59]

REACHING TOO HIGH

In these atzilic regions of such subtlety, there can be no distractions. It is clear that the Malakh was a man of extremes, single-minded in the pursuit of the higher reaches of divinity. Many people talk about going into emptiness and "the void," but most of the time it is merely the recapitulation of words. But the Malakh actually traveled the boundary between the *is* and the *is not*, between *yesh* (being) and *ayin* (nothingness), as we see from this famously ambiguous story . . .

ON THE EVENING *of Tisha b'Av, the day commemorating the destruction of the Temple in Yerushalayim, the ḥevra sat on the floor of the beit midrash in the dark, mourning for the loss of the Temple with candles in their hands. As the reader began, "Alas! Lonely sits the city once great with people!" (Lam. 1:1), Reb Avraham the Malakh cried out in a loud voice, "Alas!" and then fell silent with his head between his knees. The men looked anxiously at his silhouette in the candlelit room, but quickly returned to the service. After the lamentation was over, all of the ḥevra left the beit midrash, except the Malakh, who remained silent upon the floor. The next morning, they found him in the same place, silent with his head between his knees, and he remained thus in meditation until the end of Tisha b'Av. A tzaddik who witnessed this trembled at the sight of the Malakh in his meditation.*[60]

It is clear from this *ma'aseh* why the Maggid might have been frightened for his son. Was he reaching too high? Was he being reckless in his constant attempts to "purify" his body of its grosser elements, trying to make its substance more and more transparent? Could it become so ethereal that he might pass through the gradually thinning atmospheric zones, the temperature dropping and the oxygen thinning exponentially the higher he goes? How long before he freezes or asphyxiates?

We are not told how the Malakh died, only that he lived a mere four years after his father's death, passing away in Fastov on the 12th of Tishrei in 1776 (5537), just 36 years old. The aforementioned story and his own teachings lead us to believe that he may have passed out of this life in just such a meditation.

We are of course reminded of the well-known story from the Talmud of four sages who enter the Pardes, the mystical orchard . . .

> The Rabbis teach us that four sages entered the Pardes. They were Ben Azzai, Ben Zoma, Aher (Elisha ben Abuya, called Aher, "the other one" because of what happened to him), and Rabbi Akiva. Rabbi Akiva said to them, "When you come to the place of pure marble, do not say, 'Water! Water!' for it is said, 'One who speaks falsely shall not stand before My eyes' " (Ps. 101:7). Ben Azzai gazed and died. Concerning him, the scriptures say, "Precious in the eyes of God is the death of the faithful" (Ps. 116:15). Ben Zoma gazed and was damaged. Concerning him, the scriptures say, "If you find honey, eat only what you need, lest, surfeiting yourself, you throw it up" (Prov. 25:16). Aher cut his roots. Rabbi Akiva entered and left in peace.[61]

Did the Malakh die like Ben Azzai, "Precious in the eyes of God," in love with the Glory he witnessed in the Pardes? Did he die like Moses with a kiss "from the very mouth of God," as he described in the teaching of the Fiftieth Gate? Did he die before the open door of the *maskil?* Who can say, but I wish it for him.

A DEBT TO THE WORLD

It is not surprising that the last communication we have from Reb Avraham comes from beyond the grave. It is probably an understatement to say that his relationship with his wife was complex; how could it not be with a man who did not truly wish to live in the world?[62] But in this last *ma'aseh*, he acknowledges his guilt before her, and we see something more of the human being within the angel. Ironically, it is only when he is no longer among the living that he seems most human . . .

AFTER THE SEVEN days of mourning were ended, Gittel, the wife of Reb Avraham the Malakh had a dream in which she again beheld a great hall filled with a circle of thrones as she had 12 years before. On each throne sat sages of noble countenance. However, this time, none of them spoke. Then a door opened on the hall, and another sage entered and stood before the assembly. It was her husband, Avraham! He looked around him and said, "My friends, my wife bears a grudge against me

because I lived apart from her in my earthly existence. She has been the more right-
eous, and I must beg her forgiveness." Then, unable to restrain herself, Gittel cried
out, "My husband, I forgive you with all of my heart!" and she awoke comforted.[63]

Later we are told that Gittel and her son, Shalom Shakhna, were taken in by
Reb Nahum of Chernobyl, a disciple of the Maggid, who raised young Shalom
to be the heir of his father. Eventually, Shalom even married the
Chernobyler's granddaughter. It is also said that Reb Nahum made an offer
of marriage to Gittel, but that the Malakh appeared to him to forbid it. Was
the Malakh now her husband in death because he had not been so in life?
Somehow it appears this way, for Gittel then departed for the Holy Land and
died in obscurity, making her living as a washing woman. Her grandson, the
great Yisra'el of Rhyzhin was known to say, "If someone could only tell me
where she is buried, I would go and lay myself at the foot of her grave!"[64]

THE *TZADDIK*

It is difficult to place individuals like Reb Avraham the Malakh, or his friend
Reb Zushya of Anipol, within the structure of Hasidism, which is so oriented
toward the Hasid–Rebbe relationship. Of course, they are both clearly
Hasidim of the Maggid, but both reached a stage of accomplishment that
ranks them among the *tzaddikim,* which in Hasidism almost always ends in
the acceptance of the mantle of leadership. Hasidim begin to come to the
tzaddik, and the *tzaddikim* must look to see whether they have the *shoresh ha-
neshamah* of a Hasid and to decide if they are willing to accept the burden of
leadership. But the Malakh did not become a Rebbe. Perhaps what the
Maggid had to say to his son regarding Reb Zushya might also apply to him,
"Do not push my *talmid,* Reb Zushya, to assume any mantle of pastoral leadership, for this holy man has already transcended this possibility."[65]
     What does this mean exactly?
     Was it, as we have already discussed, that neither was a *neshamah klalit*
(aggregate soul), having a preordained karmic connection to many souls that
necessitated a pastoral vocation? That they were capable of the most elevated
holiness without having the disposition and temperament for leadership?
Who can forget Reb Zushya's deep wisdom as he says, "When I get to
Heaven, they will not ask me why I was not Moses, but why I was not
Zushya." Not Moses, the leader of the generation, but Zushya.
     Perhaps he is really drawing a parallel between himself and Moses. For

Moses talked with God, while his brother, Aaron, was the pastoral comforter of the people. There is something compelling about this idea. In some ways, we could see Reb Zushya and Reb Avraham as explorers—Zushya tunneling within to the depths of humility and the Malakh taking flight to the highest heavens.[66]

I think this is how we must think of the Malakh, as a great and lonely explorer of early Hasidism who attempted to make himself "nothing" in the "nothingness" of the *Ain Sof*. He was a *tzaddik* who worked for the "good" of the people, like the Moses of his own Torah, but also like the Moses who left the "comfort" of the people to Aaron, his brother. As he once said, "There exists a *tzaddik* who is unable to lead his generation because it cannot bear him . . . he belongs to the higher sphere of knowledge."[67]

Perhaps this was true of the Malakh.

9

Beggars and Kings: Elimelekh of Lizhensk and His Brother, Zushya of Anipol

AFTER THE DEATH OF THE MAGGID OF MEZRITCH, there would be no single successor or sole leader of the Hasidic movement in the Ukraine, nor was it necessary to have a unifying personality to hold it all together. Hasidism would now survive through numbers and diversity; the Maggid had trained a corps of uniquely talented disciples and sent them into Poland and Russia to spread the holy message of the Ba'al Shem Tov. Nevertheless, it could be argued that in the first two decades after the passing of the Maggid Hasidism had no more important leader than Elimelekh of Lizhensk, who is called the Rebbe Reb Melekh, the Rebbe King.[1]

THE PREDICTION AND A HOUSE OF PIETY

Like his predecessor, the Maggid, much of Reb Elimelekh's early life remains obscure, indeed, the first two thirds of it are mostly a mystery, as full of seeming contradictions and puzzles as his later life is well known and celebrated. What we do know is something about his birth and a few tales of his life before he became the famous *tzaddik* of Lizhensk. As with the Ba'al Shem Tov, we have a story of his father's meeting with a wandering beggar, an encounter that would likewise reveal the coming birth of a very special child . . .

ONCE, THE WEALTHY and pious businessman Eliezer Lippa was driving home in his carriage to Lapakha, near Tiktin in Lithuania, when he noticed a beggar along the roadside. As it was a cold day, Eliezer leaned out of the carriage window and offered the poor beggar a ride.

The beggar refused, saying, "I haven't yet earned what I need."

Eliezer asked, "What do you need?"

"25 rubles," the beggar answered.

"Well," said Eliezer, "accept the ride and I'll give you the 25 rubles." To his great surprise, the beggar refused even this. "Why?" he asked.

"Because you can afford it easily, and it won't 'cost' you anything; think of the mitzvah those whom it will 'cost' will be deprived of if they don't give to me."

Eliezer considered this strange and wonderful answer for a moment and then said, "Then I'll collect the money myself, and you will accept the ride; I can't stand to see you walking in this cold."

Then the beggar looked at Eliezer as if with a secret pleasure and said, "Two things will I reveal to you. You will soon have a son who will do great and holy things in the world. However, you have only one year left to live, so take the time to put your affairs in order."

Then the strange beggar walked away.

Eliezer was shaken by this strange news, but also grateful. He went home and began to reorganize his life, giving away most of his riches and slowly letting go of his stressful business interests. The next year, a son was born to him whom he named Elimelekh.

Miraculously, Eliezer did not die; he was granted 25 more years of life, which he lived in simplicity and holiness.[2]

Who was the beggar? Prophet Elijah or a hidden *tzaddik*?

Whoever it was, the message was heeded and a blessing was born from it. The beggar's answer to Eliezer shows us how merit and blessing come through sacrifice, and how wisdom can be combined with cleverness. This is often what distinguishes the Hasidic *ma'aseh* from ordinary miracle tales and good roadhouse yarns. In the Hasidic tale, cleverness is put in the service of God. In this story, the beggar's purpose was to "tease" Eliezer into a good realization leading to a holy act, even if he had to use a disguise to do it. This is something that will come up again and again in the stories of Reb Elimelekh . . . a kind of seed sown into the story of his birth.

What of the beggar's warning about Eliezer's imminent death?

Perhaps this was the course Eliezer was on at that time. Nevertheless, it seems that the beggar's warning was a prescription for healing. There is also a connection between the 25 rubles and Eliezer's 25-year reprieve. For it says in Proverbs 11:4, *"Tzedakah* (charity) saves from death."* Perhaps there was something in his lifestyle that needed to change in order to create the right environment for his future son.

There is one other small anecdote that gives us insight into Reb Elimelekh's childhood, about his mother, remembered years later by his brother, Zushya.

REB ZUSHYA OF Anipol used to say, "My sweet mother, Miresh, peace be upon her, was an unlettered woman, but she was deeply pious and a great servant of God. She could not read the prayers from a siddur *(prayer book), of course, but she had learned how to recite the* berakhot *(blessings) by heart, and she recited them with such deep longing that the place in which she recited them in the morning was filled with the radiance of the* Shekhinah *the whole day!"*[3]

Reb Elimelekh's friend and first mentor in Ḥasidut, Reb Shmelke of Nikolsburg taught: "In Torah it says, 'You shall each revere your mother and your father and keep my *Shabbat*, for I am *Y-H-V-H*, your God.' (Lev. 13:3) Thus the Talmud teaches that there are three partners in a human being: God, your mother, and your father.[4] Of course, you could certainly attain holiness if God's share predominated, but you must not forget that which you have inherited from your mother and father."[5] This is a teaching for all of us, whatever our relationships with our parents might be, but it seems especially appropriate with regard to Reb Elimelekh and his brother, Reb Zushya. For in some ways, we might see each of the brothers as the spiritual heirs of their parents—Reb Elimelekh, the heir of his father; Reb Zushya, the heir of his mother. For these two isolated stories somehow speak to the "spiritual styles" of each of these two brothers, who could not be more different. And yet, no two brothers are as inextricably linked and devoted to one another as Elimelekh and Zushya. Indeed, the story of Elimelekh of Lizhensk cannot be told in any significant way without talking about his brother, Reb Zushya of Anipol. They are a study in contrasts, but as with all contrasts, each helps to define the other's character all the more sharply.

THE EXILE

Most stories agree that both Zushya and Elimelekh studied in Tiktin, a city near their birthplace in Lithuania. We are told that Elimelekh was as brilliant and rigorous in his studies as Zushya was indifferent to them, though there is no reason to suppose that he did not complete them. There is little indication as to what happened to each of them next; it is to be supposed that they each married and were either supported by in-laws or found some work as teachers of one kind or another. When next we hear of the brothers, they are both already deeply engaged in ascetic practices. Reb Elimelekh, it is said, devoted himself completely to his studies and ascetic practices, fasting from *Shabbat* to *Shabbat* for a period of 14 years.[6] And Reb Zushya, we find in one famous anecdote, lies down on an anthill to excoriate his body, though not a single ant would bite him. After a while, he cried out in frustration, "Oh Zushya! Zushya!—even the ants despise you!"[7]

In these years, it seems, Elimelekh and Zushya were in many ways students of one another, sharing in a unique spiritual partnership. To Elimelekh, Zushya was a walking lesson in piety, and he adored him. So it was that they set out on the road of self-imposed exile together, wandering from place to place to atone for misdeeds, and to bring others to repentance. For three years they did this, suffering through great poverty and sowing the seeds of many legends.

The sense of exile for Jews at that time was acute, and for those who followed the creative and ascetic Kabbalah of Rabbi Yitzhak Luria, it was a value in itself to be experienced. For according to the Kabbalah, the Divine Presence was in exile, and thus the followers of these teachings would set out on the road in sympathy with the *Shekhinah*, seeking the deepest possible experience of exile.[8] This was the aim of Elimelekh and Zushya's three-year journey. Later Hasidim considered this journey by the brothers to be so significant that they would say, "You will find Hasidim up to the point the brothers Reb Zushya and Reb Elimelekh reached in their long wanderings; beyond that you will not find Hasidim."[9]

The following are two representative stories from that period.

ONCE, WHEN REB Zushya and Reb Elimelekh were in the midst of their self-imposed exile, they entered a roadhouse to find a little rest and warmth. Right away, they saw that the common room was full of rowdies, so they tried to make themselves inconspicuous and sat down against the wall in a corner near the woodstove. But it was already too late. The ragged wayfarers had been spotted as soon as they entered the room. No sooner had they sat down then the rowdy bunch singled out Reb Zushya for some abuse. They beat him senseless and then threw him back in the corner where they had found him.

Reb Elimelekh, knowing that they would be back for Zushya, said to him, "My *brother, now we will trade places. I will take your hat and cloak, and I'll take my turn." When the men came back for Reb Zushya a short time later, they looked at the pair of them and said, "We can't give to this one (Elimelekh disguised as Zushya) and not to that one (Zushya disguised as Elimelekkh)." So they grabbed Zushya roughly and took him away for another beating!*

This little *ma'aseh* tells us so much about these brothers and their very different destinies. Perhaps more than any other two personalities in Hasidism, they are the respective archetypal embodiments of the Holy Beggar and the Philosopher King. If there is a story where someone is carrying a stick, Reb Zushya is always the one who gets whacked with it; while Reb Elimelekh, in the same situation, either escapes or (especially later) is the person who breaks the stick in two and sends the would-be assailant running scared. The following tale, one of my favorites, shows us a little of both archetypes, and the wisdom of each.

IN THE YEARS of Zushya and Elimelekh's exile, they passed through many towns and villages. Often they were ill-treated in these places, but usually they were able to find some place to pray, a place to eat, and place to lay their heads, even if the conditions were very poor. However, once the two brothers came upon a certain town in the middle of a rainy afternoon; cold and covered in mud from the road, they could find no rest anywhere. First they went to the beit midrash to get warm while they davened Minḥah, but they were unexpectedly turned out before they could even begin to pray. So they went to houses, they went to inns, they inquired about stables, they went anywhere they possibly could and were refused even the most meager accommodations. Cold, wet, and truly miserable, they crawled into a great pile of hay and made a crude shelter in which to say their prayers and rest until the rain stopped and they could move on to the next town.

Years later, when both brothers were famous tzaddikim, and Reb Elimelekh was known to preside over a court in Lizhensk, they returned to the same town—this time by invitation. Unlike their previous "reception," their carriage was met by a pageant of official representatives of the Jewish community, and they were escorted into a great hall as a crowd of townspeople looked on. Inside a great table was set for them and for all of the dignitaries. At the head of the table, a place was set for Reb Elimelekh, and beside him a seat for his brother, Reb Zushya.

As soon as they were seated, out came a feast of wonderful foods of all kinds, and their glasses were filled with wine. The head of the community signaled Reb Elimelekh to say the blessing over the bread and wine and to speak a few words to the assembled dignitaries. When Reb Elimelekh had completed the blessings, he rose to speak. He looked out at all the faces of the assembled; he looked at the warm fire burning in the hall and at the sumptuous feast set before them. Then he looked at his brother, Reb Zushya, who smiled sweetly at him, and he raised his glass as if to make a toast. Everyone leaned forward, eager to hear some praise of their town, their reception, the food, or themselves, but their eager anticipation soon turned into gasps of shock and indignation. For Reb Elimelekh, the guest of honor, then poured the glass of wine down the front of his silk bekeshe! Worse still, he called loudly for a servant to take his plate out to the horses!

The townsfolk were horrified, and the head of the community spoke up, demanding, "What is the meaning of this?"

Reb Elimelekh replied calmly, "Once, many years ago, my brother and I visited your town and received quite another reception. In fact, we were refused all that you have granted us this day, even the right to pray in the beit midrash. As I look out at you now, seeing all of the same faces who turned us away those many years ago, welcoming us with such pomp and circumstance, I can only come to one conclusion—that you somehow wish to honor our clothing and our horses, for that is the only thing that has changed from then to now."[10]

I first heard this story many years ago from a man whose name I never learned, but I have told it with delight ever since, elaborating it here and there as I have seen fit, watching its wonderful point unfold on the faces of everyone who hears it.[11] No matter how many times I tell it, I continue to wonder, "What happened next? What could possibly follow a show-stopper like that?"

THE WOOD CUTTER AND THE PRINCE

Contrary to what many assume, most sources agree that Meshullam Zushya was the elder of the two brothers, and that it was Reb Zushya who first led his brother, Elimelekh, to the Maggid, and not the other way around. How this came about is unclear, but it seems that Reb Shmelke of Nikolsburg, who knew both brothers, may have first led Zushya to the Maggid, perhaps even while the Maggid was still in Rovno before the passing of the Ba'al Shem Tov. It is my belief that the following story comes from that time.

It seems that Zushya's natural ecstatic tendencies were immediately catalyzed by the Maggid's Torah and holy presence. Some have even said that Zushya never heard a teaching from the Maggid start to finish, for as soon as the Maggid said, "And God spoke . . ." Reb Zushya would fall into ecstasy, yelling "God spoke! God spoke!" and then had to be carried out. I suspect that this was not always so, but happened enough for it to have made an impression on the centuries. Likely, this behavior—like a match that bursts into bright flame before calming into a steady burn—was more prevalent in the early days of his association with the Maggid and less pronounced later. But this new turn of behavior seems to have concerned his brother, Elimelekh, and to my mind, likely prompted the discussion that takes place in this famous *ma'aseh* and *mashal*.

IN THE EARLY days of Zushya and Elimelekh's association with the Maggid of Mezritch, Zushya seemed to be taking another path from his brother, Elimelekh. He lived apart from the other disciples of the Maggid, wandering through the nearby woods, lying down among the trees and singing praises to God. Soon the disciples began to whisper as Zushya passed, "Be infatuated with love for her always" (Prov. 5:19). But Elimelekh was concerned and even a little disconcerted by Zushya's recent unconventional behavior, and when they were alone together, he asked him, "Brother, you have been behaving so strangely of late; why do you not stay among us and learn as the rest of us do?"

Reb Zushya looked kindly at his younger brother and said, "My brother, let me tell you a story . . .

"Once, there was a poor peasant who had a great desire to look upon the face of the king. With this purpose in mind, he left the small village where he lived and walked for many days until he came to the city of the king. Once he was there, he succeeded in finding employment with the king, cutting wood and tending to the stoves that heated the palace. Because his desire to look upon the king and serve him was so great, he put his whole heart into his work. He went to the forest himself and collected the best and most fragrant wood, split the logs himself, and stacked these in the palace stoves with perfect timing so that the palace never lacked warmth as the days grew cold. Before long, the king himself noticed the steady warmth of the palace—being never too cold, and never to hot—and asked a servant, 'Who is it that is making me so comfortable?'

"It was then that the king was told about the poor peasant they had hired to tend the palace stoves. He then asked them to bring the wood cutter before him. When the peasant stood before the king, he said, 'You have made me very comfortable; please tell me what wish can I grant for you?'

"The poor peasant replied, 'My lord, I don't want to bother you—you have so many big things to do—I only ask that you allow me to see you every once in a while.'

"So the king then commanded the royal architect to make a small peephole into the royal chamber so that the wood cutter might be able to satisfy his longing to gaze upon the king.

"Now it later happened that the prince said something that displeased the king and was banished for a time from the royal chamber. Because of this, he began to wander through the corridors of the palace in great loneliness and longing to see his father. When the wood cutter noticed the prince's sadness as he walked the corridors, he understood that he longed to see the king and so he made bold to speak to him and told him of the little peephole, and they both looked through it together for a time.

"My brother," said Reb Zushya, "You are like the prince who really belongs in the rooms of the king. All you have to do is to watch what you say, always speaking with wisdom. But I am like the wood cutter, neither wise nor learned, and so I must perform my poor service so that I may occasionally gaze upon the king's face through my little peephole."[12]

Oh, there is so much beautiful teaching in this story. Only Reb Zushya could admonish with such love and genuine humility.[13] From at least one perspective, this is a parable of the two brother's relationship with the Maggid. And while Zushya thinks of his brother as the prince who by rights may sit in the chamber of the king, his humility is not of the kind that thinks his own service is unworthy. He is aware that the "warmth he provides" is both pleasing to the king (the Maggid), as well as to the King of Kings. Nor is he above reminding his brother that it was through his (Zushya's) little "peephole" that he (Elimelekh) first beheld the king before entering the king's chamber!

SHABBAT DURING THE WEEK

The brothers remained close and continued their exploration of the spiritual world together as before, only now they had the Maggid to turn to for guidance when they entered an area that caused them confusion. For so great was their combined *kavanah* that they frequently moved Heaven and Earth and lost their bearings. What then could they do but return to the Maggid?

ONCE, THE HOLY *brothers, Reb Elimelekh of Lizhensk and Reb Zushya of Anipol, went on a journey. As they had often done in the past, they traveled incognito, living as if in galut (in exile), doing everything they could to bring God and the seek-*

ers of God together. Wherever they found themselves, in whatever town or circumstances, they would stop and celebrate Shabbat together in that place. After one particularly high Shabbat, which had filled each of them with ecstatic love, they made Havdalah, the ceremony marking the "separation" between Shabbat and the weekdays, and turned to one another wondering, "Do you suppose we have really reached so high that we have touched the very source of Shabbat in Heaven? Or is it perhaps that we have become all too adept at kidding ourselves? Maybe all that we have been doing is deceiving ourselves?"

This question is a terrifying one for the true seeker, and there is no verbal answer one can give oneself. Maybe all that we are doing here is a pious collusion? Maybe there is really nothing transcendentally divine or even immanent in the whole spiritual business, except that we are good at kidding ourselves and we have a good formula by which we do this?

THIS QUESTION TORTURED the brothers until finally they decided to make a Shabbat experiment. They would attempt to live one day during the week as if it were Shabbat! If they tried this during the week and did not reach the heights of Shabbat, it would be a sign that their Shabbat was real and sincere. But if they were able to achieve the heights of Shabbat during the week, then it would prove that it was all a sham.

The following Tuesday, they began their Shabbat experiment. They made all the same preparations and did everything that they usually did on Friday to prepare for Shabbat . . . They went to mikveh, dressed in their Shabbat finery, and began to chant the Shir ha-Shirim (Song of Songs), invoking their deepest love for God, and God's love for them and all of Yisra'el: "Oh kiss me with the kisses of your mouth, for your love is better than wine" (Songs 1:2). Then came the Minḥah prayer and the Yedid Nefesh (Soul's Friend), "Quick, my lover, the time has arrived; grant me a taste of eternity."

Then they entered into the delights of "Shabbat evening"—the table hymns, the Torah, the Shabbat food—everything that they usually did.

The next morning, and throughout the whole of the "Shabbat," they held back on nothing, soaring as they would on the most holy Shabbat, in a flight of awareness that reached to the highest heights!

After Havdalah, they looked at one another with bitter smiles—"Oy! What fakes we are! If we can do this on Wednesday, then it is clear that we have only been kidding ourselves. What are we going to do now?"

There was nothing else but to go to their Rebbe, the Maggid.

The brothers arrived in Rovno soon after and immediately went to the study of the Maggid. Before they could speak, however, the Maggid held up his hand and bade them remain silent. Then he said, "Tell me, dear ones, where does Shabbat go during the week?"

Perplexed by this question, neither could answer.

The Maggid then pointed a finger into the air and said, "Up! It rises upward. On Shabbat, holiness descends and dwells among us, but when Hasidim like you enter so deeply into the spirit of Shabbat, as you did last Wednesday, you rise up to the level where Shabbat dwells during the week! So do not trouble yourselves; you are holy, your service is holy, and the blessed and Holy One takes pleasure in your service."[14]

This is so wonderful, for at once it acknowledges the texture of time, which says that there is something special that happens on *Shabbat* and the *Yamim Tovim* (holy days), and yet also honors the possibility of raising oneself to the regions where the delights and efficacy of these holy days dwell when we need them. Only why should we thrust ourselves into those regions unnecessarily when they come down to us at the appointed times? Therefore, we must avail ourselves of the grace that happens at those times. But when there is a real need outside of them, we know that we may create the atmosphere of those days and ascend to the regions where they dwell.

GIVE OVER ALL YOUR NEEDS TO GOD, AND BE GRATEFUL

While Reb Elimelekh's great Torah was collected in the *No'am Elimelekh,* most of Reb Zushya's teaching has been transmitted in the form of tales about his life.[15] As much as anyone else in the Hasidic tradition, Reb Zushya embodied the teaching. And for Reb Zushya, everything that came out of the mouth of the Maggid, his Rebbe, was a command; every teaching turned into a practical action directive. Thus, when the Maggid taught the following,

"Leave all to God" (Ps. 37:5)

Plant this idea so firmly in your mind
That you respond to everything in life by saying,
"This is from God,"[16]

Reb Zushya followed it through to the letter, as we see in the next little anecdote.

ONCE, REB ZUSHYA arrived in a little town and immediately went to the beit midrash to sit down and rest. He was hungry and tired but said nothing to anyone about this. Finally, someone who supposed he was a beggar (because of his ragged appearance) brought him some food and set it on the bench beside him. Reb Zushya, however, didn't touch it or even look at it. Then he said suddenly, "O Ribbono shel Olam, Master of the Universe, my God—Zushya is hungry! Zushya is hungry! Please give him something to eat!" Then he sniffed the air and turned suddenly to look at the food on the bench beside him as if surprised, saying, "Barukh ha-Shem! You gave him something to eat!"

Reb Zushya took this teaching to such an extreme that he almost couldn't acknowledge an intermediary between himself and God's gift! He wanted to save all of his gratitude for God alone. This overwhelming sense of gratitude filled Reb Zushya's consciousness, coloring his entire perspective. So when his friends Reb Shmelke and Reb Pinhas came to the Maggid with a difficult question having to do with gratitude, the Maggid sent them on to Reb Zushya for the answer.

ONE DAY, REB Shmelke and Reb Pinhas came to the Maggid of Mezritch with a difficult question, "Rebbe, our sages tell us that we should thank God for suffering as much as for prosperity, and that we should receive both with joy, but we are ashamed to say that this makes no sense to us; will you please help us to understand this mystery?"

The Maggid replied, "Go and ask Reb Zushya what it means."

So they went to seek Reb Zushya in his little shack on the far end of the village where he lived in dire poverty with his wife and children. There they found him smoking his pipe. They asked him their question, "Reb Zushya, what does it mean that we should thank God for the bad as well as the good?"

Reb Zushya looked puzzled for a moment and then said with absolute seriousness, "I don't know, nothing bad has ever happened to me."[17]

With this answer, Reb Zushya became the Hasidic equivalent of Nahum ish Gamzu, the 1st-century sage of the Mishnah. Ish Gamzu—literally "man of this too"—was his nickname, for he was famous for saying *Gam zu l'tovah*, "this too is for the good," though most of his life appeared to be a misery. Rabbi Nahum was said to be a quadriplegic, that is, paralyzed in all four limbs.[18] Both Reb Zushya and Nahum ish Gamzu, through an extraordinary spiritual transformation, had become incapable of seeing any evil in the difficulties that befell them.

At some point, Reb Zushya and his brother felt themselves directed to go in separate directions. They remained in touch, but Zushya would continue to wander, a holy beggar pursuing greater and greater levels of humility, while Elimelekh would begin preparing to fulfill his destiny to be a Rebbe like the Maggid. Zushya would also be visited by Hasidim, but on a much smaller scale than his brother, Elimelekh. Reb Zushya's way was simple but profound, and like his brother's teaching, it was neatly packaged for practical use. Reb Zushya maintained that there are five verses in the TANAK that constitute the essence of Hasidism.

"OY!" HE SAID, "how could I do the big teshuvah (repentance), I can't do it all at once, so I broke it into five parts: T—tamim, 'You shall be whole-hearted with Y-H-V-H, your God' (Deut. 18:13); S—shiviti, 'I have set Y-H-V-H before me always' (Ps. 16:8); U—ve'ahavta, 'You shall love your neighbor as yourself' (Lev. 19:18); V—b'khol, 'In all your ways acknowledge God' (Prov. 3:6); and H— hatznei'a, 'To walk humbly with your God' (Mic. 6:8)." These initial letters of these five verses in Hebrew—tav, shin, vav, bet, heh—when taken together, spell the word "teshuvah!"[19]

Once there was a man who asked Reb Shneur Zalman of Liadi, the author of the *Tanya*, why he addressed Reb Zushya in a letter as "*ha-Rav ha-Ga'on*, the mighty master and prince of Torah," since Reb Zushya was said not to have been able to master all the complexities of Torah scholarship. Reb Shneur Zalman replied, "There are mitzvot that can be fulfilled with the limbs of the body. One who knows all the mitzvot, their interpretations, their laws, details, knows them from the ground up, surely deserves to be called *ga'on*. There are other mitzvot known as the mitzvot of the heart, and Reb Zushya is accomplished in all of these and is the master of this entire generation in the duties of the heart. It is for this reason that he deserves the title *ga'on*." But then, among those who knew, it was said that the Rebbe Reb Zushya also had within him the soul of Yishma'el, the high priest, and it was because of that soul that he did not lack anything, even in the manifest part of the Torah dealing with the duties of the limbs.[20]

THE FLOW OF BLESSING

Now let's return to Reb Elimelekh, the primary subject of this and the next chapter. This tale is told of various Rebbes, but I think it is probably most appropriately told of the Rebbe Reb Melekh.

BEFORE REB ELIMELEKH became "known," he davened every day in a local shul. In the same shul was a businessman who admired the great fervor of Reb Elimelekh's prayer and who would every day put a coin in Reb Elimelekh's tallit bag, so that he should not suffer want. The businessman found that from the time he began to do this, he also began to prosper in his business, until finally he became very rich!

Seeing this, he thought he would find out a little more about Reb Elimelekh. But when he discovered that Reb Elimelekh was the disciple of the Maggid of Mezritch, he thought to himself, "If this is what comes from giving to the disciple, what shall happen if I give to the master?" After that, he went to the Maggid of Mezritch and stopped giving tzedakah to Reb Elimelekh. But his fortunes did not increase; indeed, the businessman's fortunes began to fail! In desperation he went to Reb Elimelekh and asked, "What's going on here? When I gave to you, I prospered; but since I have been giving to your master, my fortunes have suffered!"

Reb Elimelekh looked at the man with a wry expression and said, "As long as you gave to me out of sincere motives, without respect to my status, the merit of my prayer accrued to your benefit; you didn't count my merits and God didn't count yours. But once you started to keep count, desiring to increase your own benefit by going to my master, God too began to count your merits, and the benefit of the prayer no longer accrued to your benefit."

This is a kind of cautionary tale for those who would like to play a numbers game with God, but there is also a message about the misapplication of human reason to holy matters, in this case, trying to factor the status of the Hasid and the Rebbe into an economic equation. It doesn't work that way. The flow of blessing (as we have seen in numerous stories and teaching) comes through the particular channels it needs to come through. For this man, that blessing was to come through Reb Elimelekh and not the Maggid.

LONG LIVE THE KING!

As we have said already, after the Maggid, there was no longer any possibility or need for a single unifying figure to lead the Hasidic movement. Nevertheless, certain of the Maggid's Hasidim wisely recognized that their training was not yet complete and looked to the most senior students of the Maggid to serve them now as Rebbes.

AFTER THE PASSING *of the Maggid of Mezritch, several of the* ḥevraya kaddisha *(holy fellowship) took counsel and decided to make Reb Elimelekh their Rebbe. In fact, many of them had already been of this mind and had decided to discuss it in secret while Reb Elimelekh was asleep. After they had finally made their decision, they sent his holy brother Reb Zushya to wake him and to tell him that they wished him to be their Rebbe. No one else would have dared to wake him, but Reb Zushya simply walked to the door of the room in which Reb Elimelekh slept, put his hand over the mezuzah, and Reb Elimelekh stirred within and soon came out of the room!*

Later, the Hasidim asked Reb Zushya why he had placed his hand over the mezuzah. Zushya replied, "As long as the last thought that a tzaddik has upon entering a room to sleep is of the Presence of God while looking at the mezuzah, they are connected to that thought, even in sleep. But when I covered the mezuzah, the connection was broken and my holy brother's sleep was disturbed."

Of course the ḥokhmah of this ma'aseh is really about deveikut, but its context is equally important for us as we tell the story of Reb Elimelekh. For here we have a Hasidic tradition regarding the choice of Reb Elimelekh as a Rebbe in the wake of the Maggid's passing, as well as the proof of his worthiness without any conscious effort on his part. It is also important to note that Rebbes do not declare themselves to be "Rebbes" or set themselves up as such; they are chosen by someone to be their Rebbe. Thus, when the man came to Reb Menachem Mendel of Kotzk saying, "Rebbe, I have had a dream in which my father came to me and told me that I shall become a Rebbe," Reb Menachem Mendel laughed out loud. "Rebbe," the man asked, "Why are you laughing?" The Kotzker replied, "That you have dreamed that your father came to you and told you that you shall be a Rebbe means little to me. Now, if he had gone to 300 other people telling them that you shall be their Rebbe, that I might take seriously!"

Did Reb Elimelekh accept these Hasidim at that time? It is hard to say. We know that several of the younger disciples of the Maggid, like Ya'akov Yitzhak Horowitz (later of Lublin) and Yisra'el Hofstein (later of Kozhnitz) would become his disciples in the years to come, but we are also told that for a period after the death of the Maggid, he took to the road, making his living as a traveling *maggid* or preacher. This period may have lasted up to three years, until the time he settled in Lizhensk. Was this another self-imposed three-year exile to purify and prepare himself for the role of Rebbe? Fortunately there are stories to tell us something of that time.

THE RENEGADE'S BLESSING

This remarkable *ma'aseh* gives us the flavor of Reb Elimelekh's day-to-day existence during this period, and even a tantalizing description of his appearance. This is the story much as it is given in the collection called *Esser Zakhzakhot*.

THE TIFERET SHLOMO, *Reb Shlomo of Radomsk, tells us that the Rebbe Reb Elimelekh, before he became famous, traveled the land as if he were in* galut *(exile), dressed like a common man with a short jacket and a belt made of straw. Now, Reb Elimelekh was also very tall, and his beard at that time was like two koltenes (dreadlocks), so one can well imagine the impression he must have made.*

It is said that during this self-imposed exile, Reb Elimelekh came to Chernovitz and went to the parnas ḥodesh, *the leader of the Jewish community for that month—for each member of a council of 12 led the community for one month of the year—seeking permission to preach to the Jewish community. But the* parnas ḥodesh, *taking one look at his outlandish appearance, turned Reb Elimelekh out of the house immediately. However, Avner, the young son of the* parnas ḥodesh, *had witnessed this scene and was much disturbed by his father's treatment of the traveling* maggid. *"Why should you care if this* Yiddeleh *earns a few rubles here?" he said. "After all, he wouldn't ask to give a sermon if he didn't know what to say, would he, Tatte?"*

The father looked at his beloved son doubtfully but decided to call the maggid *back to tell him that he could preach there after all. He then gave a note to the city* shammes *who went to bang on the doors of everyone in the Jewish community,* asking them to gather in the beit ha-knesset *(house of gathering)* to hear a sermon by a traveling maggid.

When everyone was gathered, the strange-looking maggid ascended the bimah *(dais)* in silence, but searched the room with a determined gaze as if looking for someone in particular. This went on so long that the parnas ḥodesh finally asked him, "What are you looking for?"

Reb Elimelekh did not answer him, but asked instead, "Is everyone here?"

"Yes, why?" the parnas ḥodesh asked.

Reb Elimelekh continued to gaze around the room and said, "Because there is an odor of adultery in this city."

The people gasped and immediately became angry with this crude stranger. "Who was he to condemn them? To make such assertions without evidence!" Soon the grumbling became a tumult and they began to shout at the stranger, threatening to beat him within an inch of his life. Finally, Reb Elimelekh was forced to flee the building, and several young men began to chase after him, hoping to give him the beating he deserved!

Reb Elimelekh ran this way and that, zigzagging in and out of buildings, hoping to throw the young men off of his trail. They searched everywhere, but couldn't find him. Finally, they turned to search a large horse stable, and there they found the city shoḥet fornicating with a non-Jewish woman! "Oy! The maggid was right!" they said.

Meanwhile, Reb Elimelekh continued moving from building to building, hoping to avoid the angry mob. Nevertheless, he was soon seen by the young boy, Avner, the son of the parnas ḥodesh, who had pleaded on his behalf. Now, Avner was too young to understand what all the fuss was about, but he knew that if the maggid had been allowed to give his sermon, he would have gotten a few rubles. As it was, he had nothing in his pockets and was on the run for his trouble. So the boy had run after him, and when he noticed him sneaking out from around the back of a building, he yelled, "Stop, stop, stop! They aren't after you any more!"

Hearing the voice of the little boy, Reb Elimelekh turned round and waited for the boy to approach. When he had come near, Reb Elimelekh asked him, "My child, what do you want?"

Avner said, "Look, I know you needed that money, sir—please let me give it to you. It's not your fault that the people didn't allow you to speak—you should get your pay."

Reb Elimelekh was touched, but looked doubtfully at the kindhearted boy and said, "My child, this money belongs to your father; you haven't got any right to give it to me."

"No," the boy replied, "this is my own money. My father gives me 40 groschen each day, and from that, I have saved this money!"

Reb Elimelekh looked thoughtful for a moment, then said, "Well, if that's the case, then I'll accept it."

The boy smiled and gave him the eight rubles he had been carrying, and said, "This is what they give to the traveling maggidim for sermons."

Reb Elimelekh said, "Now, my child, with what shall I bless you?"

The discerning boy replied, "With whatever you would like, sir?"

The Rebbe Reb Melekh smiled and put his hand on the boy's head and blessed him that they should one day become mehutanim (family by marriage)!

When Avner—the boy who had once helped Reb Elimelekh—grew up, he married and became a very rich man. After many years, his daughter became engaged to a grandson of the Ohev Yisra'el, Reb Avraham Yehoshua Heschel of Apt, and also of the Rebbe Reb Melekh, who had long since passed on to the next world. Because Reb Avraham Yehoshua Heschel, the elder Rebbe of the generation, himself traveled to the wedding, 70 tzaddikim in white garments were in attendance. Thus people said that the wedding in Chernovitz was as great as the great wedding as in Ostilla [a great wedding attended by many Rebbes at which the Ohev Yisr'ael showed his support for the radical Pyshysska Hasidim]. Among the Rebbes present in Chernovitz were the Hozeh (Ya'akov Yitzhak) of Lublin and the Yid ha-Kodesh, Ya'akov Yitzhak of Pyshysska, meaning that the wedding took place before 1814.

When the Ohev Yisra'el arrived at his inn, he sent for Avner, the father of the bride. When Avner entered the room, the Ohev Yisra'el immediately saw a light on him, and asked, "How is it that you have been given this light, meriting to marry into the family of the Rebbe Reb Melekh?"

Avner thought about this for a moment, and then began to tell the Ohev Yisra'el about all of the good things that he did, how he was hospitable, how he studied diligently, how he gave tzedakah liberally; but the Ohev Yisra'el only shook his head, "No, it is not for these things." Finally, Avner remembered the poor maggid who had once given him an unusual blessing and told the story to the Ohev Yisra'el, who perked up at this and said, "Describe him to me!" And when Avner had described the wandering maggid, the Ohev Yisra'el said, "Yes, yes, I see! It was the holy Rebbe Reb Elimelekh who blessed you!"[21]

This is one of those wonderful tales that we don't see as much of in later Hasidism, tales in which the master makes a journey of purification, "a descent for the sake of ascent" as Reb Nahman of Bratzlav does later. It is possible that Reb Elimelekh was doing this to prepare himself for the role of Rebbe, to do the spiritual work that was necessary for him to be able to take on such a role in humility. There is an understanding that leadership of this kind is a terrible burden and involves all manner of danger, especially with regard to the ego. So one can see how softened the ego might become in such circumstances!

THE HORSE DOCTOR

Another important tale from this period concerns his former *mashpiyya* (mentor), Reb Shmelke, who had recently taken up the post of Rav in Nikolsburg. Reb Shmelke, it turns out, was having some trouble with his new congregation when Reb Elimelekh arrived in Nikolsburg, seeking to preach as we have seen before . . .

AFTER REB SHMELKE, *the holy disciple of the Maggid of Mezritch, became the Rav of Nikolsburg, he began to give remarkably holy sermons, imagining all of his congregants to be learned, pious, and holy beings, but the people of Nikolsburg couldn't relate to them. Some felt that the sermons were over their heads, while others looked down their noses at them. The ones who looked down their noses were usually scholars who, thinking themselves quite advanced in knowledge, would take issue with one point or another in his sermon, and even occasionally interrupt the sermon to argue these points right then and there! Not only were they entirely unaware of the coarseness of such behavior, they were missing the point of the sermons, the deep and holy prescriptions Reb Shmelke was giving over for their benefit.*

When Reb Elimelekh of Lizhensk realized that his friend was having some trouble in Nikolsburg, he set out immediately to visit his former mashpiyya and friend. When he arrived, he went to the leaders of the community and asked to preach in the synagogue as a visiting maggid. They agreed, and people soon filled the synagogue.

Reb Elimelekh ascended the three steps of the bimah (dais), and said, "Once upon a time there was a prince whose father sent him to Paris to study at the university. With him, he sent a valet and a coachman. But soon after the three had started out on the road, the valet and the coachman began to plot against the prince, thinking to kill him and take his traveling funds. Thus the valet said to the coachman, 'From now on, you will be the valet and I will be the prince, and when we get to Berlin, I will send a message to the king saying that I require more funds.

Then we will go on to Paris, continuing to impersonate the prince from afar, stealing the income the king is going to send to him there while he was supposed to be
in the university!'

"So they went through with their plan and killed the prince and hired a new
coachman, but by the time they arrived in Berlin, the pretend 'prince,' who was
really the valet, had fallen ill. What could they do? They called for the best doctor
that could be found to come and cure him. Thus, the court physician to the Kaiser
himself soon arrived to treat the masquerading prince with his very refined medicines fit for royalty. But much to his surprise, the medicines didn't help. Seeing this,
the former coachman, now masquerading as the valet, suddenly realized that the
medicines weren't going to work on the valet-prince. So he sent for a horse doctor,
who quickly diagnosed the valet-prince's illness after only a few sharp questions. He
administered a good purgative to the prince, and after he had been cleared out, the
pretender quickly returned to health."

"Now, let me tell you something" said Reb Elimelekh, "my dear friend and holy
brother, Reb Shmelke, is a good doctor, but he thinks that you are all menschen,
and thus he has been giving you all refined medicines fit for princes; but I know that
you are nothing but valets in disguise, and that these medicine won't work on you.
What you really need is a horse doctor like me to come and give you some strong
medicine!" He then began to look out upon all of them, reading their foreheads and
proclaiming their sins aloud, and urging them to repent!

After that, it is said that the entire congregation repented and began to receive
Reb Shmelke's sermons with delight.

It is said that during this visit, Reb Elimelekh noticed that his former mentor,
Reb Shmelke, had a habit of sleeping in his chair after studying into the wee
hours. Seeing this, he realized that this habit probably closed more doors for
Reb Shmelke than it opened, continuing his weariness into the next day. So
as Reb Shmelke nodded off in his chair, Reb Elimelekh went to prepare Reb
Shmelke's bed and then gently led him to it for a good sleep. Too tired and
kind to deny Reb Elimelekh's wishes, he lay down and slept until daybreak.
He woke clearheaded and invigorated and thanked Reb Elimelekh, saying,
"Not until this very day did I understand that one can also serve God with
sleep!"[22]

This story should be remembered as we explore the spiritual prescriptions
(*etzot*) of Reb Elimelekh in the next chapter and we begin to feel that he is
becoming too ascetic. The prescription is for the needs of a particular patient,
and for Reb Shmelke, subduing the body was no longer an issue. Now it was
time for him to show kindness to his body.

THE *TZADDIK*

At the end of this period of wayfaring, Reb Elimelekh finally settled in Lizhensk, which would become the "Jerusalem of Hasidism" for the next 10 years. There, Reb Elimelekh trained his disciples, dispensed justice for the Jews of the region, and maintained a Hasidic court supported by *pidyonot*, contributions offered to the *tzaddik*.

In Lizhensk, Reb Elimelekh began to teach his disciples how to be *tzaddikim*, just as the Maggid had before him. But while the Maggid was a great pedagogue, a river of holy teaching continually flowing from his mouth, Reb Elimelekh's teaching was more compact and packaged for practical use. This has made his collection of discourses, *No'am Elimelekh*, one of the enduring classics of Hasidic literature, even more popular than Reb Levi Yitzhak of Berditchev's *Kedushat Levi*. The subject of most of the *No'am Elimelekh* is the *tzaddik*. And perhaps more than any other Rebbe, Reb Elimelekh emphasized the *tzaddik*'s critical role in the work of creation and the power of the *tzaddik*'s prayer to affect the divine will.

"OPEN THE GATES *of Righteousness for me that I may enter and serve Yah. This is the gate to Y-H-V-H; the Righteous shall enter it" (Ps. 118:19–20).*[23]

The great realization of the tzaddikim is that they cannot reach perfection. This is what distinguishes them as tzaddikim. The longer they are in service to God, the more they become aware of the fact that they cannot attain the level of perfect service, for theirs is a path without limits, and this awareness is itself service.

The Psalmist says, "Open the Gates of Righteousness (sha'arei tzedek) for me." The tzaddikim say, "Open the gates so that I may enter and serve God," for the tzaddikim are aware that they have not even begun to serve. Then the Psalmist replies, "This is the gate to Y-H-V-H; the Righteous (tzaddik) shall enter it." This means that this realization is itself the "gate" through which the tzaddikim become tzaddikim, for it is an act of service to know that one cannot reach a perfect level of service with regard to God, since God is Without Limits. Please, understand this well.[24]

This teaching is a perfect parallel to "The Heart Afire" teaching of the Ba'al Shem Tov discussed in Chapter 2. You see, when people read about Reb Elimelekh and other Hasidic masters being preoccupied with the concept of the *tzaddik*, it tends to sound like some sort of megalomania or radical self-absorption. But you have to read the texts to see that they are actually redefining the entire concept of righteousness around a radical humility, elevating the importance of the function of *tzaddikim* on the one hand, while at the same time saying that this function cannot be performed adequately unless the ego has been removed from the equation! This is why the Ba'al Shem Tov is saying in "The Heart Afire" that the *tzaddikim* are those who are continually doing *teshuvah* (repentance).

PRACTICAL TZADDIKISM

Another misunderstanding of Reb Elimelekh has to do with his advocacy of what the opponents of Hasidism and some scholars have called "practical tzaddikism," which is to say that he was not only a spiritual guide but also attended to the most minute and mundane needs of his followers. Not all *tzaddikim* subscribed to this kind of leadership; nevertheless, Reb Elimelekh set a precedent in this that would be followed by most Rebbes in the generations to follow.[25] Thus, he is sometimes called the "originator of practical tzaddikism" and, as such, is made responsible for various "degenerate,"[26] or more materially oriented forms of Hasidism that would come later. However, when we look at the actual practices of Reb Elimelekh himself, we see that they are quite far removed from what critics have said (with some justification) of later Hasidic courts. For never did the Rebbe Reb Melekh's court become oriented toward material power or gain. Indeed, it was said that an excess coin never remained in his house overnight. Moreover, Reb Elimelekh was certainly not one to de-emphasize the personal responsibility or spiritual transformation of the Hasid. In fact, the situation was quite the opposite (as we shall see in Chapter 10).

It is true that Reb Elimelekh's teachings in the *No'am Elimelekh* emphasize the *tzaddik's* "obligation to direct his worship, through his mystical attainment and relationship to the higher worlds, in such a way as to gratify the material needs of his Hasidim."[27] And it is also true that he does this in a way that is not represented in the teachings of the Maggid of Mezritch, as various scholars have pointed out.[28] But this emphasis is not different from the living practice and personal concerns of the Ba'al Shem Tov. Nor do I think that we can say that these were *not* the concerns of the Maggid of Mezritch, only that it was not his task to address these needs directly. For the Maggid was the one who was training those who would go out to the regions of greatest need to serve and uplift those people. But we might also ask, for what purpose did the

Maggid continually teach that "the *tzaddik* decrees and the Holy One fulfills" if not for the uplifting of the people? This is very much what Reb Elimelekh teaches in the following passage from the *No'am Elimelekh*.

"AND THESE ARE the names of the children of Yisra'el as they came into Egypt with Ya'akov, each came with their household" (Exod. 1:1).

The spirituality, or the soul of a person is what is called the "name" (shem), because the name is at the core of a person. Thus names like "Reuven" and "Shim'on" are names for the soul and not for the body. To understand this more clearly, we can see that when a person is asleep, and we try to awaken them by nudging the body without calling the name of the person, we have great difficulty bringing them to consciousness. This is because the soul leaves the body during sleep and rises up to higher spheres, making it more difficult to awaken a person by simply nudging their body. It is much easier to awaken one by calling their name.

This is why it is written, "And these are the names of the children of Yisra'el as they came into Egypt," meaning that the holy tzaddikim, who deserve to be called by the name "Yisra'el," which is a higher rung, "came into Egypt," which is on a very low rung. So how was it possible that these tzaddikim fell into such a low place as the oppression of Egypt? This is why the Torah says that "they came into Egypt with Ya'akov," because Ya'akov represents the simple people who are so called by God. Therefore, we see that it is necessary for the tzaddik to descend the higher rungs to become involved in the lives of the simple people in order to raise them up to holiness.

It is often said that the *tzaddik* or Rebbe is the "intermediary," making the connection between God and the Hasid, but this is not so. The Rebbe is the one who gets underneath the Hasid and pushes the Hasid up from below, as we see here.

IF THE TZADDIKIM would not descend in this way, there would be no connection between them and the simple people. And why is it that the tzaddik can bring them up to holiness? Because the Torah says, "each came with their household." The household, which was not on the same rung of service, arrived with Ya'akov and his sons.

This is why it is written, "I shall thank God with my mouth" (Ps. 109:30),[29] for although everything of the mouth follows after the thought, thought may grasp many things at once that the mouth can express only serially, one at a time. This is why David ha-Melekh, of blessed memory, said, "I shall thank God with my mouth," which is to say, although it is impossible to express what is in my thoughts [paradox and multidimensionality] through the lips, nevertheless, "I shall thank God with my mouth," which is a lower rung than my intention. Why is he doing this? In order that God's name shall be praised among the many, who are on the lower rung. Therefore, the tzaddik has to descend to a lower rung in order to raise the simple people up to holiness.[30]

Teachings like this (and the stories that go with them) are probably the reason that Reb Elimelekh has sometimes been called "the second Ba'al Shem Tov." For his own Rebbe, the Maggid of Mezritch, was so focused on training the elite that Reb Elimelekh's concern for the simple folk must have seemed like a "return" to the Ba'al Shem Tov's love of the people. As we have said, this is not likely true, but it is easy to see why some may have seen things in this way.

THE VIEW FROM ABOVE

I also tend to think this emphasis from Reb Elimelekh is a very personal response to the grinding poverty and terrible political vicissitudes that Jews were continually subject to at that time. There is one painful anecdote when Reb Elimelekh dreams of the Maggid and asks him why he has not intervened for the people.

ONCE, REB ELIMELEKH saw great trouble approaching the Jewish people and he began to pray very hard for God's help. Later when he was asleep, he saw the Maggid of Mezritch in his dream, and he asked him, "Rebbe, why are you silent? Why don't you cry out against this terrible catastrophe?"

The Maggid answered him, saying, "In Heaven, we do not see any evil—we see only the goodness and the kindness of judgments. You who are on Earth see the good as well as the evil, therefore, you must insist and pray very hard to move the Heavens in these matters."[31]

This is an extraordinary teaching. In it, we can see why Reb Elimelekh goes to such great lengths to stress the urgency of needs here below and to create powerful channels of mercy. Elsewhere Reb Elimelekh teaches, "'In the beginning, God created the world under the attribute of judgment (din), but later added the attribute of mercy.' So the question is, Why didn't God do this from the beginning?" Then Reb Elimelekh says, "In the beginning, God created in the world of beri'ah (world of knowing), which is mostly good. And in a mostly good world, it is good to go with judgment, but when you get down to a world of assiyah (world of action), where we live, which was created afterward, and which is mostly evil, then you need to have great mercy added."[32]

THE TRIAL OF GOD

In his own way, Reb Elimelekh is as much an advocate for justice for the people as the famous Reb Levi Yitzhak of Berditchev. The ḥutzpah of this incredible ma'aseh shows this as well as any in all of Hasidic literature and makes the point of how hard Reb Elimelekh felt he had to push in Heaven, how loudly he had to call for justice, in order to be heard above.

IN THE DAYS of Reb Elimelekh of Lizhensk, it happened that the Kaiser Oestereich [in Austria] made a royal decree that any person who wished to give their daughter in marriage must first pay a marriage tax of 400 gold pieces to the royal treasury. Now, 400 gold pieces was a fortune well beyond the reach of all but the wealthiest persons in the realm. And when that decree was finally spread over the length and breadth of the land, it caused a terrible grief and anxiety to people everywhere; there were so many girls of marriageable age who would now become like straw widows, unable to marry for lack of money.

In a city near Lizhensk at that time, there was a poor Jew of good character and a fearer of God who had a daughter only recently engaged to be married. The young man to whom she was engaged was a fine person also and ready to marry her even without a dowry, but neither he nor the father of the bride could even conceive of paying the kaiser's tax. The father of the would-be bride was driven almost to despair. "Soon," he thought, "no one will want to marry my gentle daughter because she will be poor and too old. And now this wonderful match has come to us and we cannot even accept it! My God, what have you done to us?" Angry and grief stricken he departed for Lizhensk to go to the court of the Rebbe Reb Melekh. When he arrived in Lizhensk, he burst through the doors of Reb Elimelekh's house and shouted, "Rebbe, I wish put God on trial!"

Once those words had left his mouth, his anger departed from him, and he sud-

denly became terribly self-conscious, and thought, "Oy! what did I say? What kind
of hutzpah is this? And before whom did I say such a thing? Oy! Oy! Oy!" A wave
of regret and fear washed over him as he imagined the Rebbe's terrible anger and
the punishment that would be meted out to him as a result. All of these thoughts
flashed by in an instant, and he turned to flee Reb Elimelekh's house when he heard
the Rebbe Reb Melekh's voice quietly saying, "Stay, my son, stay."

The poor man froze on the spot. Then he heard the Rebbe speak again, saying,
"You say you would like to put God on trial. . . . Good, good, good. But the Rabbis
have said that one is not supposed to conduct a trial alone, so I will ask two of my
disciples to preside over the court with me. Please tell them that they should come
and sit with me here to constitute a court."

The man began to shake, for the Rebbe Reb Melekh never said anything that did
not come about. What else could he do? He went and called two of the disciples in
the name of the Rebbe to act as the magistrates. They came without delay, and
then Reb Elimelekh said to the man, "Please go ahead and make your claim
against God, and we will listen."

The poor man took a breath and began, "God gave us the holy Torah; and the
Torah has 613 mitzvot that we are to keep and to guard; and the first mitzvah of
the Torah is to 'be fruitful and to multiply' (Gen. 1:28). Now the kaiser has decreed
that one is not to marry off a daughter without paying the kaiser 400 gold pieces;
who in our generation has this kind of money to give? And now many young women
are not getting married; they are just sitting at home and becoming old maids. I
too have a daughter whom I need to marry, and I have a good match for her, but
I cannot pay this tax! And so I say that God has put the whole Torah in question
because of this; for how can it be that that first commandment of the Torah should
fall into disuse?"

When he had finished speaking, the Rebbe Reb Melekh opened his holy mouth
and said, "What God has said is already known to us; therefore, we must now confer and come to a decision. According to the rule of the law, while we are debating
among ourselves, the two litigants must be outside of the room, but since God fills
the whole world, there is no other place for God to go. Indeed, how could we live if
God were to go away? And since God cannot leave, you cannot leave either; both
you and God must be present while we turn the situation over according to the
law."

Then the Rebbe Reb Melekh sat down in his chair and closed his eyes, and before
long, he entered into a great deveikut and his face was aflame with light. He
remained thus for a quarter of an hour before he roused himself, and said, "Bring
me the Gemara, tractate Gittin."

After a few minutes, the volume of Gemara was brought to him and he opened *it to page 41, and said, "Read with me." And the judges all began to read, "'What should be done for one who is half slave and half free? He cannot marry a maid-servant because he is free and she is not; but neither can he marry a free-woman because he is a servant and she is free. Thus he cannot fulfill the first command-ment to be fruitful and multiply. But it is also written that the world was not cre-ated for nothing . . . so we force the master to give him total freedom.' "*

And when the Rebbe Reb Melekh said the words, "we force the master to give him total freedom," he closed his eyes and raised his arms high. And when he brought them down again, he said, "Go home; the kaiser has given up on this law." The poor man went home not knowing what to think, but while he was still on the road, he learned the news from a fellow traveler that the kaiser had rescinded the tax, and so now his daughter could get married.[33]

Throughout Hasidic stories and teachings, there is much talk of how "the *tzaddik* decrees and the Holy One fulfills," but nowhere do we see it so dra-matically put into practice as in this story of the Rebbe Reb Melekh![34] In other versions, we are told that at the moment Reb Elimelekh said the words—slow-ly and with intense *kavanah*—"we force the master to give him total freedom," the kaiser in Vienna saw the face of the Rebbe Reb Melekh and heard his voice, as if by astral projection, and he was so frightened that he immediately rescinded the decree. In another similar tale, Reb Elimelekh mysteriously spills his soup (clearly on purpose) while his disciples look on in amazement. Later they find at that same moment the kaiser was about to sign an edict that would have been injurious to the Jews when his inkwell mysteriously spilled on the papers. In frustration, he tore the document up and did not seek to have it rewritten![35]

GOD'S ATONEMENT

Another wonderful *ma'aseh* also shows Reb Elimelekh's continued preoccu-pation with divine justice. For in this *ma'aseh*, a Hasid asks if he may be wit-ness to how Reb Elimelekh does his atonement on Yom Kippur but is refused. Instead, Reb Elimelekh sends him to a certain inn to observe the innkeeper closely. In this way, the Hasid's question is answered by proxy.

ONCE, A HASID arrived in Lizhensk before Yom Kippur to learn from Reb Elimelekh how he did his own kapporot (atonement), but Reb Elimelekh said, "I can't let you be present for that, but please pay a visit to the local innkeeper and watch him carefully." So the Hasid obtained a room at the inn and took a seat in the common room where he could observe the innkeeper without being noticed.

Late that night, when the rest of the guests had gone to bed, he remained in a dark corner of the room observing the innkeeper, who sat down at a table with a candle and took out two journals. He began to read from the first in a low voice. The Hasid could hear only just enough to know it was a list of wrongs he had committed during the year. Then he closed the book and opened the second book and began to read; this it seemed was a book of wrongs he had suffered during the year!

Then he closed this book as well and set the two side by side and said, "Ribbono shel Olam, if You'll forgive me for the wrong that I've done to You, then I'll forgive You for what You've done to me."

The *tzaddikim* believe that God's wisdom is perfect, but they are not less aware that the "appearance" of things does not seem even remotely perfect. So what can we do with this perceptual split between our reality and its appearance? Don't we have to honor the appearance as "real" in our experience as well?

THE EXECUTION

At the beginning of this chapter, we spoke of those who put cleverness in the service of God, and of how this service distinguishes the Hasidic *ma'aseh* from ordinary miracle tales and good roadhouse yarns. Think back on these tales of Reb Elimelekh and see how this has been done throughout; how an ingenious twist or shift in perspective has been introduced into situations of material and spiritual importance to create healing or deep understanding. For this is part of the essence of Hasidic spirituality. I am reminded of a *mashal*, a parable I once heard the Bobover Rebbe, Reb Shlomo Halberstam tell . . .

A *tzaddik* is said to be "good" and to receive the reward for the good that is done and the reward for the fruit of these actions as well. That is to say, a *tzaddik* gets the capital, the interest, and the compound interest. However, one who does evil receives punishment *only* for the evil, and not for the fruit of their action also.

Why should this be?

If a *tzaddik* gives a dollar to someone in need, it is not just the

302 A HEART AFIRE

exchange of a dollar from one person to another, but that dollar is also intended for help and for benefit, to get food, to meet the needs of a family, and for various other good things. However, the thief who steals a dollar usually means to steal a dollar to gratify only their own needs. So the one who gives good receives the reward for the many good intentions also, while the one who intends evil is punished only for that evil.

You see, this is clever, but not for the sake of cleverness. The Bobover Rebbe (who is in the lineage of Reb Elimelekh) wants to accomplish something holy with this *mashal*—to deepen one's awareness of the importance of *kavanah* behind simple acts and also to lighten the burden of judgment around those who have done wrong, making it easier for them to do *teshuvah*. This is the way of Reb Elimelekh, as we see in this *ma'aseh*—one of my personal favorites.

ONCE, A SINNER came to the Rebbe Reb Melekh saying, "Rebbe, short of murder, I've done it all. I know that I will not be accepted in Heaven as I am, and before I die, I want to make amends. Please help me, Rebbe! What can I do? I need such a great tikkun, such a great fixing for my soul or I'll surely find myself in Gehenna! What can I do to straighten out this mess that I have made of my life?"

Reb Elimelekh listened attentively to the man's confession and was quiet for a moment. Finally, he said, "My friend, atonement is a very serious matter for sins such as yours; you may not be willing to accept the punishment that is prescribed to expiate such sins."

The man was determined and said, "I assure you, Rebbe, I am."

"Very well then," said Reb Elimelekh, "the prescribed atonement is one of execution by the pouring of hot lead down one's throat. If you truly wish to make a complete atonement for these sins, we can arrange such an execution for you."

The man gulped and was silent for a moment. Then, gathering his courage, he asked, "Holy Rebbe, will I really be forgiven if I do that?"

"Yes," said Reb Elimelekh.

"Alright," said the sinner, "let's do it tomorrow!"

"Oh no, no, no . . . wait just a minute," said Reb Elimelekh. "The prescription for complete atonement is not quite as simple as that; I can't administer the hot lead until you have thoroughly purged yourself of these sins and changed your ways entirely."

"How long will that take?" asked the sinner.

Reb Elimelekh said, "You must do the teshuvah I will prescribe for an entire

year. Then, when you have done all that is asked of you, I will administer the exe-
cution myself, and pray for your complete redemption."

Reb Elimelekh then gave the sinner a detailed prescription for teshuvah to be
carried out every day for a year. The sinner followed through with all that was pre-
scribed for him that year, until the day of the execution finally arrived. The sinner
was afraid, naturally, but his desire for redemption had become so great that he
actually longed for anything that could bring it about—even his death. The man
entered the Rebbe's study with great solemnity and immediately noticed a boiling
cauldron next to a table on the far side of the room. Reb Elimelekh beckoned to him
and instructed him to lie down on the table, and the man did so without question.
A cloth was then laid over his eyes, and he began to recite his confession again, as
Reb Elimelekh had told him he must. Then he begged God's forgiveness and pre-
pared to say the final Shema. After a brief silence, slowly and deeply he began to
intone, "Shema Yisra'el, Yah Eloheinu, Yah Eḥa-a-a-a-d." He opened his mouth
wide . . . Reb Elimelekh lifted the ladle and began to pour. The man coughed with
surprise, tore the cloth from his eyes, and began to sputter and swallow.

It was honey!

"What did you do that for?" the man demanded. "I expected to die!"

Reb Elimelekh answered, "At this point, it is no longer necessary."[36]

You see, Reb Elimelekh had no desire to punish this man, but he also knew that the former sinner believed so deeply that he *deserved* punishment that he would not be able to accept outright forgiveness either.

Back in 1955 or 1956, I lost my job as a congregational rabbi. The board complained, "He is not modern enough and uses too much English." Clearly I couldn't give them what they wanted, but I had a family to provide for, so I applied for a teaching post at the University of Manitoba. But, being the 1950s, the national administration of Hillel would only take me if I cut my beard! Well, I was a card-carrying Lubavitcher Hasid at the time, and Hasidim don't cut their beards. But the situation was getting desperate, so I talked them into allowing me to keep a goatee. Well, I'll tell you, the first time I went back to Lubavitch in Crown Heights after that, I was so ashamed that I tried to keep to the shadows and avoid most of the gatherings. Finally, my friend Zalman Posner spotted me sneaking around and gestured to me to follow him. He led me over to a private corner and really let me have it—"You cut your beard and sold out your Jewishness for what? A few dollars!" But when he was done, he put his arm around me and said, "Okay, now can you come in and enjoy yourself?"

You see, he took me into the shame I was feeling so that I could let it go, which is exactly what I had to do. This is very much the way Reb Elimelekh works as well. Moreover, Reb Elimelekh knows that even more important than the shame is the transformation, thus he has to find a way for the man to unseat his former habits. For it is not enough to regret your past, you have to change the negative patterns. So he prescribed a year's worth of practices for the man to unseat the negative patterns of his past, allowing him to say at the final moment, "At this point, the punishment is no longer necessary!" What were those practices he prescribed for the sinner? This is what we will explore in the next chapter.

10

The King's Counsel: In the Court of the Rebbe Reb Melekh

IN THE PREVIOUS CHAPTER, WE EXPLORED REB ELIMELEKH'S role as an advocate for his people, but now we would like to turn to the ways in which he trained his Hasidim. For Reb Elimelekh continually emphasized the unique and intimate relationship that existed between the Hasid and Rebbe, believing that they were bound together at the level of the soul. And, as we mentioned earlier, many of the great Rebbes of the next generation were his disciples, including the Hozeh of Lublin, the Maggid of Koznitz, Reb Mendel of Rymanov, and Reb Avraham Yehoshua Heschel of Apt. All of these men (with the exception of the Apter Rav) had been among the youngest disciples of the Maggid of Mezritch, but quickly acknowledged the leadership of Reb Elimelekh after the Maggid's passing.

What was it that drew them to Reb Elimelekh, who was so different from the Maggid? One small indication comes from Yisra'el Hofstein (1733–1815), the Maggid of Kozhnitz, who tells us, "I had studied 800 books on Kabbalah, but when I arrived in the presence of the Maggid, I realized I had not even begun to study."[1] But after the Maggid of Mezritch had passed on, Reb Yisra'el took his devotion to Reb Elimelekh of Lizhensk, saying, "My knowledge of Kabbalah may be superior to that of my teacher Elimelekh, but I am not able to serve God in the way that he does, in the spirit of self-sacrifice, Love and Awe."[2]

THE *TZETTEL KATTAN*

So what did Reb Elimelekh's great service, done "in the spirit of self-sacrifice," look like? Before we can talk about this properly, we first have to introduce a different genre of Hasidic literature than we have seen heretofore in this book. Up to this point, we have mainly dealt with stories and tales—*sippurim* and *ma'asiot*—and with the Torah of the Rebbes written on kabbalistic themes—sometimes as independent *ma'amarim* (discourses) and most often as Torah *derashot* (interpretations)—usually arranged around the sections (*parshiot*) of Torah. But there is another genre of Hasidic literature that is equally important but that gets far less emphasis in most books about Hasidism. That is the literature of *etzot* (counsels) and *hanhagot* (practices).

In the Hasidic context, an *etzah* is a counsel or a piece of advice received from the Rebbe (often in the *yehidut* interview) as a solution to a problem. These I have dealt with at length in *Spiritual Intimacy: A Study of Counseling in Hasidism*.³ Here we are more concerned with *hanhagot*, the various spiritual intentions and practices recommended by the Rebbes for their Hasidim. This is the "how-to" literature of spiritual attainment.⁴ The lists of *hanhagot* that the early Hasidim were themselves most familiar with came from the great kabbalists of S'fat—Moshe Cordovero (1522–1570) and Yitzhak Luria (1534–1572)—who created lists of spiritual practices for themselves and their disciples to follow. But while these *hanhagot* were grounded in mystical thought, they were also deeply ascetic, advocating a strict regimen of self-mortification (*sigufim*), all manner of fasting (*ta'aniyot*), sleep deprivation, and withdrawal from even the most basic of sensual pleasures, all to prepare the body for mystical experience.⁵ Of course, these were time-honored practices found in different forms across the spectrum of spiritual traditions, but they were taken up with new vigor by many mystically inclined Jews in the wake of the kabbalistic revolution wrought by Yitzhak Luria, the Ari ha-Kodesh.

With the coming of Hasidism, and the Ba'al Shem Tov's emphasis on *avodah begashmiut* (service through the physical), a major shift occurred in the *hanhagot* literature. For the Ba'al Shem Tov taught that the body, which had formerly been forced into submission, could instead be used as a tool of holiness. Thus Hasidic *hanhagot* tend to deemphasize the fasting and self-mortification that is so prevalent in kabbalistic lists of *hanhagot*, while still preserving some of the ascetic flavor of those practices. In point of fact, what they have done is to raise the physical asceticism of the former practices up to the level of *kavanah*, stressing the *intention* to overcome the persistent call of the *yetzer ha-ra* (negative inclination) and the biological urges. These urges would now be addressed on the level of the heart and mind, instead of the body. In this way, Hasidism made a major shift away from the rigidly defined opposition of spirit and matter taught for centuries among kabbalists.[6]

Of all the lists of *hanhagot* preserved from the first generations of Hasidism, undoubtedly the most famous is the one known as the *Tzettel Kattan*, the "little note" written by Reb Elimelekh and appended to his book *No'am Elimelekh*. This little note was really a very specific set of spiritual "prescriptions" given to a particular disciple to read and work through every day. Let me say that again so that it is very clear: The *Tzettel Kattan* is not *necessarily* a list of Reb Elimelekh's own spiritual practices or even those practices that he recommended to all of his Hasidim.

You see, Reb Elimelekh took special care in the training of his Hasidim, writing specific *hanhagot* for each to carry out for the purification of their service to God. The *Tzettel Kattan* appears to be one of these lists. Thus it is a very specific set of spiritual instructions written out for the use of a *particular* Hasid, or at the very least for Hasidim of a particular age group, in this case, a young male disciple, anywhere from 15 to 20 years old.

Why is this relevant?

Because, as you will see, many of these *hanhagot* are tailored toward a "heroic" sense of divine service, using up a lot of energy, as is necessary for a youth in a constant state of struggle with his own libido. Many of these would not be necessary to recommend to his older disciples or those who had already brought these basic urges under control.

Nevertheless, with that qualification in mind, we can say with some assuredness that these *hanhagot* are quite representative of Reb Elimelekh, who is clearly the archetypal "ascetic hero."[7] While his *hanhagot* have turned away from the physical harshness of the earlier *hanhagot* of the kabbalists, they are still pretty strong medicine, and he knew it. This is why he compared himself to "a horse doctor" in the last chapter. He was a hard taskmaster, but he was equally skillful, which provided the balance for his Hasidim. Nevertheless, it should be remembered that Reb Elimelekh's "strong medicine" was meant as a kindness, a means of working a great healing in his patients very quickly. Thus I can easily see him prescribing this very set of *hanhagot* to the repentant sinner in the *ma'aseh* of "The Execution" presented in Chapter 9.

THESE ARE THE *things that human beings shall do and live by them!*

I. WHENEVER YOU ARE idle, sitting alone in a room, or lying in bed unable to sleep, meditate on the positive mitzvah, "And I will be made holy in the midst of the children of Yisra'el" (Lev. 22:32).[8] *Then imagine an all-consuming fire burning before you, describing it in your thought and imagination with flames reaching even to the heart of Heaven. Picture yourself for the sake of union with the blessed name, breaking free from the bonds of self-preservation and casting yourself into that holy fire! Since a good thought is reckoned as a good deed by the blessed and Holy One, the result will be that you will have accomplished the redemption of your spare time by the fulfillment of a positive mitzvah.*

When I was a teenager, I was very inspired by this *hanhagah* of Reb Elimelekh and used to do miniature meditations of this sort while riding on the BMT subway from my home in Boro Park to the *yeshiva* on Eastern Parkway. Being a good Hasid and *yeshiva bokher* (student), I didn't want to have to look at the Maidenform bra advertisements posted in the passenger cars. So I would let myself into the little cubicles at the end of the train (where the conductors sometimes sat) and do a meditation of this sort in privacy there. I would imagine that by the time we came to Pacific Avenue (where the train stopped), I would surrender my life to God and die. As we approached Pacific Avenue, I would begin to prepare myself to let go. Closer and closer it would come, and I could feel the sense of momentousness building in me. Suddenly, I would hear the brakes and know those were my last moments; the train came to a stop and I experienced for a brief moment the nothingness of death! I'll tell you, at the time, that little meditation really did something for me.

Reb Elimelekh clearly felt that an imaginal experience, if sincerely felt, could be accounted as an actual deed. In this case, he sees the imaginal experience of offering one's life for the sanctification of God's name as a kind of scouring for the "mirror of the heart," removing the ego obstructions, defying and transcending the ego and its fears by a continual confrontation with death. It is indeed "strong medicine," but the confrontation with death is not something that can be avoided. Sooner or later, one must face it. Here Reb Elimelekh gives us the opportunity to face it voluntarily, to do a "dry run" if you will. By putting it into the context of divine service and preparation for the ultimate surrender, it gives us a genuine way to begin to weaken the powerful grip of the ego.

II. WHEN READING THE first sentence of the Shema and the first blessing of the Amidah, you should practice this same meditation. Moreover, make it your intention that even if the entire world were to cause you pain, torturing you in an attempt to convince you to identify only with the surface of your skin and to deny God's blessed unity, you would never give in. Imagine this very scenario in detail with a realistic situational thinking so that it stimulates emotion. In this way, you may become attuned to the true locus of the Shema *and* Amidah.

Reb Mendel of Rymonov used to speak of the greatness of Reb Elimelekh's awe before God in prayer, saying, "Behind the ear is an artery that pulsates intensely when a person is about to die; whenever Reb Elimelekh began to *daven*, this artery could be seen pulsating wildly!"[9]

Reb Kalonymous Kalmish of Piasetzno (1889–1944), a descendant of Reb Elimelekh and a strong advocate of using visualizations, recommends this powerful meditation in his *B'nai Maḥshavah Tovah*, saying:

> In this way we actually experience the quality of giving ourselves over to God each time we recite the *Shema* prayer, which contains the words, "heart, soul, and might." This is not an empty mental exercise with no impact on the soul; we do not feed the body by imagining food. Rather, we have the intention of giving over the soul. We offer up the soul fully and willingly, and the offering itself fulfills our deepest yearning. Our bodies partake of the offering as well; both the body and the soul are cleansed by the act.[10]

Some people will be bothered by what they may consider unnecessary references to torture in this *hanhagah*, but we must remember that Reb Elimelekh lived in an era when brutality and persecution of Jews was the norm, and forced conversions were not something of the distant past. Indeed, Reb Kalonymous Kalmish, whom we have just quoted, was himself killed by the Nazis in the Warsaw Ghetto in 1943.[11]

III. THIS INTENTION IS also of value while you are eating or engaged in sexual intercourse. As soon as you begin to feel sensual pleasure, visualize and experience this holy fire in your imagination, transmuting the joy and pleasure of these acts into the mitzvah "And I will be made holy" (Lev. 22:32), thus elevating the raw experience.[12] For greater delight may be found in this than in those acts. Proof of this may be found in the fact that if great danger or trouble were to befall you, you would certainly seek God before such things. However, be careful that these intentions and statements be made with great sincerity; they must become engraved with truth on the tablets of your heart, in the innermost recesses of your heart. Do not deceive yourself in this!

In other words, as soon as you begin to feel sensual pleasure, visualize and experience this holy fire in your imagination, transmuting the joy and pleasure of these physical acts into the mitzvah "And I will be made holy," thereby burning your selfish intentions in the fire of divine sacrifice and elevating the raw experience to its root above. Through this, the soul will become so habituated to the experience and present (through this intention) that no experience of pleasure, or any deprivation of it, or any experience of pain should divide you for long from being united with the blessed name.

It is clear that Reb Elimelekh's intention is that his disciples should be able to slip into the situational thinking of this imagery at will, stimulating deep feeling in order to disassociate from their attachments to sensual pleasure. In this way, he hopes that his Hasidim will be able to transform the desire to satisfy their animal appetites into the accomplishment of a divine unification, *yiḥud*.

Now, Reb Tzvi Elimelekh of Dynov in his *Derekh Pikudekha* (in the section that deals with the first mitzvah, to "be fruitful and multiply") deals with sexual intercourse in a way that is perhaps more in line with our own values today. There he asks the question, "Why don't we make a *berakhah* over the enjoyment of sexual intercourse?" He comes to the conclusion that it is only because the Rabbis never came to a decision about this, but not because it is unhealthy or wrong. Then he says, "Since you cannot experience it without enjoying it, and to enjoy anything of this world without thanking God is not good, you should say in the vernacular, 'Thank you, God, for giving me a mitzvah that you cannot do without feeling pleasure.' "

IV. IN ALL YOUR actions—in prayer, mitzvot, or Torah—acquire the habit of saying, "I do this for the sake of the conscious uniting of the transcendent Holy One with the manifest Presence, Yud Heh with Vav Heh, thus giving pleasure to the act of creation."³ This should be said wholeheartedly, with depth and sincerity; in time, you will experience a great illumination through this practice.

By intending to bring about "the conscious uniting of the transcendent Holy One with the manifest Presence," one brings about the union of the masculine and feminine aspects of the Divine. It is as if the consciously directed effort of the individual can bring about the union of the divine parents, as it says in the Zohar, "Like the child who is devoted to their Father and Mother." This is the great work of creation, the bringing together of these two aspects of the divine being. This is our work in the world.

The pre-Hasidic "unifications" (*yiḥudim*) of the Kabbalah concerned themselves with myriad constellations of divine names and their proper pronunciation in correspondence with very specific acts. The Maggid of Mezritch likened these to highly intricate locks with corresponding keys—which is fine if you have such a key ring in your possession and a knowledge of which key fits with which lock. But what if you don't? Are you to be denied your part in the holy work of bringing worlds together? No, says the Maggid; it is not only door wardens who can open doors; thieves can do so as well. If they can't pick the lock, they can surely break it! Thus, Reb Elimelekh asks his Hasid to recite this formula, "In all your actions." It is not the key of the door warden, and it is not the hammer of the impetuous burglar, but the pick of the expert thief.[14] It is said that the Ba'al Shem Tov accomplished such *yiḥudim* even while smoking his pipe as he sat down and relaxed in the evening.[15]

V. As soon as you are aware of being goaded by habitual vices—obstinacy, self-importance, laziness, or the lack of initiative (which brings about boredom)— immediately say with all your strength, "Ha-Kena'ani, ha-Ḥitti, ha-Emori, ha-Perizi, ha-Ḥivi, ha-Yebusi, ha-Girgashi!" (Exod. 3:17; Deut. 7:1), and you will be saved from it. Also, acquire the habit of refraining from nervously glancing about outside of your own four ells (cubits) of personal space. Do this even in your own home, but especially when you are in the synagogue or the room where you study Torah, and particularly when walking about town. If any distraction calls to you, visualize the divine name A-D-N-Y upon it.

Here Reb Elimelekh prescribes a kind of mantric formula to his Hasid, the names of the seven peoples who previously occupied the land that would become Yisra'el. It would seem that the recital of these names is equivalent to crying out, "My enemies are upon me," thus bringing divine help. This counsel is of the *segullah* (charm or potency) variety. In other words, it is not intended to deal with the problem of vice on the level in which it occurs, but rather attempts through a verbal pronouncement to shield the Hasid from the evil energy system of the *kelippot* (shells) that begets them. Perhaps the method of labeling the vices is akin to the conscious labeling of preconscious urges, thus enabling the Hasid to suppress rather than to repress them.

Now, the seven tribes of Cana'an that are mentioned here also correspond in the tradition to seven vices, which are the shadow sides of the seven *sefirot* (divine attributes), and follow in the same order. Therefore, as these come up in our consciousness, we might also deal with them in the way Insight

Meditation does—labeling them and letting them go. So if it is lust, we might say, "Ah, *ha-Kena'ani*, there you are again . . . good-bye." If it is anger, "Ah, *ha-Ḥitti*, it's you . . . good-bye." This would be a very good practice.

It is interesting that Reb Elimelekh advocates the visualization of the name A-D-N-Y (*Adonai*). This has a relationship with the sweetening of divine judgments (*dinim*) here below, for this name corresponds to the *sefirah* of *malkhut* (A-D-N-Y = D-Y-N-A, as in *dina d'malkhuta*, "The judgment of the kingdom" or "sovereignty" is to be respected).

VI. WHEN A NEGATIVE or distracting sexual thought comes to you, repeat this to yourself, "Be on your guard against anything inappropriate" (Deut. 23:10),[16] remembering the teachings of our sages who said, "Think not such thoughts during the day, for they will bring pollution at night."[17] Do not permit such thoughts to remain in your mind, for they will cloud your soul's celestial mind as well.

This *hanhagah* might also be framed this way: When a negative or distracting thought comes to you—perhaps a sexual thought out of its proper context (at the appropriate time, in the appropriate place, with the appropriate person)—repeat, "Be careful to keep all things in their own time and place." Do not linger on such thoughts out of their proper context, for that will block the flow of wisdom coming from your soul in that moment, bending the shape of your mind to be ever more accommodating to these inappropriate thoughts.

VII. IF YOUR EYES should meet a disturbing or compelling sight, such as a person inappropriately uncovered, persons engaged in sexual intercourse, or uncleanness of any kind, immediately say to yourself, "Do not be led astray by your eyes" (Num. 15:39),[18] and you will be saved from defilement.

VIII. ACQUIRE THE HABIT of refraining from speaking except when necessary, and even then, do not speak more than is necessary for that moment. Sift your words through 13 sieves[19] so that there is in them neither untruthfulness nor flattery, malicious gossip nor boasting, or anything that may cause another shame or humiliation. Try to hide your good deeds from others[20] and acquire the habit that our sages have praised, teaching your tongue to say, "I do not know."[21] When those who are

unmindful and careless in their speech address you, attempt to disengage yourself,
speaking only as much as is necessary.

The control of speech and the use of silence is frequently referred to in
Hasidic *hanhagot*.[22] The idea is that the unconscious, automatic connection
between thought and word must be broken in order to reject for a time all of
those thoughts that do not belong to an intentional life of holiness. This then
allows for the upwelling of a holier kind of thought from the source of the
Hasid's soul to be stimulated and reinforced. As long as the immediate,
unconscious connection between thought and word exists, the thought cannot be properly incubated, as it were, to create a desirable emotional state and
corresponding actions in the Hasid.

Reb Elimelekh also intends with this *hanhagah* to move the gestalt of the
Hasid's being from an outer-directedness to inner-directedness. As long as
the Hasid is connected only to the periphery of their being and not to the core,
they will not be able to draw on that which is good and holy from the hidden
sources of their being.

IX. WHEN YOU AWAKEN *from sleep, make it a habit to say, "Thank You, Living God,*
for mercifully granting my soul another day of awareness; thank You for this sacred
trust."[23] *Feel free to say it in the vernacular, as it is here, if you need to. Then when*
the time comes for these mitzvot, say with a joyful heart, "Blessed is the Most High
who gave to me the mitzvah of tzitzit in which I wrap myself," or "the mitzvah of
washing my hands in the morning in order to remove the slothful kelippot (shells)
from my hands." When you say this, let your heart be filled with joy. And again,
make certain to limit your speaking, as was mentioned before.

Here Reb Elimelekh is building the attitude of thankfulness into the Hasid.
His advice to use the vernacular, the language in which the Hasid actually
thinks, is potent in that it helps bring the immediacy of feeling to the expression of gratitude. He does not want the Hasid to pass over the real feeling of
thankfulness simply because the Hebrew, as the language of the sacred, may
be abstracted from his everyday life and ordinary feelings.

X. BE DILIGENT IN *your study and make of it a regular practice. Do this immediately*
upon arising from sleep, and after having recited the Tikkun Ḥatzot (the midnight

lament).[24] *This* Tzettel Kattan *should never be removed from the book from which you study.*[25] *When you seat yourself to study, say the penitential prayer that begins, "I beseech You, my God," and the prayer before study that begins, "Behold, I desire to study," both of which are found in* Sha'arei Tzion. *With all your strength, refuse to let yourself be interrupted by a single thought that is not relevant to your study or what is contained in this* Tzettel Kattan, *which should always be before your eyes.*[26] *The light contained in this* Tzettel Kattan *will ever cause you to turn to the good.*[27]

Reb Elimelekh is aware that we tend to be driven in the direction of our past habits and natural inclinations. Therefore, he urges us to keep this *Tzettel Kattan* before our eyes and in our thoughts constantly. Remembrance is of extreme importance to the novice. The many years of habitual tendencies that drive us most of the time cause us to react immediately to our environment without awareness or discernment. If the Hasid in this case is to develop on the spiritual path, this lack of awareness must be replaced by a particular remembrance allowing him to make a conscious decision about what is truly important to him.

Now what is the "penitential prayer" that he is referring to? It is "The Prayer of the Penitent" composed by Rabbi Yonah:

I beseech You, my God,
Because I have failed You;
I have defaced your command;
I have rebelled against You
[In this place one enumerates one's sins]
From the very first day of my existence
Until this very day.

Now my heart is raised up to You
And my spirit has made me willing
To return to You in truth;
With a good and whole heart,
My soul and my being one,
Admitting all of my guilt
And ceasing to repeat the sin,
Casting away all my rebellions.

Give to me a new heart
And a new spirit
That I might be diligent
And careful in the fear of You;
You are my God,
Opening Your hand
To receive my *teshuvah*,
Helping those who come to be purified.

Open your hand and receive me
In full *teshuvah* before You;
Help me in my Awe before You;
Help me against this *Satan*,
Who wages war with me,
Using all manner of schemes,
Desiring to destroy my soul.

Help me to subvert its rule over me;
Remove it from my 248 limbs
And cast it into the depths;
Rebuke it so that he will not stand
At my right hand to oppose me.

Please, do this so that I may
Walk in your statutes;
Remove from me this heart of stone
That is within me;
Give me a heart of flesh.

Please my Master, my God,
Listen to the prayer of Your servant,
And accept my *teshuvah*;
Let no sin in failure hold me back,
Let no distortions on my part
Hold back my prayer and my *teshuvah*.

Let those who are the best advocates
Rise to the throne of Your glory

To speak well for me,
To bring my prayer to You;
If my great sins have
Caused them to reject me, ·
Then dig a passage for me
Under the throne of Your glory
To receive my *teshuvah*
So that I will not return
Empty-handed from You,
For You are the One
Who hears my prayer.
Amen.[28]

As far as the prayer before study is concerned, I would recommend this prayer from the circle of the Ari ha-Kodesh:

My God, creator of all,
Master of all worlds,
Supremely compassionate and forgiving,
Thank You for Your Torah,
And for allowing me to learn from it
So that I might know You better;
Thank You for revealing the
Mysteries of Your way to me;
I am truly amazed by Your help.

Please forgive my foolishness,
The sins of my past and present;
I vow to live in accord with Your will
That I may be ever closer to You;
Fill me with the awe of You,
Opening my capacity for love;
Open my heart to the mysteries
Of Your holy way;
Reveal Your Torah, I pray.

I pray too that this study
Will bring You joy;
It is the incense I offer
In Your holy Temple;

Bathe my soul, Your soul,
In the light of the source.

My God, please remember
The kindness and honesty
Of those who have come before me;
Remember Your promise
To care for the children of the righteous
Unto the thousandth generation;
Enlighten me, if not for my own worth,
Then for theirs, and for the future
Growth of Your people.

Let Your radiance be recognized today,
In me, and through me, that I may use
The insights and energy of these,
Your holy teachings,
For the good of all living beings,
And for the furtherance
Of Your plan for creation;
Let no one anywhere be hurt by this study;
Guard my soul to stay on the straight path
Back to You.

With King David,
The joyful singer of Yisra'el,
I pray, "Open my eyes and let me see
The wonders of Your Torah."
May the words of my mouth
And the meditation of my heart
Find favor before You, my God,
My rock and my redeemer.[29]

XI. PRAY WITH THE whole of your being in a voice that awakens kavanah, harmonizing and bringing your thoughts and emotions into accord with your words. Turn away from distractions and read your prayers from a siddur. From the beginning of the prayer until its conclusion, look neither this way nor that. Even in the reader's repetition of the Amidah, look carefully into the siddur to answer Amen at the end of each blessing. Do this with the whole of your being. At the time of the Torah read-

ing, pay attention to every word of the reader as if you were listening to the reading of the Megillah. Keep silence in the synagogue, both before and after the prayer, even until you turn to go home.[30]

During the reading of the Megillah, the book of Esther, every word is said to be so important that if you miss one, you would have to hear the reading all over again. This is how we should listen to reading of the Torah, says Reb Elimelekh.

He also tells us that idle conversation in the synagogue is liable to ruin all of the Hasid's preparation. In the *Hanhagot Adam*, which we have also translated here, Reb Elimelekh writes, "Be very careful to refrain from conversation in the holy synagogue; even if you begin to speak of things of virtue, you will find that your consciousness will eventually be drawn into vain and useless conversation."

Is there any more pervasive problem in synagogues today?

XII. AT ALL TIMES, but especially when reading this Tzettel Kattan, visualize someone standing close to you, urging you vigorously to abide by everything said therein. Do not neglect even the most minor detail of it. If you habituate yourself to these disciplines, you will find in the course of time that a great arousal, "flaming tongues of fire, a great blaze of Yah" (Sg. 8:6) will arise from the source of your soul.[31]

Hasidishe tradition says that the person whom the Hasid must visualize is the Hasid's own Rebbe (thus Reb Elimelekh himself for the Hasid who first read this). In other words, the Rebbe must be internalized in the Hasid's mind and heart. When the Rebbe becomes an integral part of the Hasid's psyche, "a great arousal, 'flaming tongues of fire, a great blaze of *Yah*' will arise from the source of your soul." *Yah* corresponds to the celestial wisdom (*hokhmah*) and understanding (*binah*), the highest rational factors in the hidden soul elements.

XIII. ALL THE THOUGHTS of negativity and distraction (running counter to the Torah) manifested by the yetzer ha-ra (the negative impulse) during the time of study and prayer, when you lie in your bed, or walk in the middle of the day, must be related to your spiritual guide who shows you God's way, or to a loyal friend. Do not hide even the slightest thought from them in pride or shame.[32] *By confessing these thoughts, you will bring them out of potential and into actuality, breaking the power of the yetzer ha-ra and weakening its future influence upon you. This benefit is great in itself, but added to this will be the benefit that you derive from the good advice and counsel of your guide and friend. This is powerful advice.³³*

It is really a good idea to have a trusted friend with whom you can share your spiritual work. Spirituality done in loneliness, without interpersonal reality checks, tends to breed harmful fantasies and wild exaggerations of attainment. As my Rebbe, Reb Yosef Yitzhak of Lubavitch used to say, "It is good for two friends to study together, for that makes two *yetzer ha-tov's* against one *yetzer ha-ra.*" That is to say, because two friends want the best for each other and are not likely to have the same emotional difficulty at the same time, they may combine their separate desires for good to overwhelm the one's desire for what is not so good.

Moreover, Reb Elimelekh advises the unburdening of one's negative thoughts in order to rob them of their neurotic compulsiveness. A grand-Hasid of Reb Elimelekh, Reb Shalom of Belz (1783–1855) urged his Hasidim to do the same . . .

> "Once," a Hasid reported, "I went to Rabbi Shalom of Belz and told him my trouble; that while I prayed, alien thoughts came and confused me, not thoughts about the business of the day, but evil and frightening visions; and I begged him to heal my soul. When I had finished, he said to me, 'Feel no shame before me, my son. Tell me everything in full that is disturbing and perplexing you.' I started right in and told him about every terror, and every lust that had attacked me. While I was speaking, he kept his eyes closed, but I looked at him and I saw his holy thoughts were laboring to draw those alien thoughts up from the depths of my soul. When I had ended, he said, 'God will help you to keep them away from now on.' And ever since they have never come into my mind."³⁴

XIV. Go over this Tzettel Kattan carefully, and in your own words several times a day. Before you engage in sexual intercourse, study the 16th chapter of the Reshit Ḥokhmah as well as the prescriptions of the Ari, Rabbi Yitzhak Luria. If you have more time, also study the 17th chapter of the Reshit Ḥokhmah. This must be a fixed practice for you, not to be broken.

These writings concern themselves with the sanctification required of a husband and a wife at the time of sexual intercourse. Rabbi Eliyahu de Vidas (1518–1592), the author of the Reshit Hokhmah, quotes the Zohar:

The blessed and Holy One dwells only where there is union, meaning, with the person who has become unified.[35] Then the blessed and Holy One rests on that person, and nowhere else. When is a human being called "one"? At the time when they are both male and female. Then when one sanctifies oneself with celestial holiness by intending to be made holy, they become one. Behold, when one is in a union of male and female, intending to sanctify this union, then one is complete and without damage; therefore, one must bring joy to one's spouse at that time, inviting them to be of one desire, intending the same end. Their intention then unites their souls, and the body, we have learned, is not complete until one marries. Before one marries, one is called "half a body." When husband and wife unite, the body becomes a whole. Thus we find that they are one soul and one body—one person. The blessed and Holy One rests upon them in oneness and invests the spirit of holiness into this oneness. This is the meaning of "Children you are unto Y-H-V-H, your God" (Deut. 14:1). Therefore, "Holy you shall be, for holy am I, Y-H-V-H, your God" (Lev. 19:2). Blessed is Yisra'el for they conceive of God as "holy am I," and by uniting with God, and not with another, all of holiness is effected.[36]

The Reshit Hokhmah also says the following:

One should regard the yetzer ha-ra (the negative impulse) that becomes aroused in sexual intercourse as a holy fire from the side of gevurah (rigor). The marital union is like the Amidah prayer, during which there must be nothing between the worshiper and the wall; thus, during the union of husband and wife there must be nothing to separate the flesh of the two.[37]

In chapter 17, de Vidas wars against the sin of onanism and discusses the difficulties of repenting for sexually motivated sins. Thus Reb Elimelekh is attempting to guide the young Hasid through this stage of life; he desires to prepare his Hasid for a higher kind of union that only consciousness and intention save from an animal-like consummation. Elsewhere, Reb Elimelekh advises the Hasid to visualize the letters A-D-N-Y at the moment of climax. This is to ensure that the union will be accompanied and coincide with the union of souls, and through them "the conscious uniting of the transcendent Holy One with the manifest Presence."

XV. *BEFORE WASHING YOUR hands to eat, recite the penitential prayer. After you have eaten the first piece of bread over which you have made your blessing, say, "For the sake of the conscious uniting of the transcendent Holy One with the manifest Presence, I eat this food so that my body may be a healthy instrument of service for the blessed name. Please God, let no polluting thought or negative attachment disturb my awareness of your Oneness as I raise the holy sparks contained in this food and drink."*

Make it your intention that the taste in your mouth be rooted in and spring from the innermost holiness of the holy sparks that dwell in this food and drink, that through eating, chewing, and digesting it, this interior holiness will be awakened in the food. Then your soul will rejoice in the innermost holiness of the food. Likewise, affirm the intention to feel gratitude for that which you have taken in and what it has been given you when you feel the urge to move your bowels.

At the time of eating, you should also imagine the letters of ma'akhal *[mem, alef, kaf, lamed, the Hebrew for "food"] written in the square Hebrew script. Keep in mind that its numerical value is 91, which is equal to Y-H-V-H (26) combined with A-D-N-Y (65).*

We might also say:

"For the sake of the conscious uniting of the transcendent Holy One with the manifest Presence, I eat this in the joyous mingling of spirit and matter, that my body may be a healthy and whole instrument of service for the blessed name. Please God, let no pollution, negative imagining, or attachment on my part disturb your Oneness! Please help me to raise the holy sparks contained in this food and drink."

Reb Elimelekh takes for granted that the Hasid will be well acquainted with the doctrine of the divine sparks (*nitzotzot*) in need of liberation (*tikkun*) through our intentions (*kavanot*). He also advises the visualization of another name, *ma'akhal,* whose numerical value corresponds to the combined numerical value of the written and the pronounced Tetragrammaton, which signifies the union of God (*Y-H-V-H*) and the *Shekhinah* (*A-D-N-Y*).

XVI. *THE HUMAN BEING was created and brought into this world in order to transmute its nature. Therefore, be diligent to correct your attitudes and emotions by these prescriptions, especially in the 18th year of your life.*

For instance, let us say that you are born with an obstinate nature. You must break through this obstinacy within yourself and for 40 consecutive days do the opposite of those things that you are naturally inclined to do.

If you are lazy by nature, you must do everything with diligence and expediency for 40 consecutive days. Whether it is going to sleep at night or waking in the morning, do it with diligence—get dressed, wash your hands, cleanse your body, pursue your studies, and go in haste to the synagogue.

If you are shy and filled with an unearned shame, you must pray in a loud voice for 40 consecutive days, moving your body with fervor, fulfilling the verse, "All my bones shall say, Yah, Who is like You?" (Ps. 35:10). With Heaven's help, this misplaced sense of shame will be removed from you.

If you are unable to speak clearly because of habit or a defect in your organs of speech, listen carefully to every word that you say for 40 consecutive days. Whether you are speaking of worldly things or engaged in holy discourse, pay close attention to everything that you say. The habitual tendency becomes the rule in one's life.

If you are not steadfast in your studies, you must study more rigorously for 40 consecutive days. Before you study, go over this Tzettel Kattan *and Heaven will help you to continue your study and to break through your habitual tendencies until they are transformed.*

Here we find Reb Elimelekh instructing the young Hasid (as he says, "especially in the 18th year of your life") on the most difficult internal issue that any of us face. Nowhere is it better described than by the Jew named Shaul, who later became known as Paul—"For the good that I would, I do not; but the evil which I would not, that I do" (Rom. 7:19).[38] What can we do about that? How is it ever going to change? Reb Elimelekh says, "Act the part of the person you would be for 40 days and this will make a shift in who you are and what you will do afterward." This is similar to what the psychologist George Kelly called "fixed-role therapy."[39]

The fact that Reb Elimelekh is addressing so young a Hasid is not so unusual when we consider the circumstances of the time. Chances are, by the age of 18, many of his Hasidim had already been married for several years and were probably *yoshevim* (sitters) at the Rebbe's court. It is only after the Hasid had rebuilt and reintegrated the personality, having learned to control both actions and intentions, that the young man would venture back into the world.

XVII. WHENEVER YOU ARE not praying or studying Torah, spend your time learning the necessary prayers, such as the Tikkun Raḥel *and the* Tikkun Leah *(said during* Tikkun Ḥatzot), *the penitential prayer, the prayer for the New Moon, and the prayer before the Torah is taken out, and all the occasional prayers that one should know by heart. In your spare time, do not forget to meditate on "And I will be made holy" (Lev. 22:32), as was mentioned in the first counsel.*[40]

ALL THIS *I found in his handwriting.*[41]

———

The last *hanhagah* of the *Tzettel Kattan* is concerned with filling the mind with the words of Torah and prayer. This discipline is highly recommended. It is as if the very words have the power to fill one's soul, to wash it out and manifest themselves in thought and inclination.

This last line, *"All this I found in his handwriting,"* suggests that Reb Elimelekh's son, Eliezer of Lizhensk, who published the *No'am Elimelekh* in Lvov in 1788, two years after his father's death, found or was given a copy of this document and decided to include it in the book.

HANHAGOT ADAM

Usually printed with the *Tzettel Kattan* is another set of *hanhagot* by Reb Elimelekh called *Hanhagot Adam* (practices of the human being), perhaps for a Hasid who was a little older. These *hanhagot* seem to be slightly more focused on "what" than on "how." It is possible that Reb Elimelekh wished to sober this Hasid a bit from "spiritual infatuation." Reb Elimelekh may have wished to test his Hasid's earnestness, to see if he was not flirting with spirituality in order to escape other responsibilities. Perhaps this is why he begins his counsels with ordinary advice, to study the revealed (not the hidden) Torah.

———

THESE ARE THE *things that human beings shall do and live by them!*

I. FIRST, YOU MUST *study the Talmud with the explanations of Rashi, Tosafot, and the other commentators. This study, and a study of the codes of law, you must pursue according to your own abilities. Of the codes, study the Shulḥan Arukh and* Oraḥ Ḥayyim *first. You should also pray to the blessed name that you should be able to reach the truth, for the sins and pollution of youth blind one's eyes. And although the blind might be able to engage in* pilpul *(clever disputational hair splitting) and tell others what laws they must obey, the blind often forget these laws and do not keep them sincerely. For this reason, you must feel profound remorse over your polluted actions and meditate by yourself before daybreak. The time before daybreak is a time of great compassion and grace. This time is also especially well suited to becoming conscious of the embrace of the Shekhinah. This you must do with the joy and tears born of a painful separation from the Beloved.*

Reb Elimelekh wishes to transform the Hasid's study life, to turn it into a devotional practice intended to help the Hasid know the truth. For he says, while the Torah contains the truth, "the sins and pollution of youth blind one's eyes" to it. This situation has to be mended; the eyes have to be opened again and the cataract of sin removed from them before the Hasid can see clearly. Having set this higher standard, Reb Elimelekh shakes the complacency from the Hasid. If the Hasid is to be readied to do something, they first have to come face-to-face with their current limitations. Only then does Reb Elimelekh begin to show them how to cleanse the "doors of perception."

We also see here that the issues the Hasidim had with the *mitnagdim* in the past are the same as those we have today. Thus Reb Elimelekh says, "And although the blind might be able to engage in *pilpul* (clever disputational hair splitting) and tell others what laws they must obey, the blind often forget these laws and do not keep them sincerely." "Sincerely" means "with the heart," living the tradition from the inside out, and not the other way around. For when it is all external, it is all too easy to tell others what they must do. But when it is reoriented to come from within, our eyes are opened, and it is revealed *to us* what *we* must do!

FROM TIME TO time, seek a bit of solitude to meditate during the day and you will soon realize how often sin draws you down unfruitful paths and blinds you, even in this very moment. Therefore, recognize and uncover all of your own tendencies toward sin and polluted action. Do not be daunted if they be as big as mountains or hills. This you must do not once, not twice, nor even a hundred times, but continually until mercy is granted to you from Heaven. Pray to the holy name that you should be led in the way of truth, that this way be shown to you so that you do not spend the rest of your life in vain. It is after such prayer that God in great mercy and grace will illumine your eyes with the light of the holy Torah, allowing you to understand and gain wisdom concerning the innermost meaning of the teachings and practices that uphold them.

Again, it is only in silence and periods of contemplation that we can begin to discern what is helpful from what is unhelpful in our behavior; to begin to see really clearly where our life is going instead of being carried on the crest of it; to discern our own authentic voice from the unhelpful, introjected voices that actually come from without.

After such a period of meditation, he says, we will be able to see the meaning of Torah in our lives. In the *Tzava'at HaRiBaSh*, there is a teaching attributed to the Ba'al Shem Tov, which likewise says the following:

> There will be times when something will come your way, and you will be uncertain whether or not to pursue it. If you have studied Torah that day, however, you will be able to determine your course of action from your learning. For this to occur, you must sustain your connection to God. Then, God will enable you to understand the connection between your studies and your life.[42]

II. BE VERY CAREFUL and guard yourself against flattery, lies, mocking, gossip, enmity, hatred, competitiveness, anger, and pride. Be wary of gazing at the opposite sex in lust and following this with dangerous flirtation.

Today we might say: Be wary of following the delight of the eyes onto paths that do not follow from and support your deepest and most holy desire, but spring instead from the appeal of external surfaces and feeding the wounded places within us.

III. ALWAYS LIVE WITH an awareness of your own mortality. When you study Talmud or any holy book, do not permit yourself to be interrupted in your studies. Pray to the blessed name that you may be able to study the Torah for her own sake.

IV. SPEND TIME IN books of musar (ethical instruction) every day, looking on them with awe and respect (b'aimah uv'yir'ah), especially the Reshit Ḥokhmah, the Shelah (Shenei Luḥot ha-B'rit), and the Ḥovot ha-Levavot.

After having the Hasid engage in a battle with the senses, Reb Elimelekh now wants the Hasid to sharpen his sensitivity by reading *musar* or ethical literature, as if to build into the Hasid a normative standard against which he can measure his behavior.

V. FROM TIME TO time, study some of the writings of the Ari, Rabbi Yitzhak Luria, with awe and respect before God. In the past, souls were guarded more carefully and people prepared their bodies and souls diligently to study this wisdom, but today, distractions abound and our bodies are disturbed, having acquired accretions of subtly obstructing filth and pollution that we must scour and wash off of our bodies and souls. Only then may we understand whether we have reached a point where our yetzer ha-ra (negative inclination) will not be able to tempt us with vanities as before. Once one has reached this level, one may study more and more of these writings.

When you have clarified your thoughts in holiness, truth, and perfection, then the blessed name opens the gates of wisdom to you. Then you will truly be able to understand the writings of the Ari, for understanding them is not given to one who is clothed in animal desires and preoccupied with the follies of time. In that state, the study of his writings can cause confusion and be co-opted by negative tendencies within you—may God prevent this from happening.

Reb Elimelekh is saying that the rewards of sublime insight, such as those that are found in the writings of the Ari, are to be doled out sparingly. The wisdom of the Kabbalah should not be read as objective concepts or academically, for this, he says, can do great harm. Thus the Hasid must work hard to attain an openhearted, deeply personal, and involved manner of study. Nevertheless, Reb Elimelekh shows wisdom in permitting the Hasid a taste of these things as a small-task reward in the midst of his exoteric study. Bis zu der Kretshme darf men oich a trink Bronfen (Even before one reaches the inn, one needs a bit of gin).

VI. CLEANSE BOTH YOUR body and soul, and study the Talmud and its commentaries, especially the aggadot in the Talmud, which are so very effective in cleansing the soul.

The aggadot, the non-legal passages of the tzaddikim in the Talmud, are especially powerful teachings; they belong, as my Rebbe, Yosef Yitzhak of

Lubavitch, put it, to the realm of *Sefer ha-Yashar*.[43] The reading of the inner life and thoughts of the *tzaddikim* straightens out the "twists" the world has made in a person's mind.

VII. GUARD YOURSELF WELL against sin of all kinds and the pollution of negative thoughts.

VIII. GUARD YOURSELF AGAINST hating anyone; only those who are undeniably wicked, in whom one cannot find a shed of merit are we permitted to hate. Anyone whom you can possibly judge on the side of merit, even if only slightly, you are duty bound to love as your own soul and possessions, your own body and your own self. This is in accordance with the mitzvah, "You should love your neighbor as your self" (Lev. 19:18).[44]

Reb Elimelekh sees that "hatred of the wicked" would only provide the novice with a projection mechanism. The Hasid's projection would exteriorize the conflicts one was feeling inside and thus only serve as an escape from the real battle raging within.

It is interesting, he says, that only those who are "undeniably wicked, in whom one cannot find a shred of merit are we permitted to hate." Which is to say, *no one*. You see, if he had begun by saying, "You are not permitted to hate anyone," without getting the person to stop and think through it first, it would probably be put aside as too difficult. This is an example of Reb Elimelekh's great skillfulness.

IX. BE ESPECIALLY CAREFUL not to speak before prayer. Conversation before prayer tends to nullify the intentions and intensity of the prayer.[45]

Re-read the *Tzettel Kattan, hanhagot* VIII and XI and the discussion that follows them, as well as *hanhagah* XXI of this list. Talking before the service moves the center of gravity to the periphery. The battle cry for the novice must always be: "inward!"

X. BE VERY CAREFUL to wash and cleanse yourself before prayer and your mealtimes. Whenever you feel that you must relieve yourself, you must not keep yourself from doing so.

Like Moshe Leib of Sassov, another great writer of *hanhagot,* he holds with even more vehemence that physical constipation is connected to spiritual constipation. The bodily urge to relieve oneself must be obeyed even, or especially, during prayer and study. One must relieve oneself and then return to study, presumably with concentration fully restored and any blockages removed. This may also be driven by the notion that thought and study are traditionally considered angelic forms that should not be sullied by mixture with thoughts of excretion. These thoughts and uncleanness, as we see in the next *hanhagah,* must give way to the *kelippot.* If they gain hold, they may clip the wings of prayer so that it cannot ascend.

XI. ALWAYS TAKE CARE to make certain that your undergarments are quite clean.

XII. DO NOT CAUSE fear or anxiety to your household, nor should you allow anger and sullenness to remain therein; harbor no anger toward any person. As soon as you are tempted to become angry, remember your own dissipated youth, saying in your heart, "As I have sown, so do I reap."46 Therefore, at all times and in all things, be aware of your own shortcomings, and through God's grace, you will subdue them, breaking the power of the yetzer ha-ra *over you.*

In *Ḥayyim V'Ḥesed,* Hayyim Heikel of Amdur quotes a *hanhagah* of the Maggid of Mezritch that adds dimension to this counsel of Reb Elimelekh:

> It is written in the Gemara (Megillah 28b), "I did not become angry in my house." At times you may have to act as if you were angry, instilling fear in others; but do not do so "in your house"—do not become angry in your body and soul. Anger emanates from arrogance, and even the slightest arrogant thought is destructive. . . . All your thoughts reverberate throughout the cosmos, and your arrogance can blemish the worlds above and displace the *Shekhinah.* As it is written, "Every haughty person is an abomination to the Lord" (Prov. 16:5).47

XIII. PRAY TO THE ONE whose name is blessed for help in achieving wholeness through teshuvah in this lifetime. Include yourself in the company of the penitents that their repentance may be of help to you in achieving a complete turning, and you should intend in your prayer to forgive and achieve forgiveness for the many contaminating sins you and others have committed.

XIV. SPEAK CALMLY, WITH deliberateness and circumspection, when talking to other human beings. If you find them praising you, go into your inner alcove of pain and ask yourself, "Why are they praising me? If only they knew of my base desires, my foolishness, and evil deeds! Oh my blessed creator, how can I even lift my head before you, you who know and see all of my secret thoughts and deeds in every moment? Nevertheless, you are 'gentle and compassionate, patient and caring with me, always' (Ps. 145:8)."

XV. VISUALIZE SOMEONE STANDING and facing you always, never ceasing to watch your every deed. If only you could feel this presence continually, surely you would act as duty requires and refrain from certain actions you formerly did in secret. How much more so if the blessed name stood over you, seeing all your deeds in every moment? For it is impossible to hide yourself from God, as it is said, "Can a human being hide from Me so that I will not see?" (Jer. 23:24).

XVI. IF ANYONE SHAMES you, you should rejoice that God has brought this opportunity before you to make an atonement for your own harmful deeds. Look upon every person you encounter with humility.[48]

Once, Reb Shneur Zalman of Liadi was forced to listen as a *mitnaged* railed against Reb Elimelekh, calling his book *No'am Elimelekh* "an arrogant work." Then the *mitnaged* placed the book under his foot to show his disdain for it and asked Reb Shneur Zalman, "What do you think of that?" Reb Shneur Zalman paused for a second and then replied, "Reb Elimelekh was such a humble soul that if you were to put him under your foot, he wouldn't say anything either."[49]

XVII. THAT WHICH YOU do not actually need for the health of your body, or for the service of God, be it in food or drink, or any bodily enjoyment, remove it far from you.

XVIII. BE ESPECIALLY CAREFUL of intoxicating drink; it is a great sickness and brings us to a very low state, as the teacher taught, "Do not pour and you will not sin."

Exodus 34:17 speaks of "gods of pouring (meaning, cast idols) you shall not make," which is interpreted here in relation to drunkenness. This warning against liquor, which is sacrilized in Judaism, may be due to the specific needs of the Hasid for whom these particular *hanhagot* were written, or perhaps, like Reb Mikeleh of Zlotchov, Reb Elimelekh was very careful when it came to alcohol.

XIX. BE EXTREMELY CAREFUL not to mention God's name in vain.

XX. BE EXTREMELY CAREFUL to refrain from speaking or thinking of any sacred thing in a defiled context. Remember, the domain of the yetzer ha-ra is not limited to those places we ordinarily think of as defiled.

This *hanhagah* would like us to avoid thinking of sacred things in the bathroom, for instance, but it also encourages us to think of "defiled" a little differently as well. Therefore, we might say, "Be extremely careful to refrain from speaking or thinking of any sacred thing in a defiled context, in a way that taints its sacredness, drawing it into lewd or ridiculous talk."

XXI. BE VERY CAREFUL to refrain from conversation in the holy synagogue; even if you begin to speak of things of virtue, you will find that your consciousness will eventually be drawn into vain and useless conversation.[50]

Reflecting on the tone of these two sets of *hanhagot*, one may be struck by their strictness and sobriety. But it is precisely for such a sober prescription that the Hasid comes to the Rebbe in the first place. Hasidim believe that the roots of their souls have been deposited with the Rebbe, and the Rebbe can gain access to the Hasid's previous lives, their specific purposes in life, their spiritual makeup and the locus of their soul on the Tree of Life, and even the physical factors of their life, and write a prescription for them that will fit the particular needs of their specific soul.

In recent years, there have appeared two wonderful collections of Hasidic *hanhagot*. The first is Yitzhak Buxbaum's magnificent tome, *Jewish Spiritual Practices*, which covers a broad spectrum of practices, drawn primarily from Hasidic sources and corresponding to one's daily activities. The second is Or Rose and Ebn Leader's collection of early Hasidic *hanhagot*, *God in All Moments*, in which they translate a variety of practices and intentions that the early masters considered most important. But for those who would like to get into the practice of using a modern set of *hanhagot*, I highly recommend Arthur Green's beautiful list of intentions and practices for neo-Hasidim in his book *Ehyeh: A Kabbalah for Tomorrow*.[51] There you will notice that Reb Arthur writes, "These are the things a person should do to live by them," giving an appropriate nod to the Rebbe Reb Melekh.

THE KING'S LEGACY

Stories of Reb Elimelekh's passing are scarce. Perhaps this is at it should be, for he lived each day as if it were his last and with utter humility. Once he said, "I am old—I am nearly 60 years of age, and I have not managed to carry out even one mitzvah with proper devotion."[52] This was just around the time of his move to Lizhensk. But even then his service to God was so great that Satan himself came to threaten him, saying, "If you do not cease harassing me, I shall see to it that everybody becomes a 'Hasid,' and then what would you do?" Reb Elimelekh dismissed this threat, but soon his court began overflowing with would-be Hasidim. He became concerned and began to weedout the half-hearted, the seekers of new experiences, and the merely curious followers of the new Hasidic fashion. But he could not stop them from coming.[53] All he could do was continue to try "to speak a little truth," to deepen his own humility and provide a model for all of the Hasidim to follow.[54] He began to erase all trace of the "Rebbe of Lizhensk," even while he was yet living. No coin that was given to him was left in the house overnight, and as he had no desire to start a dynasty, nothing was left to his children, and even Lizhensk almost disappeared entirely from the map after his passing![55]

Nevertheless, his impact could not be erased. Indeed, his legacy only grew in proportion to his great humility. In the years that followed his death, it became clear to his disciples just how far his reach had grown, so that he continued to serve God seemingly from the other side of the grave . . .

ONCE, REB MENDEL *of Rymonov was called to the bedside of a man who was having a difficult death. For three days his body had been shutting down, and yet he would not die, and he was having a very hard time of it. Thus someone had called Reb Mendel to come and help him. Reb Mendel looked at him and asked the man, "Did you ever happen to visit Reb Elimelekh of Lizhensk for a blessing?"*

The man nodded that he had visited the Rebbe Reb Melekh.

Now Reb Mendel understood what the problem was. Reb Elimelekh was known to have said, "No one who has come to me in my lifetime will die without doing teshuvah!"

So Reb Mendel said to the man, "My friend, if you will complete your teshuvah, you will certainly be able to let go of this life and enter into the next."

Nevertheless, his greatest legacy was his disciples. It is said that before Reb Elimelekh died, he bestowed four gifts on his four great disciples: to the Hozeh (Seer) of Lublin he granted his "sight"; to Reb Mendel of Rymanov he gave his "mind"; his golden "speech" he bestowed on Reb Avraham Yehoshua Heschel of Apt; and his "heart" he gave to Reb Yisra'el, the Maggid of Kozhnitz. These Rebbes would develop and spread a distinctive form of Hasidism that was based on the teachings of Reb Elimelekh. Indeed, most of the Hasidim in Brooklyn and Meah Shearim today belong to lineages of Polish and Hungarian Hasidism—Ger, Belz, Satmar, Bobov—founded by disciples of Reb Elimelekh. And if you happen to see one of them reading a favorite book, it is likely to be the *No'am Elimelekh*, which is even more popular than the *Kedushat Levi* of Reb Levi Yitzhak of Berditchev.

It is said that when Reb Elimelekh was given the manuscript that his Hasidim had assembled from their own transcripts of his teachings (the *No'am Elimelekh*), he exclaimed, "What is this? Did I really say all of this?" For, like his master the Maggid, he often spoke the words of the holy *Shekhinah* while in a state of profound *deveikut* or absorption.

Now the Torah is divided into 54 *parshiyot* (sections) for the 52 weeks of the year. Every *Shabbat*, the reader recites one *parsha* (section), and occasionally two. But the holy Rebbe Reb Melekh's *No'am Elimelekh* has teachings on all of the *parshiyot* of the Torah except one. We are told that during all the years of his leadership there was only one week in the year when he did not teach— "the week in which we read the last but one section of the second book of Moshe. And it was in this very week—on the 21st day of Adar (1786)—that the holy Rebbe Reb Melekh passed away."[56]

Epilogue: The Three Pillars

IN THIS WORK, WE HAVE ATTEMPTED TO REPRESENT the evolutionary flow of the Hasidic spirit through the stories and teachings of three early Hasidic masters and their disciples—the Ba'al Shem Tov, the well-spring of Hasidism; the Maggid of Mezritch, the teacher and organizer of Hasidism; and the Rebbe Reb Melekh, the disseminator of Hasidism. From these three Rebbes may be traced all the distinct lineages of Hasidism extant today.

From the circle of the Ba'al Shem Tov, we were introduced to Mikeleh of Zlotchov; Pinhas of Koretz; Ya'akov Yosef of Polonoyye; the Maggid of Mezritch; and the Ba'al Shem's beloved daughter, Adel. And while the majority of later Hasidic lineages derive from the Maggid, an influential minority derive from the circle of these close disciples and the family of the Ba'al Shem Tov himself. The sons of Adel, Moshe Hayyim Efraim of Sudilkov and Barukh of Mezhbizh, were raised in the house of the Ba'al Shem and became Rebbes under the tutelage of Pinhas of Koretz. And from Adel's daughter, Feiga, came one of the most original and luminous of all Hasidic Rebbes, Nahman of Bratzlav, who remains the Rebbe of Bratzlav in *absentia* to this day. Standing next to his empty chair, the descendants of Nosson of Nemirov and his other great Hasidim attest to the holiness imparted by Reb Nahman's great teaching, which I was honored to learn from the lips of my friend and mentor, Gedaliah Kenig of S'fat, of blessed memory.

From the circle of the Maggid of Mezritch, we were introduced to Zushya of Anipol; Elimelekh of Lizhensk; Ahron of Karlin; Shmelke of Nikolsburg; and the Maggid's son, Avraham the Malakh. And while the Rebbe Reb Melekh would become the most influential of the Maggid's disciples in Poland, others looked to the leadership of the Maggid's great disciple Menachem Mendel of Vitebsk in Lithuania and Russia. And when he left for Eretz Yisra'el, his place was taken by Shneur Zalman of Liadi, the founder of the great ḤaBaD lineage of Hasidism, to which I was introduced by my *mash-piyyim* in Antwerp, Moshe Chekhoval and Barukh Merzel, of blessed memory; by my *mashpiyyim* in Crown Heights, Yisra'el Jacobson, Eliya Simpson, Shmuel Levitin, Avraham Paris, and Hayyim Mordecai Hodakov, of blessed memory; and especially by my Rebbes, Yosef Yitzhak Schneersohn of Lubavitch and Menachem Mendel Schneerson of Lubavitch, may the memory of the righteous continue to illuminate us.

From the circle of the Rebbe Reb Melekh, we were briefly introduced to his four great disciples: Ya'akov Yitzhak of Lublin, Menachem Mendel of Rymonov, Yisra'el of Kozhnitz, and Avraham Yehoshua Heschel of Apt. Of the four, Reb Elimelekh's brother, Reb Zushya, tells us (interpreting the verse from Gen. 2:10), "'A river issues from Eden to water the garden, and then divides into four branches.' The Ba'al Shem Tov is 'Eden', the river is the Maggid of Mezritch, the 'garden' is Reb Elimelekh, and the 'four branches' are his four great disciples." And as we have said before, from these disciples come most of the great Polish and Hungarian lineages of Hasidism we see today, including the great Pyshysska lineages of Ger and Ishbitz, Menachem Mendel of Kotzk, the unique Rebbe of Piasetzno, as well as the Belzer lineage of my fathers and grandfathers, of blessed memory, and the Bobov line of my own avuncular Rebbe, Shlomo Halberstam of Bobov, may the memory of the righteous continue to illuminate us.

In their honor, and for the sake of the blessed *Shekhinah*, we humbly lay this book before you, which was conceived, collected, and polished in loving dialogue between a Rebbe and his Hasid, and completed on the 10th of Shevat, the yahrzeit of Rabbi Yosef Yitzhak Schneersohn, the sixth Lubavitcher Rebbe.

Zalman Meshullam Schachter-Shalomi
Netanel David Miles-Yepez

Boulder, Colorado

Appendix: The Tree of Life

THROUGHOUT THIS BOOK ARE VARIOUS REFERENCES TO *SEFIROT*, *middot*, *sikhliyot*, and *maskilim*, all of which relate to the spiritual structure called the Tree of Life, or *etz ḥayyim*. According to the Kabbalah, everything in creation reflects some combination of the 10 divine attributes or dimensions of reality that make up the Tree of Life. These 10 *sefirot* in descending order are: *keter* (crown), which is utterly transcendent; *ḥokhmah* (wisdom), the seed containing the whole; *binah* (understanding), the detailed taxonomy of all the qualities inherent in the seed; *ḥesed* (lovingkindness), open expression; *gevurah* (strength), boundaries; *tiferet* (beauty), balancing openness and boundaries; *netzaḥ* (victory), raw efficacy; *hod* (glory), aesthetic presentation; *yesod* (foundation), balancing efficacy and aesthetics; and *malkhut* (sovereignty), wholeness embodied.

The Tree of Life structure (shown on p. 338) reveals the significant relationship dynamics among the *sefirot*. The most basic of these dynamics are those defined by the Three Pillars of the Tree: the right-hand pillar, composed of *ḥokhmah*, *ḥesed*, and *netzaḥ*, is the pillar of masculine attributes; the left-hand pillar, composed of *binah*, *gevurah*, and *hod*, is the pillar of the feminine attributes; and between them is the central pillar, composed of *keter*, *tiferet*, *yesod*, and *malkhut*, which are neutral and provide the balance to the polarities on either side.

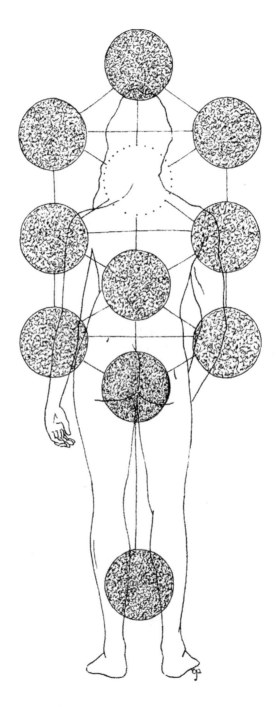

Masculine and feminine *sefirot* by Netanel Miles-Yepez.

Notes

INTRODUCTION

1. In the summer of 2005, I made a trip to the Ukraine with my youngest son, Yotam, with whom I visited the graves of numerous Rebbes. —Z.M.S-S.

2. I have pursued this theme in "Neo-Hasidism and Reconstructionism: A Not-Only Imaginary Dialogue," *Paradigm Shift: From the Jewish Renewal Teachings of Reb Zalman Schachter-Shalomi*, 127–33. —Z.M.S.-S.

3. This applies to our respective students and colleagues, Manuel Goldmann, a Christian Evangelische Pfarrer in Germany, and Thomas Atum O'Kane, a Sufi Murshid in the lineage of Hazrat Inayat Khan, who leads spiritual guidance programs around the United States and Europe.

4. I too was guilty of treating Neo-Hasidism as such. See Zalman M. Schachter, "Forward" to *Rabbi Israel Baal Shem Tov: A Monograph on the Life and Teachings of the Founder of Chassidism*, 9–11; and Zalman M. Schachter, "Hasidism and Neo-Hasidism." —Z.M.S.-S.

5. See Salomon Maimon, *Lebensgeschichte: Mit einer Einleitung und mit Anmerkungen / neu hrsg. von Jakob Fromer.*

6. The Hasidim ha-Rishonim ("the first pious ones") are referred to in the Mishnah (Berakhot 5:1) and may be related in spirit if not in lineage to the Dead Sea community at Qumran. The Hasidei Ashkenaz lived in 12th- and 13th-century Germany and were led by Yehudah the Hasid of Regensburg (d. 1217) and Eleazar of Worms (d. 1230).

7. The term "turnings" is borrowed from Vajrayana Buddhism, which speaks of "three turnings of the Wheel of Dharma." These refer to three successive evolutionary stages of Buddhist teaching through the centuries, emphasizing a greater and greater integration of life and spiritual practice.

8. Martin Buber's first book, *The Legend of the Baal-Shem*, was published in 1907.

9. There is some evidence that this was the case in the Ba'al Shem Tov's time as well. The Ba'al Shem Tov has become the symbol of Hasidism for us today, but it is well known that the Ba'al Shem Tov had many colleagues who were not disciples. It is very likely that each of them, in their own way, was participating in a Zeitgeist that desired a renewal of the spirit in their time. See Abraham J. Heschel, *The Circle of the Baal Shem Tov: Studies in Hasidism.*

10. This, of course, is a great oversimplification of a partly academic dispute having to do with determining authoritative sources for the proper interpretation of Hasidism's relationship to Jewish mysticism. Nevertheless, the basic thrust of the argument is consistent with how we have framed it here.

11. See Martin Buber, "Replies to My Critics," in *The Philosophy of Martin Buber*, ed. Paul Arthur Schlipp and Maurice Friedman, 731–41; and Maurice Friedman, *Martin Buber's Life and Work: The Later Years, 1945–1965*, 280–99.

12. See Gershom Scholem, "Martin Buber's Interpretation of Hasidism," in *The Messianic Idea in Judaism*, 228–50.

13. For a different version, see Martin Buber, *Tales of the Hasidim: The Early Masters*, 222 ("The Drayman").

14. Levi Yitzhak ben Meir of Berditchev, *Kedushat Levi*, 316.

15. Elie Wiesel's grandfather Dodye Feig; see Elie Wiesel, *Souls on Fire: Portraits and Legends of Hasidic Masters*, 7.

16. It should be noted that it was Arthur Green who once pointed out: "The controversy between Buber and Scholem as to the historical worthiness of the Hasidic tales could best be tested out around the figure of Levi Yizhak"; see his *Tormented Master: A Life of Rabbi Nahman of Bratslav*, 123–24, n. 2.

17. Still other aspects of the Rebbe's life that might round out his distinctiveness for the Hasid would be the style of the Rebbe's *davenen*, the unique flavor of the *niggunim* (melodies) he composed, or the manner of the *tish* (table) the Rebbe conducted.

18. There is no better example of this phenomenon than the Hasidic writings of Elie Wiesel; see the bibliography.

19. Sources that might be seen as non-kosher include teachings from psychology and other religions. The "enemy camp," according to traditional Hasidism, refers to the *mitnagdim* (the Orthodox opponents of Hasidism) and the *maskilim* (members of the Jewish Enlightenment movement).

20. I once heard the Bobover Rebbe, Reb Shlomo Halberstam, say, "When a person comes to see me dressed in his *Shabbat* clothes, I can't help him very much; I want to see what he looks like during the week." —Z.M.S.-S.

21. *Tanna de-Vei Eliyahu*, ch. 25.

22. See Tovia Preschel, "Farbrengen," in *The Encyclopedia of Hasidism*, ed. Tzvi M. Rabinowicz, 125.

CHAPTER 1

1. See Joseph I. Schneersohn, *Lubavitcher Rabbi's Memoirs*, for a vast body of stories on the hidden *tzaddikim* from the ḤaBaD oral tradition. The title of

the English work is misleading; *zikhronot* is more properly "remembrances" in this context—that is, stories he (the Rebbe) remembers, and not his "memoirs" in the sense of an autobiography.

2. For instance, if a Christian doesn't know about the miracles of the prophets Elijah and Elisha, Jesus' miracles seem sui generis, wholly without precedent; but when these figures are considered, Jesus is contextualized as acting in the prophetic tradition of his people.

3. See Yaffa Eliach, "Baal Shem," in *The Encyclopedia of Hasidism*, ed. Tzvi M. Rabinowicz, 34; and Gershom Scholem, *Kabbalah*, 310–11 (on the ba'alei shem.)

4. See Yitzhak Buxbaum, *The Light and Fire of the Baal Shem Tov*, 14 (on the ba'alei shem as leaders of proto-Hasidic communities), and 359 (on the ba'alei shem as eastern European folk healers).

5. Yosef Yitzhak Schneersohn, *Likkutei Dibburim*, Vol. IV: *An Anthology of Talks by Rabbi Yosef Yitzhak Schneersohn of Lubavitch*, 109.

6. Ibid., 105–6 (on spiritual practices and studies of Torah and Kabbalah), 110–11 (on the *yeshiva* of Eliyahu Ba'al Shem and its "twenty-seven handpicked scholars"), and 114–15 (on specific spiritual means employed by Eliyahu Ba'al Shem and his disciples).

7. Ibid., 108. See Yisroel Yaakov Klapholtz, *Tales of the Baal Shem Tov*, 50–90, for more information on Eliyahu Ba'al Shem collected and translated from ḤaBaD sources.

8. Even churches used to hold watch-night services in honor of the circumcision of Jesus.

9. See Scholem, *Kabbalah*, 356–61 (on the Lilith).

10. For more tales of Reb Yoel Ba'al Shem, see Klapholtz, *Tales of the Baal Shem Tov*, 90–100, 113–20.

11. See Buxbaum, *The Light and Fire of the Baal Shem Tov*, 13–14 ("The Pre-Beshtian Hasidim and the Hidden Tzaddikim"), 36–39 ("The Secret Manuscript of Rabbi Adam Baal Shem"), and 103–5 ("The Besht Is Chosen as Leader and Perceives the Limitations of the Camp of Israel").

12. Jacob Immanuel Schochet, *Rabbi Israel Baal Shem Tov: A Monograph on the Life and Teachings of the Founder of Chassidism*, 41–42.

13. The basic tale is found in *Shivḥei ha-Besht*. For variations on the tale, see Dan Ben-Amos and Jerome R. Mintz, eds. and trans., *In Praise of the Baal Shem Tov [Shivhei ha-Besht]: The Earliest Collection of Legends about the Founder of Hasidism*, 7–9 ("Rabbi Eliezer"), 9–10 ("Rabbi Eliezer, A Second Version"), 10 ("Rabbi Eliezer and the Viceroy's Daughter"), and 11 ("The Birth of the Besht").

14. This is the story as I have heard it. — Z.M.S.-S. For different versions,

see Buxbaum, *The Light and Fire of the Baal Shem Tov*, 16–18 ("The Besht's Parents Tested"); Martin Buber, *Tales of the Hasidim: The Early Masters*, 35–36 ("The Test"); and Elie Wiesel, *Souls on Fire: Portraits and Legends of Hasidic Masters*, 10–11.

15. See Ben-Amos, *In Praise of the Baal Shem Tov*, 11 ("The Birth of the Besht"); Buxbaum, *The Light and Fire of the Baal Shem Tov*, 19–20 ("His Father's Last Words"); Buber, *Tales of the Hasidim: The Early Masters*, 36 ("His Father's Words"); and Wiesel, *Souls on Fire*, 11.

16. See Buxbaum, *The Light and Fire of the Baal Shem Tov*, 292 ("The Cantor"), for a story of a Reb Mordechai of Zaslov, a hidden *tzaddik* and a disciple of the Ba'al Shem Tov who became a cantor.

17. See Buxbaum, *The Light and Fire of the Baal Shem Tov*, 22–26 for another version of the Ba'al Shem Tov's being orphaned and why he left the town of his birth. In Buxbaum's retelling, the Ba'al Shem Tov "succeeded in his studies" and later runs away because of the untenable conditions at the *ḥeder*. It is his running away that wears on the nerves of his guardians, until the boy eventually takes up with a hidden *tzaddik*, who becomes his new guardian. Another story of this period worth reading is Martin Buber, *Legend of the Baal-Shem*, 51–55 ("The Werewolf").

18. See Buxbaum, *The Light and Fire of the Baal Shem Tov*, 39–43 for another version of the story of the Ba'al Shem Tov's marriage to the sister of Reb Gershon. In Buxbaum she is called "Sarah," and in many HaBaD sources she is "Leah Rahel"; however, she is generally thought to have been called Hannah.

19. See Buxbaum, *The Light and Fire of the Baal Shem Tov*, 39–43 (on Gershon's initial contempt for the Ba'al Shem Tov), and 110–11 ("Rabbi Gershon Complains about the Besht").

20. Buxbaum, in *The Light and Fire of the Baal Shem Tov*, 88–90, uses a storyteller's prerogative and calls this book the Zohar (376, n. 75), but the original tale says only "a book." There are reasons for suspecting it may have been the Zohar, and there are other reasons for suspecting it was not. We prefer to follow the original and leave it as a mystery for the reader.

21. See Buxbaum, *The Light and Fire of the Baal Shem Tov*, 36–39 ("The Secret Manuscript of Rabbi Adam Ba'al Shem").

22. Often Naqshbandi Sufis will not share the name of their sheikh with anyone except the *fuqara* (the fellowship) of Naqshbandi Sufis.

23. See Glitzenstein, *Sefer ha-Toldot: Rabbi Yisra'el Ba'al Shem Tov*. A version of this was previously published in Zalman Schachter, *Fragments of a Future Scroll: Hassidism for the Aquarian Age*, 63–67. See Buxbaum, *The Light*

and Fire of the Baal Shem Tov, 88–90 (another English version of this story), and 376, n. 75 (on how Buxbaum adapted the story).

24. See Buxbaum, *The Light and Fire of the Baal Shem Tov*, 105–6 ("The Besht Refuses to Be Revealed").

25. For another version of this story, see Buber, *Legend of the Baal-Shem*, 202–8 ("The Shepherd").

26. This letter is found in *Kovetz ha-Tamim*, in which was published much of the material from the Herson Genizah. The Herson Genizah was a large collection of letters and manuscripts attributed to hidden *tzaddikim*, the Ba'al Shem Tov, and many of his leading disciples. It was unearthed in the city of Herson in 1918 and was said to have been a collection of papers confiscated many years before from the home of Yisra'el of Rhyzhin (1797–1851) at the time of his arrest. These papers were purchased by Shalom Dov Baer Schneersohn, the fifth Lubavitcher Rebbe, examined, and considered by him to be authentic (if badly copied from original documents and thus filled with errors). Scholars generally consider them to be forgeries. Whatever one's opinion, they are a wonderful part of the ḤaBaD Hasidic tradition. Here, I cite these papers as *Kovetz ha-Tamim*. A version of this story was previously published in Schachter, *Fragments of a Future Scroll*, 69–71. For an alternate version of the story, see Buxbaum, *The Light and Fire of the Baal Shem Tov*, 107 ("Ahiyah Tells Him of the Previous Incarnation of His Soul").

27. For a version of this story with regard to the Ba'al Shem Tov, see Buxbaum, *The Light and Fire of the Baal Shem Tov*, 18 ("Sixty Heroes"). Buxbaum wrote (based on *Sefer Ba'al Shem Tov*, 1:198, no. 8): "R. Yaakov Yosef of Polnoye explained, based on the teachings of the Ari in *Sefer HaGilgulim*, that a great soul that descends to elevate others is reluctant to do so for fear it may be led to sin; it only descends when promised that it will not sin" (ibid., 368, n. 5).

28. "Karass" is a term from Kurt Vonnegut's novel *Cat's Cradle:* "A group of people who, unbeknownst to them, are collectively doing God's will in carrying out a specific, common, task. A karass is driven forward in time and space by tension within the karass."

CHAPTER 2

1. See Richard H. Robinson and Willard L. Johnson, *The Buddhist Religion: A Historical Introduction* 30–31; and John S. Strong, *The Experience of Buddhism: Sources and Interpretations*, 32–33.

2. The story does not identify this great rabbi, but there were many such Torah luminaries among the disciples of the Ba'al Shem Tov, including Rabbis Meir Margoliot, Gershon of Kittov, Ya'akov Yosef of Polonoye, Dov Baer, the Maggid of Mezritch, and Hayyim Rappaport of Lemberg. Of course, Gershon of Kittov can be ruled out simply by the context, and the conversion stories of Ya'akov Yosef of Polonoye and the Maggid of Mezritch are too well known to be confused with this one. So for the student of Hasidism, the identity of this rabbi remains a tantalizing mystery. See Yitzhak Buxbaum, *The Light and Fire of the Baal Shem Tov*, 137–38 ("Rabbi Yaakov Yosef of Polnoye") and in chap. 6 ("Words and Reality").

3. "Be careful to observe only that which I enjoin upon you: neither add to it nor take away from it" (Deut. 13:1), *JPS Hebrew-English TANAKH: The Traditional Hebrew Text and the New JPS Translation*. All translations given in the notes are from the new JPS translation.

4. For a more detailed version of this tale, see Buxbaum, *The Light and Fire of the Baal Shem Tov*, 19–20 ("His Father's Last Words"). Conspicuous in its absence is the oft-quoted, "Fear nothing other than God."

5. Rashi's commentary on Bamidbar (Numbers) 22:35.

6. See Buxbaum, *The Light and Fire of the Baal Shem Tov*, 241–42 ("Divine Providence with a Leaf").

7. Karlfried Graf Durkheim, quoted by Joseph Campbell in *The Hero's Journey: Joseph Campbell on His Life and Work*, 40. This is also the notion behind the *mahamudra tantra* of Buddhism: Everything is a symbol of itself, which is to say, of *shunyata* (emptiness).

8. This notion is close to the title and content of G. I. Gurdjieff's great trilogy *All and Everything*. See J. G. Bennett, *Gurdjieff: Making a New World*, 203 ("God Is All and Everything—*Deus est omne quod est*").

9. Most of the statements the Ba'al Shem Tov uses in this passage are based on Maimonides, whose thought became foundational to much of the Kabbalah of the 13th and 14th centuries in Spain.

10. Berakhot 60b.

11. See Bennett, *Gurdjieff*.

12. "Know therefore this day and keep it in mind that the Lord alone is God in heaven above and on earth below; there is no other" (Deut. 4:39).

13. Midrash Rabbah, B'reishit 10

14. Hazrat Inayat Khan, *The Sufi Message*, pt. 4, chap. 13 ("Intuition and Dream").

15. C. G. Jung, *Memories, Dreams, Reflections*, 51.

16. "Come and see what the Lord has done, how He has wrought desolation on the earth" (Ps. 46:9)

17. "If a man seduces a virgin for whom the bride-price has not been paid, and lies with her, he must make her his wife by payment of a bride-price" (Exod. 22:15).

18. See Joseph Campbell, *The Masks of God: Primitive Mythology*, 229–42; and Joseph Campbell, *The Flight of the Wild Gander: Explorations in the Mythological Dimension*, 157–63.

19. " 'Remove yourself from this community, that I may annihilate them in an instant' " (Num. 17:10).

20. Talmud, Berakhot, 19b.

21. " 'His presence fills all the earth!' "(Isa. 6:3).

22. "I am ever mindful of the Lord's presence" (Ps. 16:8).

23. I am no longer certain of the source from which I translated this story almost 50 years ago, but versions are found in *Ikkarei Emunah*, 9–23; and *Kol Sippurei Ba'al Shem Tov*, 4:10, no. 4. — Z.M.S.-S. For another version of this story, see Buxbaum, *The Light and Fire of the Baal Shem Tov*, 243–48 ("A Debate with a Misnagid").

24. A description of the circumstances of this disputation between Shneur Zalman of Liadi and the *mitnagdim* is found in Nissan Mindel, *Rabbi Schneur Zalman*, Vol. I: *Biography*, 68–70.

25. "An angel of the Lord appeared to him in a blazing fire out of a bush. He gazed, and there was a bush all aflame, yet the bush was not consumed. Moses said, 'I must turn aside to look at this marvelous sight; why doesn't the bush burn up?' " (Exod. 3:2–3).

26. Jean Houston (b. 1937) is one of the most respected integral spiritual thinkers in the world. She is the author of *Lifeforce: The Psycho-Historical Recovery of the Self-Mythic Life: Learning to Live Our Greater Story* and *The Passion of Isis and Osiris: A Union of Two Souls*.

27. "When the Lord saw that he had turned aside to look, God called out to him out of the bush: 'Moses! Moses!' He answered, 'Here I am.' And He said, 'Do not come closer. Remove your sandals from your feet, for the place on which you stand is holy ground' " (Exod. 3:4–5).

28. See Rudolf Otto, *The Idea of the Holy*.

29. "Now Mount Sinai was all in smoke, for the Lord had come down upon it in fire" (Exod. 19:18).

30. "When he calls on Me, I will answer him; I will be with him in distress" (Ps. 91:15).

31. This is an example of *t'murah*, letter manipulation or re-arrangement.

32. "Are trees of the field human to withdraw before you into the besieged city?" (Deut. 20:19).

33. Talmud, Ta'anit 7a.

34. Talmud, Ta'anit 7a; Mekhilta to Exod. 19:18.

35. I heard a version of this teaching from Rabbi Miles Krassen, who said it was from *Likkutei Maharan Tinyana*. — N.M.-Y.

36. Similarly, Yisra'el of Rhyzhin said, "He who speaks does not know, and he who knows does not speak." In the *Tao Te Ching* it says, "The Tao that can be known is not the true Tao."

37. *Kuntres Bikkur Chicago*, 22. I first published a version of this teaching in Zalman M. Schachter, "Two Facets of Judaism." For other translations of this teaching, see Jacob Immanuel Schochet, *Rabbi Israel Baal Shem Tov: A Monograph on the Life and Teachings of the Founder of Chassidism*, 99–100; and Mindel, *Rabbi Schneur Zalman*, 70–72.

38. "Now Moses was a very humble man, more so than any other man on earth" (Num. 12:3).

39. This is not a criticism of Shneur Zalman of Liadi, who basically made the *tzaddik gamur* beyond his system.

40. This is a paraphrase of a quotation from Pir Vilayat Inayat Khan from *The Leader's Manual: Volume One: Leadership in the Sufi Order*.

41. See Martin Buber, *Tales of the Hasidim: The Early Masters*, 50 ("Trembling").

42. "Make an opening for daylight in the ark, and terminate it within a cubit of the top" (Gen. 6:16).

43. "This is how you shall make it: the length of the ark shall be three hundred cubits, its width fifty cubits, and its height thirty cubits. Make an opening for daylight in the ark, and terminate it within a cubit of the top. Put the entrance to the ark in its side; make it with bottom, second, and third decks" (Gen. 6:15–16).

44. "Then the Lord said to Noah, 'Go into the ark, with all your household, for you alone have I found righteous before Me in this generation" (Gen. 7:1).o

45. Translated from Yisra'el ben Eliezer in *Sefer ha-Ba'al Shem Tov*, 119 ("Parshat Noaḥ"). For another version of this teaching, see Arthur Green and Barry W. Holtz, eds. and trans., *Your Word Is Fire: The Hasidic Masters on Contemplative Prayer*, 40.

46. Actually, the text says, *Vayomer Yah" l'Noaḥ bo-atah v'khol-beytkha el-ha-tevah ki-otkha ra'iti tzaddik l'fanai bador ha'zeh*, "Then *Yah* said to Noah, 'Come into the ark, with all your household, for you alone have I found righteous before Me in this generation.' " It is also relevant to this reading that God says, *bo el-ha-tevah*, "*come* into the ark [*tevah*]" and not "*go* into the ark," for God is actually inside the ark, inside of the word.

47. For a story of how the Ba'al Shem Tov learned soul ascent from the manuscript of Adam Ba'al Shem, see Buxbaum, *The Light and Fire of the Baal Shem Tov*, 92 ("Soul-Ascent").

48. See Yakov Travis, "Adorning the Souls of the Dead: Rabbi Nahman of Bratslav and Tikkun Ha-Neshamot," 155–92.

49. Later updated and considerably revised as Zalman M. Schachter-Shalomi, *Gate to the Heart: An Evolving Process*.

50. See Zalman M. Schachter, "Segullah," *The Encyclopedia of Hasidism*, ed. Tzvi M. Rabinowicz, 437; and Zalman Meshullam Schachter-Shalomi, *Spiritual Intimacy: A Study of Counseling in Hasidism*, 243–44.

51. In Ya'akov Yosef of Polonoye's *Toldot Ya'akov Yosef*, Va-'era' A is found: "And as I have heard, in the name of my teacher, how it was told him from Heaven, why the coming of *Mashiaḥ* is delayed: because people do not take their time in the great love and the mystery of kisses, which is before the genital union. This is done in order to arouse her passion, so that she will seed first and thus give birth to a male, which represents compassion. The words of the wise have great and deep meaning. May God forgive me for bringing this to our attention."

52. "Instruct a wise man, and he will grow wiser" (Prov. 9:9). Appended to Ya'akov Yosef of Polonoye, *Ben Porat Yosef*. See Buxbaum, *The Light and Fire of the Baal Shem Tov*, 303–5 ("His Soul-Ascent to the Messiah"), where this account is given as a story.

CHAPTER 3

1. A ḤaBaD Lubavitch rabbi and emissary. A good story of him, which is pertinent to the message and type of stories presented here, can be found in Eliyahu Touger and Malka Touger, *To Know and to Care*, chap. 13 ("Beyond Nature's Limits").

2. "A. What is a large town? B. Any in which there are ten men available at all times [to form a quorum]. C. [If there are] fewer than this number, lo, this is a village." See Jacob Neusner, ed. and trans., *The Mishnah: A New Translation*, 317 (Megillah 1:3 A–C); also three "rows" of disciples attended and were to be available to the *beit din* (rabbinical court); see Sanhedrin 4:4 A–G.

3. "Others go down to the sea in ships, ply their trade in the mighty waters; / they have seen the works of the Lord and His wonders in the deep. / By His word He raised a storm wind that made the waves surge. / Mounting up to the heaven, plunging down to the depths, disgorging in their misery, / they

reeled and staggered like a drunken man, all their skill to no avail" (Ps. 107:23–27), *JPS Hebrew-English TANAKH: The Traditional Hebrew Text and the New JPS Translation*. All translations given in the notes are from the new JPS translation.

4. Because the Torah portions within the tefillin can be arranged as they appear in the Torah or according to the way in which they make sense with regard to meaning, Rashi and Rabbeinu Tam argued about which order should be followed. Now because these two great masters are of two opinions and because the mitzvah is of great importance, some people are inclined to wear two different sets of tefillin, one arranged according to Rashi's opinion and one arranged according to Rabbeinu Tam's. The Ari, Rabbi Yitzhak Luria, tells us that it is not because of doubt that we do this but because of the powerful impact that these variations may make on the soul. Thus many people (mainly Sephardim) lay two sets of tefillin simultaneously, one according to Rashi and the other according to Rabbeinu Tam, and others (mainly Hasidim) first lay the Rashi-style tefillin and then the style of Rabbeinu Tam. I myself used to *daven* with both the Rashi and the Rabbeinu Tam on one strap. These tefillin have now been given over to my son, Rabbi Sholem Dov Baer, and he has taken up the practice of wearing both Rashi and Rabbenu Tam tefillin. The Lubavitcher Rebbe actually had four pairs of tefillin, which he would wear for similar reasons of halakhic purity and spiritual effect. — Z.M.S.-S.

5. From the weekday liturgy, *Pesukei de-Zimrah* (Verses of Praise): "And David worshiped."

6. "And God saw all that He had made, and found it very good. And there was evening and there was morning, the sixth day" (Gen. 1:31).

7. *Nishmat*, from the *Shabbat* liturgy.

8. "Instead of bulls we will pay The offering of our lips" (Hosea 14:3).

9. Talmud, Ḥullin 91b; Sanhedrin 95a.

10. When I first published this story in the *Yiddishe Heim*, my Rebbe, Menachem Mendel Schneerson (1902–1994), looked it over and didn't like the ending when Reb Hayyim says, "Murderer, let go of my hand!" He wanted me to soften that ending, and I did. Today I have returned to the original telling as I heard it from Reb Berel Baumgarten, stressing how terrified Reb Hayyim was that catastrophe would befall him if he did not rid himself of the name. — Z.M.S.-S.

11. Frank Herbert, *Dune*, 12.

12. Alan Jay Lerner's play *Brigadoon* is based on this story.

13. The first version of this story was published in the Winnipeg *Jewish Post*. Later it was revised and edited for the HaBaD-Lubavitch journal *Yiddishe*

Heim and then again for *The Holy Beggars' Gazette,* a journal published by the House of Love and Prayer in San Francisco, Rabbi Sholmo Carlebach's Bay Area *shtibl.* The version included here is completely revised.

14. For a story about Alexi the coachman, see Yitzhak Buxbaum, *The Light and Fire of the Baal Shem Tov,* 266 ("Without Questions or Doubts").

15. This same story is also told in the Sufi tradition, except that it is Khidr who takes Moses (Arabic: *Musa*) on his journeys. In the Sufi tradition, Khidr, the "green man of the desert," is a figure much like Elijah, descending from another dimension to instruct the initiates in hidden wisdom.

16. "Praise the Lord, for He is good; His steadfast love is eternal! / Thus let the redeemed of the Lord say, those He redeemed from adversity" (Ps. 107:1–2). The recitation of Psalm 107 in thanksgiving at the end of the week was an innovation of the Ba'al Shem Tov; before his time this was not a custom.

17. "Do not laugh at one who moves his body, even violently, during prayer. A person drowning in a river makes all kinds of motions to try to save himself. This is not a time for others to laugh." Quoted in Arthur Green and Barry W. Holtz, eds. and trans., *Your Word Is Fire: The Hasidic Masters on Contemplative Prayer,* 96.

18. See Martin Buber, *Tales of the Hasidim: The Later Masters,* 101–2 ("Miriam's Well").

19. Some have said that my late Rebbe, Reb Menachem Mendel Schneerson, the seventh Lubavitcher Rebbe, was the Messiah-designate during his lifetime. I have often been asked about this matter, and the most I would want to say is this: After the many Messianic disappointments and failures in Jewish history, at least Reb Menachem Mendel bore the weight of those projections honorably and, in many ways, redeemed the image of the Messiah-designate in our time, whether he was that person or not. — Z.M.S.-S.

20. See "The Execution" on p. 301 herein.

21. "God, You will not despise / a contrite and crushed heart" (Ps. 51:19).

22. Yitzhak of Drohobitch seems to have been more of a friend and colleague of the Ba'al Shem Tov, but this is the way the Rebbe told the story. Nevertheless, it is said that he encouraged his son to become a disciple of the Ba'al Shem Tov. See Abraham J. Heschel, *The Circle of the Baal Shem Tov: Studies in Hasidism,* chap. 4 ("Rabbi Isaac of Drohobycz").

23. "Let not the foot of the arrogant tread on me, / or the hand of the wicked drive me away" (Ps. 36:12).

24. See Martin Buber, *Tales of the Hasidim: The Early Masters,* 85 ("The Fiery Mountain").

CHAPTER 4

1. With gratitude to Rabbi Leah Novick and Maggid Yitzhak Buxbaum who gathered many of these stories and contributed their insights on them.

2. See Yitzhak Buxbaum, *The Light and Fire of the Baal Shem Tov*, 136 ("The Birth of His Son, Tzvi").

3. "Lightning flashing at them from His right" (Deut. 33:2), *JPS Hebrew-English TANAKH: The Traditional Hebrew Text and the New JPS Translation*. All translations given in the notes are from the new JPS translation.

4. Adapted with permission from Buxbaum, *The Light and Fire of the Baal Shem Tov*, 83 ("His Infant Daughter Edel Grasps Her Father's Beard").

5. Adapted with permission from Buxbaum, *The Light and Fire of the Baal Shem Tov*, 128–29 ("The Sleeping Child").

6. Adapted with permission from Buxbaum, *The Light and Fire of the Baal Shem Tov*, 129 ("The Gates of Divine Help").

7. See Zalman Alpert, "The Rebbetzin Who Became a Rebbe: The Chentsiner Rebbetzin"; Zalman Schachter-Shalomi, *Wrapped in a Holy Flame: Teachings and Tales of the Hasidic Masters*, 297–306 (on the Maid of Ludmir); and Tirzah Firestone, *The Receiving: Reclaiming Jewish Women's Wisdom*, 9–41 (on the Maid of Ludmir), 76–108 (on Malkah of Belz).

8. See Nissan Mindel, *Rabbi Schneur Zalman:* Vol I, *Biography*, 98–101 (on Devorah's sacrifice).

9. I learned this Adel-oriented version of this famous tale of the Ba'al Shem Tov (with minor differences) from Rabbi Leah Novick in Boulder, Colorado, in 2002. — N.M.-Y. For another more traditional, telling of this *ma'aseh*, see Buxbaum, *The Light and Fire of the Baal Shem Tov*, 130–35.

10. I learned this unique variation on a traditional story (with minor differences) from Rabbi Leah Novick in Boulder, Colorado, in 2002. — N.M.-Y. For an alternate story of the match, see Buxbaum, *The Light and Fire of the Baal Shem Tov*, 153–54 ("The Perfect Groom").

11. For an account of how this accusation came about, see Buxbaum, *The Light and Fire of the Baal Shem Tov*, 182 ("A False Rumor").

12. Another accusation followed along the same lines with the *mitnagdim*: It was said that the Hasidim were seen drinking wine on Tisha b'Av, the day of mourning. Of course, they neglected to mention that Tisha b'Av fell on *Shabbat* that year, and when Tisha b'Av and *Shabbat* coincide, not only is it permitted to drink wine but one is supposed to drink wine. Because the specific dates and circumstances of both of these supposed heresies were "omitted" from the official accusations, it was easy for many to conclude that these Hasidim were really heretical Sabbatians.

13. I learned this version of the traditional story (with minor differences) from Rabbi Leah Novick in Boulder, Colorado, in 2002. — N.M.-Y. For another story on the shoes theme, see Buxbaum, *The Light and Fire of the Baal Shem Tov,* 154–55 ("Shoes in the Garden of Eden").

14. See Elie Wiesel, *Somewhere a Master: Further Hasidic Portraits and Legends,* 129.

15. For the Herson Genizah, see n. 26 to Chapter 1.

16. In the original source, the Ba'al Shem Tov's wife is called "Leah Rohel," which we have changed to the more accepted Hannah.

17. *Kovetz ha-Tamim,* vol. 3.

18. *Kovetz ha-Tamim,* vol. 4, letter 104, no. 228.

19. Ibid., letter 111, no. 134 (Wednesday of Devarim, in the year 5515).

20. See "Wine Drops on the Eyelashes," in Chapter 3.

21. Adapted with permission from Buxbaum, *The Light and Fire of the Baal Shem Tov,* 154 ("Edel and the Book of Remedies").

22. I learned this version of the traditional story (with minor differences) from Rabbi Leah Novick in Boulder, Colorado, in 2002. — N.M.-Y.

23. *Kovetz ha-Tamim,* vol. 4, 28, no. 562.

24. We will translate more of this will and discuss the succession thoroughly in "A Bear in the Forest" in Chapter 6.

25. I learned this story of Adel and the Ba'al Shem Tov (with minor differences) from Rabbi Leah Novick in Boulder, Colorado, in 2002. — N.M.-Y.

26. Shlomo Yosef Zevin, *Sippurei Hasidim,* 138. For another version of this story, see Buxbaum, *The Light and Fire of the Baal Shem Tov,* 213 ("The Death of a Baby").

27. I learned this story (with minor differences) of Adel and her daughter, Feiga, from Rabbi Leah Novick in Boulder, Colorado, in 2002. — N.M.-Y.

28. It may be possible to speculate a birthday for Adel, based on the year of her birth and from the possibility that the Ba'al Shem Tov named her from a verse in the *sedra* of the week.

CHAPTER 5

1. Abraham J. Heschel, *The Circle of the Baal Shem Tov: Studies in Hasidism,* 1–2.

2. Ibid., 4–5.

3. Ibid., 4, n. 17.

4. Ibid., 5.

5. A variation on this story is found in Elie Wiesel, *Somewhere a Master:*

Further Hasidic Portraits and Legends, 11–13. Whatever the original source, this story from Heschel seems the most complete and personal in all details. It is interesting that he did not include it in his essay on Reb Pinhas in his *The Circle of the Baal Shem Tov*. We discussed this story at the Jewish Theological Seminary in his office while looking over the works of Reb Pinhas. For another story on this theme about Reb Pinhas, see Yitzhak Buxbaum, *The Light and Fire of the Baal Shem Tov*, 264 ("Praying for Faith").

6. See Martin Buber, *Tales of the Hasidim: The Early Masters*, 119.

7. For a story that places Reb Pinhas in Mezhbizh before the Ba'al Shem Tov's passing, see Buxbaum, *The Light and Fire of the Baal Shem Tov*, 340 ("The Koretzer Neglects the Mitzvah").

8. Heschel, *The Circle of the Baal Shem Tov*, 11. See also *Kovetz ha-Tamim*, vol. 4, letter 165, no. 116: "To Reb Tzvi, the son of his holiness, my Rebbe, the Ba'al Shem Tov. As it is known to me that his holiness, my master and teacher is not in his home at this time, nevertheless, I will ask of you, may you live long, that you should make it known to the Ba'al Shem Tov that I have gathered the sum of 100 Polish guilders. I have them in safe keeping in the city of Ostrog in the hands of the Torah scholar Reb Borukh Segal. When the Ba'al Shem Tov comes there, he should receive that money, since it is clear that one should not change from one charitable item to another, because I gathered them together only for one purpose, to feed and to sustain the hidden *tzaddikim*. [signed] The words of the least of the least of the disciples of my teacher the Ba'al Shem Tov, Pinhas Shapira of Koretz."

9. Heschel, *The Circle of the Baal Shem Tov*, 14 (based on ms. Cincinnati, fol. 81b).

10. For more information on David of Ostrog and his questions to the Ba'al Shem Tov, see Heschel, *The Circle of the Baal Shem Tov*, 41–42, 149.

11. See Wiesel, *Somewhere a Master*, 20–21.

12. As I no longer own the copy of *Midrash Pinḥas* that these were originally translated from many years ago, we have chosen to given the citations as they occur in the more readily available, *Imrei Pinḥas*, which contains the same teachings. Versions of these stories were previously published in Zalman Schachter, *Fragments of a Future Scroll: Hassidism for the Aquarian Age*, 73–75.

13. Koretz, *Imrei Pinḥas*, gate 6, 158.

14. "Practical Wisdom from Shlomo Carlebach."

15. Koretz, *Imrei Pinḥas*, gate 6, 158.

16. "The Lord bless you and protect you! . . . Thus they shall link My name with the people of Israel, and I will bless them" (Num. 6:24,27), *JPS Hebrew-*

English TANAKH: The Traditional Hebrew Text and the New JPS Translation. All translations given in the notes are from the new JPS translation.

17. Koretz, *Imrei Pinḥas,* gate 3, 82.

18. Paraphrasing Yehudah Leib Alter of Ger as quoted in Arthur Green, ed. and trans., *The Language of Truth: The Torah Commentary of the Sefat Emet, Rabbi Yehudah Leib Alter of Ger,* 20: "By properly mending our deeds, we can come to hear more and more. This goes on forever. The ḥasid serves God in order to become attached to the root of the mitzvah, ever seeking to hear new things. . . . *all* hearing and listening should be attuned only to God."

19. Koretz, *Imrei Pinḥas,* gate 6, 148.

20. See Buxbaum, *The Light and Fire of the Baal Shem Tov,* 68–71 ("The Besht Opposes Preachers of Rebuke"), 183–85 ("He Admonishes a Preacher" and "Rebuking God's Children").

21. Koretz, *Imrei Pinḥas,* gate 3, 72.

22. *Maḥzor, Seliḥot* for Monday through Thursday. After the sin of the Golden Calf, God said to Moses, "When you find me adamant, recite these words and I will have to change my mind." It was a way of saying, "If you see that the *sefirot* have locked you out, then go to *keter;* it is not in the Ten, it is in the Thirteen; you go higher and then you will prevail."

23. Koretz, *Imrei Pinḥas,* gate 5, 28.

24. Paul Arthur Schlipp and Maurice Friedman, eds., *The Philosophy of Martin Buber,* 24.

25. Martin Buber, *I and Thou,* 75.

26. Koretz, *Imrei Pinḥas,* gate 2, 161.

27. Talmud, Megillah 25a; Berakhot 33b.

28. Koretz, *Imrei Pinḥas,* gate 6, 150.

29. Samuel Lewis, writing in October 1967 and quoted in Wali Ali Meyer, "A Sunrise in the West: Hazrat Inayat Khan's Legacy in California," 434–35; also Samuel L. Lewis, *Sufi Vision and Initiation: Meetings with Remarkable Beings,* 322.

30. As far as we know, this quotation does not exist in Torah, but this is how Pinhas of Koretz and others quote it. In the TANAKH it is *aḥen ru' ḥ hi' b'enosh v'nishmat shadday t'vinem,* "But truly it is the spirit in men, / The breath of Shaddai, that gives them understanding" (Job 32:8).

31. See "A Journey of Heavenly Ascent."

32. Author translation from an informal "table talk" of Rabbi Yosef Yitzhak Schneersohn, the sixth Lubavitcher Rebbe, from Shmini Atzeret and Simḥat Torah in 1932.

33. "Do not uncover the nakedness of your father's sister; she is your

father's flesh. Do not uncover the nakedness of your mother's sister; for she is your mother's flesh" (Lev. 18:12–13).

34. "Every part of you is fair, my darling, /There is no blemish in you" (Sg. 4:7).

35. Rabbi Obadiah diBertinoro, a commentator on the Mishnah (second half of the 15th century, in Italy).

36. Talmud, Shabbat 1:1.

37. 10 + 6 + 4 + 5 + 1 (for the *alef*) = 26.

38. 10 + 5 + 40 + 30 + 1 (for the *alef*) = 86.

39. 40 + 6 + 40 = 86.

40. Avraham ben Dov Baer of Fastov and Avraham of Kalisk, *Ḥesed L'Avraham*, 100–2.

41. A. Kahane, *Sefer ha-Ḥasidut*, 279.

42. See Louis I. Newman and Samuel Spitz, *The Hasidic Anthology: Tales and Teachings of the Hasidim*, 71; and Buber, *Tales of the Hasidim: The Early Masters*, 136 ("Mourning").

43. Part of this tale is related in David Kaetz, *Making Connections: Hasidic Roots and Resonance in the Teachings of Moshe Feldenkrais*, 65–68. Feldenkrais family tradition held that they were directly descended from Pinhas of Koretz; see Avrom Shuchatowitz, "Moses Shapira of Slavuta," in *The Encyclopedia of Hasidism*, ed. Tzvi M. Rabinowicz, 449.

CHAPTER 6

1. See Martin Buber, *Tales of the Hasidim: The Early Masters*, 98; Jacob Immanuel Schochet, *The Great Maggid: The Life and Teachings of Rabbi Dov Ber of Mezhirech*, 19.

2. Today, because of Hasidic marriage alliances, this lineage is carried on in many different dynasties but is especially found in the Chortkov, Sadigora, Husiatyn, and Boyan lineages of America and Israel.

3. When the Rhyziner would see someone enter the room, he would turn to his *gabbai* and say, *"Ehr fohrt tzu ehr feehrt?"* *"Ehr fohrt"* (he travels), meaning he is a Hasid, or *"ehr feerht"* (he leads), meaning a Rebbe.

4. I. Klapholtz, *Ha-Maggid Mi'Mezritch*, 8.

5. There are some who say that it is unlikely that Dov Baer studied with either Rabbi Shlomo Dov Baer or Rabbi Ya'akov Yehoshua in his youth, but other Hasidic sources indicate that Dov Baer visited the P'nai Yehoshua to discuss intricate passages in the Talmud and held the latter in great esteem. See Schochet, *The Great Maggid*, 21–22, n. 3.

6. See Buber, *Tales of the Hasidim: The Early Masters*, 98–99 ("The Curse").

7. This story comes from the ḤaBaD oral tradition. See Schochet, *The Great Maggid*, 24–25.

8. See Yitzhak Buxbaum, *The Light and Fire of the Baal Shem Tov*, 312–13 ("He Refuses to Visit the Besht"); and Schochet, *The Great Maggid*, 24–25.

9. A version of this story was previously published in Zalman Schachter, "The Besht and the P'ney Yehoshua," 50. The version given here is completely revised.

10. The implication here is that, for what is about to happen, standing is the appropriate posture, just as standing is the appropriate posture for the *Amidah*, which is to say, for *atzilut*.

11. The Maggid is quoted as saying, "The whole house was filled with light, a fire was blazing up all around him, and we actually saw the angels referred to!" Schochet, *The Great Maggid*, 47.

12. The story as given here is a blending of the versions in *Keter Shem Tov*, part II, sect. 424; in *Shivḥei ha-Besht*, 75; and from the oral tradition. For other English versions of this famous story, see Schochet, *The Great Maggid*, 44–49; Buxbaum, *The Light and Fire of the Baal Shem Tov*, 313–15 ("The First Visit"); Buber, *Tales of the Hasidim: The Early Masters*, 99–100 ("His Reception"); and Elie Wiesel, *Souls on Fire: Portraits and Legends of Hasidic Masters*, 54–55.

13. I first learned this story from Acharya Judith Simmer-Brown, the author of *Dakini's Warm Breath*. —N.M.-Y. See Herbert Guenther, *The Life and Teaching of Naropa* (Oxford: Oxford University Press, 1963/1974) for another version of the story.

14. "*Pashute*" is related to the word "*p'shat*," the basic meaning of something.

15. See Buxbaum, *The Light and Fire of the Baal Shem Tov*, 168 ("The Besht Teaches His Disciples to Appreciate Simple Jews"), and 177 ("The Besht Sends Scholarly Disciples to Learn from Simple Jews").

16. Talmud, Berakhot 34b.

17. Actually, "lip of truth."

18. For another teaching of the Ba'al Shem Tov on this topic, see Buxbaum, *The Light and Fire of the Baal Shem Tov*, 204 ("The Prayers of Simple People").

19. Midrash Rabbah, B'reishit Rabbah 47:4.

20. Talmud, Shabbat 63a.

21. For an English translation of this story by my former ḤaBaD colleague Zalman Posner, see Yosef Y. Schneersohn, *Saying Tehillim*, 11–16 ("The Baal Shem Tov and the Simple Folk"). For a version without reference to the Maggid, see Buxbaum, *The Light and Fire of the Baal Shem Tov*, 318–20 ("Hearing with an Open Ear").

22. *Kovetz ha-Tamim*, vol. 6, 27, no. 561.

23. Ibid., vol. 6, 28, no. 562.

24. Ibid., vol. 6, 27, no. 561.

25. See Dan Ben-Amos and Jerome R. Mintz, eds. and trans., *In Praise of the Baal Shem Tov [Shivhei ha-Besht]: The Earliest Collection of Legends about the Founder of Hasidism*, 84.

26. *Kovetz ha-Tamim*, vol. 2. 30, no. 124. The letter was written in the summer of 1759, the last summer of his life.

27. Eminent disciples who don't seem to have been mentioned as serious candidates include his brother-in-law, Gershon of Kittov (d. ca. 1761); Nahman of Horodenka (d. ca. 1780); Menachem Mendel of Premyshlan (1728–1771); Yitzhak of Drohobitch (1700–1768); and Meir Margoliot of Lvov (1700–1790). It may be that some were unwilling, whereas others were simply past the years of their greatest activity. Gershon of Kittov was great among the disciples but had emigrated to the Holy Land as early as 1747. Nahman of Horodenka is sometimes called the Ba'al Shem Tov's majordomo, but he was likewise committed to traveling to the Holy Land and like Reb Yitzhak Drohobitcher, as much a friend and colleague as a disciple. Menachem Mendel of Premyshlan was extremely self-effacing and followed Nahman of Horodenka to the Holy Land. Meir Margoliot held various important rabbinic posts and was more useful as a defender of the movement in that capacity.

28. The first quotation is reported by Pinhas Shapira of Koretz, *Midrash Pinḥas;* the second is quoted in Aryeh Kaplan, *Chasidic Masters: History, Biography and Thought*, 20; and the third is quoted in Harry M. Rabinowicz, *Hasidism: The Movement and Its Masters*, 47.

29. See Abraham J. Heschel, *The Circle of the Baal Shem Tov: Studies in Hasidism*, 16.

30. Samuel H. Dresner, *The Zaddik: The Doctrine of the Zaddik According to the Writings of Rabbi Yaakov Yosef of Polnoy*, 39, 43, 61.

31. Heschel, *The Circle of the Baal Shem Tov*, 18

32. For an excellent introduction to the man and his writings, see Kaplan, *Chasidic Masters*, 20 ("The First Revelation"); for the definitive study of the Polonoyer, see Dresner, *The Zaddik*.

33, See Buxbaum, *The Light and Fire of the Baal Shem Tov*, 141 ("A Yossele Like This").

34. Heschel, *The Circle of the Baal Shem Tov*, 9–10 (translated from *Sippurim Yekarim*); and Harry Rabinowicz, *The World of Hasidism*, 48.

35. Heschel, *The Circle of the Baal Shem Tov*, 17 (quoting *Pe'er Leyeshayim*, 14a).

36. Ibid., 19.

37. Ibid., 33, based on *Mazkeret Lig'doley 'Ostroha*, 338.

38. See Buxbaum, *The Light and Fire of the Baal Shem Tov*, 136 ("The Birth of His Son, Tzvi"). It should also be mentioned that some say that Tzvi Hirsh also inherited a book, the mysterious *Sefer ha-Zoref.*

39. *Kovetz ha-Tamim*, vol. 5, 29, no. 227.

40. Yaffa Eliach, "Tzvi Hirsch," *The Encyclopedia of Hasidism*, 513.

41. *Kovetz ha-Tamim*, vol. 2, 46, no. 146.

42. See Yosef Yitzchak Schneersohn, *HaYom Yom* . . . *"From Day to Day,"* 21, which tells us that this *ma'amar* was memorized by Menachem Mendel of Horodok and told to Shneur Zalman of Liadi, who gave over the *ma'amar* as *Umareihem uma'asseihem*, which is preserved in his *Torah Or*, Yitro.

43. This may have been in remembrance of his first great meeting with the Ba'al Shem Tov during which they experienced the *Ma'aseh Merkavah.*

44. Yisra'el ben Eliezer, *Sefer ha-Ba'al Shem Tov*, vol. 2, 106, n. 13.

45. "The Lord is king, / He is robed in grandeur; / the Lord is robed, / He is girded with strength" (Ps. 93:1), *JPS Hebrew-English TANAKH: The Traditional Hebrew Text and the New JPS Translation*. All translations given in the notes are from the new JPS translation.

46. Klapholtz, *Ha-Maggid Mi'Mezritch*, 49. See Buber, *Tales of the Hasidim: The Early Masters*, 100 ("The Succession"). It should be noted that Rafael of Bershad asked this question of Reb Pinhas of Koretz as well, and he gave the very same answer, even using the same quotation; ibid., 128 ("Endless Struggle").

47. See "Reb Mikeleh's *Niggun* of Great Longing and the Passing of the Ba'al Shem Tov" in Chapter 3.

48. Dresner, *The Zaddik*, 60.

49. Schochet, *The Great Maggid*, 93.

50. Also Aryeh Leib of Polonoye (d. 1769), Yissakhar Baer of Lubavitch (d. 1787), and David Farkes.

51. Talmud, Avot 6:1.

52. Schochet, *The Great Maggid*, 106; and Buber, *Tales of the Hasidim: The Early Masters*, 196 ("The Letter").

53. Among Hasidim, he is called "Ahron the Great," and he was succeeded by his disciple Shlomo of Karlin (1738–1792) and later his son, Asher of Karlin (1760–1828).

54. A reference to a character and a scene in the novel *Tristram Shandy* by Laurence Sterne, the first parts of which were published in 1760.

55. Mishnah, Avot 2:10.

56. "Personal names are not acquired accidentally or simply because the parents wish to confer a certain name. The Holy One, blessed is He, inspires the parents with a spirit of wisdom and knowledge to call their child by that name which corresponds to the root of its soul. . . . That is why a person is aroused when called by his name [even when preoccupied or sleeping], for one's name is related to one's very soul," Maggid of Mezritch quoted in Schochet, *The Great Maggid*, 29.

57. Yud-Beit (12) Tammuz is celebrated by HaBaD Hasidim as both the birthday of the sixth Lubavitcher Rebbe, Yosef Yitzhak Schneersohn (1880–1950), and the day on which he was informed that he was free from the exile that followed his imprisonment by the Soviet government for "sacred activity."

58. Salomon Maimon, *Lebensgeschichte: Mit einer Einleitung und mit Anmerkungen / neu hrsg. von Jakob Fromer*, 198–204.

CHAPTER 7

1. Dov Baer ben Avrahahm of Mezritch, *Maggid D'varav L'Ya'akov*, Introduction.

2. When I hear the Maggid say *"giddim,"* it brings to mind that which in the Torah goes against a human being's unregenerate nature (abstinences)—*neged*—and that which tells us how (observances)—*maggid*.

3. There is a *Gemara* (Eruvin 21b) that says, "Whoever is diligent in studying Torah tastes the taste of meat, which suggests that the taste of meat is inside the self (*etzem* = bone)." Likewise, Yosef Hayyim of Baghdad (Ben Ish Hai) in his commentary on the Talmud (Ben Yehoyada) on Ta'anit 30b mentions the quote as follows, "It is a well known quote that since the day the *Beit ha-Mikdash* was destroyed, taste has been taken out of the flesh and put into the bones." But he does not give the source. It may be a quote from the Zohar.

4. This reading was suggested by my student Rabbi Bahir Davis, the spiritual director of Rocky Mountain Hai in Lafayette, Colorado. — Z.M.S.-S.

5. Talmud, Sanhedrin 75a.

6. A fantastic example of this is Chaim Kramer with Avraham Sutton, eds. and trans., *Anatomy of the Soul: Rebbe Nachman of Breslov.*

7. Midrash Rabba, Va-yikra', 13:3. See also "For teaching shall go forth from Me" (Isa. 51:4), *JPS Hebrew-English TANAKH: The Traditional Hebrew Text and the New JPS Translation*. All translations given in the notes are from the new JPS translation. And "See, a time is coming—declares the Lord—when I will make a new covenant with the House of Israel and the House of

Judah . . . I will put My Teaching into their innermost being and inscribe it upon their hearts" (Jer. 31:31,33).

8. This is based on the Aramaic translation (*Targum Onkelos*) of "The Lord spoke those words—those and no more—to your whole congregation at the mountain, with a mighty voice out of the fire and the dense cloud" (Deut. 5:19). See also Talmud, Sanhedrin 17a. "*V'Lo Yasaf*" means "*V'Lo Pasak*."

9. Midrash Rabbah, Vayyikra Rabbah 13:3.

10. Reb Pinhas of Koretz was another Rebbe who understood that there was something "new" coming down and who likewise struggled to say this without seeming to abrogate *Torah mi'Sinai*.

11. "He said to me, 'O mortal, can these bones live again?' " (Ezek. 37:3).

12. Talmud, Hullin 63b: "R. Meir said, a person should always teach his students the short way." Talmud, Berakhot 29b: "Aherim say, (i.e., R. Meir in the name of Aher) He should pray a short prayer," etc. Both opinions are endorsed by Rav Huna.

13. "May the glory of the Lord endure forever; may the Lord rejoice in His works!" (Ps. 104:31).

14. "He fulfills the wishes of those who fear Him" (Ps. 145:19).

15. Midrash Rabbah, B'reishit Rabbah 8:7.

16. Dov Baer, *Maggid D'varav L'Ya'akov*, 9.

17. See Chapter 6, "The Magic Circle of the Ba'al Shem Tov and the Maggid's *Teshuvah*."

18. Talmud, Shabbat 118a.

19. Talmud, Shabbat 118a: "Whoever gives pleasure to the Shabbat enjoys Inheritance without end . . . (*Nahlah bli m'tzarim*)."

20. See the blind beggars tale in "The Seven Beggars" of Rebbe Nahman of Bratzlav in Adin Steinsaltz, *Beggars and Prayers*, 152–54.

21. The Maggid's disciple Nahum of Chernobyl also teaches that everything has to return to that nothing in order to become again like the butterfly in chrysalis, or is it the seed that has to rot before it can grow.

22. *Pri Etz Hayyim*, Sha'ar Hag ha-Matzot 1, Likkutei Torah, Shemot.

23. "By knowledge are its rooms filled / With all precious and beautiful things" (Prov. 24:4).

24. John R. Kohlenberger III, ed. *The Precise Parallel New Testament*.

25. "Vast floods cannot quench love" (Sg. 8:7).

26. Based on Talmud, Berakhot 40a.

27. Zohar II: 183b.

28. "Pharaoh will say of the Israelites, 'They are astray in the land; the wilderness has closed in on them' " (Exod. 14:3).

29. *Pri Etz Hayyim*, Sha'ar Mikra Kodesh 4.

30. Talmud, Yoma 69b.

31. "And who is like Your people Israel, a unique nation on the earth, whom God went and redeemed as His people, winning renown for Himself and doing great and marvelous deeds for them [and] for Your land—[driving out] nations and their gods before Your people, whom You redeemed for Yourself from Egypt" (Exod. 7:23).

32. *Toldot Ya'akov Yosef*, Va-yishlaḥ, 31d. See Aryeh Kaplan, *The Light Beyond: Adventures in Hassidic Thought*, 32–33.

33. Talmud, Ketubbot 5a.

34. "You shall be free to set a king over yourself, one chosen by the Lord your God" (Deut. 17:15).

35. Talmud, Ketubbot 17a.

36. Mishnah, Avot 2:13.

37. *Tikkunei Zohar Hadash* 102d or *Tikkunei Zohar* 21 62b.

38. "One thing I ask of the Lord, only that do I seek" (Ps. 27:4).

39. *Kedushat Levi*, Rosh Hashanah, 273. See Kaplan, *The Light Beyond*, 49.

40. See Chapter 9, "Give Over All Your Needs to God."

41. *Or ha-Meir* by R. Zev Wolf of Zhitomir (d. 1800).

42. See Arthur Green, *Ehyeh: A Kabbalah for Tomorrow*, 1–3.

43. Just as we speak of Y-H and V-H, where the upper *heh* is *binah*, and the lower *heh* is *malkhut*. So sometimes we speak of *Hokhmah ila'ah*, and *malkhut* as *Hokhmah tata'ah*. What is happening is that the name *Adonai* is in *Malkhut*. So the word "*teva*" has a Hebrew root in there, which means "sunken," which is like saying that the Divine Presence is covered by water, as it were, is sunken into nature. And the promise is that the day will come when the world will be filled with the knowledge of the Lord as the water covers the sea. And so "*teva*" is that which is sunken in deep. Therefore, because all that we see is the surface of the water, we don't notice the depth.

44. Talmud, Shabbat 11a.

45. Joseph Campbell with Bill Moyers, *The Power of Myth*, 95–97.

46. *Sha'arei Orah*, gate 1.

47. Talmud, Hagiga 4a.

48. Zohar I:71a.

49. Talmud, Sotah 3a.

50. Aryeh Kaplan, *Chasidic Masters: History, Biography and Thought*, 23–24; see Zalman Schachter-Shalomi, *Wrapped in a Holy Flame: Teachings and Tales of the Hasidic Masters*, 41.

51. We were unable to find a source for this quote, though it is clearly related to Lev. 21:1.

52. Zohar III:124a.

53. "The Lord said to Moses: Speak to the priests, the sons of Aaron, and say to them: None shall defile himself for any [dead] person among his kin, except for the relatives that are closest to him" (Lev. 21:1).

54. "[T]hat Your way be known on earth"(Ps. 67:3).

55. "Now the man knew his wife Eve" (Gen.s 4:1).

56. "How a man has his way with a maiden" (Prov. 30:19).

57. "O maidens of Zion, go forth / And gaze upon King Solomon" (Sg. 3:11).

58. Martin Buber, *I and Thou.*

59. "While he was still speaking with them, Rachel came with her father's flock; for she was a shepherdess" (Gen. 29:9).

60. "One such day, he came into the house to do his work" (Gen. 39:11).

61. Talmud, Sotah 36b.

62. Talmud, Yoma 35b.

63. "The majesty of Israel" (Lam. 2:1).

64. "[S]he caught hold of him by his garment and said, 'Lie with me!' But he left his garment in her hand and got away and fled outside" (Gen. 39:12).

65. "When you take the field against your enemies, and the Lord your God delivers them into your power and you take some of them captive" (Deut. 21:10).

66. "[A]nd you see among the captives a beautiful woman and you desire her and would take her to wife" (Deut. 21:11).

67. Talmud, Yoma 38b.

68. Chapter 6, "The Magic Circle of the Ba'al Shem Tov and the Maggid's *Teshuvah.*"

69. Tosefta, Yoma 4:11.

70. See the teachings "Outer and Inner" and "The Beauty of Rahel" in this chapter.

71. "The sun rises, and the sun sets— / And glides back to where it rises" (Eccles. 1:5)

72. See Kaplan, *Chasidic Masters,* 43.

73. We were unable to locate a source for this quotation.

74. "He discoursed about trees, from the cedar in Lebanon to the hyssop that grows out of the wall; and he discoursed about beasts, birds, creeping things, and fishes" (1 Kings 5:13).

75. "[B]ut the Lord values those who fear Him, / those who depend on His faithful care" (Ps. 147:11).

76. Dov Baer, *Maggid D'varav L'Ya'akov,* 221.

77. A story I heard at a HaBaD *farbrengen.* —Z.M.S.-S. See Martin Buber, *Tales of the Hasidim: The Early Masters,* 112 ("The Left Foot").

78. In Jacob Immanuel Schochet, *The Great Maggid: The Life and Teachings of Rabbi Dov Ber of Mezhirech*, 49–50; he translates a prayer request for healing from the Maggid to the Ba'al Shem Tov.

79. See Chapter 6, "Words and Reality."

80. A story I heard at a ḤaBaD *farbrengen*. —Z.M.S.-S. See Schochet, *The Great Maggid*, 209–10; and Buber, *Tales of the Hasidim: The Early Masters*, III ("Conjuring").

81. This is based on "and the name of the city from that day on shall be 'The Lord Is There' " (Ezek. 48:35).

82. Zohar II:59b.

83. *Pri Etz Ḥayyim*, Inyan Tefillah 15.

84. *Sha'ar ha-Kavanot*, Inyan Kavanot ha-Amidah.

85. "He had a dream; a stairway was set on the ground and its top reached to the sky, and angels of God were going up and down on it" (Gen. 28:12).

86. Dov Baer, *Maggid D'varav L'Ya'akov*, 141.

87. As we find in the permutations of Counting the Omer.

88. This was the key question behind my minor dissertation "Kabbalistic Prayer Intentions in the Amidah," which was based on a teaching of Reb Menachem Mendel of Lubavitch I, the Tzemah Tzedek. —Z.M.S.-S.

CHAPTER 8

1. One might rightly look on Reb Shneur Zalman of Liadi as a *talmid* of Reb Avraham in one sense, but the truth is, theirs was a relationship of mutuality, one learning equally from the other. Nevertheless, I suspect no one learned more from Reb Avraham the Malakh than Reb Shneur Zalman of Liadi.

2. Yet another useful distinction from the Hindu tradition is that of the *Bhakti* yogin and the *Jnani* yogin, the person who approaches God devotionally and the one who approaches God through the intellect. Avraham the Malakh was deeply intellectual, trying to understand the ways in which the universe operates.

3. The Komarner Rebbe in the past and perhaps the Tasher Rebbe today might be considered to be of this type.

4. See Martin Buber, *Tales of the Hasidim: The Early Masters*, 113 ("The Mothers"). This miracle of the four Matriarchs suggests that this would be no ordinary child. For as much as it may have been occasioned by the great merit of the Maggid or his wife, it also spoke of the future of Hasidism, perhaps of the many great *Rebbeim* who would be descended from the angel, or perhaps

of the great *tikkunim* (heavenly adjustments) he would accomplish for Yisra'el in his short lifetime.

5. Buber, *Tales of the Hasidim: The Early Masters*, 133 ("Origin").

6. See Chapter 7, "The Glory Revealed to the World."

7. See Chapter 6, "A Sojourner in the World."

8. Buber, *Tales of the Hasidim: The Early Masters*, 113–14 ("The Face").

9. See Buber, *Tales of the Hasidim: The Early Masters*, 114 ("Marriage").

10. Harry M. Rabinowicz, *Hasidism: The Movement and Its Masters*, 85.

11. Rabinowicz, *Hasidism*, 85–86 quoting from Horodezky, *Leaders of Hasidism*, 49.

12. For another version of this part of the story, see Buber, *Tales of the Hasidim: The Early Masters*, 267 ("Concerning Ardent Zeal"). For another version and explanation, see Nissan Mindel, *Rabbi Schneur Zalman*, 133–34. In Abraham J. Heschel, *The Circle of the Baal Shem Tov: Studies in Hasidism*, 21, the Malakh says, "*Fohr, fohr, kuk nit oif die ferd*" (Ride, ride, pay no attention to the horses)—that is to say, ignore the animal body and outrun it instead of trying to discipline it.

13. This is why Reb Nahman of Bratzlav tells us, "Whatever the soul learns, teach it to the body."

14. See Buber, *Tales of the Hasidim: The Early Masters*, 114 ("His Wife's Dream").

15. See Chapter 5, "Eavesdropping on a Journey Out-of-Body."

16. "The dove came back to him toward evening, and there in its bill was a plucked-off olive leaf!" (Gen. 8:11), *JPS Hebrew-English TANAKH: The Traditional Hebrew Text and the New JPS Translation*. All translations given in the notes are from the new JPS translation.

17. Toldot 151a.

18. "The Lord founded the earth by wisdom; / He established the heavens by understanding; / By His knowledge the depths burst apart, And the skies distilled dew" (Prov. 3:19–20).

19. Literal translation: "the one who causes you to succeed."

20. "My body and soul shout for joy to the living God" (Ps. 84:3).

21. "God will not take away the life of one who makes plans so that no one may be kept banished" (2 Sam. 14:14).

22. Talmud, Rosh Hashanah 12a.

23. Zohar, Tzav 96:34a.

24. In the Hebrew, the Malakh is executing a play on words using the letters *kaf* and *ḥet* of *koaḥ* (potential), which equal the number 28 to speak of the 28 times mentioned in Ecclesiastes.

25. New JPS translation.

26. Zohar III:258a.

27. We were unable to trace the source of this quotation.

28. Pirkei Avot 5:2. Jacob Neusner, ed. and trans., *The Mishnah: A New Translation*, 685 (Abot 5:2: "There are ten generations from Adam to Noah, to show you how long-suffering is [God]").

29. See Chapter 2, "The Word-Ark."

30. Actually, the text says, *Vayomer Yah" l'Noah bo-atah v'khol-beytkha el-ha'tevah ki-otkha ra'iti tzaddik l'fanai bador ha-zeh,* "Then *Yah* said to Noah, 'Come into the ark, with all your household, for you alone have I found righteous before Me in this generation.' "

31. B'reishit Rabbah 36.

32. Avraham ben Dov Baer of Fastov and Avraham of Kalisk, *Hesed L'Avraham,* 26–28.

33. As Annie Dillard, in *Pilgrim at Tinker Creek, 96,* writes: "Hasidism has a tradition that one of man's purposes is to assist God in the work of redemption by 'hallowing' the things of creation. By a tremendous heave of his spirit, the devout man frees the divine sparks trapped in the mute things of time; he uplifts the forms and moments of creation, bearing them aloft into that rare air and hallowing fire in which all clays must shatter and burst."

34. Psalms 1–4 are recited on Yom Kippur night so that you will not have a seminal emission that night (because you are not supposed to go to *mikveh* on Yom Kippur). But I have heard other Hasidim say, if it happens, go to *mikveh* anyway. — Z.M.S.-S.

35. *Kovetz ha-Tamim,* vol. 7, 26, no. 662. This material from the Herson Genizah, primarily used by HaBaD Hasidim, is historically suspect, especially as the disciples of the Maggid mentioned play a special role in the life of Rabbi Shneur Zalman of Liadi (the founder of HaBaD). For instance, Menachem Mendel of Vitebsk is Reb Shneur Zalman's mentor, and Zushya and Yehudh Leib give *haskamot* for the *Tanya* of Reb Shneur Zalman. These are singled out, and none of the other great disciples are mentioned.

36. See Or Rose and Ebn D. Leader, ed. and trans., *God in All Moments: Mystical & Practical Spiritual Wisdom from Hasidic Masters,* 9.

37. *Kovetz ha-Tamim,* vol. 7, 27, no. 663.

38. *Kovetz ha-Tamim.* See Elie Wiesel, *Sages and Dreamers: Biblical, Talmudic, and Hasidic Portraits and Legends,* 391–92.

39. For an alternate version, see Buber, *Tales of the Hasidim: The Early Masters,* 116 ("The Mountain").

40. Ibid.

41. Readers may wish to revisit "Noah and the Hot Water" after studying this Torah.

42. See Chapter 6, "Words and Reality."

43. See Eliot Deutsch, *Advaita Vedanta: A Philosophical Reconstruction;* and John K. Sheriff, *Charles Peirce's Guess at the Riddle: Grounds for Human Significance.*

44. See Buber, *Tales of the Hasidim: The Early Masters,* 115–16 ("The Inheritance"), 116 ("The White Pekeshe").

45. Another person who explored this territory independently, basing himself on the Ba'al Shem Tov, was Reb Nahman of Bratzlav. We hope to examine these aspects of Shneur Zalman and Reb Nahman in a second volume.

46. "The one no less than the other was God's doing" (Eccles. 7:14).

47. Reb Shneur Zalman concretizes and brings down into psychology what the Malakh has in the very high and abstract theology. —Z.M.S.-S.

48. There may also be said to be a set of *sikhliyot* (*sefirot*) corresponding to each of the four worlds (*arba olamot*). See also the appendix "The Tree of Life."

49. B'reishit 151a.

50. "Those who love Your teaching enjoy well-being; / they encounter no adversity" (Ps. 119:165).

51. See the excellent discussion of the *partzufim* in Aryeh Kaplan, *Innerspace: Introduction to Kabbalah, Meditation and Prophecy,* 92–109.

52. See Chapter 7, "Ya'akov's Inheritance."

53. Ken Wilber, *Sex, Ecology, Spirituality: The Spirit of Evolution: Second, Revised Edition.*

54. "He chose for himself the best, / For there is the portion of the revered chieftan, / Where the heads of the people come. / He executed the Lord's judgments / And His decisions for Israel" (Deut. 33:21).

55. *Prakriti* (primordial nature) in Hindu philosophy, as contrasted with *purusha* (spirit), as in spirit and matter.

56. This is a pun: *ha-mishim* is "50"; *ha-mushim* is "well armed."

57. *Hesed L'Avraham,* 11–14.

58. Michael Kagan, "The King's Messenger," 56–58.

59. It is possible to see all 10 *sefirot* in each of the four worlds, in the manifest world, in the emotive world, in the world of the intellect, or the spiritual world, or to see *hokhmah* as being *atzilut, binah* as *beri'ah,* the 6 as *yetzirah,* and *malkhut* as *assisyah,* but the Malakh tends to deal with all 10 *sefirot* in *atzilut.*

60. For alternate versions of this story, see Buber, *Tales of the Hasidim: The Early Masters,* 115 ("Anniversary"); and Wiesel, *Sages and Dreamers,* 395–96.

61. Talmud, Hagiga, 14b.

62. See Wiesel, *Sages and Dreamers,* 398–99 (on this complex relationship from his perspective).

63. See Buber, *Tales of the Hasidim: The Early Masters,* 117 ("The Other Dream"); and Wiesel, *Sages and Dreamers,* 398–99.

64. See Buber, *Tales of the Hasidim: The Early Masters,* 117 ("Sanctified").

65. Nevertheless, Reb Zushya was visited by Hasidim and did have Hasidic heirs.

66. Wiesel, *Sages and Dreamers,* 394. This seems to have been an issue between them. For Reb Avraham writes to Reb Zushya: "To the friend of God and mine, a living *tzaddik* who embodies the sacredness of this generation and its grandeur, Rabbi Zushya, may his candle continue to burn . . . I am surprised as a *tzaddik* such as he . . . he and Reb Zalmenke [Shneur Zalman] and I have heard from my holy father and teacher that a man must see himself as nothing—but not as something small. Quite the contrary—man must at times see himself as great in order to perceive the greatness of the Eternal One. Therefore my advice to him is not to yield. . . . And all those who fight us will fall like straw, and we shall rise and be courageous. These are the words of a friend who loves him truly and who is waiting for his people's salvation. . . . Avraham son of Reb Dov Baer."

67. See Wiesel, *Sages and Dreamers,* 394.

CHAPTER 9

1. It is said that there are only eight persons to have been called "Rebbe Reb," which is a title of extraordinary respect.

2. See Elie Wiesel, *Souls on Fire: Portraits and Legends of Hasidic Masters,* 113–14.

3. See Martin Buber, *Tales of the Hasidim: The Early Masters,* 235 ("The Blessings").

4. Talmud, Kiddushin, 30.

5. Louis I. Newman and Samuel Spitz, *The Hasidic Anthology: Tales and Teachings of the Hasidim,* 304.

6. Harry M. Rabinowicz, *Hasidism: The Movement and Its Masters,* 108.

7. See Jiri Langer, *Nine Gates to the Chassidic Mysteries,* 117. I have also heard this in the name of Reb Elimelekh, with him saying, "Melekh, Melekh even the ants don't want you!" —Z.M.S.-S.

8. See Chapter 1, "Adam, the Ba'al Shem of Ropshitz and the *Tzaddikim Nistarim.*"

9. See Buber, *Tales of the Hasidim: The Early Masters,* 240 ("The Fruits of Wandering"). My father would also tell me that when they reached Oswiecim (Auschwitz), they were not comfortable and turned back. —Z.M.S.-S.

10. See Buber, *Tales of the Hasidim: The Early Masters*, 240 ("The Horses").

11. The man from whom I heard this story, told it, if I remember correctly, as a story of Reb Levi Yitzhak of Berditchev and Reb Moshe Leib of Sassov. Nevertheless, I tend to think it is a story of Reb Elimelelkh of Lizhensk and Reb Zushya of Anipol, for a similar tale is told of them making the same point with horses and a carriage (see n. 10). —N.M.-Y.

12. Avraham Hayyim Simcha Bunem Michaelson, ed., *Ohalei Tzaddikim*, 3–144 ("Ohel Elimelekh," supplemented by other versions).

13. See the Maggid's teaching in Aryeh Kaplan, *Chasidic Masters: History, Biography and Thought*, 44–45 (Likkutim Yekarikm no. 22), which fits Zushya of Anipol like a glove.

14. A version of this was previously published in Zalman Schachter, *Fragments of a Future Scroll: Hassidism for the Aquarian Age*, 47–48.

15. There is a book *Menorat Zahav* (Warsaw, 1902) in which his aphorisms and some teachings are found, but mostly his stories are remembered.

16. Or Rose and Ebn D. Leader, eds. and trans., *God in All Moments: Mystical & Practical Spiritual Wisdom from Hasidic Masters*, 61.

17. See Samuel H. Dresner, *Prayer, Humility, and Compassion*, 157–58.

18. Talmud, Ta'anit, 21a.

19. See Yosef Yitzchak Schneersohn, *HaYom Yom . . . "From Day to Day,"* 92a; Alexander Tobias, "Zusya (Meshullam Zusya) of Anopol," in *The Encyclopedia of Hasidism*, ed. Tzvi M. Rabinowicz, 563–64.

20. Heard at a ḤaBaD *farbrengen*. — Z.M.S.-S.

21. *Esser Zakhzakhot*, 16–41.

22. See Buber, *Tales of the Hasidim: The Early Masters*, 187–88 ("Sleep").

23. "Open the gates of victory for me that I may enter them and praise the Lord. / This is the gateway to the Lord—the victorious shall enter through it" (Ps. 118:19–20), *JPS Hebrew-English TANAKH: The Traditional Hebrew Text and the New JPS Translation*. All translations given in the notes are from the new JPS translation.

24. Elimelekh of Lizhensk, *No'am Elimelekh*, Likkutei Shoshanah, 98a. Elsewhere, Reb Elimelekh interprets a passage using the very same key, saying: "'And *Y-H-V-H* appeared to Abraham in the Oak grove of Mamreh, while he was sitting in the opening of the tent, because it was a hot day' (Gen. 18:1). Sitting at the opening of the tent, Abraham thought that he hadn't even yet entered into holiness. That is to say, he was still sitting on the outside of the tent."

25. Specifically Menachem Mendel of Kotzk and Shneur Zalman of Liadi.

26. Read (with a grain of salt) Martin Buber's description in *Hasidism and Modern Man*, 47–55 ("My Way to Hasidism").

27. Rachel Elior, *The Mystical Origins of Hasidism*, 147.

28. Rivka Schatz Uffenheimer, *Hasidism as Mysticism: Quietistic Elements in Eighteenth-Century Hasidic Thought*, 155–56.

29. "My mouth shall sing much praise to the Lord" (Ps. 109:30).

30. Elimelekh of Lizhensk, *No'am Elimelekh*.

31. Michaelson, *Ohalei Tzaddikim*, 3–144 ("Ohel Elimelekh").

32. Elimelekh of Lizhensk, *No'am Elimelekh*.

33. Michaelson, *Ohalei Tzaddikim*, 3–144 ("Ohel Elimelekh"). See also Langer, *Nine Gates to the Chassidic Mysteries*, 130–33.

34. Talmud, Shabbat 59b.

35. See Buber, *Tales of the Hasidim: The Early Masters*, 259 ("Upsetting the Bowl"); and Langer, *Nine Gates to the Chassidic Mysteries*, 124.

36. Based on M. Unger, *Ḥasidus Un Lebn*, 77. For an alternate translation, see Zalman Meshullam Schachter-Shalomi, *Spiritual Intimacy: A Study of Counseling in Hasidism*, 226–27. Compare this with Parnas, *Sippurei ha-Ari*, 62.

Chapter 10

1. Tzvi M. Rabinowicz, "Israel Hofstein Kozienice," in *The Encyclopedia of Hasidism*, ed. Tzvi M. Rabinowicz, 270.

2. Harry M. Rabinowicz, *Hasidism: The Movement and Its Masters*, 115–16.

3. See especially 125–26 and 233–307 ("The Etzah and the Blessing").

4. George I. Gurdjieff (ca. 1866–1949) once said that all the exoteric religions teach the "what," while it is left up to the esoteric traditions to teach the "how."

5. Lawrence Fine, ed. and trans.), *Safed Spirituality: Rules of Mystical Piety, the Beginning of Wisdom;* and Or Rose and Ebn D. Leader, eds. and trans., *God in All Moments: Mystical & Practical Spiritual Wisdom from Hasidic Masters,* xi–xii.

6. In point of fact, the *hanhagot* of Hasidism and the S'fat *hanhagot* are not so very different. Many of them are in quite the same spirit and equally powerful. The central difference seems to lie in an emphasis on physical austerities and the way in which the pre-Hasidic kabbalists of the Ba'al Shem Tov's time approached and engaged them, taking them to physical extremes. For a full treatment of the S'fat *hanhagot* in English, see Fine, *Safed Spirituality*.

7. See Schachter-Shalomi, *Spiritual Intimacy*, 82–83 on the ascetic hero.

8. "You shall not profane My holy name, that I may be sanctified in the

midst of the Israelite people—I the Lord who sanctify you" (Lev. 22:32), *JPS Hebrew-English TANAKH: The Traditional Hebrew Text and the New JPS Translation.*

9. Avraham Hayyim Simcha Bunem Michaelson, ed., *Ohalei Tzaddikim,* 3–144 ("Ohel Elimelekh"). See Martin Buber, *Tales of the Hasidim: The Early Masters,* 263–64 ("The Artery").

10. Kalonymus Kalman Shapira, *Conscious Community: A Guide to Inner Work,* 56.

11. Nehemia Polen, *The Holy Fire: The Teachings of Rabbi Kalonymus Kalman Shapira, the Rebbe of the Warsaw Ghetto,* 1999.

12. See Rose and Leader, *God in All Moments,* 111 ("God Loves the Body").

13. *L'Shem Yihud Kudshah Berikh Hu u'Shekhintei b'Dhilu u'Rehimu l'Yhed Shem Y"H b' V"H b'Yihudah Shelim b'Shem Kol Yisra'el.*

14. See Martin Buber, *Ten Rungs: Hasidic Sayings,* 55–56 ("The Ten Principles").

15. See Yitzhak Buxbaum, *The Light and Fire of the Baal Shem Tov,* 142–43 ("Lighting His Pipe with a Candle of Non-Kosher Fat").

16. "[B]e on your guard against anything untoward" (Deut. 23:10).

17. Talmud, Avorah Zarah, 20b.

18. "[D]o not follow your heart and eyes in your lustful urge" (Num. 15:39).

19. This was the required number of siftings for the Omer.

20. See Rose and Leader, *God in All Moments,* 81 ("Concealed and Revealed Acts of Piety").

21. Talmud, Berakhot 4a.

22. See Rose and Leader, *God in All Moments,* 15 ("The Importance of Silence"), 138.

23. See ibid., 3 ("A Meditation Upon Arising"), 5 ("Creative Awakening").

24. See ibid., 131 ("Joining Day and Night").

25. Back in 1942, when I was about 18, I read Reb Elimelekh's *Tzettel Kattan* for the first time and got very excited by it. When I read, "This *Tzettel Kattan* should never be removed from the book from which you study," I immediately cut it out of the book I was reading and pasted it into my big Lubavitcher *Torah Or siddur* so I could recite it every day from my prayer book. — Z.M.S.-S.

26. See Rose and Lander, *God in All Moments,* 125 ("A Single Thought").

27. See ibid., 91 ("Fear, Love, and Torah Study").

28. Sha'arei Tzion, 82b.

29. A prayer to be recited before studying Kabbalah found in the opening pages of the *Etz Hayyim.* A version of this was previously published in

Zalman Schachter, *Fragments of a Future Scroll: Hassidism for the Aquarian Age*, 52–53.

30. See Rose and Leader, *God in All Moments*, 15 ("The Importance of Silence").

31. For another version of this, see ibid., 133 ("Your Inner Voice").

32. In the morning blessings, we say *galui v'yadu'a* (it is all manifest and known by You), meaning, I am totally transparent to You. It is this transparency that Reb Elimelekh wants to talk about.

33. See Rose and Leader, *God in All Moments*, 127 ("Spiritual 'Talk Therapy' ") and, for another version of this, 83 ("Know Who Stands before You").

34. See Martin Buber, *Tales of the Hasidim: The Later Masters*, 206–7 ("The Confession").

35. This refers to a condition of harmonious existence and relationships.

36. Zohar, Kedoshim, 81; see Rose and Leader, *God in All Moments*, 111 ("God Loves the Body").

37. *Reshit Ḥokhmah*, chap. 7.

38. *The Precise Parallel New Testament*, KJV.

39. George A. Kelly, *Psychology of Personal Constructs*.

40. For another translation of the *Tzettel Kattan*, see Aryeh Kaplan, *Chasidic Masters: History, Biography and Thought*, 63–68.

41. Elimelekh of Lizhensk, *No'am Elimelekh*, 614–18.

42. See Rose and Leader, *God in All Moments*, 97 ("The Guidance of Torah").

43. The book mentioned in Joshua 10:13 and 2 Samuel 1:18 of which there are no extant copies.

44. See Rose and Leader, *God in All Moments*, 79 ("Love Your Neighbor").

45. See ibid., 15 ("The Importance of Silence").

46. It was the Roman statesman, philosopher, and orator Cicero who made the statement, "As you have sown, so shall you reap."

47. See Rose and Leader, *God in All Moments*, 75 ("Arrogance Begets Anger"), 77 ("Righteous Indignation").

48. Ibid., 71, 73 ("All God's Creatures"), 83 ("Know Who Stands before You").

49. I heard this story at a ḤaBaD *farbrengen*. —Z.M.S.-S.

50. Elimelekh of Lizhensk, *No'am Elimelekh*, 611–13.

51. Arthur Green, *Ehyeh: A Kabbalah for Tomorrow*, 102–5; also found in Rose and Leader, *God in All Moments*, 141–44.

52. Rabinowicz, *Hasidism*, 110.

53. See Jiri Langer, *Nine Gates to the Chassidic Mysteries*, 129–30; Buber, *Tales of the Hasidim: The Early Masters*, 257 ("Satan's Threat")

54. See ibid., 263 ("The Hidden Zaddikim").

55. Rabinowicz, *Hasidism*, 109; Elie Wiesel, *Souls on Fire: Portraits and Legends of Hasidic Masters*, 129, 130; Kaplan, *Chasidic Masters*, 55.

56. Langer, *Nine Gates to the Chassidic Mysteries*, 134–35.

Glossary

adam kadmon **(primeval human)** The human being in God's conception; also the pre-atzilic level of divine emanations.

Adonai **(my lords)** A name of God in the plural connected with the attribute of sovereignty (*malkhut*).

aggadah **(Aram., lore; pl. *aggadot*)** Nonlegal material in the rabbinic literature.

ahavah **(love)** Love, often paired with fear/awe (*yirah*).

aliyat ha-neshamah **(ascent of the soul)** A journey of the consciousness to elevated worlds of divinity.

Ain Sof **(without end)** The Infinite Nothing; the kabbalistic designation for the absolute, transcendent Godhead.

am ha-aretz **(a person of the land)** Before the coming of the Ba'al Shem Tov, someone who was judged a peasant and, therefore, an ignoramus or a boor.

Amidah **(standing)** The prayer of *atzilut* in Jewish liturgy, the 18 benedictions recited three times daily; on *Shabbat* and *Yamim Tovim*, the *Amidah* has only 7 benedictions.

assiyah **(deed)** The world of doing or action according to kabbalistic teachings; the lowest world, just below *yetzirah*.

atzilut **(emanation)** The world of being according to kabbalistic teachings; the highest of the four worlds. In the kabbalistic cosmogony, it is the archetypal world.

atzmiut **(bone-ness)** The absolute essence.

avodah **(service)** Often used as a synonym for prayer, as in "*avodah sh'b'lev*" (heart service), or as in "*shlemut ha-avodah*" (true and complete service) to God.

ayin **(nothingness)** The quality of divine transcendence, no-thing-ness.

ba'al mofet (miracle worker) A Hasidic Rebbe known for working wonders or producing miracles.

ba'al teshuvah (master of the turning; pl. *ba'alei teshuvah*) One who has turned back to God, a penitent or repentant person, a person who has undergone a conversion experience.

ba'alei shem (masters of the name; sing. *ba'al shem*) Typically itinerant folk healers of one sort or another thought to use the names of angels and demons as well as the names of God to create miraculous outcomes; also the title of proto-Hasidic leaders, such as Eliyahu Ba'al Shem, Yoel Ba'al Shem, and Adam Ba'al Shem.

balagula (coachman) A professional driver of coaches.

Barukh ha-Shem (blessed is the name) A statement of gratitude to God.

bashert (destiny) One whom destiny has ordained as a life-partner.

batlan (idler; pl. *batlanim*) Though called an "idler" or a "loafer," the *batlan* is actually one who is supported by the community as a professional religious.

behelfer (Yid., helper) Assistant to the *melammed* (teacher), usually in charge of small children.

beit din (house of judgment) A Jewish court of law made up of three *dayyan-im* (judges).

beit midrash (house of study or investigation; also *beit ha-midrash*) Place for religious services and study.

bekeshe (Yid.) A long-sleeved gown or caftan fastened by a sash (*gartel*) worn by Hasidim on *Shabbat* and festivals.

berakhah (pl. *berakhot*) Blessing.

beri'ah (creation) The world of knowing according to the kabbalistic teachings; the world above *yetzirah* and produced from *atzilut*.

binah (understanding) The second/third of the *sefirot* (divine emanations) or *maskilim*.

bittul ha-yesh (annihilation of existence) Self-annihilation, effacing or making the ego transparent.

bokher (unmarried youth) A poor student or an unmarried youth.

da'at (knowledge) Intimate knowledge; an intermediary *sefirah* very important in the HaBaD system of thought.

daven (pray), *davenen* (prayer, praying) More colloquial way to speak of *tefillah* (prayer), and yet *davenen* is also more than merely formal prayer, or prayer as a formality; it is living the liturgical life in truth. The word itself is possibly derived from the Latin *divinum*, "the divine," as in doing divine work.

dayyan (judge) A judge of Jewish communal affairs.

derashot (interpretations) Torah interpretations.

devar Torah (a word of Torah) A teaching.

deveikut (adhering, clinging) Intimate absorption in God, adhering, sticking, or clinging to God in deep devotion and love.

etrog (citron; pl. *etrogim*) Citrus fruit ritually employed during the holy day of Sukkot.

etzah (counsel, advice, pl. *etzot*) Spiritual counsel or advice; direction to be followed, solution to a problem, those points of advice with which you can make for a change and a difference.

farbrengen (Yid., time spent together) A session of Hasidic fellowship, at times presided over by a *mashpiyya* or, occasionally, the Rebbe, during which Hasidim gather for the purpose of telling stories, singing, drinking, and learning the teachings of the Rebbes.

galut (exile) Referring to the exile of the *Shekhinah* or Divine Presence from the world.

Gan Eden (garden of delight) The Garden of Eden, Paradise.

ga'on (pride, splendor; pl. *ge'onim*) Genius; a title given to an exceptionally brilliant talmudist.

gevurah (strength, severity) One of the 10 *sefirot,* also called *din* (judgment).

goyim (nations) Non-Jews.

Gufa d'Malka (Aram., body of the king) In Kabbalah, the body of the sovereign, God.

HaBaD (wisdom, understanding, knowledge) An acronym for three *sefirot*— *hokhmah, binah, da'at;* the name of a Hasidic school of thought and practice, as well as a lineage founded by Shneur Zalman of Liadi (1745–1813).

ha-ala'at ha-middot (raising up of the emotions) The practice wherein the devotee overcomes temptation by pursuing a stimulus to its most sublime source in the Divine.

hagim (holy days) The holy days of the Jewish liturgical year.

hakirah (philosophy of religion) Probing with the mind, or philosophy of religion with reference to Judaism.

halakhah (way to walk) The process; Jewish law.

ha-motzi Bread over which the blessing is made.

hanhagot (practices) Spiritual practices recommended by the Rebbes for their Hasidim.

ha-Shem (the name) A term used in place of the unpronounceable name of God, *Y-H-V-H.*

hashgahah pratit (specific providence) Divine providence as it relates to the most specific and minute details of our lives.

Hasid (one who is pious) A member of the Hasidic movement; a person who has a Hasidic Rebbe.

Hasidim (**pious ones**) Followers of the third religious movement by that name, founded by Yisra'el, Ba'al Shem Tov in the 17th century. The earlier Hasidim were the desert Hasidim mentioned in the Talmud, the Hasidim ha-Rishonim, and the Hasidim of medieval Germany, followers of Yehudah HeHasid, the Hasidei Ashkenaz, and the Sufi-influenced Egyptian Hasidism of Avraham Maimonides in the 13th century.

Hasidut (**piety**) Hasidism, the teachings of the Hasidim.

Havayah (**existence**) The way in which the divine name is rearranged and substituted (*Y-H-V-H* is made *H-V-Y-H*) in Hasidic texts so as to prevent its abuse.

Havdalah (**separation**) Ritual separating the *Shabbat* from the week.

heder (**room**) A traditional school of elementary Jewish education.

heksher (**approval**) Usually referring to a kosher approval or certification.

herem (**ban**) Excommunication.

hesed (**lovingkindness**) One of the 10 *sefirot*. Also known as *gedulah* (largesse).

hevra (sing. *haver*) Fellowship.

hevraya kaddisha (**holy fellowship**) The inner circle of a Rebbe's disciples.

hitbonenut (**self-inspection**) Contemplation, discursive meditation, looking deeply into oneself or into a sublime idea; a general term for meditation in the Jewish tradition, and a technical term in HaBaD Hasidism.

hitkashrut (**self-binding**) Commitment to a Rebbe.

hod (**glory**) One of the 10 *sefirot* (divine emanations).

hokhmah (**wisdom**) The first/second of the *sefirot* (divine emanations) or *maskilim*.

Humash (**fifth**) A book-bound edition of the Torah, as opposed to a scroll.

hush ha-tziyur (**imaginal faculty**) The use of the imaginative ability or faculty of the mind.

Kaddish (**Aram., holy**) The mourner's prayer after the death of a close relative, usually after the death of a parent; the child who recites the prayers after the death of their parent.

kadmut ha-sekhel (**beginning of awareness**) The causative source in Divinity analogous to preverbal awareness for us, which is before we are able to think in words.

kappote (**Yid.**) A long-frock coat worn by Hasidim.

kashrut (**fitness**) Laws that define what is ritually fit and prepared, as opposed to *treif* (unfit).

kavanah (**intention, aiming; pl. *kavanot*) Divine intentionality, the spiritual concentration invested in the service of God.

kelippah (**shell, husk; pl. *kelippot*) A metaphysical husk or shell formed around and obscuring a spark (*nitzotz*) of divinity; a synonym for the energy system of evil.

Kiddush (**sanctification**) The prayer of sanctification recited over wine on the *Shabbat* and festivals.

kiddush ha-Shem (**sanctification for the name**) Sanctification or sacrifice for God, often refers to martyrdom.

kohen (**priest**) Of the priestly caste of Judaism.

k'tav hitkashrut (**writ of self-binding**) A group *kvittel* given to a Rebbe-to-be announcing that the undersigned wish to be led by the one named.

kvittel (**Yid. short note**) A brief but formal communication or request from a Hasid to a Rebbe written on a slip of paper.

lamdan (**learned person; pl.** *lamdanim*) Scholar of the Torah.

leben (**heart**) An affectionate appellation.

lekakh (**Yid.**) From the German *lebkuchen,* a honey and spice cake.

levush (**garment**) A covering; a technical term for the cloak one becomes invested (thought, word, or deed) in in the ḤaBaD philosophy.

l'shem shamayim (**for the sake of Heaven**) The attitude that a Hasid takes toward sacred activity.

ma'amar (**oral discourse; pl.** *ma'amarim*) Oral discourses of the Hasidic Rebbes.

Ma'ariv (**evening prayer**) The evening prayer service.

ma'aseh (**deed, work, story; pl.** *ma'asiot*) A story of deeds in the Hasidic tradition; the outermost garment of the soul.

maftir (**conclusion**) The prophetic portion of the Torah reading.

maggid (**speaks**) An endowed or itinerant preacher of sermons.

mahshavah (**thought; pl.** *mahshavot*) The innermost garment of the soul.

mahshavot zarot (**strange thoughts**) Disturbing thoughts during prayer.

Makom (**space**) A synonym for God.

malakh Angel, messenger.

malkhut (**kingdom, sovereignty, majesty**) One of the 10 *sefirot,* specifically representing the feminine, the *Shekhinah.*

mamash So being-ness, palpable.

mashal (**parable; pl.** *mashalim*) An analogue or parable used in teaching.

Mashiah (**anointed**) The Messiah.

mashpiyya (**influencer; pl.** *mashpiyyim*) A guide, spiritual director, or mentor in Hasidism.

maskil (**that which causes success; pl.** *maskilim*) In the Torah of Avraham the Malakh, the primal cause of awareness, analogous to *kadmut ha-sekhel* in the Torah of his father, Dov Baer, the Maggid of Mezritch. Also an enlightened one, one who is erudite—in Hasidic terminology, an intellectual whose contemplative endeavor turns to significance instead of service, and in the Haskalah movement, a follower of the Haskalah.

melammed (teacher) A Hebrew-school teacher.

mensch (Yid., human being; pl. *menschen*) An exemplary human being.

meshugge (Yid.) Mentally disturbed, "crazy."

middot (attribute; sing. *middah*) Emotional attributes of Divinity; the modes of being, investment, attitude, and affect. Generally they correspond to the lower seven *sefirot* on *sikhliyot* in the thought of Avraham the Malakh; in HaBaD thought, each *middah* is a consequence of a *sekhel* (an intelligence, a thought sequence, or idea syndrome), consisting of *hokhmah, binah,* and *da'at.*

midrash (interpretation; pl. *midrashim*) Method of interpreting Torah, or a collection of such interpretations.

mikveh (gathering of water; pl. *mikvaot*) Ritual immersion pool for purification; ritual bath.

Minhah (gift) The afternoon prayer service.

minyan (number) Quorum of 10; the minimum number of Jews required for communal prayer.

mitnaged (opponent; pl. *mitnagdim*) An opponent of the Hasidim, anti-Hasid.

mitzvah (connection; pl. *mitzvot*) A commandment or God-connection in the Jewish tradition, popularly equated with a good deed.

m'malleh kol almin (Aram., fills all worlds) The immanent light of God in creation.

mohin d'gadlut (expansive mind) The mind of enlightenment, inclusion, or expanded awareness.

mohin d'katnut (constricted mind) The limiting mind, or narrow awareness.

nahat (also *nahas*) A feeling of deep satisfaction.

nebukh (Yid., alas!) Poor, pitiful; an expression of sympathy or alarm.

nefesh (anima) The lowest soul level; the animative function of the soul.

Ne'ilah (closing) Special prayer in Jewish liturgy recited at the conclusion of the Day of Atonement, Yom Kippur.

neshamah (soul; pl. *neshamot*) The level of the soul coming between *ruah* and *hayyah*; the intellectual or communicating manifestation of the soul.

neshamah klalit (general soul) A collective soul, a soul connected in its root to many other souls; a Rebbe.

netzah (victory) One of the 10 *sefirot;* denotes effectiveness.

niggun (melody; pl. *niggunim*) A Hasidic melody, often wordless, which

Abraham Joshua Heschel once described as "a tune in search of its own unattainable end."

nigleh **(revealed)** Revealed Torah or a revealed master.

nistar **(hidden)** Hidden, concealed, or secret, as in hidden Torah, or a hidden *tzaddik* (*tzaddik nistar*).

nitzotz **(spark; pl.** *nitzotzot*) Sparks of divinity buried in the dense and subtle substances of creation, sparks captive in *kelippot.*

nokhah p'nai ha-Shem **(facing the name)** Being in the presence of God, done as if in the presence of God.

olam **(pl.** *olamot*) The world, universe.

olam ha-ba **(the world to come)** Heaven, Paradise.

olam ha-mashal **(world of the imagination)** Imaginal world of metaphysical possibility.

PaRDeS **(orchard, paradise)** An acrostic denoting a fourfold approach to Torah interpretation, including *peshat,* the "simple" reading of the text; *remez,* the "hint," leading to a search for meaning by which our daily life is enhanced; *derash,* the allegorical "interpretation" that turns us away from the superficial and helps us live a more spiritually meaningful life; and *sod,* the "secret" hidden deep and undisclosed.

parnas hodesh **(leader of the month)** One of the 12 members of the board who lead the community for a month each; an alderman.

parsha **(portion)** Torah portion of the week.

pashute Yidden **(Yid., uncomplicated Jews)** Simple Jews of uncomplicated faith.

penimi **(inward)** An inner-directed person.

penimiut ha-Torah **(innermost part of the Torah)** The way in which Hasidim refer to the teachings of Hasidism.

peshat **(simple)** Simple meaning of the Torah.

pidyon nefesh **(soul ransom; pl.** *pidyonot*) The monetary donation given to a Rebbe.

pilpul **(sharp analysis)** Sharp intellectual discernment; casuistic argument, hair splitting.

rav A city's chief rabbi and authority on legal matters.

reb A term of respect and friendly admiration.

Rebbe The spiritual leader of a Hasidic community.

Rebbetzin **(rabbi's wife)** A rabbi's or Rebbe's wife.

Ribbono shel Olam **(master of the universe)** An appellation for the Divine.

ruah **(spirit, breath)** In kabbalistic terminology, the spirit in human beings; the emotive function of the soul.

ruah ha-kodesh (spirit of holiness) The holy spirit, also the *Shekhinah*.

sedra (section) Torah section of the week; same as *parsha*.

sefer (pl. *sefarim*) Book.

sefirot (expressions; sing. *sefirah*) The 10 divine emanations or attributes that manifest themselves in the 4 worlds; the lower 7 *sefirot* are the same as *sikhliyot* and *middot*.

segullah (charm; pl. *segullot*) A charm, such as an amulet, that a Rebbe gives a Hasid, especially charged with healing, guarding, or enriching powers.

seudah (pl. *seudot*) Meal.

Shaharit (dawn) The morning prayer service.

shaliah (emissary) An emissary of a Rebbe.

Shalom aleikhem (peace be unto you) A greeting.

shalosh seudot (third meal) The third meal of *Shabbat*.

sharayim (Yid.) Food favors from the Rebbe to the Hasid; leftovers from the Rebbe's meal distributed to or taken by his followers.

sheidim (m. sing. *sheid*, f. sing. *sheidah*) Demons.

Shekhinah (dwelling, presence) The divine in-dwelling, the Presence of God in creation.

Shema (hear) The statement that says, "Hear O Yisra'el, *Y-H-V-H* is our God, *Y-H-V-H* is One."

shiddukh (match) A martial match.

shivah (seven) The seven days of mourning.

shnorrer (Yid.) Beggar, sponger.

shofar (horn) Ram's horn blown on Rosh Hashanah as part of the ritual.

shohet (slaughterer) Jewish ritual slaughterer.

shoresh ha-neshamah (root of the soul) A phrase denoting an intimate connection to a Rebbe on the level of the soul.

shtetl (Yid.) Small town or village.

shtibl (Yid. little room) A Hasidic conventicle.

shtreimel (probably old High German) Festive fur hat worn on *Shabbat* by most Rebbes and some Hasidim.

shuckelen (swaying in prayer) A swaying movement associated with Hasidic prayer.

shul (Yid.) House of worship, synagogue.

siddur (order) A Jewish prayer book.

sikhliyot (intelligences; sing. *sekhel*) The creative conceptualizer, that which transforms the abstract into the concrete concept; also that which abstracts from the concrete model. In HaBaD thought, a *sekhel* is an intelligence, a thought sequence, consisting of *hokhmah*, *binah*, and *da'at*; in modern parlance, *sekhel* has come to mean "common sense." See also *middot* and *sefirot*.

simha **(joy)** Joy; a joyous occasion.

Sitra Ahra **(the side of the otherness)** The negative or evil aspect of the universe.

smikhah **(ordination)** A rabbinic ordination.

sovev kol almin **(Aram., surrounds all worlds)** The light of God that transcendently encompasses the world.

sukkah **(booth)** Temporary hut constructed for Sukkot.

tallit Prayer shawl.

talmidim **(disciples)** In this context, disciples of the Rebbe.

tefillah Prayer.

tefillin Small leather boxes attached to the head and arm for prayer containing scrolls with Exod. 13:1–10, 13:11–16, Deut. 6:4–9, 11:13–21.

tehillim Psalms.

teshuvah **(turning)** Repentance, penitence.

tevilah **(immersion)** The act of dipping in a *mikveh*.

tiferet **(beauty)** One of the 10 *sefirot*.

tikkun **(ordering, repairing)** Divine attunement and the act of making spiritual reparations.

Tikkun Hatzot **(midnight repair)** A midnight service of lamentation over the destruction of the Temple.

tish **(Yid. table)** The public table of the Rebbe; ritual meal with the Rebbe.

Torah (instruction) Specifically the five books of Moses, but generally any Jewish teaching.

tzaddeket **(f. righteous one)** A righteous woman.

tzaddik **(the righteous one; pl. *tzaddikim*)** A term for a saintly, righteous person, a charismatic leader, and particularly for a Hasidic leader or teacher, a Rebbe.

tzaddik gamur **(complete *tzaddik*)** A perfect *tzaddik* in the system of HaBaD who no longer even feels an urge to sin.

tzaddik ha-dor **(the righteous person of the generation)** The leader of the generation.

tzaddikim nistarim **(sing. *tzaddik nistar*)** Hidden righteous ones.

tzedakah **(righteousness)** Charity.

tzimtzum **(contraction; pl. *tzimtzumim*)** The self-concealment of God.

tzitzit **(fringes)** The ritual threads hanging from the tallit to signify the 613 mitzvot and to remind one to observe them.

yahrzeit **(Yid., time of year)** A death anniversary, usually celebrated in memory of saints or special persons.

yehidut (one-ing) A Hasid's private encounter with the Rebbe.

yesh (being) Manifestation.

yeshiva (pl. *yeshivot*) An advanced academy for studying Torah, especially for the training of rabbis.

yesh mi'ain (something from nothing) An expression of how God created the universe; the same as *creatio ex nihilo*.

yesod (foundation) One of the 10 *sefirot*.

yetzer ha-ra (evil inclination) Negative impulse; the opposite of the *yetzer ha-tov* (positive impulse).

yetzirah (formation) The world of feeling according to kabbalistic teachings; the world of angels, formed from *beri'ah*.

Yid (Yid., sing. dimin. *Yiddeleh;* pl. *Yiddelakh*) Jew.

Yiddishkeit (Yid.) Judaism, Jewish culture.

yihudim (unifications; sing. *yihud*) Bringing the diverse manifestations of the material world together with Divinity.

yirah (awe) Awe/fear, often paired with love (*ahavah*).

Yisra'el (God-wrestler) The community of Jews and the mythic landscape of Judaism.

yoshev (sitter) A Hasid who studies at the Rebbe's *yeshiva*.

yoshev ohel (tent dweller) A contemplative supported by others.

zemirot (sing. *zemer*) Hymns.

Bibliography

HEBREW WORKS

Avraham ben Dov Baer of Fastov and Avraham of Kalisk. *Ḥesed L'Avraham*. Jerusalem: Siftei Tzaddikim, 1995.

Biber, M. M. *Mazkeret Lig'doley 'Ostroha*. Berditchev: H. Y. Sheftel, Mifitzey Haskalah, 1907.

De Vidas, Eliyahu. *Reshit Ḥokhmah ha-Shalem*. Jerusalem: Or Ha-Musar, 1984.

Dov Baer ben Avraham of Mezritch. *Maggid D'varav L'Ya'akov*. Jerusalem: Toldot Ahron, 1971.

Elimelekh ben Eliezer of Lizhensk. *No'am Elimelekh*. 2 vols. Critical ed. Gedaliah Nigal. Jerusalem: Mossad Harav Kook, 1978.

Esser Zakhzakhot. Piatrikov: ca. 1879.

Glitzenshtein, A.H. *Sefer ha-Toldot: Rabbi Yisra'el Ba'al Shem Tov*. Vol. I. Kfar Habad: Kehot, 1986.

HaKohen, Aharon Tzvi Hirsh, ed. *Keter Shem Tov*. Brooklyn: Kehot, 1972.

Horodetzky, Samuel. *Ha-Ḥasidut V'ha-Ḥasidim*. Vol. 2. Tel Aviv: Dvir, 1928.

Ikkarei Emunah. Lodz: 1933; reprinted Brooklyn: 1961.

Kahane, A. *Sefer ha-Ḥasidut*. Warsaw.

Klapholtz, Yisroel Yaakov. *Ha-Maggid mi'Mezritch*. B'nai Brak: Pe'er Ha-Sefer, 1972.

———. *Kol Sippurei Ba'al Shem Tov*. Vol. IV. Israel: Pe'er Ha-Sefer, 1976.

Kovetz ha-Tamim. 8 vols. Otwock-Warsaw: Yeshivot Tomhej Temimim, 1938.

Kuntres Bikkur Chicago. Brooklyn, NY: Kehot Publications, 1944.

Levi Yitzhak ben Meir of Berditchev. *Kedushat Levi*. Jerusalem: Torat Ha-Netzaḥ, 1993.

Michaelson, Avraham Hayyim Simcha Bunem. *Ohalei Tzaddikim.* New York: E. Grossman's.

Mordechai ben Yehezkel. *Sefer ha-Ma'asiyot.* Tel Aviv: Dvir Company, 1955.

Nehora Ma'alya Siddur. Warsaw: 1906.

Parnas, B. *Sippurei ha-Ari.* New York: Star Hebrew Book Company.

Pinhas ben Avraham Shapira of Koretz. *Imrei Pinhas.* B'ai Brak: Ha-Shalem, 1988.

———. *Midrash Pinhas.* Jerusalem: Yom-Tov Zipa Weiss Publishers, 1953.

Raphael, Yitzhak. *Sefer ha-Hasidut.* Tel Aviv: Avraham Zioni, 1972.

Shimon Menachem Mendel of Gavartchov. *Sefer ha-Ba'al Shem Tov.* 2 vols. Tel Aviv: Alter-Bergman.

Shivhei ha-Besht. Ed. Israel Jaffe. Kopusht: 1814.

Tzvi Elimelekh of Dynov. *Derekh Pikudekha:* 1851.

Ya'akov Yosef of Polonoye. *Ben Porat Yosef.* Israel: 1970.

———. *Toldot Ya'akov Yosef.* Jerusalem: 1973.

Zevin, Shlomo Yosef. *Sippurei Hasidim.* Vol. 1. Tel Aviv: A. Tzioni, 1959.

Zev Wolf of Zhitomir. *Or ha-Meir.* New York: Ziv Publishing Co., 1954.

Meshullam Zushya of Anipol. *Menorat Zahav.* Warsaw: 1902.

German and Yiddish Works

Maimon, Salomon. *Lebensgeschichte: Mit einer Einleitung und mit Anmerkungen / neu hrsg. von Jakob Fromer.* München: Georg Müller, 1911.

Unger, M. *Hasidus un Lebn.* New York: 1946.

Hasidic and Kabbalistic Works in English

Alpert, Zalman. "The Rebbetzin Who Became a Rebbe: The Chentsiner Rebbetzin." *The Chasidic Historical Review* 6, no. 3 (April/May 1996): 8–11.

Ben-Amos, Dan, and Jerome R. Mintz, eds. and trans. *In Praise of the Baal Shem Tov [Shivhei ha-Besht]: The Earliest Collection of Legends about the Founder of Hasidism.* Bloomington: Indiana University Press, 1970.

Buber, Martin. *Hasidism and Modern Man.* Trans. Maurice Friedman. New York: Horizon Press, 1958.

———. *Legend of the Baal-Shem.* Trans. Maurice Friedman. New York: Harper & Brothers, 1955.

———. *Tales of the Hasidim: The Early Masters.* Trans. Olga Marx. New York: Schocken Books, 1947.

————. *Tales of the Hasidim: The Later Masters*. Trans. Olga Marx. New York: Schocken Books, 1948.

————. *Ten Rungs: Hasidic Sayings*. Trans. Olga Marx. New York: Schocken Books, 1947.

Buxbaum, Yitzhak. *Jewish Spiritual Practices*. Northvale, NJ: Jason Aronson, 1990.

————. *The Light and Fire of the Baal Shem Tov*. New York: Continuum, 2005.

Carlebach, Shlomo. "Practical Wisdom from Shlomo Carlebach." *Tikkun Magazine* (fall 5758).

Cooper, David A. *God Is a Verb: Kabbalah and the Practice of Mystical Judaism*. New York: Riverhead Books, 1997.

Dresner, Samuel H. *Levi Yitzhak of Berditchev: Portrait of a Hasidic Master*. New York: Hartmore House, 1974.

————. *Prayer, Humility, and Compassion*. Philadelphia: Jewish Publication Society of America, 1957.

————. *The Zaddik: The Doctrine of the Zaddik According to the Writings of Rabbi Yaakov Yosef of Polnoy*. New York: Abelard-Schuman.

Elior, Rachel. *The Mystical Origins of Hasidism*. Trans. Shalom Carmi. Portland, OR: The Littman Library of Jewish Civilization, 2006.

Fine, Lawrence, ed. and trans. *Safed Spirituality: Rules of Mystical Piety, the Beginning of Wisdom*. Ramsey, NJ: Paulist Press, 1984.

Green, Arthur. *Ehyeh: A Kabbalah for Tomorrow*. Woodstock, VT: Jewish Lights, 2003.

————. *Tormented Master: A Life of Rabbi Nahman of Bratslav*. Tuscaloosa: University of Alabama Press, 1979.

————. ed. and trans. *The Language of Truth: The Torah Commentary of the Sefat Emet, Rabbi Yehudah Leib Alter of Ger*. Philadelphia: Jewish Publication Society, 1998.

Green, Arthur, and Barry W. Holtz, eds. and trans. *Your Word Is Fire: The Hasidic Masters on Contemplative Prayer*. Woodstock, VT: Jewish Lights, 1993.

Heschel, Abraham J. *The Circle of the Baal Shem Tov: Studies in Hasidism*. Ed. Samuel H. Dresner. Chicago: University of Chicago Press, 1985.

Kaetz, David. *Making Connections: Hasidic Roots and Resonance in the Teachings of Moshe Feldenkrais*. Victoria, BC, Canada: River Centre, 2007.

Kagan, Michael. "The King's Messenger." *Spectrum: A Journal of Renewal Spirituality* 2, no. 1 (winter–spring 2006): 56–58.

Kaplan, Aryeh. *Chasidic Masters: History, Biography and Thought*. 2nd ed. rev. New York: Moznaim, 1984.

————. *Innerspace: Introduction to Kabbalah, Meditation and Prophecy*. Ed. Avraham Sutton. Jerusalem: Moznaim, 1991.

————. *The Light Beyond: Adventures in Hassidic Thought*. New York: Maznaim, 1981.

————. *Until the Mashiach: The Life of Rabbi Nachman*. Jerusalem: Breslov Research Institute, 1986.

Klapholtz, Yisroel Yaakov. *Tales of the Baal Shem Tov*. Vol. 1. Trans. Sheindel Weinbach. New York: Feldheim, 1970.

Kramer, Chaim, with Avraham Sutton, eds. and trans. *Anatomy of the Soul: Rebbe Nachman of Breslov*. New York: Breslov Research Institute, 1998.

Langer, Jiri. *Nine Gates to the Chassidic Mysteries*. Trans. Stephen Jolly. New York: David McKay, 1961.

Matt, Daniel, ed. and trans. *The Zohar: Pritzker Edition*. Stanford, CA: Stanford University Press, 2004.

Mindel, Nissan. *Rabbi Schneur Zalman*. Vol. 1: *Biography*. Brooklyn, NY: Kehot Publication Society, 1969.

Newman, Louis I., and Samuel Spitz, eds. and trans. *The Hasidic Anthology: Tales and Teachings of the Hasidim*. New York: Schocken Books, 1968.

Polen, Nehemia. *The Holy Fire: The Teachings of Rabbi Kalonymus Kalman Shapira, the Rebbe of the Warsaw Ghetto*. Lanham, MA: Roman & Littlefield, 1999.

Rabinowicz, Harry M. *Hasidism: The Movement and Its Masters*. Northvale, NJ: Jason Aronson, 1988.

————. *The World of Hasidism*. Hartford, CT: Hartmore House, 1970.

Rabinowicz, Tzvi M., ed. *The Encyclopedia of Hasidism*. Northvale, NJ: Jason Aronson, 1996.

Rose, Or, and Ebn D. Leader, eds. and trans. *God in All Moments: Mystical & Practical Spiritual Wisdom from Hasidic Masters*. Woodstock, VT: Jewish Lights, 2004.

Schachter-Shalomi, Zalman M. "The Besht and the P'ney Yehoshua." *The Holy Beggars' Gazette: A Journal of Chassidic Judaism* (winter–spring [special double issue] 1975).

————. *A First Step: A Primer of a Jew's Spiritual Life*. Winnipeg: David Jackson, ca. 1958.

————. "Foreword." *Rabbi Israel Baal Shem Tov: A Monograph on the Life and Teachings of the Founder of Chassidism*. Toronto: Lieberman's, 1961.

————. *Fragments of a Future Scroll: Hassidism for the Aquarian Age*. Ed. Philip Mandelkorn and Stephen Gerstman. Germantown, PA: Leaves of Grass Press, 1975.

———. "Hasidism and Neo-Hasidism." *Judaism: A Quarterly Journal* 9, no. 3 (summer 1960): 216–21.

———. *Spiritual Intimacy: A Study of Counseling in Hasidism.* Northvale, NJ: Jason Aronson, 1991.

———. "Two Facets of Judaism." *Tradition: A Journal of Orthodox Jewish Thought* 3, no. 2 (spring 1961): 191–202.

———. *Wrapped in a Holy Flame: Teachings and Tales of the Hasidic Masters.* Ed. N. Miles-Yepez. San Francisco: Jossey-Bass, 2003.

Schachter-Shalomi, Zalman M., with Daniel Siegel. *Credo of a Modern Kabbalist.* Victoria, Canada: Trafford Publishing, 2005.

Schatz Uffenheimer, Rivka. *Hasidism as Mysticism: Quietistic Elements in Eighteenth-Century Hasidic Thought.* Trans. Jonathan Chipman. Princeton, NJ: Princeton University Press, 1993.

Schneersohn, Yosef Yitzchak. *HaYom Yom . . . "From Day to Day."* Ed. Menachem Mendel Schneerson. Trans. Zalman I. Posner and co-workers. New York: Kehot Publication Society, 2000.

———. *Likkutei Dibburim.* Vol. 4: *An Anthology of Talks by Rabbi Yosef Yitzhak Schneersohn of Lubavitch.* Trans. Uri Kaploun. New York: Kehot Publication Society, 1997.

———. *Lubavitcher Rabbi's Memoirs.* Trans. Nissan Mindel. 2 vols. New York: Kehot Publication Society, 1993.

———. *Saying Tehillim.* Trans. Zalman I. Posner. New York: Kehot Publication Society, 1988.

Schochet, Jacob Immanuel. *The Great Maggid: The Life and Teachings of Rabbi Dov Ber of Mezhirech.* New York: Kehot Publication Society, 1990.

———. *Rabbi Israel Baal Shem Tov: A Monograph on the Life and Teachings of the Founder of Chassidism.* Toronto: Lieberman's, 1961.

Scholem, Gershom. *Kabbalah.* New York: Quadrangle, 1974.

———. *The Messianic Idea in Judaism.* New York: Schocken Books, 1971.

Shapira, Kalonymus Kalman. *Conscious Community: A Guide to Inner Work.* Trans. Andrea Cohen-Kiener. Northvale, NJ: Jason Aronson, 1999.

Steinsaltz, Adin. *Beggars and Prayers.* Ed. Jonathan Omer-Man. Trans. Yehuda Hanegbi, Herzlia Dobkin, Deborah French, and Freema Gottlieb. New York: Basic Books, 1979.

Touger, Eliyahu, and Malka Touger. *To Know and to Care: An Anthology of Chassidic Stories about the Lubavitcher Rebbe, Rabbi Menachem M. Schneerson.* 1996.

Travis, Yakov. "Adorning the Souls of the Dead: Rabbi Nahman of Bratslav and Tikkun Ha-Neshamot." In *God's Voice from the Void: Old and New*

Studies in Bratslav Hasidism. Ed. Shaul Magid. Albany: State University of New York Press, 2001.

Wiesel, Elie. *Sages and Dreamers: Biblical, Talmudic, and Hasidic Portraits and Legends.* Trans. Marion Wiesel. New York: Summit Books, 1991.

———. *Somewhere a Master: Further Hasidic Portraits and Legends.* Trans. Marion Wiesel. New York: Summit Books, 1982.

———. *Souls on Fire: Portraits and Legends of Hasidic Masters.* Trans. Marion Wiesel. New York: Random House, 1972.

NON-HASIDIC AND NON-KABBALISTIC WORKS

Bennett, J. G. *Gurdjieff: Making a New World.* San Francisco: Harper & Row, 1973.

Buber, Martin. *I and Thou.* Trans. Ronald Gregor Smith. 2nd. ed. New York: Charles Scribner's Sons, 1958.

———. *Two Types of Faith.* Trans. Norman P. Goldhawk. New York: Macmillan, 1986.

Campbell, Joseph. *The Flight of the Wild Gander: Explorations in the Mythological Dimension.* New York: Viking Press, 1969.

———. *The Hero's Journey: Joseph Campbell on His Life and Work.* Ed. Phil Cousineau. San Francisco: Harper & Row, 1990.

———. *The Masks of God: Primitive Mythology.* New York: Viking Press, 1959.

Campbell, Joseph, with Bill Moyers. *The Power of Myth.* Ed. Betty Sue Flowers. New York: Doubleday, 1988.

Deutsch, Eliot. *Advaita Vedanta: A Philosophical Reconstruction.* Honolulu: East-West Center Press, 1969.

Dillard, Annie. *Pilgrim at Tinker Creek.* New York: Harper Perennial, 1998.

Firestone, Tirzah. *The Receiving: Reclaiming Jewish Women's Wisdom.* San Francisco: HarperSanFrancisco, 2003.

Friedman, Maurice. *Martin Buber's Life and Work: The Later Years, 1945–1965.* New York: E. P. Dutton, 1983.

Gerstäcker, Friedrich. "Germelshausen" (English translation). *Zoetrope* 6, no. 1 (spring 2002).

Guenther, H., ed. and trans. *The Life and Teaching of Naropa.* Oxford: Oxford University Press, 1963, 1974.

Herbert, Frank. *Dune.* New York: Ace Books, 1999.

Heschel, Abraham Joshua. *God in Search of Man: A Philosophy of Judaism.* New York: Farrar, Straus and Cudahy; Philadelphia: Jewish Publication Society of America, 1955.

JPS Hebrew-English TANAKH: *The Traditional Hebrew Text and the New JPS Translation.* 2nd ed. Philadelphia: The Jewish Publication Society, 1999.

Jung, C. G. *Memories, Dreams, Reflections.* Ed. Aniela Jaffe. Trans. Richard and Clara Winston. Rev. ed. New York: Vintage Books, 1989.

Kelly, George A.. *Psychology of Personal Constructs.* 2 vols. New York: W. W. Norton, 1955.

Khan, Inayat. *The Complete Sayings of Hazrat Inayat Khan.* New Lebanon, NY: Sufi Order Publications, 1978.

———. *The Sufi Message.* Vol. 2: *The Mysticism of Music, Sound and Word.* Delhi: Motilal Banarsidass, 1994.

Khan, Vilayat Inayat. *That Which Transpires behind What Appears: The Experience of Sufism.* New Lebanon, NY: Omega Publications, 1994.

Kohlenberger, John R. III, ed. *The Precise Parallel New Testament.* New York: Oxford University Press, 1987.

Lao Tsu. *Tao Te Ching.* Trans. Gia-Fu Feng and Jane English. New York: Vintage, 1972.

Lewis, Samuel L. *Sufi Vision and Initiation: Meetings with Remarkable Beings.* Ed. Neil Douglas-Klotz. San Francisco: Sufi Islamia/Prophecy Publications, 1986.

Meyer, Wali Ali. "A Sunrise in the West: Hazrat Inayat Khan's Legacy in California." In *A Pearl in Wine: Essays on the Life, Music and Sufism of Hazrat Inayat Khan,* ed. Zia Inayat Khan, 395–435. New Lebanon, NY: Omega Publications, 2001.

Neusner, Jacob, ed. and trans. *The Mishnah: A New Translation.* New Haven, CT: Yale University Press, 1988.

O'Kane, Thomas Atum, ed. *The Leader's Manual.* Vol. 1: *Leadership in the Sufi Order.* Seattle, WA: North American Secretariat of the Sufi Order, 1990.

Otto, Rudolf. *The Idea of the Holy.* Oxford: Oxford University Press, 1923.

Robinson, Richard H., and Willard L. Johnson. *The Buddhist Religion: A Historical Introduction.* 4th ed. Belmont, CA: Wadsworth, 1997.

Schachter-Shalomi, Zalman M. *Gate to the Heart: An Evolving Process.* Ed. Robert Michael Esformes. Philadelphia: ALEPH: Alliance for Jewish Renewal, 1993.

———. *Paradigm Shift: From the Jewish Renewal Teachings of Reb Zalman Schachter-Shalomi.* Ed. Ellen Singer. Northvale, NJ: Jason Aronson, 1993.

Schachter-Shalomi, Zalman M., with Joel Segel. *Jewish with Feeling: A Guide to Meaningful Jewish Practice.* New York: Riverhead Books, 2005.

Schlipp, Paul Arthur, and Maurice Friedman, eds. *The Philosophy of Martin Buber.* La Salle, IL: Open Court, 1967.

Sheriff, John K. *Charles Peirce's Guess at the Riddle: Grounds for Human Significance.* Bloomington: Indiana University Press, 1994.

Simmer-Brown, Judith. *Dakini's Warm Breath: The Feminine Principle in Tibetan Buddhism.* Boston: Shambhala, 2001.

Strong, John S. *The Experience of Buddhism: Sources and Interpretations.* Belmont, CA: Wadsworth, 1995.

The Upanishads: Breath of the Eternal. Trans. Swami Prabhavananda and Frederick Manchester. Hollywood, CA: Vedanta Press, 1947.

Vonnegut, Kurt, *Cat's Cradle.* New York: Holt, Rinehart & Winston, 1963.

Wilber, Ken. *Sex, Ecology, Spirituality: The Spirit of Evolution.* 2nd rev. ed. Boston: Shambhala, 2000.

About the Authors

ZALMAN SCHACHTER-SHALOMI, BETTER KNOWN AS REB ZALMAN, was born in Zholkiew, Poland, in 1924. His family fled the Nazi oppression in 1938 and finally landed in New York City in 1941. Descended from a distinguished family of Belzer Hasidim, he became a HaBaD Hasid as a teenager while still living in Antwerp, Belgium. He was later ordained by HaBaD-Lubavitch in 1947 and became one of the Lubavitcher Rebbe's first generation of outreach workers. He later earned his MA in psychology from Boston University in 1956 and a DHL from Hebrew Union College in 1968. He is professor emeritus of Psychology of Religion and Jewish Mysticism at Temple University and is World Wisdom Chair holder emeritus at Naropa University. Today he is primarily known as the Rebbe and father of the neo-Hasidic Jewish Renewal movement and is widely considered one of the world's foremost authorities on Hasidism and Kabbalah. He is the author of *Spiritual Intimacy: A Study of Counseling in Hasidism* (1991), *Wrapped in a Holy Flame: Teachings and Tales of the Hasidic Masters* (2003), and *Jewish with Feeling: Guide to a Meaningful Jewish Practice* (2005). Reb Zalman currently lives in Boulder, Colorado.

NETANEL MILES-YEPEZ was born in Battle Creek, Michigan, in 1972, and is descended from a Sefardi family of crypto-Jews (*anusim*, "forced converts"), who trace their ancestry from Mexico all the way back to medieval Portugal and Spain. He studied History of Religions at Michigan State University and Contemplative Religion at Naropa University, specializing in comparative religion and nondual philosophies. He has been a personal student of Rabbi Zalman Schachter-Shalomi since 1998 and co-founded the Sufi-Hasidic Inayati-Maimuni Tariqat with him in 2004, fusing the Sufi and Hasidic principles of spirituality and practice espoused by Rabbi Avraham Maimuni in

13th-century Egypt with the teachings of the Ba'al Shem Tov and Hazrat Inayat Khan. He collaborated with Reb Zalman on *Wrapped in a Holy Flame: Teachings and Tales of the Hasidic Masters* (2003) and is the editor of *The Common Heart: An Experience of Interreligious Dialogue* (2006). He lives in Boulder, Colorado, where he is a spiritual counselor, writer, and painter of religious icons.

How This Book Was Written

WHEN PEOPLE READ THE *LIKKUTEI MAHARAN* OF REB Nahman of Bratzlav, the great open secret is that much of what is being read comes from his Hasid, Reb Nosson of Nemirov. Only occasionally do we find the original writing of Reb Nahman. It is not that one is not learning Reb Nahman's teaching, but that the work *Likkutei Maharan* is itself a fusion of the two. In this way, Reb Nosson has made Reb Nahman accessible to the generations. If one reads the writings of Reb Nahman alone, it is difficult to know how he moves from one sentence or one thought to the next. It took the genius of Reb Tzadok HaKohen of Lublin 50 years later to find the ligatures between the ideas in Reb Nahman's personal writing. But with the *Likkutei Maharan* we are spared that burden and thus may all benefit from the combined skill and wisdom of Reb Nahman and Reb Nosson. While we cannot hope to compare ourselves with these holy masters, I would like to say that this has been our relationship, both in writing and in spiritual intimacy. Because of our relationship as teacher and student, or perhaps because of my status as an elder of Judaism, there may be some people who will tend to see Reb Netanel as some kind of a ghostwriter or as an editor of this work. Nothing could be further from the truth. He is a deep collaborator. There are moments when it is so colloquial, and moments when it is very subtle and high, and Reb Netanel's own light is represented equally in both. This is really *emes* (true). What is written on every page of this book is from a mind-meld between us; it is very difficult at this point for either of us to know who said what on any given page, and the book is better for it. For this reason, I wanted the opportunity to say how much I truly appreciate what he has done.

— Z.M.S.-S.

Index

Note: Dates given, when known, for Hasidic masters and their disciples

A

Cohen, Hermann (1842–1918), 6
Cooper, David A., xxvi
Corbin, Henri (1903–1978), 144
Cordovero, Moshe ben Ya'akov (1522–1570), 139, 306

D

da'at (knowledge), 143, 205–206, 213, 217–218, 251, 259
dakini (Buddhist feminine embodiment of wisdom), 159–161, 355
darkei ha-ḥasidut (the ways of Hasidism), 167
davenen (praying with feeling; sing., *daven*): 74, 90, 103, 124, 131, 133, 183, 348; and breath-work, 138; and distinctiveness of a Rebbe, 340; and diverting thoughts, 222; of Elimelekh of Lizhensk, 279, 287, 309; of Maggid of Mezritch, 179, 242; as service of the heart, 167; in *shtibl* and *kloiz*, 214–215; teaching of Ba'al Shem Tov on, 54–56, 65, 66;
David ha-Melekh (the king): 246, 297, 317; 348; ancestor of Yohanan ha-Sandlar, 152; as descendant of Ruth, 39; and Nathan the Prophet, 99; and Seven Shepherds, 61, 136; soul in the Ba'al Shem Tov, 134
David of Ostrog (18th century C.E.), 134–136, 171, 352
dayyan (judge), 170
deveikut (divine absorption), 38, 108, 164, 165, 170, 218, 288, 299, 332
Devorah Leah bat Shneur Zalman (d. 1790), 112, 350
divine name, the: adjuration of, 57; creation of, 256; and gender inclusivity, xiv; intention of uniting, 310–312; invoked by Moses, 140; of *Kefitzat ha-Derekh*, 79, 80, 82, 83; not to mention in vain, 330; not to profane, 368–369; published in the world, 208; the Tetragrammaton, xiv, 146, 213–214, 245; and use of *Yah*, xiv, 214
Doctor Faustus, 52
Don Juan, 47
Dov Baer ben Avraham. *See* Maggid of Mezritch
Dov Baer ben Shneur Zalman of Lubavitch (1773–1828), 68
Dubno, 153
Durkheim, Karlfried Graf (1896–1988), 344

E

ecology, xx, xix, 53, 81, 209, 246
ecumenism, ix, xx, 139
Edwards, Jonathan (1703–1758), 139
Efraim of Brod, 14–15
Eleazar ben Yehudah Rokeah of Worms (ca. 1176–1238), 4, 339
Eliezer (father of the Ba'al Shem Tov), 8–12, 17, 29, 30, 341
Eliezer Lippa (father of Elimelekh of Lizhensk), 276–277
Elimelekh ben Eliezer Lippa of Lizhensk (the Rebbe Reb Melekh, 1717–1786): 178, 230–231, 335, 370; and asceticism, 278–280, 289–292, 293, 306–307, 366; on atonement, 300–304; becoming a Rebbe, 288–289; and blessings, 287–288; disciples of, 305, 331–332, 336; and ecstasy of *Shabbat*, 282–284; exile of, 277–280, 289–292; and *Hanhagot Adam*, 323–331; legacy of, 331–333; and Maggid of Mezritch, 280–284, 287–288, 294, 295, 296, 297, 305, 332; and *mezuzah*, 288–289; parents of, 275–277; practices of, 306–331; and Shmelke of Nikolsburg, 277, 280, 292–293; and silence of Heaven, 297–298; as traveling *maggid*, 289–293; and trial of God, 298–300; on the *tzaddik*, 294–297; on *tzaddik*'s decree, 298–300; and *Tzettel Kattan*, 306–323, 369; and Zushya of Anipol, 178, 277–284, 286, 288, 367
Elisha ha-Navi (the prophet), 185, 341
Elisha ben Abuya (Aher, 1st century C.E.), 272
Eliyahu ben Moshe Loanz (Ba'al Shem of Worms, 1565–1636), 4–5, 7, 341
Eliyahu ben Shlomo Zalman (Ga'on of Vilna, 1720–1797), 53, 176, 177, 180
Eliyahu de Vidas (1518–1592), 320–321
Eliyahu ha-Navi (Prophet Elijah), xxii, 12, 17, 20–23, 78
emunah (faith): doubts about the, 128–132; faith-ing, 224–226; levels of, 34, 37, 42, 161, 162, 165, 167; and *matzah*, 207; need of great, 55–56; no flattery in matters of, 27; simple, 57, 161, 162, 165, 167
Erhard, Werner (b. 1935), 207
etrogim (citrons; sing., *etrog*), 134–136, 171
etz ḥayyim (tree of life), 220, 245, 260, 337
etzot (counsels; sing., *etzah*), 240, 241, 293, 306